I0096373

HIS SOURCE YOUR SOURCE

Alpha Omega: The Beginning The End – God Proving Himself Through Science and Everything Else

God, Quantum Mechanics, and Consciousness, God

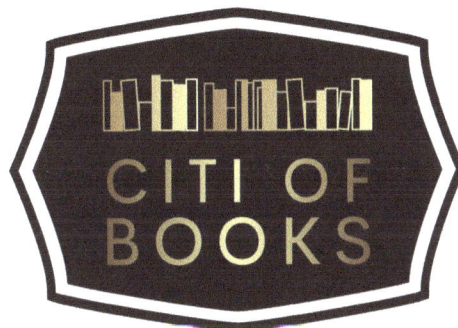

CITI OF BOOKS

Copyright © 2024 by John Bako.

All rights reserved. No part of this publication may be reproduced, distributed, or transmitted in any form or by any means, including photocopying, recording, or other electronic or mechanical methods, without the prior written permission of the copyright owner and the publisher, except in the case of brief quotations embodied in critical reviews and certain other noncommercial uses permitted by copyright law. For permission requests, write to the publisher, addressed "Attention: Permissions Coordinator," at the address below.

CITIOFBOOKS, INC.
3736 Eubank NE Suite A1
Albuquerque, NM 87111-3579
www.citiofbooks.com
Hotline: 1 (877) 389-2759
Fax: 1 (505) 930-7244

Ordering Information:
Quantity sales. Special discounts are available on quantity purchases by corporations, associations, and others. For details, contact the publisher at the address above.

Printed in the United States of America.

ISBN-13: Softcover 979-8-89391-006-3

eBook 979-8-89391-007-0

Library of Congress Control Number: 2024904826

1 Corinthians 2:9-12

Spiritual Wisdom

[9] But as it is written:

"Eye has not seen, nor ear heard,
Nor have entered into the heart of man
The things which God has prepared for those who love Him."

[10] But God has revealed *them* to us through His Spirit. For the Spirit searches all things, yes, the deep things of God. [11] For what man knows the things of a man except the spirit of the man which is in him? Even so no one knows the things of God except the Spirit of God. [12] Now we have received, not the spirit of the world, but the Spirit who is from God, that we might know the things that have been freely given to us by God.

Ephesians 1:15-23

Prayer for Spiritual Wisdom

[15] Therefore I also, after I heard of your faith in the Lord Jesus and your love for all the saints, [16] do not cease to give thanks for you, making mention of you in my prayers: [17] that the God of our Lord Jesus Christ, the Father of glory, may give to you the spirit of wisdom and revelation in the knowledge of Him, [18] the eyes of your understanding being enlightened; that you may know what is the hope of His calling, what are the riches of the glory of His inheritance in the saints, [19] and what *is* the exceeding greatness of His power toward us who believe, according to the working of His mighty power [20] which He worked in Christ when He raised Him from the dead and seated *Him* at His right hand in the heavenly *places,* [21] far above all principality and power and might and dominion, and every name that is named, not only in this age but also in that which is to come.

[22] And He put all *things* under His feet and gave Him *to be* head over all *things* to the Church, [23] which is His body, the fullness of Him who fills all in all.

A Prayer for Understanding

Heavenly Father, I pray in the Name of Jesus Christ that you wash me and cleanse me thoroughly from my sins. Search my heart and try my thoughts, like you did for David and if you find anything that is contrary to your nature, I authorize you to remove it from me. Fill me with thy Holy Spirit and open the eyes of my understanding that I may read and understand this as your Spirit wills. Help me to receive the truths in this writing exactly as it was inspired and written by your Spirit so that if I should ever communicate it to another, I will also be able to do that in your Spirit and in truth. Amen!

Table of Contents

World's Most Famous Equation by Albert Einstein

$E = mc^2$

E, or energy, is the entirety of one side of the equation and represents the total energy of the system.

m, or mass, is related to energy by a conversion factor.

And c^2, is the speed of light squared: the right factor we need to make mass and energy equivalent.

This is the world's most famous equation by Albert Einstein. "Energy equals mass times the speed of light squared". On the most basic level, the equation says that energy and mass (matter) are interchangeable; they are different forms of the same thing. Under the right conditions, energy can become mass, and vice versa. We humans don't see them that way – how can a beam of light and a walnut, say, be different forms of the same thing? But nature knows why. Who or what is nature? God is both supernature (light) and nature (mass) at the same time. The same applies to all human beings. So, when we say God is light, God is spirit, and God in physical form is Jesus, we are correct.

So why would you have to multiply the mass of that walnut by the speed of light to determine how much energy is bound up inside it? The reason is that whenever you convert part of a walnut or any other piece of matter to pure energy, the resulting energy is moving at the speed of light. Pure energy is electromagnetic radiation – whether light or X-rays or whatever – and electromagnetic radiation travels at a constant speed of 300,000 km/sec (186,000 miles/sec).

Why, then, do you have to square the speed of light? It has to do with the nature of energy. When something is moving four times as fast as something else, it doesn't have four times the energy but rather 16 times the energy – in other words, that figure is squared. So, the speed of light squared is the conversion factor that decides just how much energy lies within a walnut or any other chunk of matter. And because the speed of light squared is a huge number – 90,000,000,000 (km/sec)^2 – the amount of energy bound up into even the smallest mass is truly mind-boggling. Can you then imagine how much energy is trapped within a human being?

So, now I want you to think about the singularity of the beginning of the universe as Georges proposed in 1931. Singularity is a physics word, but I call it sovereignty. Quantum systems can exist in a superposition of all possible states simultaneously, and classical reality emerges when this superposition collapses into a single state. God is mighty but imagine Him even as this walnut – He Himself is light and the source of all things, so do the math. Think about the amount of energy bound up inside of you.

Here's an example. If you could turn every one of the atoms in a paper clip into pure energy – leaving no mass whatsoever – the paper clip would yield 18 kilotons of TNT (trinitrotoluene). That's roughly the size of the bomb that destroyed Hiroshima in 1945. On Earth, however, there is no practical way to convert a paper clip or any other object entirely to energy. It would require temperatures and pressures greater than those at the core of our Sun. That's correct – that is why until this day, there is no physical means to convert even the smallest objects entirely into energy. As you keep reading, you will know and understand the source of the universe and the proof for that.

What Is Light? Matter or Energy?

Einstein and the Photoelectric Effect

Light is both a particle and a wave. Light has properties of both a particle and an electromagnetic wave but not all the properties of either. It consists of photons that travel in a wave-like pattern.

The debate has raged for generations amongst the giants of the physics community regarding the nature of light, namely whether it is a particle or an electromagnetic wave. For centuries, this mysterious and elusive phenomenon left scientists baffled because with each experiment conducted to define its nature, it seemed to change the way it behaved. This will always be the case. We can never learn all that there is about light – it is the biggest mystery that we live in and even in eternity, we will not be able to fully understand. God is light and light is a mystery.

In simple terms, light is one of nature's freaky exceptions, and is both a wave and a particle. This variability is also one of the fundamental tenets of the theory of Quantum Mechanics. Let's look at what happened over the years as people came to this important conclusion.

Light Is a Particle

Light, depending on the measurement (visible or invisible) can either be matter or not matter. In other words, it can either have mass or no mass. An example is the Moon. We all agree that the Moon is light, yet it can be walked upon. So, it's light that has matter. Others say light is both a particle and a wave. Light has properties of both a particle and an electromagnetic wave but not all the properties of either. It consists of photons that travel in a wave-like pattern. Think about this and how we have for example, the laser technology, which can cut through even the thickest matter (metals etc.). With this, we can already agree that light is a form of energy.

The idea that light may be a particle was first advocated by Sir Isaac Newton, but the idea didn't catch on particularly well until the 19th century, when Albert Einstein revived the view. He argued that properties such as the reflection and refraction of light could only be explained if light was made up of particles. I argue both of their claims because they are only partially correct. God is light and God is everything – that means, light can be whatever it wants to be. It could be matter or antimatter or even what we do not know yet because God is called, "*I am*" but truly the full name is "*I am becoming*". He is whatever He wants to be or becoming whatever, He is becoming.

Waves do not travel in straight lines and cannot exhibit those properties outlined by Newton and Einstein. However, if that's true, then why was light rejected as a particle? The partial answer is that it did not fulfill or have all the properties that define a particle. A particle is a minute fragment or a quantity of matter with certain properties, such as mass and volume. The smallest unit of light is a photon, which does not have mass. Also, results of experiments by other researchers during the period between Newton and Einstein showed light having wave-like properties, which made them conclude that light was energy, instead of matter. That is also true – light is energy, and we will get into that as we keep going.

Physics can never learn or understand the fullness of light because in it is our biggest mystery – the God of the Heavens and the Earth is light. You and I are light beings because we came from Him. I say that, if there is a smallest unit of light then there must also be a bigger unit of this same light. Physicists think they can measure bigger units of light but that's false. They have tried but they can never get to the end of it. The same way they can never have the right amount of energy to convert matter into pure energy.

1 John 1:5

Fellowship with Him and One Another

[5] This is the message which we have heard from Him and declare to you, that God is light and in Him is no darkness at all.

Astronomers typically use gigaparsecs to express the sizes of large-scale structures such as the size of, and distance to, the CfA2 Great Wall; the distances between galaxy clusters; and the distance to quasars. This is one of the ways that light is measured but it is not enough because that's not the end or the fullness of light. That is why God is in unapproachable light – light is a big mystery.

Here are some example measurements in Megaparsec (Mpc):

- The Andromeda Galaxy is about 0.78 Mpc (2.5 million ly) from the Earth.
- The nearest large galaxy cluster, the Virgo Cluster, is about 16.5 Mpc (54 million ly) from the Earth.
- The galaxy RXJ1242-11, observed to have a supermassive black hole core like the Milky Way's, is about 200 Mpc (650 million ly) from the Earth.

Nope, Light Is an Electromagnetic Wave

Several scientists, including Fresnel, Young and Maxwell, are credited with investigating the wave-like properties of light. A wave is a transfer of energy from one point to another without the transfer of material between the two points. Young performed the single-slit experiment, which was instrumental in establishing the wave-like properties of light, such as interference and diffraction. He passed a beam of light through a slit and observed the image it formed on the screen placed behind the slit screen.

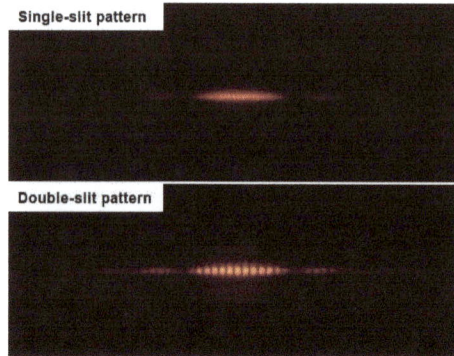

Image Source – Public Domain

If the corpuscular theory of light (light is a particle) proposed by Newton was true, then the pattern on the screen should have been light in the shape and size of the slit. However, the light pattern on the screen was more diffused/ diffracted, which indicated that light has an interference property, just like those exhibited by energy waves. Interference is a phenomenon in which two waves (considered to be linear systems) either have an additive or subtractive effect on each other's intensity, which make the resultant wave either greater or lower in amplitude.

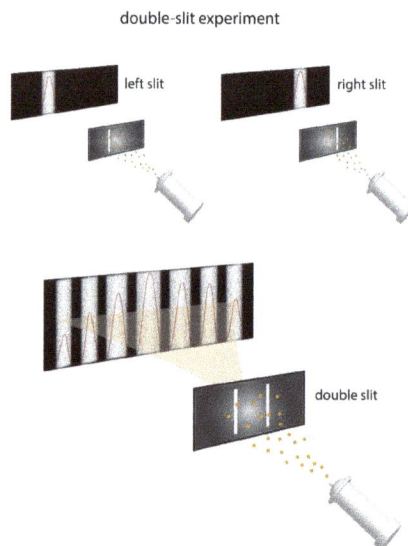

Image Source – Public Domain

Einstein observed that when light is exposed to metal, electrons fly out of the metal surface, which is very unusual if light was only a wave. The strange thing about the photoelectric effect is that the energy of the electrons (photoelectrons) that fly out of the metal does not change, regardless of whether the light is weak or strong (If light were a wave, strong light should cause photoelectrons to fly out with great power).

Einstein then proposed that light is made up of tiny packets of energy that travel or propagate in a wave-like manner. The particle he conceived was a photon, and he speculated that when electrons within matter collides with photons, the former takes the latter's energy and flies out. He went on to argue that the higher the oscillation frequency of the photons that strike, the greater the electron energy that will come flying out. This fact is perfectly illustrated through the double-slit experiment.

Using the same method as the single slit, the only modification is that the screen with the slit now has two parallel slits and light behavior is again observed on the screen placed behind the double-slit plate. The wave-like nature of light causes the light waves passing through the two slits to interfere, producing bright and dark bands on the screen – a result that would not be expected if light consisted of classical particles. However, the light is always found to be absorbed at the screen at discrete points, meaning as individual particles (not waves). Later, when detectors were installed at the slits, it was observed that each photon only passed through one of the slits, which is again a particle behavior, rather than a wave-like behavior.

In other words, light may have Dissociative Identity Disorder (DID), but at least we can stop arguing about it now. You can research the meaning of that on your own.

It's clear that physicists don't always get the answers they want or need or at least don't know or understand everything about physics or the universe. There are still things they can't figure out yet and are very confused about because to them, it makes no sense. It will continue to make no sense to them if they think that everything can be fully explained and understood with physics.

Sunlight and Moonlight

Unlike the Sun, the Moon doesn't produce its own light (that's what science says). Moonlight is Sunlight that shines on the Moon and bounces off. The light reflects off old volcanoes, craters, and lava flows on the Moon's surface. Let's do some learning on solar energy because this is how science also traps the Sunlight from the Sun and stores it in batteries or thermal storage to use as electrical energy. God's universal principle of the male and female energies.

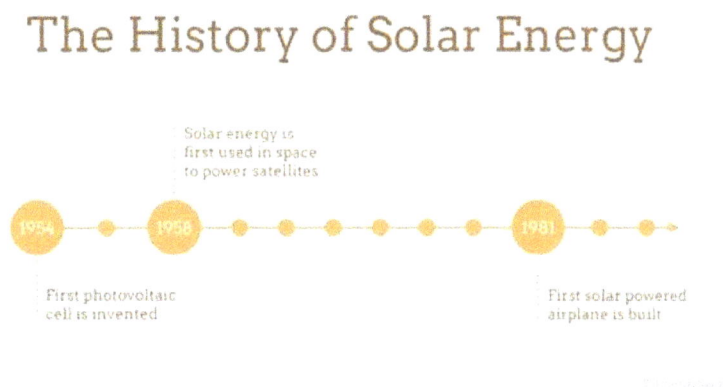

The History of Solar Energy

Solar energy is first used in space to power satellites

1954   1958   1981

First photovoltaic cell is invented

First solar powered airplane is built

Image Source – Public Domain

When Was Solar Energy First Used and How It Works?

In theory, solar energy was used by humans as early as 7th century B.C. when history tells us that humans used Sunlight to light fires with magnifying glass materials. Later, in 3rd century B.C., the Greeks and Romans were known to harness solar power with mirrors to light torches for religious ceremonies. These mirrors became a normalized tool referred to as "burning mirrors." Chinese civilization documented the use of mirrors for the same purpose later in 20 A.D.

Solar panels in outer space – Some of the earliest uses of solar technology were in outer space where solar was used to power satellites. In 1958, the Vanguard I satellite used a tiny one-watt panel to power its radios. Later that year the Vanguard II, Explorer III and Sputnik-3 were all launched with PV technology on board. In 1964, NASA was responsible for launching the first Nimbus spacecraft, a satellite able to run entirely on a 470-watt solar array. In 1966, NASA launched the world's first Orbiting Astronomical Observatory, powered by a one-kilowatt array.

The main point here is that solar technologies convert Sunlight into electrical energy either through photovoltaic (PV) panels or through mirrors that concentrate solar radiation. This energy can be used to generate electricity or be stored in batteries or thermal storage.

Now, let us look at the origin of how the Moon gets its light from the Sun and how God started demonstrating how He goes about using the male and female energies as the basis for creation. Right from the beginning of creation, God creates with two dimensions of Himself (male and female), and we can see that in the creation of the Sun and the Moon.

Genesis 1:14-16

[14] Then God said, "Let there be lights in the firmament of the Heavens to divide the day from the night; and let them be for signs and seasons, and for days and years; [15] and let them be for lights in the firmament of the Heavens to give light on the Earth"; and it was so. [16] Then God made two great lights: the greater light to rule the day, and the lesser light to rule the night. *He made* the stars also.

The Sun and the Moon are both power sources – God calls them two great lights. The Sun is the greater light, to rule the day, and the Moon is the lesser light, to rule the night. But physics for a long time have not been able to tell that the Moon also has its own power source – it is just lesser than the Sun. They are wrong. The Sun still energizes the Moon with its light. As you keep reading, you will learn something about how God created the Sun as a male and the Moon as a female. They are both in existence to support the entire universe. They are living things just as we are but live in their own space due to their nature. A man is the head of the family and typically uses his authority to rule the household. A woman is lesser to the man in terms of authority and rulership in the household. The woman still supports the man but when the man is not around, the woman takes full authority over the household. Makes sense? That's how God created things to be. A woman is supposed to submit to the man and not the other way around. It doesn't mean that the woman is a slave to the man. They both play very important roles to support each other and to ensure that there's order and continuity (reproduction). Let's keep reading.

Mark 13:24

The Coming of the Son of Man

²⁴ "But in those days, after that tribulation, the Sun will be darkened, and the Moon will not give its light; ²⁵ the stars of Heaven will fall, and the powers in the Heavens will be shaken.

This is my illustration of when the man is not at home to exercise his authority and the wife should be taking over. Don't misunderstand this as just because the Moon makes its own light, it doesn't get anything at all from the Sun. No, it doesn't work that way.

When a man impregnates his wife, you can't call that child as belonging to only the man. Can you? Same with the Sun and the Moon and how they function in the universe. The Sun is the head and the Moon, the deputy. They are there to support each other. God created His entire universe with the principle of male and female. It's all over around us – you can't deny it.

The Book of Enoch

Chapter 77:1-21

1 The names of the Sun are these: one Aryares, the other Tomas. **2** The Moon has four names. The first is Asonya; the second, Ebla; the third, Benase; and the fourth, Erae. **3** These are the two great luminaries, whose orbs are as the orbs of Heaven; and the dimensions of both are equal. **4** In the orb of the Sun there is a seventh portion of light, which is added to it from the Moon. By measure it is put in, until a seventh portion of the light of the Sun is departed. They set, enter the western gate, circuit by the north, and through the eastern gate go forth over the face of Heaven. **5** When the Moon rises, it appears in Heaven; and the half of a seventh portion of light is all which is in it. **6** In fourteen days the whole of its light is completed. **7** By three quintuples light is put into it, until in fifteen days its light is completed, according to the signs of the year; it has three quintuples. **8** The Moon has the half of a seventh portion. **9** During its diminution on the first day its light decreases a fourteenth part; on the second day it decreases a thirteenth part; on the third day a twelfth part; on the fourth day an eleventh part; on the fifth day a tenth part; on the sixth day a ninth part; on the seventh day it decreases an eighth part; on the eighth day it decreases a seventh part; on the ninth day it decreases a sixth part; on the tenth day it decreases a fifth part; on the eleventh day it decreases a fourth part; on the twelfth day it decreases a third part; on the thirteenth day it decreases a second part; on the fourteenth day it decreases a half of its seventh part; and on the fifteenth day the whole remainder of its light is consumed. **10** On stated months the Moon has twenty-nine days. **11** It also has a period of twenty-eight days. **12** Uriel likewise showed me another regulation, when light is poured into the Moon, how it is poured into it from the Sun. **13** All the time that the Moon is in progress with its light, it is poured into it in the presence of the Sun, until its light is in fourteen days completed in Heaven. **14** And when it is wholly extinguished, its light is consumed in Heaven; and on the first day it is called the new Moon, for on that day light is received into it. **15** It becomes precisely completed on the day that the Sun descends into the west, while the Moon ascends at night from the east. **16** The Moon then shines all the night, until the Sun rises before it, when the Moon disappears in turn before the Sun. **17** Where light comes to the Moon, there again it decreases, until all its light is extinguished, and the days of the Moon pass away. **18** Then its orb remains solitary without light. **19** For three months it affects in thirty days each month its period; and for three more months it affects it in twenty-nine days each. These are the times in which it affects its decrease in its first period, and in the first gate, namely, in one hundred and seventy-seven days. **20** And at the time of its going forth for three months it appears thirty days each, and for three more months it appears twenty-nine days each. **21** In the night it appears for each twenty days as the face of a man, and in the day as Heaven; for it is nothing else except its light.

From this, we can we know and understand that God created the male and female to work together as one to achieve His divine purposes. There is a reason behind everything – nothing is without meaning. These are supernatural and natural sources of light and how they function in the universe according to God's divine laws and principles. Their existence and the science behind them have helped humanity to advance in the areas of light and energy in general. Let us see how light is defined or perceived in the natural world.

What Is Light in Physics?

Light or *visible light* is electromagnetic radiation within the portion of the electromagnetic spectrum that is *perceived* by the human eye.

So, even the physicist agrees that light can be visible or invisible. Britannica defines light as the electromagnetic radiation that can be detected by the human eye. Take note of the word detected. This means that it can also be undetected. Why do we believe that there is still light that we cannot see with our eyes? Just like in what the physicist call quantum, our current technologies cannot access the possibilities in there. What you call quantum, is a higher spiritual or supernatural dimension – God's realm. He is an invisible purest light that can never be approached. He is too Holy.

Light and Color

To this point, "light" has been used loosely. Technically, light is only electromagnetic waves that fall within the visible spectrum. In other words, light corresponds to photons that can be detected by the human visual system. Photons falling outside of the *visible spectrum* are technically not light, although the terms ultraviolet light and infrared light are often used. The term visible light is also commonly used, but it is redundant. Light corresponds to wavelengths from approximately 380 nm to 780 nm (nanometers), with the shorter wavelengths being perceived as the blue end of the spectrum and the longer wavelengths evoking the perception of the red end of the spectrum. If a person is presented with individual wavelengths ranging from 380 nm to 780 nm, he or she will perceive all the possible colors found in the spectrum. Most light sources, however, do not emit a single wavelength, but simultaneously emit photons of many different wavelengths. Photoreceptors in the retina absorb these photons and convert them into a signal we can perceive. So, this means that our physical bodies cannot see certain wavelengths of light.

There are three types of photoreceptors associated with color vision. These are known as the L- (long), M- (middle) and S- (short) cones. The cones control our color vision. The long, middle, and short monikers refer to the wavelengths of the visible spectrum. Thus, the S-cones respond predominantly to the blue end of the spectrum. The M-cones respond to the middle, or green, portion of the spectrum, while the L-cones respond to the long wavelengths or the red end of the spectrum. Two light sources can emit drastically different spectrums of photons, yet still appear to be the same color. Although different wavelengths of light for the two sources are entering the eye, the absorption of the photons by the various types of cone receptors can occur in the same proportions. In this manner, the signals sent to the visual cortex from the two light sources are identical. The two light sources in this case are known as metamers. This effect means that the light itself is not colored, but that color is a property of the way the visual system detects light. Below is a visual representation of light.

VISIBLE AND INVISIBLE LIGHT

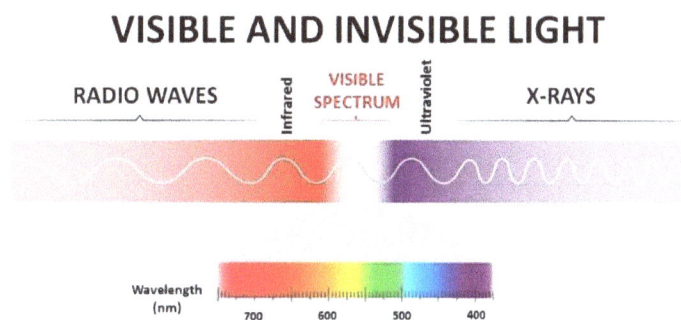

Image Source - Public Domain

From these facts, we can all agree that there is visible and invisible light. We can also track the Big Bang theory to a very small source (of a size that blows physicists minds). Earlier, we also looked at how even a tiny object hosts mighty energy if only it could be converted into pure energy. We agree in physics that our human eyes can only see where it says "visible spectrum" in the image above. Anything outside of these ranges, cannot be seen with the physical eyes. Do you now know why God exists and yet cannot be seen with the physical eyes?

For hundreds of years, there was an immutable law of physics that was never challenged: that in any reaction occurring in the universe, mass was conserved. That no matter what you put in, what reacted, and what came out, the sum of what you began with and the sum of what you ended with would be equal. But under the laws of special relativity, mass simply couldn't be the ultimate conserved quantity, since different observers would disagree about what the energy of a system was. Instead, Einstein was able to derive a law that we still use today, governed by one of the simplest but most powerful equations ever to be written down, $E = mc^2$. When God gives you something, He simplifies it.

What this equation means is thoroughly world changing. As Einstein himself put it:

It followed from the special theory of relativity that mass and energy are both but different manifestations of the same thing — a somewhat unfamiliar conception for the average mind.

This is the same way that God is light, God is spirit, and God is man and came in human form as Jesus – these are different manifestations of the same God. And just like Einstein said, this is "a somewhat unfamiliar conception for the average mind".

Here are the three biggest meanings of that simple equation. To the non-scientists, please don't feel intimidated. When you have finished reading everything, it will all make sense.

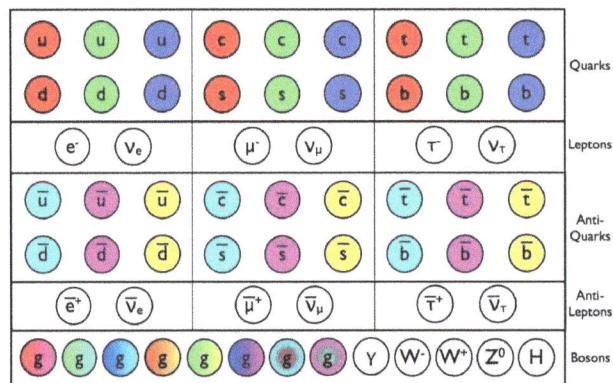

The quarks, antiquarks, and gluons of the standard model have a color charge, in addition to all the other properties like mass and electric charge. Only the gluons and photons are massless; everyone else, even the neutrinos, have a non-zero rest mass. E. SIEGEL / BEYOND THE GALAXY

Even masses at rest have an energy inherent to them. You've learned about all types of energies, including mechanical energy, chemical energy, electrical energy, as well as kinetic energy. These are all energies inherent to moving or reacting objects, and these forms of energy can be used to do work, such as run an engine, power a light bulb, or grind grain into flour. But even plain, old, regular mass at rest has energy inherent to it: a tremendous amount of energy. For example, a sleeping human being still has enormous amount of energy in him or her body. This carries with it a tremendous implication: that gravitation, which works between any two masses in the universe in Newton's picture, should also work based off energy, which is equivalent to mass via $E = mc^2$.

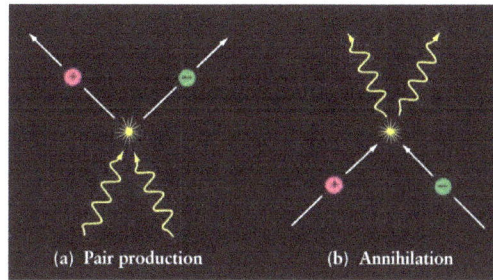

(a) Pair production   (b) Annihilation

The production of matter/antimatter pairs (left) from pure energy is a completely reversible reaction (right), with matter/antimatter annihilating back to pure energy. This creation-and-annihilation process, which obeys $E = mc^2$, is the only known way to create and destroy matter or antimatter. DMITRI POGOSYAN / UNIVERSITY OF ALBERTA

Mass can be converted into pure energy. This is the second meaning of the equation, where $E = mc^2$ tells us exactly how much energy you get from converting mass. For every 1 kilogram of mass you turn into energy, you get 9×10^{16} joules of energy out, which is the equivalent of 21 Megatons of TNT. When we experience a radioactive decay, or a nuclear fission or fusion reaction, the mass of what we started with is greater than the mass we wind up with; the law of conservation of mass is invalid. But the amount of the difference is how much energy is released! That's true for everything from decaying uranium to fission bombs to nuclear fusion in the Sun to matter-antimatter annihilation. The amount of mass you destroy becomes energy, and the amount of energy you get is given by $E = mc^2$.

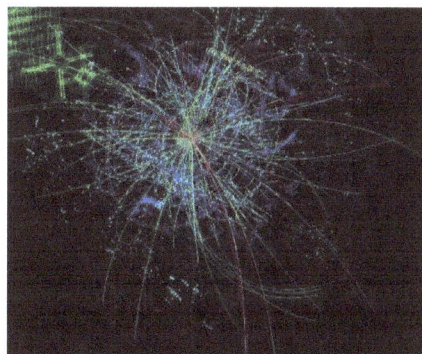

Image Source – Public Domain

In the image above, the particle tracks emanating from a high energy collision at the LHC in 2014. Composite particles are broken up into their components and scattered, but new particles are also created from the available energy in the collision.

Does what you see in the image and what you read about it draw your attention to anything else – the Big Bang or creation in general, including how we as humans all look different in terms of physical features, traits etc., and how we keep discovering new species that we have never seen before? That's right. Let's look at another example.

Recently, researchers studying subatomic particles have found something extraordinary. For the first time, they have seen a new particle changing into antiparticle and back again. But why is this observation so unique? Why has it created such hype? And most importantly, how did scientists arrive at this conclusion? Don't worry, I will explain everything to you. In this explanation, you will see the scale at which we have explored nature – they said.

Image Source – Public Domain

The particles moving towards each other.

Image Source – Public Domain

When they finally collide.

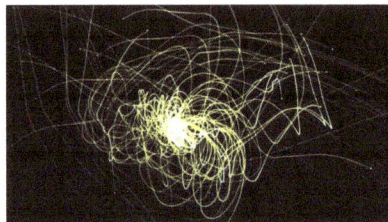

Image Source – Public Domain

The after effect of the collision – something extraordinary happens.

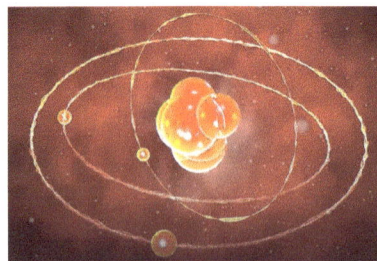

Image Source – Public Domain

For the first time, they have seen a new particle changing into antiparticle and back again.

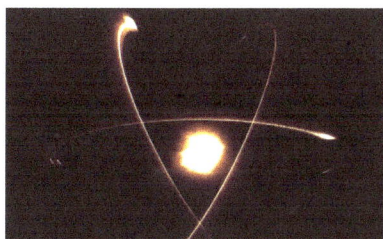

Image Source – Public Domain

You will see as you continue this reading, how this collision, supports my vision (revelation) from God and how that shows what happened before the Big Bang and confirms the Big Bang theory by Georges in 1931 to be true. In other words, the beginning of the universe before the Big Bang.

Most of you might be wondering what an antiparticle is. Here is a simple explanation. Everything you see around you is made up of particles. Some of these particles are positively charged such as the protons, while others (not all) are negatively charged, like the electrons. An antiparticle is one having similar properties to that of particles but an opposite electric charge.

Image Source – Public Domain

So, if a proton is a particle with a positive charge, it's corresponding antiparticle is an antiproton with a negative charge.

Image Source – Public Domain

Do you remember starting your chemistry classes with Dalton's atomic theory? Dalton said that the atom was indivisible.

QUICK OXFORD REFERENCE

A theory of chemical combination first stated by John Dalton in 1803. It involves the following postulates: (1) Elements consist of indivisible small particles (atoms). (2) All atoms of the same element are identical; different elements have different types of atoms. (3) Atoms can neither be created nor destroyed. (4) 'Compound elements' (i.e., compounds) are formed when atoms of different elements join in simple ratios to form 'compound atoms' (i.e., molecules). Dalton also proposed symbols for atoms of different elements (later replaced by the present notation using letters).

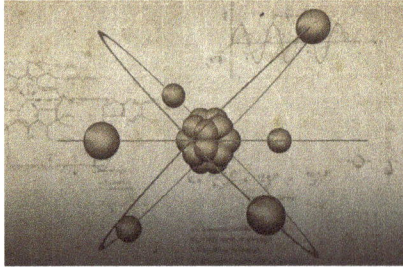

Atom

Image Source – Public Domain

It's the smallest entity. Well, now we know it isn't – oops! He stated that in 1803. The quark model was independently proposed by physicists Murray Gell-Mann and George Zweig in 1964. Quarks were introduced as parts of an ordering scheme for hadrons, and there was little evidence for their physical existence until deep inelastic scattering experiments at the Stanford Linear Accelerator Center in 1968. I will let you do the math on how long it took for the Dalton theory to get disproven.

An atom is made up of a nucleus around which electrons revolve. The nucleus is composed of protons and neutrons, which are further made up of particles called quarks. So far, quarks are known to be the most fundamental particles that constitute matter that we see around us. There are six quarks in the standard model of physics. They are up, down, top, bottom, strange, and charm quarks. Pay attention to the names of the last two quarks. Fancy names! Right? Yeah, right.

Image Source – Public Domain

Forget about all the quarks except the charm quarks. They are the ones behind this grand discovery. Different combinations of these quarks make up different particles.

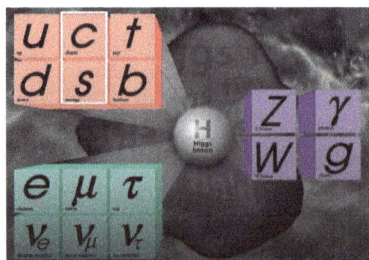

Image Source – Public Domain

For example, some pairs of quarks and antiquarks form a family of particles called the mesons.

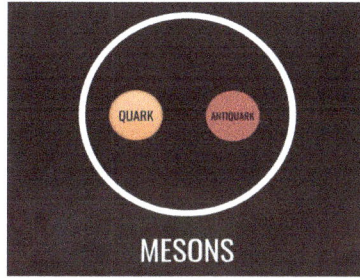

Image Source – Public Domain

A meson is a particle made up of a quark and an antiquark, held together by the strong force. What's the "strong force" here? I will let you think about that. You will find out soon.

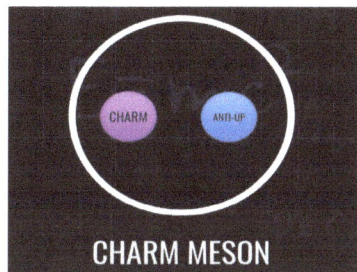

Image Source – Public Domain

The charm meson is made up of a charm quark and anti-up quark. Observations had revealed that the charm meson lives in a state of superposition of being itself and its antiparticle, this superposition results in two particles, one being a heavier one and a lighter version of charm mesons, allowing the particle to oscillate into its antiparticle and back again. Strange right?

Why then is it difficult for most scientists to believe when the Bible and Christianity say that God is three persons: father, son, and the holy spirit – that God is both matter and antimatter? Or to better relate in the previous paragraph, God is both particle and antiparticle? Or why is it so difficult for you to accept that all creation started from God as our one and only Source? This is the Holy Trinity like the Bible presents. You can never separate science from God. But when you separate God from science, you have absolutely no science at all left and science will make no sense. Keep reading.

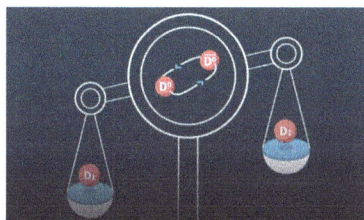

Image Source – Public Domain

Image Source – Public Domain

For more than ten years, it was known that the charm mesons could travel as a mixture of their particle and antiparticle state. However, for the first time, they have been found to oscillate between the two states. Furthermore, measurements have shown that these particles differ by $10^{(-38)}$ grams – ($D2 - D1 = 10^{-38}$ g).

$$D2 - D1 = 10^{-38} g$$

0.0000000000000000000
0000000000000000001
grams

Image Source – Public Domain

That's a hundred trillion trillion trillion times smaller than a gram. Such a negligible value, isn't it? But this minute mass difference is the critical quantity that controls the speed of a charm meson oscillation into an anti-charm meson and vice versa. So, how is such a tiny quantity measured? Wouldn't it have been challenging to do so? Well, it was. A measurement of this precision and certainty requires a copious number of observations, and even the analysis method must be extremely precise. In laboratory systems, charm meson particles are produced in proton-proton collisions in particle accelerators. This is because God is a male being (male energy) and He truly generated the female being (female energy) from within Himself. Remember Adam and Eve? OK.

Genesis 2:22-24

22 Then the rib which the Lord God had taken from man He made into a woman, and He brought her to the man.

23 And Adam said:

"This *is* now bone of my bones
And flesh of my flesh;
She shall be called Woman,
Because she was taken out of Man."

24 Therefore a man shall leave his father and mother and be joined to his wife, and they shall become one flesh.

In physics, and chemistry, a proton is a stable subatomic particle occurring in all atomic nuclei, with a positive electric charge equal in magnitude to that of an electron, but of opposite sign and a rest mass of 1.67262×10^{-27} kg, which is 1,836 times the mass of an electron. Most importantly, note that it is a positively charged elementary particle that is a fundamental constituent of all atomic nuclei. The Bible clearly states this.

Don't be surprised when you see the clear difference between the male and female body mass etc., because out of the man or male component, came the female but the female is the gateway for all. This is a standard principle and law by God. Let's continue.

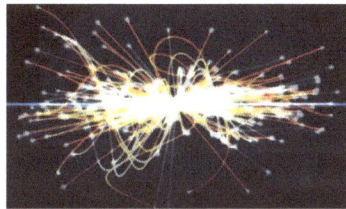

Image Source – Public Domain

Before decaying or transforming into other particles, they travel only a few millimeters. Does this ring any bell? Why humans die and then become only spirits and enter higher dimensions? Or why our Bible says that you die to self before transforming into the image of God? Or why seeds die in the soil before they germinate? It doesn't just decay, but it transforms into other particles. A seed for example, doesn't need a male seed and female seed to germinate. In certain plants, there are male and female seeds, and or a hermaphrodite – even in animals too. You can read more on self and cross pollination in plants. There is also what is called a male cone and a female cone. There is what is also called asexual reproduction. There are reproductive structures. Life and science are not random. Sounds familiar about God and the entire universe and how He says everything works. Keep reading.

The researchers compared the charm meson particles that decayed after traveling a short distance with those that travel a little further to measure the mass difference between the two classes of the particles. Apart from the charm meson, only one particle has been seen to oscillate in this way: the strange beauty meson. Sounds like a germinating seed to you right or the one sperm that travels further to fertilize the female egg in humans and other living things? But what makes the discovery impressive is that in the case of charm mesons, the oscillation is very slow, making the transition extremely difficult to be measured within the short time of 40 picoseconds that the meson takes to decay. This discovery has opened a new door for particle exploration.

Image Source – Public Domain

It can potentially prove to be a significant step in solving the mystery of matter-antimatter asymmetry and shed some light on why our universe is entirely made up of matter, even though matter and antimatter were created in equal amounts after the Big Bang.

Image Source – Public Domain

That is right – physics has gotten far enough but will soon learn that the beginning is also the end, and the end is also the beginning. That's God – Alpha Omega. Therefore, the Venn diagram or Vesica Pisces is the birthplace of the entire universe and confirms that the vision that God showed me is exactly what happened in the beginning before the Big Bang and why everything in this dimension is made up of mostly matter. Also, most importantly, why He gave us the Vesica Pisces as the foundation of our geometry. This 3D world is the physical dimension. Physics is very important here, but physics will always have to rely on the supernatural to fill in the gaps. The supernatural can always survive here even without physics. But physics cannot survive without the supernatural.

Energy can be used to make mass out of nothing... except pure energy. The final meaning is the most profound. If you take two billiard balls and smash them together, you get two billiard balls out. If you take a photon and electron and smash them together, you get a photon and an electron out. **But if you smash them together with enough energy, you'll get a photon, and electron, and a new matter-antimatter pair of particles out. In other words, you will have created two massive new particles:**

- **a matter particle, such as an electron, proton, neutron, etc.,**
- **and an antimatter particle, such as a positron, antiproton, antineutron, etc.,**

whose existence can only arise if you put in enough energy to begin with. We can get into details of this but let's save the non-scientists the headache. This is good enough and gives you the idea and the science behind creation. The bolded lines above are exactly what happened in the Big Bang by God according to His supreme power through the spoken word joined with the power of the Holy Spirit.

Einstein's greatest equation, $E = mc^2$, is a triumph of the power and simplicity of fundamental physics. Matter has an inherent amount of energy to it, mass can be converted (under the right conditions) to pure energy, and energy can be used to create massive objects that did not exist previously. There are fundamental particles that make up our universe, to invent nuclear power and nuclear weapons, and to discover the theory of gravity that describes how every object in the universe interacts. This science can be found as you read on that this is exactly how the universe was born. The key thing to note here is that energy can be used to create massive objects that did not exist previously. So, we can all agree that the creation of any new object won't be considered as "magic". Just like how you and your siblings all have unique physiques and characteristics. Also, all the different things in creation that God spoke into being. We can't call it magic, but it can be called a miracle because everything was created through the manifestation power of God.

Einstein discovered something very special, except that He took God out of his equations, or he just didn't want to disclose or admit it or give God the glory. He would have found the "God Equation" – not in a working or practical sense, but to at least know and understand that we are governed by way more than our eyes can see. God is real and the universe is not an accident – you are not an accident or a random object that popped out of nowhere.

There are several things that result from Einstein's theory of relativity, but I will talk about one of them as it relates more to this writing with respect to space-time. Take note of the gyroscopes' directions.

Proof From Orbiting Earth

In 2004, NASA launched a spacecraft called Gravity Probe B specifically designed to watch Einstein's theory play out in the orbit of Earth. The theory goes that Earth, a rotating body, should be pulling the fabric of space-time around it as it spins, in addition to distorting light with its gravity.

The spacecraft had four gyroscopes and pointed at the star IM Pegasi while orbiting Earth over the poles. In this experiment, if Einstein had been wrong, these gyroscopes would have always pointed in the same direction. But in 2011, scientists announced they had observed tiny changes in the gyroscopes' directions because of Earth and its gravity, dragging space-time around it.

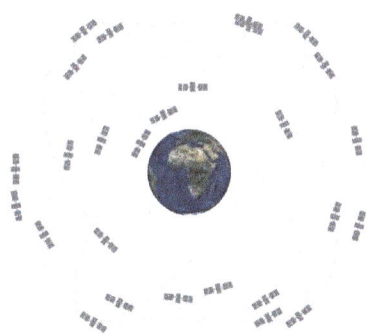

Global Positioning System or GPS is a United States space-based radionavigation system that helps pinpoint a three-dimensional position to about a meter of accuracy (for example latitude, longitude, and altitude) and provide nano-second precise time anywhere on Earth. Credit: NASA

Speaking of time delays, the GPS (global positioning system) on your phone or in your car relies on Einstein's theories for accuracy. To know where you are, you need a receiver – like your phone, a ground station and a network of satellites orbiting Earth to send and receive signals. But according to general relativity, because of Earth's gravity curving spacetime, satellites experience time moving slightly faster than on Earth. At the same time, special relativity would say time moves slower for objects that move much faster than others.

When scientists worked out the net effect of these forces, they found that the satellites' clocks would always be a tiny bit ahead of clocks on Earth. While the difference per day is a matter of millionths of a second, that change really adds up. If GPS didn't have relativity built into its technology, your phone's guidance and directions would be several miles off.

What Scientists Say About the Quantum

Quantum's actual meaning is a specific amount or quantity of something, but the story of the quantum is bizarre – defy all common sense. Well, common sense should be called uncommon sense because it's not common as people think.

Why Is the Quantum So Strange?

I was listening to a series of interview to physicists by Robert Lawrence Kuhn and here are some of the things they talked about. I will try to understand the quantum – he said. He started asking some of his friends at the Foundational Questions Institute – visionary scientist, unafraid to challenge current belief. He met Wojciech Zurek, a leading authority of Quantum theory – originally from Poland. He explores the deep meaning of the quantum. My comments are in bold.

He started by saying the reason we need to understand quantum theory before we understand reality is that quantum theory is the only theory which is encompassing everything – it has no limits. **That is correct – this is a limitless problem. It is an eternal or infinity problem. God is limitless and you cannot solve or calculate Him with mere science. He only gave us science to help us understand Him and our physical world. Mathematics and science are technologies from Heaven – a much higher dimension. He gave it to us through grace.** Quantum theory is weird. It is weird because it is so egalitarian and in quantum theory, any superposition of state is a legal state. Then he said, I know that sounds mysterious. Well, it is mysterious – something scientists don't want to encounter because they believe everything is physical. **Well, now scientists will believe that everything is not physical. They must understand this else it will only make life harder for them.** The interviewer asked him what that means. He then used a glass on the table for illustration – this glass can be here on this side and then there on that side. It can also be here and there at the same time. **That's how things work in the spirit when you ascend into higher dimensions – you can be in multiple places at the same time. That is why the Bible says that God is omnipotent, omniscient, and omnipresent. That is why His prophets mostly or people with prophetic gifts can see things about the world or individuals and relay God's mind or message to them.** We don't see things which are here and there – we see things which are localized, which are in definite places. **That's how things work in the physical but in the spiritual, things can be nonlocal (remote) without the need for any cables whatsoever. Don't compare it to the internet because behind the internet are still a lot of cables. In this case, I mean no cables**

at all needed for anything. The interviewer said, and we see that no matter how small we look at things; in microscopes etc., we never see things in two places. The interviewee continued; in microscopes, you have evidence of things being in two places. So, in some sense, for example, electron microscopy works because things are in many places at the same time and then get recombined. So, electron microscopy is there because quantum mechanics is there. He added that in fact, if you look at applications, a lot of that is because of quantum mechanics – transistors, and computers run because of quantum mechanics.

The interviewer said, he understood the weirdness – the weirdness is superposition. **Yes, the superposition is God.** The interviewee said, the place where the weirdness starts is the superposition. **Of course, you can never understand the fullness of God's supremacy. That's why He is the Almighty and for eons, the Heavenly beings bow down on their faces and worship Him day and night, and say Holy, Holy, Holy.**

Revelation 4:6-11

[6] Before the throne *there was* a sea of glass, like crystal. And in the midst of the throne, and around the throne, *were* four living creatures full of eyes in front and in back. [7] The first living creature *was* like a lion, the second living creature like a calf, the third living creature had a face like a man, and the fourth living creature *was* like a flying eagle. [8] *The* four living creatures, each having six wings, were full of eyes around and within. And they do not rest day or night, saying:

"Holy, holy, holy,
Lord God Almighty,
Who was and is and is to come!"

[9] Whenever the living creatures give glory and honor and thanks to Him who sits on the throne, who lives forever and ever, [10] the twenty-four elders fall down before Him who sits on the throne and worship Him who lives forever and ever, and cast their crowns before the throne, saying:

[11] "You are worthy, O Lord,
To receive glory and honor and power;
For You created all things,
And by Your will they exist and were created."

The interviewee added, it gets weird. The weirder part has to do with the fact that in classical physics, if you have a well-defined state of an object which consists of several pieces, this means that you have a well-defined state of each of the pieces. In quantum mechanics, that's not the case. In quantum mechanics, you can know everything that is to be known about a collection of objects and yet you can be left in a situation where you know nothing about any of the parts. So, these are the entangled states. **That is correct – the entangled state is when your spirit becomes** one with God's spirit. Although you are one with Him, He still chooses to show or tell you only what He wants you to know for a moment or time.

1 Corinthians 13:9-10

[9] For we know in part, and we prophesy in part. [10] But when that which is perfect has come, then that which is in part will be done away.

This means that a time will come, and we will not be limited to knowledge and understanding – the perfect time in and with Christ. This time will be in eternity – forever and ever, everlasting to everlasting.

The interviewee continued. So, entanglement is an intimate knowledge of two particles about each other and that knowledge is so intimate that it precludes any communication with anything else. So, these two particles know about each other so well that indeed if you ask a question of one of them, it gives you the answer, the other one will give you a correlating answer – no matter how far away. The interviewer was surprised so, he asked again, no matter how far? The interviewee responded, no matter how far away. **That is correct – therefore, as believers, we keep a continuous relationship, communion, and fellowship with our father, God, through prayers, worship, and praises, and holy living. We are never out of sync this way. We literally walk with the mind of God and God dwelling in us. Our spirits become entangled with His spirit and that gives us His all-seeing and all-knowing power.** So, the interaction doesn't matter. The state is a shared property. The interviewer asked, so particles could be so far apart that even light would not have a chance to communicate between them. The interviewee responded that this has been confirmed experimentally. The interviewer said that he was more mystified – now how do we make progress in understanding this? Is it possible? The interviewee responded, it is possible, and he thinks that one of the links they were missing recently had to do with their prejudices of how they understood classical theories. **This means that physicists have now realized that there is more to the universe than just classical physics theories – that is great. Good progress.** In classical physics, we always thought that a system by itself is something to be understood really in separation from the rest of the universe. Now in quantum mechanics, it turns out that because of entanglement, the nature of the interactions, the consequences of interactions are so subtle that the fact of even very weak interactions exist can change the behavior of the system in very dramatic ways. So, in fact, the most quantum aspect of quantum mechanics, which is entanglement, can help one understand how quantum mechanics ends up explaining what they see classical. **So, my advice to you is to learn about God and how He deals with those who worship Him, and you will understand this piece of the puzzle – you will truly understand the meaning of quantum mechanics.** The interviewer said, so, help me understand how superposition, how entanglement can help us understand how the micro world explains the macro world. **This is exactly what we mean by that the spiritual world supersedes the physical world and that everything or every reaction in the physical world is to an action in the spiritual world. I believe this is Newton's third law of motion. He called it action-reaction force pairs. For every action, there is an equal and opposite reaction. Now you will know and understand**

that spiritual people are not crazy after all. The interviewee responded that the key point is that quantum systems are not isolated. They interact with the environment. Once they interact with the environment, they leave records, they leave memory in the environments – so there is the transfer of information. So, the interaction with the environment allows the environment to know where an object of interest is. The interviewer said, and before that it was just a probability of where it may be. The interviewee said, it's worse than that – so, before the interaction with the environment happened, you had oodles of possibilities. Essentially, all of them incompatible with what they see in the real world. After that interaction happens, you end up being offered a menu, but the menu has only on it, positions which are "classical" – it doesn't tell you which one of them happens, but it tells you the set of possibilities. **That is correct.**

Remember that I mentioned earlier that the Venn diagram or Vesica Pisces is the source of all creation. In mathematics, a set is a collection of elements. The elements that make up a set can be any kind of mathematical objects: numbers, symbols, points in space, lines, other geometrical shapes, variables, or even other sets. The set with no element is the empty set; a set with a single element is a singleton. God is both a singleton and a collection. A set may have a finite number of elements or be an infinite set. Two sets are equal if and only if they have precisely the same elements. So, it shouldn't surprise you when Christians say that they are One with God and when God says He is Elohim: the father, the son, and the holy spirit. Now let us look at the Venn diagrams below.

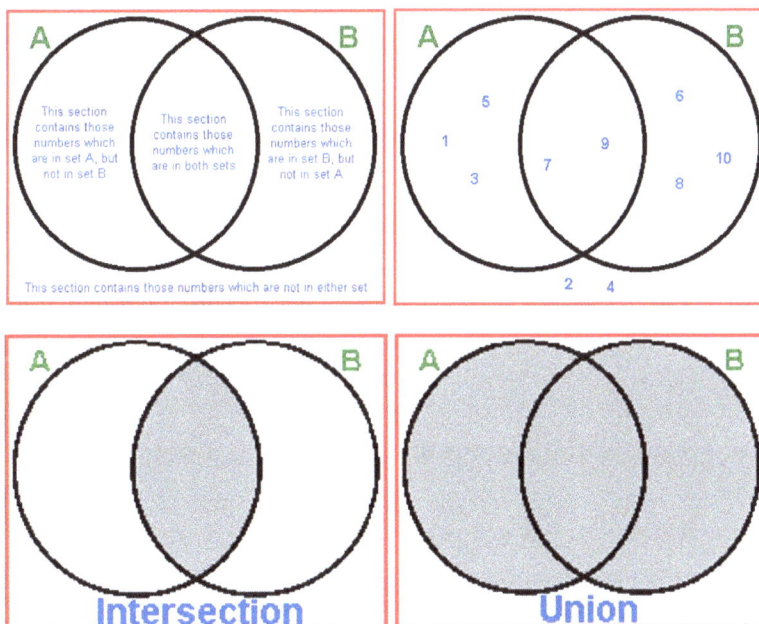

Image Source – Public Domain

Sets are ubiquitous in modern mathematics. Indeed, set theory, more specifically Zermelo–Fraenkel set theory, has been the standard way to provide rigorous foundations for all branches of mathematics since the first half of the 20th century. So, you see, we are back to the basics or fundamentals of our mathematics or science. This is how it all started, and this is how it all ends – alpha omega.

A Venn diagram is a widely used diagram style that shows the logical relation between sets, popularized by John Venn in the 1880s. The diagrams are used to teach elementary set theory, and to illustrate simple set relationships in probability, logic, statistics, linguistics, and computer science. Mathematics and science all came from God – and they are discovered, not invented. God gives the knowledge and understanding. He gave us mathematics and science (they are the same thing) because it helps us and to know and understand Him much better.

Look at the Vesica Pisces below. The union also represents the union between eternity and time. I will explain it to you in depth as we go.

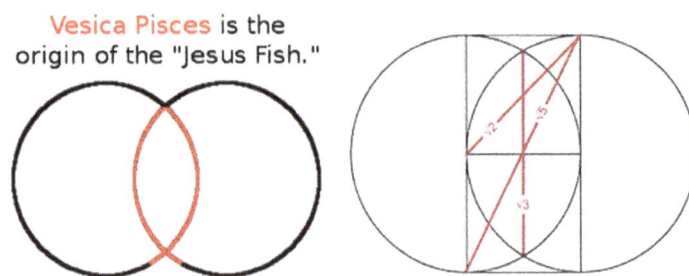

Vesica Pisces is the origin of the "Jesus Fish."

Image Source – Public Domain

The interviewee continued. And the sets in models that we can calculate is classical – and that's the probability, the interviewer completed the Interviewee's statement. The interviewee said, and then you can say you assign probability to this set of possibilities. The interviewer asked, so, how then can we go back and say what is really happening in quantum theory – is it just a mathematical formulation that is a kind of a way to understand some reality or is this really what's happening? **I say it has all been programmed in the agenda of God to help humans understand reality. I am very thankful to God that He has given me the revelation and the privilege to represent this purpose for Him as part of my divine purpose and assignment in my time.** The interviewee responded, now, we know that components which make objects which we deal with are quantum. So, the question that arise is does anything strange happen when these objects get bigger and bigger? Nothing seems to – everything seems to be still quantum. So, if you are in a controlled situation, when the system is isolated, it behaves as if quantum laws were sacrosanct. **Similar words for sacrosanct are sacred, hallowed, respected, inviolable, inviolate, or unimpeachable. Hence, the relationship between God and man.** The isolation of the environment is the key, the interviewer added. It's not just the size because the size gets bigger, and the quantum weirdness is maintained. The interviewee said, absolutely. The interviewee said, so, you put your finger on the key thing. If the system gets bigger, it's harder to isolate from the environment. So, if something is as small as an atom or electron, it's easy to make it separate and keep it carefully away from everything else. But if something is as big as a glass or as you or me, that's impossible. *End of first interview.*

So, we see that is it no surprise that God keeps His children controlled and isolated if we submit to Him, to be one with Him and you become untouchable and full of His divine knowledge, understanding, wisdom, and power. If you decide to go in the world and violate the word of God, then it's harder to isolate you from the environment and you become vulnerable and easily gets destroyed by the devil or you can't host God and prove Him tangibly.

After the interview, the interviewer talked about some quantum basics – he said, energy is not smooth, it occurs in steps like climbing up a stair, not walking up a ramp. Quantum describes the smallest unit or discrete packet of energy. But then the quantum goes weird – superposition: things in more than one state or place at the same time. Entanglement: objects related to each other irrespective of distance. This he said, makes no sense. Ah, his physics friends reply, now you are starting to get it. It means that if you understand quantum then you don't understand quantum. Find out about the "uncertainty principle", they suggest – it's fundamental and it's wild.

In another interview, he went to Harvard to meet with Nima Arkani-Hamed; an innovative physicist linking theory and experiment. He hears that Nima embodies the excitement of his grand quest to dig into deep reality. You will have to deal with the uncertainty principle. Perhaps, it's part of the history of the quantum.

What Is the Uncertainty Principle?

In physics, this is defined as the principle that the momentum and position of a particle cannot both be precisely determined at the same time. It is represented by the formula below.

Formula

$$\Delta x \Delta p \geq \frac{h}{4\pi}$$

Δx = uncertainty in position

Δp = uncertainty of momentum

h = Planck's constant

π = pi

Image Source – Public Domain

He asked, Nima, how can we understand quantum theory? Nima replied, in the late 1800s, we had two basic kinds of phenomenon that we see in nature – things like light and sound waves and other exhortations of different media were described by waves but things like billiard balls didn't have enough carbs but if they had carbs then carbs and other things could be described as particles. **Therefore, it is important to know and understand a little bit about light and how it works, as it was provided at the beginning of this writing because everything is connected to light.** He continued – having these two different kinds of descriptions for a phenomenon in nature started leading to some confusion. What people realized in the early part of the 20th century was that these two different things that were being described by classical physics; wave-like property on one hand and particle-like properties on the other, at the end of the day, all describing particles but particles that don't move according to the laws of classical mechanics but move instead according to the laws of quantum mechanics, which are very different than the classical laws that govern particles. For example, there was the famous uncertainty principle that said that while in the world of classical physics we associate the movement of a particle through space and time by specifying its position and its velocity in any given point, that we can't in fact, specify the positional velocity to infinite accuracy and if we know the position very well, we don't know the velocity very well and vice versa. And all of this happened in conjunction with the realization that there is a new fundamental concept of nature. Planck's constant – which determined when classical approximations to the real underlying quantum physics was good and when that classical approximation broke down. **This already tells us that there is more to life than what mere physics can explain. When we look at the uncertainty principle, my question is, how can we attain certainty from a formula in which two variables are labeled as uncertain? This is very tough and unrealistic.**

The interviewer said, now today we know that from this there are many observations, which we know to be true but seem counterintuitive to our normal microscopic lives – particles entangled, tunneling effects where things seem to jump from one place to the other. This seems to be impossible, but it is real. **Yes, that is correct. They seem impossible but very real except that they are not merely physical. This is both the fundamental and the advanced, this is how we were made, how we live, and how we will continue to live until we leave the Earth to a higher dimension (eternity) where these things will be normal. That is why it is both the fundamental and the advanced at the same time unless you take the spiritual realm as non-existing.**

Nima responded, it is absolutely real and one of the unfortunate things about the way sometimes quantum mechanics is described is there is an awful lot of mysticism associated with it and uncertainty means we can't make sure of anything and maybe consciousness has something to do with the way the world is and there is an awful lot of nonsense said about quantum mechanics whereas in fact, quantum mechanics is responsible for the absolute stability of everything we are made of like atoms, for example. **That stability he talks about is God. I laughed at this statement. The awful lot of mysticism is valid, that is correct because what you call quantum is not purely physical, it is spiritual. And yes, consciousness also has something to do with it. I have added a section in this writing about consciousness. I am glad that Nima at least knows that quantum mechanics is responsible for the absolute stability of everything we are made of like atoms, for example. That is correct, because the spiritual world is where we all came from and that's what rules the physical world.**

The interviewer, added, we could see electrons can't occupy the same position. Nima responded, right. There was this old classical picture that an atom was like a little solar system, when an electron is orbiting around a nucleus, and there were a variety of problems with that picture. One of them was that the electrons will quickly lose energy and spiral into the nucleus and the atoms will be completely unstable. And another one, a regulated one is that even if you ignore that problem, you could imagine lots of different solar systems, lots of different spirals and why were all the atoms identical? Why is everything made up of the same stuff? And both mysteries were solved by quantum mechanics with the realization that it was impossible for the electron to fall into the nucleus because if it did then you would know both where it was and how quickly it was moving at the same time and the uncertainty principle tells you that that's not possible. **Is a solution provided by the uncertainty principle truly considered a solution? Something to think about, especially in "physics". I thought everything must be certain in physics. But here, we are uncertain, so, is it still physics?**

The interviewer added, so, the uncertainty principle creates stability and absolute confidence in the modern world.

Nima responded, exactly. The uncertainty principle far from introducing all kinds of fuzzy garbage, allows things to be stable and is responsible for all the gross properties of matter. *End of interview.*

That is right. There is a reason why the best name that physics could give it is the "uncertainty principle". It doesn't matter how stable it makes things, even they (physicists) accept that it introduces all "kinds of fuzzy garbage" – this is what you call anything that doesn't make sense to you. God made things that way. We cannot know everything, even in eternity. Mankind is so messed up that if God should ever allow these secrets to come out, imagine what would happen to the world. Even with the little we know, look around you and all the mess.

After the interview, their conclusion was atoms are not little solar systems. Little solar systems will be unstable. Only the uncertainty principle can create stability. Only because it is impossible to know the precise location and velocity of a particle, that's why atoms do not collapse, wow. Yeah, it sounds well, too perfect, too packed. There I say, too simple – he said. There must be problems lurking somewhere. Take note of what the interviewer said, "**There must be problems lurking somewhere". Yes, there are problems lurking somewhere.**

The third interview was with Lee Smolin, who has very controversial ideas about fundamental physics, which many of his colleagues don't like. Which is why the interviewer thought he should get to him. **In cases like this, sometimes it's best to be controversial because our reality that most people are still looking for lies in something that's considered far more controversial by the natural man who doesn't believe in God and the supernatural.**

Lee is at the Perimeter Institute in Canada. The interviewer started – Lee, everybody talks about quantum mechanics, particularly, what you call the foundations of quantum mechanics: the relationship between quantum mechanics and general relativity. How can we begin to understand these fundamental problems?

Lee responded, what I will say is that if you think that physics is supposed to give you a picture of reality independent of us, that tells you in every experiment exactly what is happening and why, which is what Einstein and everybody before Einstein thought physics was about, quantum mechanics doesn't do that. **That's correct because what you call quantum mechanics is both the fundamentals and the advanced. Fundamentals to those who live in it and understand it well and the advanced to those who practice it consistently daily and have matured in it through a close relationship with God.** Lee said, Quantum mechanics talks in terms of probabilities, and not even probabilities, some things prior to probabilities. **"Some things prior to probabilities." That's correct – it's our basics, our foundations (the fundamentals), how we were created and how we should be living and how we shall leave the Earth. This is how we will continue to live in eternity.** He continued – if you scatter two particles off each other, quantum mechanics doesn't tell you what's happening in an individual event. It tells you in a class of events, what are the probabilities for different outcomes. Einstein never liked that, including half of the founders of the subject. They thought that certainly it works, it gives correct predictions as far as it has been tested, it is the basis of one more technology, it's extraordinarily successful, but they didn't believe it and many of us still don't believe it. **I don't blame you because physics idea of quantum is how things work in the spiritual and most importantly, how they manifest and hold the natural.** He continued – this was controversial in the 1930s and it has been controversial since. **It will always remain controversial until people finally accept that it isn't just about the physical, but it also involves the spiritual – with the spiritual part being the controller.** He said, if you talk to different of us, there are some people who have bought the whole thing, which means that they have found a way of thinking, a way of talking that accommodates the weirdness of quantum mechanics. **Yes, they have but it doesn't mean they totally know and understand it or even at all know and understand it.**

The interviewer said, but no experimental evidence is contradictive. Lee responded, sure but the controversy remains. **It's like somebody saying show me God in His physical form so that I will believe that He truly exists. It's a stupid idea because He can be proved through everything around us if you know and understand. Or you can be taught of how to be spiritual, and you can know Him the quantum way.** He continued – some of us continue to think that it's a good tool, it's a good bookkeeping device, it's a good predictive device but it's not a fundamental theory because the fundamental theory should describe what's happening in detail in each experiment. **So, if science can't explain what is happening in detail in each experiment but still claim the theory to be true, then how different are the unbelieving scientists from the Christians who they think can't prove God due to lack of evidence? It is the fundamental theory, and it is describing everything in detail in each experiment. If you know, you know but if you don't know, you don't know. It is as simple as that. The problem is that you don't know and understand it.** He continued – Einstein never bought it as a fundamental theory, Schrödinger never bought it, de Broglie, and many others, and I have never been able to buy them – maybe I'm dumb. **It is a fundamental theory. You all just don't understand it. That's why. You are overthinking it with your physical brains. Once you understand God and how things work in the spiritual realm (a higher dimension), quantum will make a lot of sense to you as it does to me right now by the grace through revelation and wisdom of God.**

The interviewer said, but at least it's accommodating, it's a prejudice because the probabilistic way of looking at the world; the world being all smeared in some way – it's uncomfortable in our modern way of thinking but if no experimental data contradicts it then it looks impressive. **This has been the curse of science – "experimental data". You won't find that in quantum mechanics although spiritual people clearly see it. You need a different set of eyes to see and a different kind of mind to understand. Well, I call it spiritual mechanics. By the way, the experimental data is everywhere – in you and all around you.**

Lee responded, it is impressive and the key thing that we have learned is that any theory that goes beyond quantum mechanics gives a deeper explanation, a deeper description must be fundamentally non-local. **Exactly, it is fundamental, both local and non-local. The quantum aspect is mostly non-local but creates and controls both the non-local and local.** The interviewer said, right. Lee added, this is the spooky action at distance that Einstein talked about. **So, Einstein even called it "spooky". Albert Einstein famously said that quantum mechanics should allow two objects to affect each other's behavior instantly across vast distances. Think about God and man – our relationship with Him, although He "sits" on His throne, which is in a whole different dimension. And you shouldn't compare it to your ability to talk to someone on the phone from far away. Behind the phone technology are still a lot of physical cables. Although the phone technology was given to us through this same intelligence provided by God. There are no physical cables involved in talking to God.** The interviewer asked, what does that mean, specifically?

Lee responded, it means that if you have an atom in an excited state and it decays and spits out two photons, the state of those two photons remains what we call, entangled. That means that if I make a measurement on this one, and I make a measurement on the other one, the probabilities of the outcome of the first measurement depends on which measurement I choose to make on the second one. The interviewer added, even though the distance between them could be vastly greater than the speed of light could travel. Lee confirmed, yes. That experiment has been done.

An excited-state atom is an atom in which the total energy of the electrons can be lowered by transferring one or more electrons to different orbitals (orbitals equals dimensions). In other words, when an electron temporarily occupies an energy state greater than its ground state, it is in an excited state. An electron can become excited if it is given extra energy, such as if it absorbs a photon, or packet of light, or collides with a nearby atom or particle. The following is how it is represented in chemistry. We are back to the basics, the fundamentals. By the time you finish reading this writing, you will know that all branches of sciences and mathematics are all one.

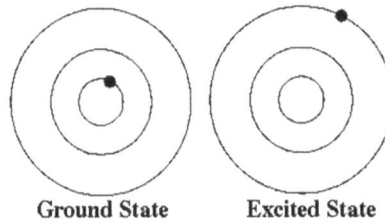

Ground State   Excited State

Image Source – Public Domain

Now, it is no coincidence that the eternal "time" ring or circle revelation that God gave to me looks exactly like this. Think about the universe or creation, most importantly, human beings as occupying the ground state. What science mean by *"when an electron temporarily occupies an energy state greater than its ground state, it is in an excited state. An electron can become excited if it is given extra energy, such as if it absorbs a photon, or packet, of light, or collides with a nearby atom or particle"* **is that, in the lives and experiences of Christians or believers, there is a state we get to during prayer or worship and we tap into God's power. We can also walk perpetually in this, depending on how serious you keep your relationship with God. This is where we usually say that the anointing is strong on us. At that energy level or frequency, all possibilities are made available to us – we can heal the sick, we can have all kinds of miracles etc. We tap into an eternal God state. This state in quantum mechanics is when the electron temporarily occupies the energy of the superposition. At this stage, we can call anything to come into being with the spoken word. This is where we can even have creative miracles. For example, we can instantly create bones where bones are lacked or do not exist, heal all kinds of diseases, raise the dead etc.**

Lee continued, plutonium physics worked and still works and it's our understanding of how the bridges stay up and why the water is different from the air and so forth but it's fundamentally misconstrued, it's fundamentally wrong, totally wrong when it comes to the description of nature. **Maybe what you have always called to be fundamental, isn't quite fundamental. Think about that.** He added, so, there's no problem in my mind with quantum mechanics working very well but being totally wrong. The interviewer added, by working at a certain level. Lee responded, yes. Now, if you believe it's wrong then you must believe that there's a crunch somewhere. One place I believe the crunch is likely to be is cosmology, quantum cosmology. **That is correct.** That is, we use quantum theory to study systems which are tiny compared to the universe. **That is correct. Even if you have adequate systems to study cosmology in depth, you will end up at the same thing – the same problem. You cannot separate quantum mechanics from cosmology. It's all intertwined or entangled. You cannot separate anything from God.** He continued – some of us, and I certainly I'm guilty of this; I have the potential to study the subject of quantum cosmology. We'll try to put the description of cosmology in the language of quantum mechanics; so, we talk about the quantum state of the universe. My bet is that that's completely wrong. **He is wrong here – his bet is not completely wrong. The fundamental of all science is one, so if he bets against his bet, scientists will make head way in quantum studies.** He continued – that at some point between our laboratory and the universe, quantum mechanics breaks down. **He is correct because the problem is spiritual, not mere science. If you understand the spiritual realm (higher dimension), you will understand quantum in a physical sense.** The interviewer asked, what's the alternative? Lee responded, one of the oldest hypotheses in the subject is that when you include quantum mechanics together with general relativity, the singularity goes away, and there is a time before the Big Bang singularity. **Again, he is correct**. **That is why whatever scientists are trying to do to merge everything together to get an equation of everything or the God equation as Einstein called it or the string theory practically, is simply impossible.** He added – that there was a universe before the Big Bang and that rather than having to talk about the initial conditions of the universe, is the explanation for why everything is the way it is, one must talk about how the universe passed through these events. What was before the Big Bang? Because what was before the Big Bang evolve to become this very gradient state, which then began to expand, which made everything. So, if you like, you push the explanation back and maybe that's a good thing, maybe that's a bad thing but it's the scientific questions. *End of interview*.

I say, Lee is a smart man and I like his reasoning although he was wrong a few times. He has reasoned the closest to what quantum mechanics truly mean. He understands it to some extent.

After the interview, the interviewer asked himself – quantum mechanics working very well but being totally wrong? **It's not totally wrong – it's just misunderstood. It's normal to mature Christians or spiritual people.** He continued – Quantum cosmology, the quantum state of the entire universe? My head is spinning. Talk about an uncertainty principle, that describes me. How to make sense of all these? **Yes, I understand your confusion. Everything is linked together – both the spiritual and the physical worlds. Once you separate them, then all you have left is the classical physics. And even that still is a result of the spiritual (quantum) physics. Without the spiritual, there is no physical. Without quantum physics, there is no classical physics. Classical physics depend on quantum physics just as how the physical world depend on the spiritual world. Your confusion starts when you separate them.**

The interviewer finally went to MIT to see a pioneer in quantum computing; Seth Lloyd, who uses the weirdness of the quantum to make radically powerful computers. He said he knows Seth, can he help? They met in his lab. **I honestly don't know and understand how quantum products are made when quantum is very much misunderstood.**

The interviewer asked, Seth, how can I begin to understand this weirdness of quantum theory?

Seth responded, well, maybe you shouldn't even try. Nobody understands it, he said. That's the way I feel about it. You know, I have studied this for years. I did my master's degree in Cambridge in Philosophy of Science Study in quantum mechanics, trying to understand what it was that I can have an electron that was here and there at the same time. Forget about it. I never understood it but however, you can if you try, you can become more comfortable with it over time. **No, you**

will never understand it if you think about it as physics or classical physics alone. He continued – so, you know, one way to become more comfortable unfortunately, is to learn the math behind quantum theory because there's a very nice straightforward mathematical background for quantum theory. And the math says, hey electron here, electron there at the same time, no problem. Ok, but unfortunately, if we want to do this intuitively then it's tough. Our intuitions are poor classical intuitions – are never going to understand this. In fact, I think that our intuition for quantum theory is ruined at the very early age around three months because it's at three months when they do studies on infant cognition, it's around three months that babies start to believe in the permanence of objects. Right, you go like "cover your face with both hands", and "remove your hands" – peekaboo, right? Both the interviewer and interviewee laughed. When you play peekaboo with the kid younger than three months old, it's no fun. You cover your face, and they go like, oh, daddy is gone. But after three months, they know you are there. But their intuitions for quantum mechanics have now been ruined so I think you should just forget about getting a good intuition about it. **You see; therefore, the Bible talks about becoming like a child before you can enter the Kingdom of God, which requires being born again. Through that you will become a new creation, have a renewed mind and be able to know and understand the spiritual things of God. Then, quantum mechanics will become normal stuff to you. Apparently, majority of scientists are way "too smart" that their ego would be stung by this word of God but that's their only way to fully understand quantum mechanics.**

Matthew 18:2-4

[2] Then Jesus called a little child to Him, set him in the midst of them, [3] and said, "Assuredly, I say to you, unless you are converted and become as little children, you will by no means enter the kingdom of Heaven. [4] Therefore whoever humbles himself as this little child is the greatest in the kingdom of Heaven.

Don't forget about it. Believe in God and become spiritual and you will have a better intuition about it. The interviewer said, ok - alright. Seth added, in fact, many noble prize winners; people who got their noble prizes in quantum mechanics, like Einstein, he didn't really believe in quantum mechanics at some level. I think that is because if quantum mechanics is just intrinsically counterintuitive, and if you are Einstein, you believe your intuition. The interviewer laughed. His intuition is like, hey, this quantum mechanics stuff is weird, and I don't believe it right. So, he didn't believe it even though he got a noble prize for it, for photoelectric effect. The interviewer added, I think Richard Feynman once said, "if you think you understand quantum theory, that proves that you don't. The interviewee added, Niels Bohr said, "anybody who thinks they can contemplate quantum mechanics without getting dizzy hasn't properly understood it." They both laughed about it. *End of interview.*

Yes, but the sons and daughters and friends of God, understand it crystal clearly and we don't get dizzy contemplating it. We don't even have to contemplate it. It is the lives we live – that's our abode. It is normal stuff to us like in the physical. In fact, it is very tangible to us.

The interviewer said to himself after the interview, this stuff is hard, I have struggled but to no reality, I must deal with the quantum. So, here is what I know, quantum mechanics is how the world works at its most fundamental level. Uncertainties: all is probability. Superposition: particles having two states at once. Entanglement: particles instantly linked, non-locally. None of this happens in the ordinary world. **That is right because it is fully spiritual and once you understand it, you will know that this is reality – the reality that most people have been very eager to find.** He continued – but everything in the ordinary world is constructed from the quantum world. **Very smart, you got it.** How is this possible? How does quantum weirdness transform into normal stuff? Is decoherence the answer; the collapse of the quantum wave function when it hits the larger environment? Or do we need so-called hidden variables to solve the puzzle? Or is quantum theory not fundamental? Our deeper true is yet to be found. Like it or not, the quantum gets us closer to truth. **Absolutely, the quantum has brought you to truth. The whole truth is one word, God. It's all written in the Word of God. He is the creator of the universe and that is how he designed it. He showed it to me.**

On Consciousness

I read an article which was titled "The Origin of Consciousness" in which a few important subjects were discussed.

"MuZero is an algorithm with a superhuman ability to learn. It has learned to play 57 different Atari video games as well as Chess, Go and Shogi, and defeated the greatest human masters in every one of them. Yet, this amazing algorithm and the computer in which it is implemented are as conscious as your washing machine. Its "intelligence", manifest in its learning ability, has nothing to do with consciousness – the ability to feel, perceive and think in the deeply subjective sense that we cherish. If you were told that you would become deprived of all subjective perceptions and feelings, you would be devastated and consider such a life to be meaningless. Intelligence – having the ability to learn and solve complex problems like MuZero does – and consciousness – being the subject of experience – seem to be unrelated."

"But are intelligence and consciousness really unrelated? Most people have the strong intuition that clever animals like chimpanzees, dolphins, elephants, and dogs are conscious, whereas they are less sure about animals like sea anemones, worms and slugs that show only very simple forms of learning."

"In the 19th century George John Romanes, an ardent follower of Charles Darwin, articulated this intuition. He interpreted animal psychology within the Darwinian evolutionary framework and defined mind (which he and others of his time used as a synonym for consciousness) in terms of the ability to make learning-based choices:"

"The criterion of mind, therefore, which I propose, […] is as follows: – Does the organism learn to make new adjustments, or to modify old ones, in accordance with the results of its own individual experience?" (Romanes 1883).

My question is, if living things and their consciousness were not intentionally programmed by God into them in levels according to the type of being that they are and how they should function, how then does the newly born baby of any living thing, immediately know where the mother's breast is and how to feed on it, and the mother knowing exactly what to do with that baby? Something to think about. At this early stage, you can't say that the baby already has a living experience and making learning-based choices based on that experience. Yes, all living things can learn and, in the future, make learning-based choices but there are learnings or experiences that are already programmed in them prior to birth, including humans. It's time to throw away the Darwinian theory about human beings evolving from apes etc. – it's nonsense.

The Merriam-Webster defines consciousness as, at its simplest, is sentience or awareness of internal and external existence. Despite millennia of analyses, definitions, explanations and debates by philosophers and scientists, consciousness remains puzzling and controversial, being "at once the most familiar and [also the] most mysterious aspect of our lives". Perhaps the only widely agreed notion about the topic is the intuition that it exists. Opinions differ about what exactly needs to be studied and explained as consciousness.

Let me tell you this, consciousness exists in all life forms. When we look at how God created the Heavens and the Earth and everything that is in it, it confirms this. Even the luminaries; the Sun, the Moon, the stars etc., are very conscious of their existence because they follow instructions or programming as the Creator Himself put in them. They rise and fall at specific times of the day throughout the year. Now, that is consciousness. At the very basic level, you can say the same thing about our technologies – we make them conscious by giving them very specific instructions to follow and expect them to act that way. If you press the on button of your phone or computer and it doesn't turn on while you know that the battery isn't dead, you will become upset because it is failing to follow the instructions given to that device or as programmed into it.

The reason why I use these examples is that God has many creations. He put them in order of least to highest. We are the highest of His creation because He created us in His image. Let me be very clear on this subject – our consciousness is at the highest level when we serve God and serve Him properly, in spirit and in truth. You will go from the basic consciousness that all human beings have (which is still higher than all other things) to a much superior, higher dimensional, or spiritual consciousness, where you will even know things that you are not supposed to know. This is when some people will even start calling you strange or weird.

Science is trying to weigh consciousness equally almost among all living things and that is a mistake. You don't even have to compare the consciousness of animals to humans if you want to save yourself time. Or you can do it just for studies sake to learn about the differences but even that, you won't find all the answers you need because our consciousness is at different dimensions. Even among humans, we grow into higher consciousness based on our closeness to God. This and the problem of quantum mechanics are very linked.

That is why God is God because He lives in His own realm all by Himself and knows, sees everything etc. His consciousness is superior (limitless) to all and it's from His that He gave us our own different levels of consciousness when it comes to His creations. That is why sometimes you know everything about some elements and sometimes, you don't know anything at all when it comes to quantum mechanics and entanglement. Attempting to build a robot to have the same consciousness as a human being is a total waste of time. I'm sorry to disappoint you. If you understand spirituality, you will not even waste your time to try certain things. If you want to just research something to publish a paper or as a PhD requirement or dissertation then go ahead, try something because you need to put something in writing to get your degree. God is the Master designer and creator, and He does it with precision – perfection. Therefore, there will be nothing like a perfect robot ever through Artificial Intelligence. I'm sorry to disappoint you but that's the reality.

In another article, I read that, on the opposite side of this empiric bias is the point of view that consciousness will never be explained unless there is some supernatural force present to explain the mystery. This implies that the fundamental building blocks of reality are conscious – everything is conscious. That's correct. There is some scientific truth to this. Richard Feynman used to wonder if an electron had its own mind. There is a mathematical proof of something very similar by Conway and Kochen, who basically say that if we (humans) have free will to choose to measure something, which basically means our decisions are not based completely on the past (a real deterministic universe) then the particles must also have free will. This is also correct. Therefore, scientists are facing an impenetrable wall that they can't get through with regards to quantum mechanics and consciousness. We are back to both the fundamentals and the advanced because the fundamental is the advanced – those are the roots of all things. That's why God says, He is alpha omega; the beginning the end.

We want to use science to explain pure spiritual things and to some extent we can but in its fullness, no we can't because spiritual things are spiritually discerned, and they are foolishness to the natural or carnal man. Everything you will ever want to understand is already in the Bible.

1 Corinthians 2:14

[14] But the natural man does not receive the things of the Spirit of God, for they are foolishness to him; nor can he know *them,* because they are spiritually discerned.

"The hard problem is understanding what it feels like to be conscious. The defining essay, written in 1972, was entitled, "What is it like to be a bat?" Many argue that no matter how much we discover in neuroscience we will never understand a bat's inner feelings. There is a bit of a linguistic debate here, and some say *experience* is a better word than *understand*. "

Both words are correct, but I also agree that experience is a better word to use here because you can only understand best when you have experienced it. There is a saying that goes, "the person who is sitting next to the fire knows how hot it feels." You can sit or watch from a distance and think you understand how that person would be feeling but it would only be to a certain degree. Maybe you have touched something very hot before or in the past, so you at least have an idea of how it feels like. But in that moment, maybe the person sitting right next to the fire is literally roasting. That is a different pain level than just touching a hot substance and immediately dropping it.

"The best way to understand consciousness is the religious or spiritual way of thinking about it, which started long before any other ways, and says floating somewhere above your body/brain is your mind or soul and, that the soul never really dies."

That is correct. This is what in quantum mechanics, physicists see it as a mystery to be alive in "multiple universes". We never really die. Death is basically your soul leaving your body permanently. Your body is just a vessel or a host so that you can live in the Earth without restrictions. The laws of the Earth require the legal inhabitants to have a physical body. That's why even God Himself had to come as Jesus. That is why our bodies are made up of the same substances as our universe and scientists wonder why everything is made from the same stuff. To sum this up, consciousness is the most mysterious thing in the universe because that is who we truly are. Anybody without this is considered as dead. The breath of God in us is what we call consciousness.

Genesis 2:7

7 Then the LORD God formed a man from the dust of the ground and breathed into his nostrils the breath of life, and the man became a living being.

The 2nd Book of Enoch

Chapter 30:10-11

10 [Friday]. On the sixth day I commanded my wisdom to create man from seven consistencies: one, his flesh from the Earth; two, his blood from the dew; three, his eyes from the Sun; four, his bones from stone; five, his intelligence from the swiftness of the angels and from cloud; six, his veins and his hair from the grass of the Earth; seven, his soul from my breath and from the wind.

11 And I gave him seven natures: to the flesh hearing, the eyes for sight, to the soul smell, the veins for touch, the blood for taste, the bones for endurance, to the intelligence sweetness [enjoyment].

Are you still wondering why a body that is not actively breathing is considered dead? Now you know better. So, the soul (consciousness) is used to smell – and how do we smell? We smell through our nostrils as an active result of the air that we breathe into our bodies.

Another paper says this. "Consciousness is arguably the most important scientific topic there is. Without consciousness, there would after all be no science. But while we all know what it is like to be conscious – meaning that we have personal awareness and respond to the world around us – it has turned out to be near impossible to explain exactly how it arises from the hardware of the brain. This is dubbed the "hard" problem of consciousness."

"Solving the hard problem is a matter of great scientific curiosity. But so far, we haven't even solved the "easy" problems of explaining which brain systems give rise to conscious experiences in general – in humans or other animals. This is of huge clinical importance."

That is correct. God in His infinite wisdom designed it to be so. That is why it is hidden knowledge. He chooses to share the secret things with His Sons and friends if He wants to or as He wills. Therefore, there will never be any robot which consciousness will get even close as to the consciousness of a human being.

"Consciousness they say, is not localized; it is widely distributed, at least in the brain. Panpsychists say it is distributed throughout the whole universe."

The Panpsychists claim is more accurate. Therefore, what we call dreams are not always dreams. There are a few times that maybe a medication you take can screw this up and it would just be the side effect of the medication. But true dreams are your "consciousness" roaming about somewhere in the spirit. That is why there are so many spiritual laws that can be used to kill people by separating this "consciousness" from their human bodies or vessels. Everything will always link back to the spiritual world because that is the engine for the natural world whether you believe or like it or not. This is reality.

Let me ask you this. Do you know of a country called Ghana? In Ghana, do you know of a very small town called Adawso? Maybe you know Ghana or have heard of it and the small town too. If you have then great. That means you are conscious of it. But if you don't then that's too bad. You are unconscious of it and the fact that you don't or didn't know about it doesn't change the fact that it's true or it exists.

Knowledge and understanding are the beginning of higher consciousness.

Proverbs 9:10

[10] "The fear of the Lord *is* the beginning of wisdom,
And the knowledge of the Holy One *is* understanding.

At the physical level, an unknown sickness or disease has a higher probability of killing you than a sickness or disease that is commonplace to you and you already know about. At a spiritual level, just because you choose not to believe God, or His existence or the devil's existence doesn't change that fact or reality. That's why even when the devil is inflicting you with evil stuff or diseases, you call it cancer and keep trying to cure it until it finally kills you. Look at the statistical data and count the number of patients who successfully beat cancer, even after going through all the painful chemotherapy treatments, then you will know that even science has limits. There are no limits in the spiritual – it all depends on how much you want to grow or develop. These are both the blessings and curses of free will. You are free to think, do, accept, or believe, or disbelieve whatever you want. It's not by force. God in His righteousness made it so.

You would see all kinds of people with cancers and other diseases. When you look at them physically, that's all you can see but if you can see in the spiritual realm, you would know that the things you call diseases can be all kinds of demonic beings and activities attached to people. Physical treatments just become a way to manage them for a while but eventually a waste of time, money, and effort. I am not saying that all diseases are from demons. If for example, there is a particular substance in a food you like to eat which causes a certain disease and you are stubborn enough to keep eating it then you will face the consequences. In other words, it is easier to solve cancers or diseases from physical causes in the physical with science but even if a migraine is sent to you from the spiritual realm, it can kill you instantly because the solution can't be found in the physical. The solution can only come from the spiritual.

If only doctors or professionals in the medical field will also be spiritual enough, they will learn and know when to apply physical medication and when to lay hands on the sick and cast out devils to set their patients free from affliction. This is the bridge or balance between the spiritual and the physical realms – both worlds help each other but the physical depends more on the spiritual.

I heard Neil deGrasse Tyson in an interview titled "Neil deGrasse Tyson on God". The interviewer asked him, do you believe in God, the creator? He responded and said that me, so, the more I look at the universe, the less convinced I am that there is something benevolent going on. So, if your concept of a creator is someone who is all powerful and all good – that's not an uncommon pairing and powers that you must describe to a creator. All powerful and all good, and I look at disasters that afflict Earth, life on Earth, volcanoes, hurricanes, tornadoes, Earthquakes, disease, pestilence, congenital birth defects – you look at this list of ways that life is made miserable on Earth by natural causes, and I just ask, how do you deal with that? So, philosophers rose and said if there is a God, God is either not all powerful or not all good. I have no problems if as we probe the origins of things we bump up into the bearded man. If that shows up, we are good to go, ok. Not a problem. There is just no evidence of it, and this is why religions are called faiths, collectively because you believe something in the absence of evidence. That's what it is. That's why it's called faith. Otherwise, we will call all religions evidence, but we don't, for exactly that reason. So, I'm giving what everyone describes to be the properties that will be expressed by an all-powerful being in the Gods that they worship. I look for that in the universe and I don't find it, so I remain unconvinced but if you got some good evidence, bring it. So, I don't lead with that information because what I believe should be irrelevant to anyone. It's not about me, it's about the real world. *End of interview.*

This is the gap that most scientists and philosophers have in God (spirituality) and science. In response to his words in the interview, so, we live in a world where we are governed by very clear and specific laws. We try as much to abide by these laws, and it's almost programmed as parts of our lives here on Earth while we are alive. For example, the government says don't drink and drive. If you drink and drive, you will get a DUI. That's exactly what will happen if you drink and drive. This is what Neil doesn't get. Christianity is a way of life. You first believe in God, and you read the Bible which has all the rules or laws and their conditions. If you don't even believe in God, let alone to read His word, and apply it to your life, just like your government laws, you are breaking the laws of God whether knowingly or unknowingly. Maybe you don't know but be aware that the Earth is in this state because of sin (breaking laws). Just like spirits, whether you intentionally or unintentionally invite them into your life doesn't mean the consequences will change – they will be the same or even worst.

Therefore, the greatest thing the word of God advises us to possess, and practice is love. Look around you, all these places that have wars, if and only if everybody loved everybody like you love your family and are at peace with them, then the world will become a better place. Don't you think so? The reason why you see a lot of pestilence, natural disasters etc., in the world is because we are not living according to the word, laws, statutes, and the commandments of God. You will find a lot of examples when you read the Bible. The Bible is supposed to be a human life manual for practical and to be practiced daily. You don't just read it as a story or history book. The Bible is alive when you believe, and God will show you Himself when you believe. In this writing, I show you how you scientists or physicists have proved God – He has proved Himself through His works to let you know how little you know when you think you know a lot. The spiritual world rules the physical world.

You may think that God is truly not all powerful and all good, but I tell you that everything is done according to spiritual laws. Maybe you did not know. God cannot do anything for humanity until somebody prays. Therefore, we have intercessors in the Body of Christ. It is illegal for God to interfere in the affairs of men if nobody is praying or without any intercession. This is due to the spiritual laws on the rules of engagement.

Prayer or intercession gives God authorization to intervene in the affairs of men here on Earth. Satan has the right to accuse the justice system of Heaven if God intervenes without somebody praying on Earth because this would be a violation to God's own divine laws. These same strict laws apply to everything else in the universe. For example, you can be very sure to wake up the next day to see the Sun shining or to have your seeds germinate or your plant grow when you plant them or to be sure that an early pregnancy will result to a baby and then into a mature man or woman over a period. If there were no laws, then everything would be out of course. Things don't just happen, and God is Almighty, faithful, righteous etc., because He doesn't break the laws He set. Therefore, He is God. Prayer grants Him the legal access to operate for us here on Earth. If God does anything here on Earth without the people of God praying to authorize Him first, then He would be trespassing. He already gave us dominion over the Earth upon creation in Genesis 1.

Psalm 115:16

[16] The Heaven, *even* the Heavens, *are* the LORD's;
But the Earth He has given to the children of men.

God has given the Earth to men so even Jesus had to be born through the womb of a woman before He could come here. You can't come to planet Earth without a womb of a woman. If any spirit comes here without a body, they are here illegally. No spirit or spirits can operate here without flesh and blood – you need a vehicle or vessel on Earth to work through. This applies to both the Holy Spirit, who is the Spirit of God, and demonic or evil spirits. This is a war going on and Satan needs your bodies as much as God does.

Isaiah 66:1:2

True Worship and False

66 Thus says the LORD:

"Heaven *is* My throne,
And Earth *is* My footstool.
Where *is* the house that you will build Me?
And where *is* the place of My rest?
[2] For all those *things* My hand has made,
And all those *things* exist,"
Says the LORD.
"But on this *one* will I look:
On *him who is* poor and of a contrite spirit,
And who trembles at My word.

Acts 7:49

[49] 'Heaven *is* My throne,
And Earth *is* My footstool.
What house will you build for Me? says the LORD,
Or what *is* the place of My rest?

Hebrews 10:5

[5] Therefore, when He came into the world, He said:

"Sacrifice and offering You did not desire,
But a body You have prepared for Me.

God is not talking about physical houses made with the hands of men. He is talking about human bodies. Apostle Paul confirms and advises the same thing in the book of Romans.

Romans 12:1-2

Living Sacrifices to God

12 I beseech you therefore, brethren, by the mercies of God, that you present your bodies a living sacrifice, holy, acceptable to God, *which is* your reasonable service. **²** And do not be conformed to this world, but be transformed by the renewing of your mind, that you may prove what *is* that good and acceptable and perfect will of God.

Man was initially given governance over the Earth but lost it to Satan because of disobedience. Satan has power over this Earth but through the sacrifice of Jesus, man has the authority back and can exercise and demonstrate it. I can give you scripture after scripture to prove to you how much power Satan has over this world. Unfortunately, Satan doesn't have the authority anymore because of the sacrifice of Jesus Christ for man. Below are some proofs of Satan's power over the world.

2 Corinthians 4:3-4

³ But even if our gospel is veiled, it is veiled to those who are perishing, **⁴** whose minds the god of this age has blinded, who do not believe, lest the light of the gospel of the glory of Christ, who is the image of God, should shine on them.

Ephesians 2:1-3

2 And you *He made alive,* who were dead in trespasses and sins, **²** in which you once walked according to the course of this world, according to the prince of the power of the air, the spirit who now works in the sons of disobedience, **³** among whom also we all once conducted ourselves in the lusts of our flesh, fulfilling the desires of the flesh and of the mind, and were by nature children of wrath, just as the others.

Matthew 4:8-10

⁸ Again, the devil took Him up on an exceedingly high mountain and showed Him all the kingdoms of the world and their glory. **⁹** And he said to Him, "All these things I will give You if You fall down and worship me."

¹⁰ Then Jesus said to him, "Away with you, Satan! For it is written, 'You shall worship the LORD your God, and Him only you shall serve.'"

It's only through true knowledge and understanding of the Word of God that grants man the dominion over the Earth through the authority given to us by Jesus Christ. Authority is what moves things in the spirit to manifest in the physical. Before you can use this power of attorney or delegated authority of Jesus, you must first be under His authority. You can't be a judge in the supreme court of the United States if you are not under the authority or government of the United States. This is how things work. The court system of God is stricter than the joke we have here on Earth. Even God Himself obeys His own laws and doesn't make Himself an exception. We have the authority to command all creation into obedience, but it requires submission and obedience to the authority of God first. Below is the wisdom of a centurion in the Bible regarding authority.

Matthew 8:5-10

Jesus Heals a Centurion's Servant

[5] Now when Jesus had entered Capernaum, a centurion came to Him, pleading with Him, [6] saying, "Lord, my servant is lying at home paralyzed, dreadfully tormented."

[7] And Jesus said to him, "I will come and heal him."

[8] The centurion answered and said, "Lord, I am not worthy that You should come under my roof. But only speak a word, and my servant will be healed. [9] For I also am a man under authority, having soldiers under me. And I say to this *one,* 'Go,' and he goes; and to another, 'Come,' and he comes; and to my servant, 'Do this,' and he does *it.*"

[10] When Jesus heard *it,* He marveled, and said to those who followed, "Assuredly, I say to you, I have not found such great faith, not even in Israel!

Below is a plea to God from someone several years ago, who understood the secrets and how things work in the courts of Heaven and in this world. For the same reasons that Neil deGrasse Tyson and other atheists think that God doesn't exist. Look at the prayer of a saint because he knew that people of this world did not understand spiritual things. You need knowledge and understanding to know why everything is the way it is. This is the kind of consciousness that God wants all of us to have.

Psalm 82

A Plea for Justice

A Psalm of Asaph.

82 God stands in the congregation of the mighty;
He judges among the gods.
[2] How long will you judge unjustly,
And show partiality to the wicked? *Selah*
[3] Defend the poor and fatherless;
Do justice to the afflicted and needy.
[4] Deliver the poor and needy;
Free *them* from the hand of the wicked.

⁵ They do not know, nor do they understand;
They walk about in darkness;
All the foundations of the Earth are unstable.
⁶ I said, "You *are* gods,
And all of you *are* children of the Most High.
⁷ But you shall die like men,
And fall like one of the princes."
⁸ Arise, O God, judge the Earth;
For You shall inherit all nations.

I will suggest to you, to repent of your words and come to God. God is not just science but if you still want to see more evidence of His works, let me know and I will show you. What you even call science is God's intelligence given to man by grace. You didn't invent it. You discovered it. That is why your scientific books always get updated, but the Bible has never even once been updated. It is written forever and ever and for everlasting to everlasting.

Matthew 24:35

³⁵ Heaven and Earth will pass away, but My words will by no means pass away.

I read another article on consciousness with the title "Can Quantum Physics Explain the Science of Creating Miracles?". Now scientists even regard miracles as science and this is very interesting.

"It seems human thoughts determine reality. It is one of the fundamental principles of quantum physics and was proved in the 1900s with the double-slit experiment and proved recently by Dr. Larry Farwell. It conclusively determined that the behavior of energy particles at the quantum level is the human observer's conscious intent. For example, it has been observed that the electrons under the same conditions would sometimes act like particles. Moreover, at other times, they would switch to working like waves, formless energy – completely dependent on what the human observer intended and imagined was going to materialize. Whatever the observed believed would happen is what the quantum field did in the experiments conducted over the years."

"When we make a conscious decision, the quantum world knows what to do and how to obey the command. Furthermore, as a result, it is we humans who are directing and controlling our quantum world. Our collective human energy field is interacting, instructing, and always influencing the quantum field all around us. Our conscious beliefs, desires, and intentions are infused into our energy field because they are defined and directed by the energy of our thoughts and emotions."

This was told a long time ago by the Bible – it is not new.

Numbers 13:33

33 There we saw the giants (the descendants of Anak came from the giants); and we were like grasshoppers in our own sight, and so we were in their sight."

Proverbs 4:23

23 Keep your heart with all diligence,
For out of it *spring* the issues of life.

Another translation says,

Proverbs 4:23

23 Be careful what you think,
   because your thoughts run your life.

Proverbs 23:7

7 For as he thinks in his heart, so *is* he.
"Eat and drink!" he says to you,
But his heart is not with you.

Mark 7:20-23

20 And He said, "What comes out of a man, that defiles a man. 21 For from within, out of the heart of men, proceed evil thoughts, adulteries, fornications, murders, 22 thefts, covetousness, wickedness, deceit, lewdness, an evil eye, blasphemy, pride, foolishness. 23 All these evil things come from within and defile a man."

"The emerging experimental evidence suggests that conscious human intentions and our universe are intertwined. Since everything in the universe is made from an interconnected web of energy, quantum physicists discovered that physical atoms are made of currents of energy that are constantly spinning and vibrating. Now the matter at its tiniest level is energy, and human consciousness is connected to it. So, human consciousness can instruct and influence its intentions and even restructure them."

You will hear scientists using the vibration of guitar strings or any other musical instrument to explain their quantum theories and how an instrument playing at a similar frequency can interact or vibrate along. They got that right. This is a fundamental principle in the Kingdom of God and how everything works in the universe. Music is a vital part of Heaven and the throne of God. It has been part of the worship and praise of God since the beginning. In fact, Lucifer was created as a beautiful and wise archangel, an anointed cherub, and music was an integral part of his being. Why do you think God did that? Although Lucifer is not part of God's Kingdom now, this example should help you understand that there's something about sound, music and vibrations, and God's Kingdom.

Ezekiel 28:13

[13] You were in Eden, the garden of God;
Every precious stone *was* your covering:
The sardius, topaz, and diamond,
Beryl, onyx, and jasper,
Sapphire, turquoise, and emerald with gold.
The workmanship of your timbrels and pipes
Was prepared for you on the day you were created.

Isaiah 14:11

[11] Your pomp is brought down to Sheol,
And the sound of your stringed instruments;
The maggot is spread under you,
And worms cover you.'

Isaiah says "the sound of your string instruments" when referring to Lucifer. This phrase illustrates an extraordinary mastery of stringed instruments by Lucifer and the use of them to accomplish his wicked purposes. They must have been quite valuable to Lucifer for him to declare them as his own.

Now let's look at a good example. Elisha used sound from the minstrel instrument to synchronize with the Spirit of God and prophecy. Maybe physicists should ask themselves, why is music this important in the Kingdom of God and why did prophets like Elisha used the minstrel to prophecy? The string musical instruments are very common in the Bible and there's a reason for that. We people of God know and understand the power of sound because it is one of our primary ways to contact and connect and synchronize with our Father God.

2 Kings 3:14-16

[14] And Elisha said, As the LORD of hosts liveth, before whom I stand, surely, were it not that I regard the presence of Jehoshaphat the king of Judah, I would not look toward thee, nor see thee.

[15] But now bring me a minstrel. And it came to pass, when the minstrel played, that the hand of the LORD came upon him.

[16] And he said, thus saith the LORD, Make this valley full of ditches.

"Our consciousness has a seamless interface with the universe and can accomplish any complexity necessary to carry out the desired result. Moreover, the conscious human intention has the power to command change in our universe. So, if we can consciously command even a very slight shift in the quantum-mechanical events that arise, provided that this change is consistent, that would be enough to explain not only how we exercise free will and drive our brains at will, but also how we potentially can create any world we desire. Great discoveries for our collective good will come when we are in harmony with the universe. So, how can the emerging understanding of Quantum Physics be applied to bring peace and security to our world?"

Quantum Physics cannot bring peace and security to the world. The answer to what they are trying to look for is the LOVE of CHRIST. That is the only thing that brings peace, joy, and harmony. Again, the Bible talks about this. We can read about love at least a hundred plus times in the Bible.

1 John 4:7-12

Knowing God Through Love

[7] Beloved, let us love one another, for love is of God; and everyone who loves is born of God and knows God. [8] He who does not love does not know God, for God is love. [9] In this the love of God was manifested toward us, that God has sent His only begotten Son into the world, that we might live through Him. [10] In this is love, not that we loved God, but that He loved us and sent His Son *to be* the propitiation for our sins. [11] Beloved, if God so loved us, we also ought to love one another.

Seeing God Through Love

[12] No one has seen God at any time. If we love one another, God abides in us, and His love has been perfected in us.

Without God, currently the Earth can be described in three words – darkness, lies, and corruption or hatred or wickedness. All these words are related. But with God, we have the opposite – light, truth, and love. Within these words, we can have righteousness, mercy, a forgiving heart, kindness, and a lot more.

Dr. Michio Kaku says, if you understand deeply the laws of physics then you know what is possible, plausible, and impossible. Having a good foundation in physics made all the difference in the world. All biology can be explained in the language of chemistry. All of chemistry can be explained in the language of physics. But all of physics can be explained in the language of relativity like the Big Bang and the quantum theory, which gives us transistors, and lasers, and the internet. The goal is to merge these two great theories to create an equation, that would allow us to unravel the universe itself – he calls it the holy grail of science. He quoted Galileo, who once said that "the purpose of science is to determine how the Heavens go. But the purpose of religion is to determine how to go to Heaven – how the Heavens go; how the planets move, how the galaxy moves, how to be a good person, how to obey the laws and help your neighbors. So, if we keep these two things relatively separate, they are complementary to each other, so, I don't see any contradiction between the two".

It is such a fine quote except that there are still some things missing in the "religion" aspect of the quote. I put religion in quotes because I call it Christianity because that's the only truth about what we call religion. The rest are bogus. The fathers of old knew that you couldn't separate science from God. After all the research, you will end up about God. I say that we have already unraveled the universe, just not all of it but at least from all of science discoveries, there is not a single doubt that there is a supreme being called the God of the Heavens and the Earth – a sovereign God who created all things, including what we call the universe. And truly, there is no separation of science from God – it's just impossible. But as always, the people of God have already unraveled the universe and they did that several years ago through the Spirit of God.

Dr. Kaku said that he begins to realize that science is closing in on mortality – genetic immortality is a possibility and digital immortality is a possibility. For example, everything known about us can be digitized – credit card transactions, emails, to give an approximation of who we are (our digital soul). Why do we die? We die because of the buildup of error – error in our DNA, errors in our cells because of chaos; the second law of thermodynamics. This law shows that things rust, things fall apart, things die but if you get energy from the outside, you can get around the second law of thermodynamics. For example, with gene therapy, we'll be able to attack aging at three levels – telomeres: is also used by cancer cells. Cancer cells are also immortal, that's why they kill you. That's one way cancer cells become immortal, so we must control telomeres etcetera.

Is it not interesting to learn that where science has reached and where it's heading all prove that God truly exists? Therefore, the Bible mentions that we are in this state because of sin. Cancer cells kill us through corrupting our organs (interfering and impairing their function). Sin is what started the entire buildup of error that Dr. Kaku talks about. There is only one way to total immortality – a life in Christ Jesus, which then becomes a holy life that is free from sin and death. That's the mystery of the cross. There's no way around that, not even science can solve it through biochemistry. Someday, science will understand this fact. According to both the Bible and the laws of physics, this is impossible to attain in mere science.

Romans 2:7

7 eternal life to those who by patient continuance in doing good seek for glory, honor, and immortality;

1 Corinthians 15:51-58

51 Behold, I tell you a mystery: We shall not all sleep, but we shall all be changed— 52 in a moment, in the twinkling of an eye, at the last trumpet. For the trumpet will sound, and the dead will be raised incorruptible, and we shall be changed. 53 For this corruptible must put on incorruption, and this mortal *must* put on immortality. 54 So when this corruptible has put on incorruption, and this mortal has put on immortality, then shall be brought to pass the saying that is written: "Death is swallowed up in victory."

55 "O Death, where *is* your sting?
O Hades, where *is* your victory?"

56 The sting of death *is* sin, and the strength of sin *is* the law. 57 But thanks *be* to God, who gives us the victory through our Lord Jesus Christ.

58 Therefore, my beloved brethren, be steadfast, immovable, always abounding in the work of the Lord, knowing that your labor is not in vain in the Lord.

Ezekiel 18:4

4 "Behold, all souls are Mine;
The soul of the father
As well as the soul of the son is Mine;
The soul who sins shall die.

Romans 6:23

23 For the wages of sin *is* death, but the gift of God *is* eternal life in Christ Jesus our Lord.

At least science knows now that it is a possibility to live forever and ever. It has always been like that – eternal life. It was like that in the beginning, before man sinned for the first time in the Garden of Eden. It's also interesting to read science talk about "digital immortality" or our digital soul. Again, it has always been like that. Our souls existed even before we were born, and it will continue to exist in eternity. There are several scriptures on this but below are a few.

Jeremiah 1:5

5 "Before I formed you in the womb, I knew you;
Before you were born, I sanctified you;
I ordained you a prophet to the nations."

Jeremiah 29:11

11 For I know the thoughts that I think toward you, saith the Lord, thoughts of peace, and not of evil, to give you an expected end.

Romans 8:29-30

29 For whom He foreknew, He also predestined *to be* conformed to the image of His Son, that He might be the firstborn among many brethren. 30 Moreover whom He predestined, these He also called; whom He called, these He also justified; and whom He justified, these He also glorified.

This is the same way you predestine your robots before you sell them to customers or send them to space for explorations. You have an expectation for them, and as long as they follow your programming, you can be very sure of their success. We are eternal or immortal beings. There is no question about whether this is true or false. It is a fact. The question you should ask yourself is where will I spend eternity or immortality? There are only two precise locations – Heaven or hell. You decide and choose for yourself today, which location you want to spend eternity.

Isaiah 65:17

The Glorious New Creation

[17] "For behold, I create new Heavens and a new Earth;
And the former shall not be remembered or come to mind.

This is how awesome our God is – He knows how messed up this current Earth is and how there are still contaminations in some Heavenly places because of activities of the devil and wickedness. We will not remember our experiences here; they will not come to mind at the new Heavens and the new Earth. All these will come pass and your negative or opposite opinion about it won't change anything.

Isaiah 66:22

[22] "For as the new Heavens and the new Earth
Which I will make shall remain before Me," says the LORD,
"So shall your descendants and your name remain.

Revelation 21:1

All Things Made New

21 Now I saw a new Heaven and a new Earth, for the first Heaven and the first Earth had passed away. Also, there was no more sea.

Just like the prophecies about the birth of Jesus came to past, so shall every other prophecy come to past. If the Lord tarries in His return, in a hundred years from now, records somewhere could show that you once existed. These records could be your so-called "digital soul" or anything you may have written. People in that generation may choose to believe whether you existed or not. Their opinion wouldn't change the fact that you existed because you truly existed and would still be existing in another dimension. Perhaps, scientists should investigate why there will be no more sea in the new Heaven and the new Earth. In what form will we live that will not require us to have the sea as our primary life support system as we do right now on Earth?

Jesus spoke a lot about hell. Here are a few examples but you can research the rest on your own. The same way you gained consciousness here on Earth at a certain age, that's the same way you will have full consciousness on the other side when you leave the Earth. You don't know how you came by that consciousness or how it worked for you as a child – you just found yourself alive suddenly. It'll be the same thing. Spiritual things are foolishness to only the carnally minded.

Revelation 21:8

[8] But the cowardly, unbelieving, abominable, murderers, sexually immoral, sorcerers, idolaters, and all liars shall have their part in the lake which burns with fire and brimstone, which is the second death."

Matthew 10:28

[28] And do not fear those who kill the body but cannot kill the soul. But rather fear Him who is able to destroy both soul and body in hell.

Matthew 13:41-42

[41] The Son of Man will send out His angels, and they will gather out of His kingdom all things that offend, and those who practice lawlessness, [42] and will cast them into the furnace of fire. There will be wailing and gnashing of teeth.

Matthew 25:46

[46] And these will go away into everlasting punishment, but the righteous into eternal life."

Everything that science is "discovering and proving", is already in the Bible – they all come from God. What scientists call quantum is a spiritual technology – it works by first, having free will and using that free will to believe through faith but I don't see how physics or science in general can build a system or technology that can have and exercise these spiritual attributes. It's impossible because even human beings who have been given freely these abilities are rebelling.

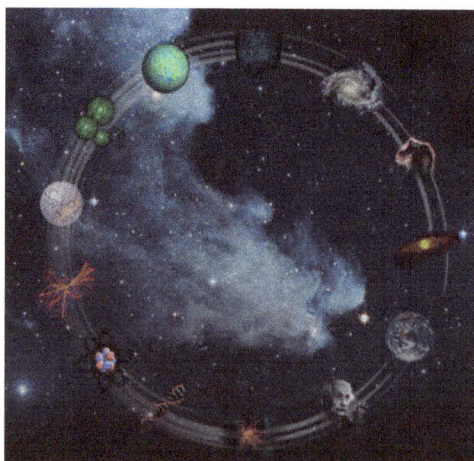

Image Source – Public Domain

Science or physics belong to God. He knew that our current state wasn't His original plan for us so He revealed His science to us through mysteries so that we can use it to advance ourselves and live well while we await His return. It is given to us for our good, not to disprove that God exists. I don't think most scientists even know how what they are studying started – the history or background or the foundations of it. That is why we are having this quantum theory fundamental problem. It's right there but they can't see it. It started from God, and it will end with God.

This image above is from the Foundational Questions Institute's website. FQXi catalyzes, supports, and disseminates research on questions at the foundations of physics and cosmology, particularly new frontiers, and innovative ideas integral to a deep understanding of reality, but unlikely to be supported by conventional funding sources.

The foundational or fundamental questions that seem mysterious and they don't have answers to is the purpose for this writing. God is both the fundamental and the advanced of the universe. It's interesting that the image here is a circle – they have an idea of God but it's either they don't want to accept, or they still think everything is about science. Well, God is spirit and God is science, and everything is science except that you can't fully understand science until you understand the spiritual because the spiritual is the aspect of science you cannot see or explain with mere science or physics. In other words, the spiritual can be thought of as the invisible science. It is the foundation of everything we see in the physical as both matter and antimatter. We can all agree that till today, this one pursuit about the universe proves that scientists do not even understand how science works. This is not meant to be an insult. Scientists have done a great job so far, but the missing link isn't science – it is spiritual. Once they fit that into this image you see above, everything will start making sense to them and you will truly understand that the problem they are dealing with or trying to solve is an eternal or infinity problem. Put what I am telling you in this writing before, inside, and after the picture of the Earth or globe in the circle, and you will know that God is truly alpha omega – the beginning, the end. Out of Him, came all things and through Him came everything that was made and without Him was nothing that was ever made.

John 1:3

[3] All things were made through Him, and without Him nothing was made that was made.

Colossians 1:16-17

[16] For by Him all things were created that are in Heaven and that are on Earth, visible and invisible, whether thrones or dominions or principalities or powers. All things were created through Him and for Him. [17] And He is before all things, and in Him all things consist.

The fear had always been that once we discover that indeed the universe had a singularity (sovereign) beginning, that will imply that physics had broken down. Well, that's if physicists will want to see it that way. But it doesn't necessarily mean that physics has broken down – it means that physics has a beginning, and the beginning explains physics even much better. Physicists will have a much better understanding of things and to the high schoolers, physics won't be as hard or that bad anymore after all.

This writing is to confirm that Albert Einstein was also right – his general theory of relativity is correct. That means that there was singularity, a point of infinite density and space-time curvature, where time in fact, has a beginning. This is to also confirm that Georges Lemaître was right – the universe started off in a Big Bang and expanded quickly. This is called "inflation" and it was extremely rapid: the universe doubled in size many times in a tiny fraction of a second. Inflation made the universe very large, very smooth and very flat. However, it was not completely smooth: there were tiny variations from place to place. These variations eventually gave rise to galaxies, stars, and solar systems because God's creations were orderly – one thing after the other. He did not create it all in the first day. We don't owe our existence to these variations (evolution) as scientists say: we owe our existence to the one and only Source, God. Scientists add that if the universe had been completely smooth, there would be no stars and so life could not have developed. That's accurate. That is why God created life (land animals and finally humans) as the last beings on day six in the days of creation. So, human life was God's final creation in the order of creation. Finally, we are the product of primordial quantum, like physics will call it. You have put in great and enough effort but that is how far you can go because the rest are all mysteries (spiritual). I call it the end of the 3D. God is your legal access into the 4D and beyond.

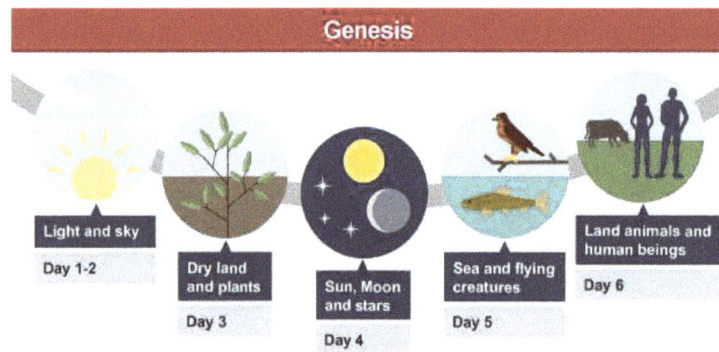

Image Source – Public Domain

Genesis 1

The Beginning

The History of Creation of the World

1 In the beginning God created the Heavens and the Earth. **2** The Earth was without form, and void; and darkness *was* on the face of the deep. And the Spirit of God was hovering over the face of the waters.

3 Then God said, "Let there be light"; and there was light. **4** And God saw the light, that *it was* good; and God divided the light from the darkness. **5** God called the light Day, and the darkness He called Night. So, the evening and the morning were the first day.

6 Then God said, "Let there be a firmament in the midst of the waters, and let it divide the waters from the waters." **7** Thus God made the firmament and divided the waters which *were* under the firmament from the waters which *were* above the firmament; and it was so. **8** And God called the firmament Heaven. So, the evening and the morning were the second day.

9 Then God said, "Let the waters under the Heavens be gathered together into one place, and let the dry *land* appear"; and it was so. **10** And God called the dry *land* Earth, and the gathering together of the waters He called Seas. And God saw that *it was* good.

11 Then God said, "Let the Earth bring forth grass, the herb *that* yields seed, *and* the fruit tree *that* yields fruit according to its kind, whose seed *is* in itself, on the Earth"; and it was so. **12** And the Earth brought forth grass, the herb *that* yields seed according to its kind, and the tree *that* yields fruit, whose seed *is* in itself according to its kind. And God saw that *it was* good. **13** So the evening and the morning were the third day.

14 Then God said, "Let there be lights in the firmament of the Heavens to divide the day from the night; and let them be for signs and seasons, and for days and years; **15** and let them be for lights in the firmament of the Heavens to give light on the Earth"; and it was so. **16** Then God made two great lights: the greater light to rule the day, and the lesser light to rule the night. *He made* the stars also. **17** God set them in the firmament of the Heavens to give light on the Earth, **18** and to rule over the day and over the night, and to divide the light from the darkness. And God saw that *it was* good. **19** So the evening and the morning were the fourth day.

20 Then God said, "Let the waters abound with an abundance of living creatures, and let birds fly above the Earth across the face of the firmament of the Heavens." **21** So God created great sea creatures and every living thing that moves, with which the waters abounded, according to their kind, and every winged bird according to its kind. And God saw that *it was* good. **22** And God blessed them, saying, "Be fruitful and multiply, and fill the waters in the seas, and let birds multiply on the Earth." **23** So the evening and the morning were the fifth day.

24 Then God said, "Let the Earth bring forth the living creature according to its kind: cattle and creeping thing and beast of the Earth, *each* according to its kind"; and it was so. **25** And God made the beast of the Earth according to its kind, cattle according to its kind, and everything that creeps on the Earth according to its kind. And God saw that *it was* good.

26 Then God said, "Let Us make man in Our image, according to Our likeness; let them have dominion over the fish of the sea, over the birds of the air, and over the cattle, over all the Earth and over every creeping thing that creeps on the Earth." **27** So God created man in His *own* image; in the image of God, He created him; male and female He created them. **28** Then God blessed them, and God said to them, "Be fruitful and multiply; fill the Earth and subdue it; have dominion over the fish of the sea, over the birds of the air, and over every living thing that moves on the Earth."

²⁹ And God said, "See, I have given you every herb *that* yields seed which *is* on the face of all the Earth, and every tree whose fruit yields seed; to you it shall be for food. ³⁰ Also, to every beast of the Earth, to every bird of the air, and to everything that creeps on the Earth, in which *there is* life, *I have given* every green herb for food"; and it was so. ³¹ Then God saw everything that He had made, and indeed *it was* very good. So, the evening and the morning were the sixth day.

So, this was our beginning. There have still been questions regarding our universe. Most people have been asking, where did we come from? And are we the only beings in the universe? We came from God – we came from His light. We are spirit beings in Earthly (matter) bodies. That's where our consciousness come from – the breath of God. When you believe in Him and serve Him, you become one spirit with Him, and you know what He knows. That's why we had prophets in the Bible, and we still have them today. They know the deep things of God through the Holy Spirit.

1 Corinthians 6:17

¹⁷ But he who is joined to the Lord is one spirit *with Him.*

1 Corinthians 2:10-16

¹⁰ But God has revealed *them* to us through His Spirit. For the Spirit searches all things, yes, the deep things of God. ¹¹ For what man knows the things of a man except the spirit of the man which is in him? Even so no one knows the things of God except the Spirit of God. ¹² Now we have received, not the spirit of the world, but the Spirit who is from God, that we might know the things that have been freely given to us by God.

¹³ These things we also speak, not in words which man's wisdom teaches but which the Holy Spirit teaches, comparing spiritual things with spiritual. ¹⁴ But the natural man does not receive the things of the Spirit of God, for they are foolishness to him; nor can he know *them,* because they are spiritually discerned. ¹⁵ But he who is spiritual judges all things, yet he himself is *rightly* judged by no one. ¹⁶ For "who has known the mind of the LORD that he may instruct Him?" But we have the mind of Christ.

These things – these natural and supernatural abilities have been freely given to us by God. That is why in quantum mechanics, you have learned and expect an object to be here and there at the same time, but it makes no sense to you. Why? Because you want to solve or understand it from a physical perspective, but these things are spiritual. That is why a prophet can be in His room and be somewhere else at the same time. It is not magic or weird or bizarre. It is the spirit of God joined together with your spirit and working in synchronicity. With this supernatural ability, you can have the all-seeing eyes because you can be in multiple places at the same time. This is what you are trying to solve as quantum, but it is not for physics to solve. Life is not just physics. Life is spiritual and the spiritual rules over the physical because out of the spiritual came all things, including you.

2 Kings 6:12

¹² And one of his servants said, "None, my lord, O king; but Elisha, the prophet who *is* in Israel, tells the king of Israel the words that you speak in your bedroom."

How was Elisha in His room but also in the king's bedroom in Syria at the same time but the King did not know it? In your physics, you call it quantum. That is how best physics can name it. It is not quantum – it is the spirit of God, joining with the spirit of the man of God to be one spirit. So, next time you see a prophet or any men or women of God, honor them as truly a people of God because God lives in them, and they know the secret things of God that you do not know. When one tells you that you will be blessed then you shall surely be blessed but when he or she tells you that you shall die then you shall surely die. Get a Bible and read it for more examples and turn to God and be saved and transformed.

And are we the only beings in the universe? You should know the answer by now and yes, your guess is correct – no, we're not the only beings in the universe. The scary and dangerous part is that most of these beings, you cannot see with the physical eyes. So, when we say demons or evil spirits or Satan is real, yes, they are real. They all exist in different forms. The sad part is that you are just a vessel, or a host and they can possess your body if you don't allow God to live in you because you can't be an empty vessel in this universe – a spirit must occupy and use you. Get yourself a Bible and read about it.

Ephesians 6:10-12

The Whole Armor of God

¹⁰ Finally, my brethren, be strong in the Lord and in the power of His might. ¹¹ Put on the whole armor of God, that you may be able to stand against the wiles of the devil. ¹² For we do not wrestle against flesh and blood, but against principalities, against powers, against the rulers of the darkness of this age, against spiritual *hosts* of wickedness in the Heavenly *places.*

The Bible calls these present times darkness. God is real my people. Satan and his devils are real. Heaven and Earth are also real. When you ignore the Bible and God, you are meant to be destroyed at the final day and hour of the Earth. And that day will surely come. There is no doubt or question about that. You can believe it or leave it. We will live forever and ever in eternity and there we will not be limited by our physical bodies but limitless with our spiritual bodies. To help you understand, we will be living in our quantum bodies where there is no space or time. We are currently living in darkness as the Bible says and science is finally proving that we live in a black hole (darkness). We (children, sons and daughters, and men and women of God) are supposed to be the light in this darkness. That's why we bring you the good news about Christ's sacrifice to bring us out of this darkness forever and ever. Christianity isn't a fairy tale or joke or something that is meant to waste your time. It is meant to save you and it works by first offering your free will as a sacrifice and using it to accept this by faith. For without faith, it is impossible to please God.

Hebrews 11:1-3

By Faith We Understand

11 Now faith is the substance of things hoped for, the evidence of things not seen. [2] For by it the elders obtained a *good* testimony.

[3] By faith we understand that the worlds were framed by the word of God, so that the things which are seen were not made of things which are visible.

Science is already proving this, and this is what we call reality. We know that out of the unseen realm did the seen realm fully emerge and fully depend.

Hebrews 11:4-6

Faith at the Dawn of History

[4] By faith Abel offered to God a more excellent sacrifice than Cain, through which he obtained witness that he was righteous, God testifying of his gifts; and through it he being dead still speaks.

[5] By faith Enoch was taken away so that he did not see death, "and was not found, because God had taken him"; for before he was taken, he had this testimony, that he pleased God. [6] But without faith *it is* impossible to please *Him,* for he who comes to God must believe that He is, and *that* He is a rewarder of those who diligently seek Him.

Now science is even thinking about time travel as a possibility. This technology existed several thousands of years ago for the people of God. It is the real deal – it is reality and now, let this be your reality about the universe and your existence whether you like it or not. Whether you believe it and practice it or not, it doesn't change the prophecy that is to come. You will be doomed at the final hour no matter what unless you accept Christ. He is your one and only way – you have no other better options. That's the only condition that will save you forever and ever. Everything we are dealing with here in this quantum physics mystery is eternity or infinity – it is always going to be forever and ever. Nothing more, nothing less. The fact that you are even reading this writing means when that final hour comes, you will not have any excuse that the gospel didn't reach you. Be mindful of that. It wouldn't matter if you are male or female, young or old, rich, or poor. Being a billionaire won't save you on that day if you refuse to come to Christ. Let this day be your decision point and come to Christ.

Dr. Martin Luther King Jr. and Albert Einstein

"Science investigates; religion interprets. Science gives man knowledge which is power; religion gives man wisdom which is control. Science deals mainly with facts; religion deals mainly with values. The two are not rivals. They are complementary." – Dr. Martin Luther King Jr.

Please be advised that religion as Dr. King was referring to here is Christianity with its associated spirituality. This man knew something, and he is very on point.

"Science without religion is lame, religion without science is blind." – Albert Einstein. Einstein was confident in science's ability to afford new information and knowledge, even to the extent of producing a reconstruction of existence. He also said, "Though science is the attempt at the posterior reconstruction, science can never succeed in such an aim unless it is guided by judgments beyond science".

This is a very strong and powerful statement by Einstein. He knew that there was more to science than what meets the eye. He knew something – he was a smart man indeed. The judgements beyond science that he's referring to is Christianity and a life in Christ to serve the one and only true God of the Heavens and the Earth. It is only from the spiritual realm that we get such revelation and wisdom from God. It is very uncommon.

"We know nothing about [God, and the world] at all. All our knowledge is but the knowledge of school children. Possible we shall know a little more than we do now. But the real nature of things, that we shall never know, never."

These words came from the one who discovered the world's most famous equation – Einstein. Think about it very carefully. The people of God will know because He reveals it to them just as He revealed the theory, $E = mc^2$ to Einstein. It is said that the year 1905 was a landmark year for science is grossly underselling it. Einstein, still working as a "technical expert" in the Swiss patent office, published four revolutionary scientific papers in a span of 7 months that would establish him as one of the greatest scientific minds of the time. Einstein later described the period by saying that it was when "a storm broke loose in my mind". He just wasn't spiritually grown enough to know that that was God. That is why the idea symbol in science is represented by a light bulb. When you are spiritually mature enough and know these things, you will know when God drops and turns on the light bulb in your mind. There's a reason for that but that's a lecture for another time.

Einstein continued. "I see a pattern, but my imagination cannot picture the maker of the pattern. I see a clock, but I cannot envision the clockmaker. The human mind is unable to conceive of the four dimensions, so how can it conceive of a God, before whom a thousand years and a thousand dimensions are as one?"

Einstein was either knowingly or unknowingly quoting some scriptures – these words are in the Bible. The wisdom that he possessed, and his reasoning tells me that he knew God because when every wise person sits down quietly to look around him or her and think properly, they cannot deny that there is no maker or creator of the universe.

Psalm 90:4

[4] For a thousand years in Your sight
Are like yesterday when it is past,
And *like* a watch in the night.

2 Peter 3:8

[8] But, beloved, do not forget this one thing, that with the Lord one day *is* as a thousand years, and a thousand years as one day.

When asked whether he was influenced by Christianity, he said, "As a child I received instruction in both the Bible and the Talmud. I am a Jew, but I am enthralled by the luminous figure of the Nazarene (Jesus Christ)."

When asked whether he accepted the historical existence of Jesus, he replied, "Unquestionably! No one can read the Gospels without feeling the actual presence of Jesus. His personality pulsates in every word. No myth is filled with such life."

Just right here in this statement, Einstein confirms without a doubt that the gospel is the truth and Jesus truly exists. Albert Einstein wasn't a fool as we all know; he believed in a higher intelligence – he believed in God. He did not preach the gospel, so we did not know his secret life. It is hard to know what men do in the secret, whether they do good or bad things. One can only discern the hearts or true lives of people by the Spirit of God – the Holy Spirit. But from what he contributed to the world, he met God but didn't know it or didn't want to disclose it or give Him glory.

He said of the creator's existence, "I am not an atheist. I don't think I can call myself a pantheist. The problem involved is too vast for our limited minds. We are in the position of a little child entering a huge library filled with books in many languages. The child knows someone must have written those books. It does not know how. It does not understand languages in which they are written. The child dimly suspects a mysterious order in the arrangement of the books but doesn't know what it is. That, it seems to me, is the attitude of even the most intelligent human being toward God. We see the universe marvelously arranged and obeying certain laws but only dimly understand these laws. What separates me from most so-called atheists is a feeling of utter humility toward the unattainable secrets of the harmony of the cosmos."

Einstein was humble because he knew that there are unattainable secrets of the harmony of the cosmos. When there are secrets, you discover, you don't invent. He surely believed that he was only a discoverer, not an inventor. Nothing is new – everything already exists. Whatever we see as new has already existed. The following are the words of the wisest man, King Solomon in the Bible.

Ecclesiastes 1:9-10

[9] That which has been *is* what will be,
That which *is* done is what will be done,
And *there is* nothing new under the Sun.
[10] Is there anything of which it may be said,
"See, this *is* new"?
It has already been in ancient times before us.

Einstein also knew immediately that putting himself under the category of atheists would only make him a fool after all that he had learned about the marvelous arrangements, patterns, and laws of the universe and how the universe obeys these laws. We all know that even physically here on Earth, we only obey laws from higher authorities – the federal and local governments. Think about the rest. There is a sovereignty over the Heavens and the Earth and that is God.

He wrote in a letter, "The fanatical atheists, are like slaves who are still feeling the weight of their chains which they have thrown off after hard struggle. They are creatures who in their grudge against traditional religion as the 'opium of the masses', cannot hear the music of the spheres."

In other words, because of the hatred of traditional religion, they refuse to see the supremacy and genius of God's work anywhere, including their own bodies (human anatomy) and around them. Your body was perfectly made by the hands of God. You are a piece of divine artistry.

At the age of 34, a young Albert Einstein proudly boasted of something that seemed right to him. "I have firmly resolved to bite the dust, when my time comes, with the minimum of medical assistance, and up to then I will sin to my wicked heart's content."

So, Einstein believed that there is something called sin. You only believe that there is sin if you believe that there is righteousness. You only believe that there is darkness if you believe that there is light. And you also only believe that there is lie if you believe that there is truth. This is how it works. This is reality.

As he grew older, he became more philosophical, "To one bent on age, death will come as a release. I feel this quite strongly now that I have grown old to regard death like an old debt, at long last, to be discharged. Still, instinctively one does everything possible to postpone the final settlement. Such is the game that nature plays with us."

He spoke biblical truths unawares. But people of God even look forward to going home to their Lord. Death to the true Christian is only the beginning – it is merely a transition from one dimension into another. He accepted that upon all the wisdom, death was inevitable. Again, even the wisest man in the Bible (King Solomon) towards the end of his life, talked this way.

Ecclesiastes 1:12-18

The Grief of Wisdom

¹² I, the Preacher, was king over Israel in Jerusalem. ¹³ And I set my heart to seek and search out by wisdom concerning all that is done under Heaven; this burdensome task God has given to the sons of man, by which they may be exercised. ¹⁴ I have seen all the works that are done under the Sun; and indeed, all *is* vanity and grasping for the wind.

¹⁵ *What is* crooked cannot be made straight,
And what is lacking cannot be numbered.

¹⁶ I communed with my heart, saying, "Look, I have attained greatness, and have gained more wisdom than all who were before me in Jerusalem. My heart has understood great wisdom and knowledge." ¹⁷ And I set my heart to know wisdom and to know madness and folly. I perceived that this also is grasping for the wind.

¹⁸ For in much wisdom *is* much grief,
And he who increases knowledge increases sorrow.

The sorrow in Einstein's case was that he knew that there was more to life and the universe, but he wasn't given access to them and at the end of his life, he knew that he couldn't escape death. He also knew that at the end of your life, every physical thing in this universe; whether fame or riches wouldn't matter – all would be vanity. His attempt to have a God Equation or the Equation of Everything was even proof of that. His only option was to accept death because it didn't matter whether his life was extended through medical means, death would still come someday. Reality still kicks in for every person on Earth at the point of death and only the meek and humble in heart can truly repent and see the light so that they can spend eternity in a better place.

So, we can all agree that Dr. Martin Luther King Jr. and Albert Einstein both concluded that religion and science complimented each another. Religion (Christianity) fills in the blanks that science cannot answer. The scriptures fill in the blanks that science cannot offer. You ignore the scriptures, and you live in total darkness and confusion.

I say that science is only an attempt or the process to discover, reveal, and manifest spiritual things in the physical as designed by God according to His divine specific patterns, laws, and principles.

Important Findings of the Big Bang Theory

Science proves the universe to be made up of space, time, and matter. Scientists initially thought that the universe was made up of only one galaxy. But they got that wrong. Until the 1920s, science, astronomers, and philosophers, including professors all mocked the Bible. They unanimously agreed that science, space, and matter had always existed. They believed that the galaxies, the universe had always been, but they got it all wrong. They basically mocked at the creation story of the Bible. In 1929, an Astronomer by name Edwin Hubble observed that the universe was expanding. His observation was only a confirmation to what the Belgian Catholic priest, Georges Lemaître had already observed earlier in the year 1927. You shouldn't be surprised that it was a priest who first discovered all these – it was not only science. Hubble documented galaxies that were rapidly moving away from one another. He noticed that the ones further away from the Earth were moving away at a rapid pace. This makes us believe that the universe has a beginning. To the natural world, they believe that it all started with just the Big Bang theory. Now even science believe that the universe has a beginning before the Big Bang. Of course, because even human beings have a beginning – there was a specific creation day.

The Big Bang theory proved the creation of time, space, and matter. This is a trinity but a trinity of several trinities. Time consists of past, present, and future. Space consists of length, width, and height. Matter consists of liquids, gas, and solids. So, we see, it consists of three things, hence, the triune nature of God and the triune nature of man.

Man is made up of six elements, according to science. The human body is made mostly of water (a molecule composed of two hydrogen and one oxygen atom) and of "organic" molecules, which consist of a skeleton of carbon atoms bound to other elements. The organic molecules include mainly proteins (mostly carbon, hydrogen, oxygen, and nitrogen, but also sulfur and selenium), carbohydrates (mostly carbon, oxygen, and hydrogen), fats (as above), and nucleic acids (carbon, hydrogen, nitrogen, oxygen, and phosphorus). It is thus no wonder that 99% of the atoms in the human body come from six elements: Hydrogen (62.9%), oxygen (almost 24%), carbon (nearly 12%), nitrogen (nearly 0.6%), calcium (0.24%) and phosphorus (0.14%).

Hydrogen can be physically stored as liquid or gas. Storage as a gas typically requires high-pressure tanks (5000–10,000 psi tank pressure). Oxygen as we all know or very familiar with is mostly gas. It can be stored in all three states (liquid, solid, and gas) at different temperatures. And phosphorus is a solid. This is to help you understand that the human body is made up of the same elements of the universe, specifically, the Earth. On a natural level, the human being is still triune. Traditionalists also understand this concept in terms of spirituality; Higher Self – Conscious Self – Lower Self. Christians believe that man's triune nature is the Body – Mind/Soul – Spirit. The human being has a triune nature just like God – Father, Son, and the Holy Spirit.

The only attempt to prove the source of the universe has been from NASA, the Big Bang Theory. The following is the image illustration of what it means.

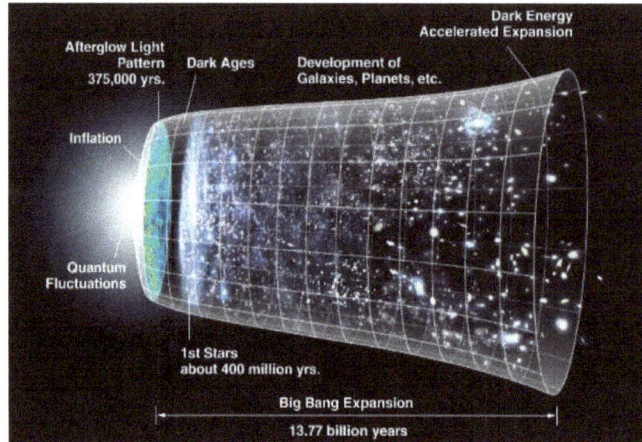

The Big Bang Theory

Image Source – Public Domain

The Bible Is Reliable in Proving Science

Pastor Tyson once gave a teaching that was titled "Modern Science Proves the Bible is Accurate". It had some very good content, and I will expand on it. God created everything in specific order according to specific patterns under divine laws and principles. God existed outside of space, time, and matter right from the beginning because you can't be within or inside what you create.

John 1:1-5

The Eternal Word

1 In the beginning was the Word, and the Word was with God, and the Word was God. **2** He was in the beginning with God. **3** All things were made through Him, and without Him nothing was made that was made. **4** In Him was life, and the life was the light of men. **5** And the light shines in the darkness, and the darkness did not comprehend it.

The universe has a beginning. The Big Bang theory starts the illustration of the origin of the universe with the light. They suggest that light and matter radiated from the beginning and gave motion to rest of creation, including man.

Genesis 1:1-5

The History of Creation

1 In the beginning God created the Heavens and the Earth. **2** The Earth was without form, and void; and darkness *was* on the face of the deep. And the Spirit of God was hovering over the face of the waters.

3 Then God said, "Let there be light"; and there was light. **4** And God saw the light, that *it was* good; and God divided the light from the darkness. **5** God called the light Day, and the darkness He called Night. So, the evening and the morning were the first day.

Biblical tradition says that the Book of Genesis was written by Moses during the Exodus from Egypt, between 1440 and 1400 BCE. An uneducated, unlearned Hebrew scribe wrote Genesis under the inspiration of God. The Bible preceded astronomy by too many years – over 3000 years. Now, science proves this by the Big Bang theory illustration in the figure above. It was released by NASA in 2001.

Scientists got it mostly correct – except that they didn't and still don't know and can't link their "Bing Bang Theory" to the Supreme Source – Almighty God. Science wants to see to believe, which is the difference between spirituality and science. But there is a relationship between the two. We believe by faith; we don't have to see it physically to believe, for the Word of God says:

Hebrews 11:1-7

By Faith We Understand

11 Now faith is the substance of things hoped for, the evidence of things not seen. **2** For by it the elders obtained a *good* testimony.

3 By faith we understand that the worlds were framed by the word of God, so that the things which are seen were not made of things which are visible.

Faith at the Dawn of History

4 By faith Abel offered to God a more excellent sacrifice than Cain, through which he obtained witness that he was righteous, God testifying of his gifts; and through it he being dead still speaks.

5 By faith Enoch was taken away so that he did not see death, "and was not found, because God had taken him"; for before he was taken, he had this testimony, that he pleased God. **6** But without faith *it is* impossible to please *Him,* for he who comes to God must believe that He is, and *that* He is a rewarder of those who diligently seek Him.

7 By faith Noah, being divinely warned of things not yet seen, moved with godly fear, prepared an ark for the saving of his household, by which he condemned the world and became heir of the righteousness which is according to faith.

Before and within the light in the Big Bang representation image is what our Bible describes in the book of 1 Timothy.

1 Timothy 6:11-16

The Good Confession

11 But you, O man of God, flee these things and pursue righteousness, godliness, faith, love, patience, gentleness. **12** Fight the good fight of faith, lay hold on eternal life, to which you were also called and have confessed the good confession in the presence of many witnesses. **13** I urge you in the sight of God who gives life to all things, and *before* Christ Jesus who witnessed the good confession before Pontius Pilate, **14** that you keep *this* commandment without spot, blameless until our Lord Jesus Christ's appearing, **15** which He will manifest in His own time, *He who is* the blessed and only Potentate, the King of kings and Lord of lords, **16** who alone has immortality, dwelling in unapproachable light, whom no man has seen or can see, to whom *be* honor and everlasting power. Amen.

So, you see, this is the light that is being described in the Big Bang theory – the unapproachable light. It is interesting for them to point out that that space, realm, or dimension is quantum. We have already learned about quantum earlier in this writing, but we will discuss a bit more again later as we keep going.

Psalm 119:130

130 The entrance of Your words gives light;
It gives understanding to the simple.

The Big Bang theory was first proposed in the 1920s by Georges Lemaître, (1894-1966): Belgian cosmologist, Catholic priest, and father of the Big Bang theory. This startling idea first appeared in scientific form in 1931, in a paper by Georges Lemaître. The theory, accepted by nearly all astronomers today, was a radical departure from scientific orthodoxy in the 1930s. Many astronomers at the time were still uncomfortable with the idea that the universe is expanding. That the entire observable universe of galaxies began with a bang seemed preposterous. Do not be surprised that a man of God is the father of the Big Bang theory. He is accurate in trying to explain how God did it.

Isaiah 40:22

22 *It is* He who sits above the circle of the Earth,
And its inhabitants *are* like grasshoppers,
Who stretches out the Heavens like a curtain,
And spreads them out like a tent to dwell in.

Pay attention to how Isaiah described where God sits. A prophet knew in 700 BC that God sits on the circle of the Earth – so he knew at that time that the Earth is a circle. The Bible proved in 700 BC (over 2000 years ago before science proved this) that the Earth was a sphere.

Job 26:7

[7] He stretches out the north over empty space;
He hangs the Earth on nothing.

Job is the oldest book in the Bible chronologically, which was written in 1445 BC, around the same time as the book of Genesis. The writer made a bold declaration and said that God made the Earth and suspended it on nothing. The idea that the Earth is a sphere was all but settled by ancient Greek philosophers such as Aristotle (384–322 BC), who obtained empirical evidence after traveling to Egypt and seeing new constellations of stars. Eratosthenes, in the third century BC, became the first person to calculate the circumference of the Earth. Islamic scholars made further advanced measurements from about the 9th century AD onwards, while European navigators circled the Earth in the 16th century. Images from space were final proof, if any were needed. Many had argued that the Earth was flat. The book of Job preceded science by over 3000 years. So, science and astronomy proved that the Earth is a sphere in the 17th century AD.

What Job means is that God stretched the abode of the stars; Heavens (north) over the empty space (nothing).

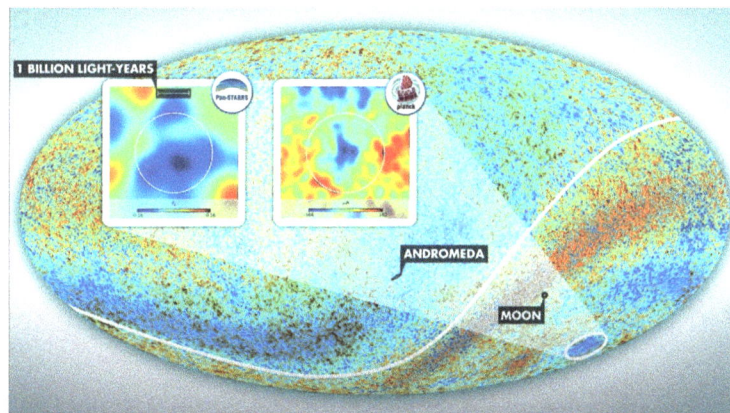

NASA WMAP

Image Source – Public Domain

This radiation map of the universe has been divided into hemispheres. It is an observation of the universe limited to our current technology. The conclusion has been that the universe is way larger than we can ever imagine or comprehend. What to pay attention to here is the very deep dark blue spot on the right bottom part of the map. NASA calls it the cold spot. Astronomers call it the super void. In other words, there is a gigantic empty place in the southern hemisphere in the universe, which is over 1 billion light years across and there is nothing in it – not even a star or any light. The dark matter that forms the universe is even sparse there. It is a cold spot called the super void of the southern hemisphere. Directly to the north of it is that red trace, which is picking up radiation of a plethora of stars, galaxies etc. This again confirms what Job says in the Bible.

Job 26:7

7 He stretches out the north over empty space;
He hangs the Earth on nothing.

It was not until 2004 that astronomers discovered the super void at the southern part of the universe and to the north of the empty space, the abode of the stars that illuminated the Heavens. Job knew this several thousands of years ago with no technology as we have today. My question to you is, who showed him? He had no electricity or modern technology. And remember, most importantly, he had no Google – the place for the most abundant but finite human information. I'm beginning to believe that there was a reason why God only allowed significant technological advancements the last 20+ years, just to show us how much we still do not know upon all the technology we think we have. We are only discovering, revealing, reproducing the best way we can, what have already been made available to us by God. The Bible is very accurate, extremely accurate.

The Book of Enoch

Chapter 18:1-5

1 And I saw the storehouses of all the winds, and I saw how with them He has adorned all creation, and I saw the foundations of the Earth.

2 And I saw the cornerstone of the Earth. And I saw the four winds which support the Earth and the sky.

(Job 38:4-7), (Zechariah 10:3-4), (Isaiah 28:16)

(Zechariah 6:1-5), (Revelation 7:1)

3 And I saw how the winds stretch out the height of Heaven, and how they position themselves between Heaven and Earth; they are the Pillars of Heaven.

4 And I saw the winds which turn the sky and cause the disc of the Sun and all the stars to set.

5 And I saw the winds on the Earth which support the clouds and I saw the paths of the Angels. I saw at the end of the Earth, the firmament of Heaven above.

When the Bible talks about the winds that hold the Earth, I can only imagine the mightiest supernatural wind that in natural terms is the similitude of the winds of the most powerful rocket engines. The law of aerodynamics. Just because you don't see it with your physical eyes does not mean that it is not there. You can see it by faith or if God opens your spiritual eyes to see it. Is the law of aerodynamics still a surprise to you? According to physics, the Bernoulli Principle is a foundational principle of aerodynamics. Aerodynamics involves a combination of four different forces (winds): lift, weight, drag, and thrust. Lift is the opposite force of weight, and it occurs as air moves on wings. So, are the four different forces needed for aerodynamics to be perfected a coincidence? We see it again in the book of Revelation.

Revelation 7:1

The Sealed of Israel

7 After these things I saw four angels standing at the four corners of the Earth, holding the four winds of the Earth, that the wind should not blow on the Earth, on the sea, or on any tree.

So, you see why there are angels positioned at the four corners of the Earth to make sure that the four winds stay on course and not blow to the Earth? Imagine the mightiest spiritual hurricane, Katrina. I will leave that for you to think about. The Earth is not stagnant. I am sure that by now you have an idea of what keeps the Earth in orbital motion. Again, science has unintentionally proved this scripture to be true.

According to science, the Earth moves in two different ways. Earth orbits the Sun once a year and rotates on its axis once a day. The Earth's orbit makes a circle around the Sun. At the same time the Earth orbits around the Sun, it also spins. Imagine a line passing through the center of Earth that goes through both the North Pole and the South Pole. This imaginary line is called an axis. Earth spins around its axis, just as a top spin around its spindle. This spinning movement is called Earth's rotation. While the Earth spins on its axis, it also orbits, or revolves around the Sun. This movement is called revolution. Therefore, I mentioned earlier in this writing to pay attention to the orbiting Earth image through the gyroscopes, which proves Einstein's theory of space-time to be true.

So, science even wants us to "imagine" a line passing through the center of the Earth that goes through both the North Pole and the South Pole. Isn't that interesting to read? So, now, we imagine things by faith in science, but science cannot believe God by faith that He exists and that with his supreme divine law of aerodynamics, he truly has his four angels keeping the Earth in course and order through four different winds as stated in multiple scriptures earlier.

Isaiah 14:9

⁹ "Hell from beneath is excited about you,
To meet *you* at your coming;
It stirs up the dead for you,
All the chief ones of the Earth;
It has raised up from their thrones
All the kings of the nations.

The prophet Isaiah wrote this book in 700 BC. He makes it clear that hell is beneath us. Jesus preached more on hell than Heaven. Science and geologists in 1898, confirmed that the Earth's core is directly beneath you no matter where you stand in the world, and it is made up of molten magma. Magma is extremely hot liquid and semi-liquid rock located under Earth's surface. When magma flows onto Earth's surface, it is called lava.

Job 28:5-6

5 *As for* the Earth, from it comes bread,
But underneath it is turned up as by fire;
6 Its stones *are* the source of sapphires,
And it contains gold dust.

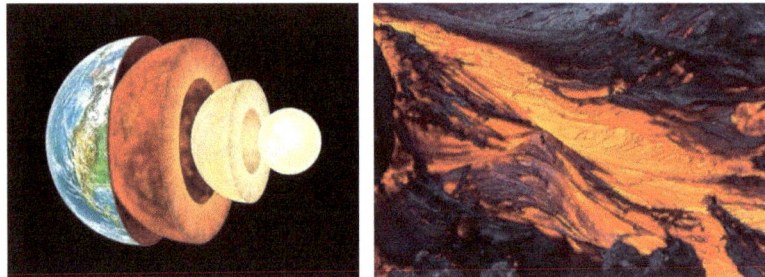

Layers of Earth and Lava

Image Source – Public Domain

Lava (magma that has erupted onto the Earth's surface) – as the molten rock flows downhill, lava exposed to the air cools to a deep black color, while the molten rock beneath glows bright orange. We see this a lot in volcanic eruptions. The core of this planet is as hot as the temperature of the Sun – about 10000 degrees Fahrenheit (5600 degrees Celsius). The Bible preceded geology about 2600 years.

Matthew 25:41-43

41 "Then He will also say to those on the left hand, 'Depart from Me, you cursed, into the everlasting fire prepared for the devil and his angels: 42 for I was hungry, and you gave Me no food; I was thirsty, and you gave Me no drink; 43 I was a stranger, and you did not take Me in, naked and you did not clothe Me, sick and in prison and you did not visit Me.'

Therefore, the Gospel is a serious deal. There indeed, is hell. Hell was not created for you in mind. It was and still meant for Satan and his cohorts. But if you reject the ways of truth and identify with self-governing, doing as you wish or whatever you want because you think your life belongs to you, you will end up where the devil ends up because followers go to where their leaders take them to.

Therefore, Jesus came and died on the cross to save us from our sins. We must be constantly changing every single day into better persons so that we will spend eternity in a better place.

Please don't tell yourself what you want to hear or what makes you feel better. You must believe in Jesus so that you can have your salvation.

The Bible has never changed since it was written although there are some missing books, which in modern theology, is strongly argued but I disagree. There are other books that we must consider when we talk about the scriptures. The Lord has told me this. A good example is the Book of Enoch. There have not been any updates whatsoever made to the Word of God. You cannot add to it nor take from it. But I believe that the early discoverers of the Bible took from it for a selfish reason and an attempt to hide the truth. This shows us how true and concrete the Word of God is.

Matthew 24:32-35

The Parable of the Fig Tree

[32] "Now learn this parable from the fig tree: When its branch has already become tender and puts forth leaves, you know that summer *is* near. [33] So you also, when you see all these things, know that it is near—at the doors! [34] Assuredly, I say to you, this generation will by no means pass away till all these things take place. [35] Heaven and Earth will pass away, but My words will by no means pass away.

My Revelation About the Source of the Universe

This startling idea which first appeared in scientific form in 1931, in a paper by Georges Lemaître, a Belgian cosmologist and Catholic priest, is accurate. I was in the place of prayer and suddenly, the "light bulb", which signifies insight, illumination, and revelation, lit up in my spirit/mind that, scientists got it correct through their explanation of creation through what they named the "Big Bang Theory". It was after that I learned that the father of the Big Bang theory was a Catholic Priest. A couple of days afterwards, during one of my customary fasting days; Wednesday, the 11th of August 2021, God showed me in a vision, a Venn diagram. I was wondering why He would show me that. I began to seek for His interpretation to gain understanding. It was through that I learned that the Venn diagram is popularly known as Vesica Pisces. He finally interpreted the meaning to me.

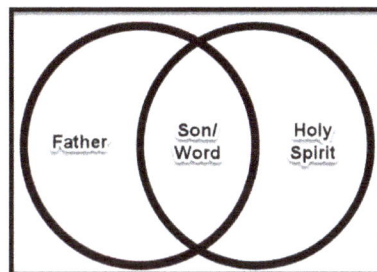

The Beginning of Creation (Universe)
Image Source – Revelation given to me by God

In the beginning, before the creation, God divided Himself into a male and female (male and female energies) and out of these energies came (birthed) the universe, through the intersection (Vesica Pisces). The intersection represents Jesus (The Son). So, in this we have the first part of the two big circles as God the Father, the middle part as God the Son, and the third part as God the Holy Spirit. The universe was created with the spoken Word of God but behind it are high dimensional mathematical, engineering, scientific formulas, patterns, laws, principles, and power.

It was the same intelligence and pattern that God used to put Adam to sleep and removed his rib bone to create Eve – in essence, He divided Adam to create Eve then out of the intercourse between the two, Cain and Abel were born.

Genesis 1:26-28

26 Then God said, "Let Us make man in Our image, according to Our likeness; let them have dominion over the fish of the sea, over the birds of the air, and over the cattle, over all the Earth and over every creeping thing that creeps on the Earth." 27 So God created man in His *own* image; in the image of God, He created him; male and female He created them. 28 Then God blessed them, and God said to them, "Be fruitful and multiply; fill the Earth and subdue it; have dominion over the fish of the sea, over the birds of the air, and over every living thing that moves on the Earth."

Genesis 4:1-2

4 Now Adam knew Eve his wife, and she conceived and bore Cain, and said, "I have acquired a man from the LORD." 2 Then she bore again, this time his brother Abel. Now Abel was a keeper of sheep, but Cain was a tiller of the ground.

Take note from the scriptures that God's image is both male and female. The Bible proves this. They represent God's dimensions separated into two beings. He first created man and then removed a part of the man to create the woman. God follows the spiritual laws, principles, and patterns that He used to birth the universe and everything else in it. The same way your biological father and your biological mother had an intercourse to give birth to you. God is a being of order. It is also written in the book of Enoch that the Sun represents the male, and the Moon represents the female in the luminaries.

The Book of Enoch

The Book of the Heavenly Luminaries

Chapter 72:1-4

1 The book of the courses of the luminaries of the Heaven, the relations of each, according to their classes, their dominion and their seasons, according to their names and places of origin, and according to their months, which Uriel, the holy angel, who was with me, who is their guide, showed me; and he showed me all their laws exactly as they are, and how it is with regard to all the years of the world and unto eternity, till the new creation is accomplished which dureth till eternity. 2 And this is the first law of the luminaries: the luminary the Sun has its rising in the eastern portals of the Heaven, and its setting in the western portals of the Heaven. 3 And I saw six portals in which the Sun rises, and six portals in which the Sun sets, and the Moon rises and sets in these portals, and the leaders of the stars and those whom they lead: six in the east and six in the west, and all following each other in accurately corresponding order: also, many windows to the right and left of these portals. 4 And first there goes forth the great luminary, named the Sun, and his circumference is like the circumference of the Heaven, and he is quite filled with illuminating and heating fire.

Chapter 73:1-8

1 And after this law I saw another law dealing with the smaller luminary, which is named the Moon. 2 And her circumference is like the circumference of the Heaven, and her chariot in which she rides is driven by the wind, and light is given to her in (definite) measure. 3 And her rising and setting change every month: and her days are like the days of the Sun, and when her light is uniform (i.e., full) it amounts to the seventh part of the light of the Sun. 4 And thus she rises. And her first phase in the east comes forth on the thirtieth morning: and on that day she becomes visible and constitutes for you the first phase of the Moon on the thirtieth day together with the Sun in the portal where the Sun rises. 5 And the one half of her goes forth by a seventh part, and her whole circumference is empty, without light, with the exception of one-seventh part of it, (and) the fourteenth part of her light. 6 And when she receives one-seventh part of the half of her light, her light amounts to one-seventh part and the half thereof. 7 And she sets with the Sun, and when the Sun rises the Moon rises with him and receives the half of one part of light, and in that night in the beginning of her morning [in the commencement of the lunar day] the Moon sets with the Sun and is invisible that night with the fourteen parts and the half of one of them. 8 And she rises on that day with exactly a seventh part and comes forth and recedes from the rising of the Sun, and in her remaining days she becomes bright in the (remaining) thirteen parts.

The Book of Enock is a valid book of the Bible with immense secrets and vast amount of knowledge. So, we can see that the Sun is a male, and the Moon is a female. God is a God of patterns, principles, and laws. This is where most people in the past and present got it wrong, and they think the Sun and Moon are gods but that is a very big error. They are all living things like us. In the book of Joshua, he commanded the Sun to stand still. Why do you think he was able to do that? Because he knew something that you don't know – the luminaries and creation in general are made up of living things and they listen to our commands because we have dominion if we have the knowledge and the understanding.

Joshua 10:12-15

The Sun Stands Still

[12] Then Joshua spoke to the LORD in the day when the LORD delivered up the Amorites before the children of Israel, and he said in the sight of Israel:

"Sun, stand still over Gibeon;
And Moon, in the Valley of Aijalon."
[13] So the Sun stood still,
And the Moon stopped,
Till the people had revenge
Upon their enemies.

Is this not written in the Book of Jasher? So, the Sun stood still in the midst of Heaven, and did not hasten to go *down* for about a whole day. [14] And there has been no day like that, before it or after it, that the LORD heeded the voice of a man; for the LORD fought for Israel.

[15] Then Joshua returned, and all Israel with him, to the camp at Gilgal.

From all these references, we can see that the Sun is a male, and the Moon is a female. So, side note and question – why don't we see the Book of Jasher as referenced in these scriptures in the sixty-six books of the Bible? There are several books that should be part of the sixty-six books of the Bible that we currently use but where are they? It saddens my heart when I hear all kinds of arguments justifying why they have been removed and condemning these other books when we have not inquired from the Lord ourselves on the answers to these questions. This will be a writing for another day, but the sixty-six books are not all that our widely accepted Bible should have. I know this from the place of prayer by the Spirit of God. This is the same way we have several denominations, and they choose to believe and teach what seems right to them. There needs to be consistencies in the Body of Christ. This is where and how Christianity is being weakened and being mistaken for a religion but it's not a religion. The doctrine should be the same across the board, in every household, Church, village, town, nation, etc. The only changes should be the language in which it is communicated. This discussion also, is for another day.

Mankind in collaboration with the devil always like to hide the truth because when you know the truth it shall set you free. It is very hard to hide the truth because even if you decide to burn it all down, God in His infinite Wisdom will still give it to His people in visions and dreams and revelations of all kinds. One way or the other, it shall be made known to them. This is how the Bible was written.

John 8:31-32

The Truth Shall Make You Free

[31] Then Jesus said to those Jews who believed Him, "If you abide in My word, you are My disciples indeed. [32] And you shall know the truth, and the truth shall make you free."

John 1:5

[5] And the light shines in the darkness, and the darkness did not comprehend it.

Physicists talk about matter and antimatter – yes, they are correct. The collision of matter and antimatter releases energy. I was in the place of prayer on August 17, 2021, and the Spirit of God started teaching me – I started downloading. He said His light joined with His Spirit. I did not quite understand what that meant so I was wondering, and He said, My light hit My gas – go and find out what energy is produced and released when light becomes one with gas. So, I went on Google to search for the energy produced when light hits gas and I found the answer. I had learned this many years ago in school but had forgotten. In other words, the collision of God the Father and God the Holy Spirit released Supreme supernatural energy. I am not a physicist, but I will use their science to explain. In other words, light collides with gas then absorption occurs when the photons from the light hits atoms and molecules to cause them to vibrate. The more the object's molecules vibrate, the hotter it becomes. This heat is then emitted from the object as thermal energy because of the internal energy. Internal energy, in thermodynamics, is the property or state function that defines the energy of a substance in the absence of effects due to capillarity and external electric, magnetic, and other fields. Then thermal energy occurs. Thermal explosion theory is based on the idea that progressive heating raises the rate at which heat is released by the reaction until it exceeds the rate of heat loss from the area. At a given composition of the mixture and a given pressure, explosion will occur at a specific ignition temperature that can be determined from the calculations of heat loss and heat gain.

This is the time in Genesis where God created the Heavens and the Earth and the Spirit of God was hovering upon the waters, and He said let there be light and there was light. The moment He said let there be light was when the Word (God/Light) hit the Spirit (God/Holy Spirit/Gas) and thermodynamics started happening. Everything that God did, He did it from this type of energy when we look at it in physical terms because He is light joined with His spirit – each time He wants to create, He speaks, and His word is light, so this light joins with His spirit and then there are manifestations. This is the same way miracles happen. Without the Spirit of God in someone or environment, God can never do anything. Therefore, this same spirit He has given to men is the reason why you see men moving on the Earth in high energies like high voltage electricity. I add this to let you know that He created the Heavens and the Earth with this same energy but for the Earth to be properly formed and to separate light from darkness so that everything we see as creation here and now on Earth to follow, His final words regarding the light – "let there be light", was the Big Bang. That explosion immediately happened at the command of God Almighty through the power of the Holy Spirit.

I could only imagine how powerful that explosion was because I know how much God hates darkness and deformity. Take note that the Earth before God spoke was formless and empty, and darkness was over the surface of the deep as we can see below in the scriptures. For light to come meant that space and time was created – He called the light, "morning" and the darkness, "night". And there was morning and there was evening – the first day. We already see a problem here for quantum physicists – how can there be a day and within that day we have light (day) and night (darkness)? That means God has encapsulated time within time. Within a day, we already have another day, and then we have night. I see what looks like three rings of eternal nature – a ring within a ring within another ring (nested rings). Because He separated light (day) from darkness (night), I see a problem; a disconnection between those double-times rings, which were originally supposed to be all in one ring.

This tells me that in eternity, there is nothing like day or night – this is a higher dimension not meant for physical forms (matter). Even if God will allow quantum physics to be true, man will first have to figure out how to travel between day and night and night and day because they are meant to be one time ring but technically separated, so encapsulated in the space between day and night, is eternity. For example, when you talk about what happened in the day during the night, you would be talking in the past tense – this is an illusion by the wisdom of God because when you add multiple days together when you are in another day, you will be referring to what technically is infinity time past because even when someone is dead and gone, somebody in the future can still count this time past to even before the dead person was born – it never ends. This is an infinity problem. The same idea applies to future time. The trickier part is present time – within this time, you have access to both time past, and future time, including the present time. So, you are already technically standing in eternity (past, present, future) except that at a 3-dimension (3D) level, you don't have the ability to see or experience all the events happening in your present time, including those to happen in the future. In the realm of God, He sees eternity (past, present, future) all at the same time. All I see is the eternity (infinity) problem so I doubt that quantum will ever become a real practical science in terms of time travel and all that. Another evidence is in these scriptures.

Exodus 33:20-22

20 But He said, "You cannot see My face; for no man shall see Me, and live." 21 And the LORD said, "Here is a place by Me, and you shall stand on the rock. 22 So it shall be, while My glory passes by, that I will put you in the cleft of the rock and will cover you with My hand while I pass by.

The God - "Time" Eternity Ring/Circle

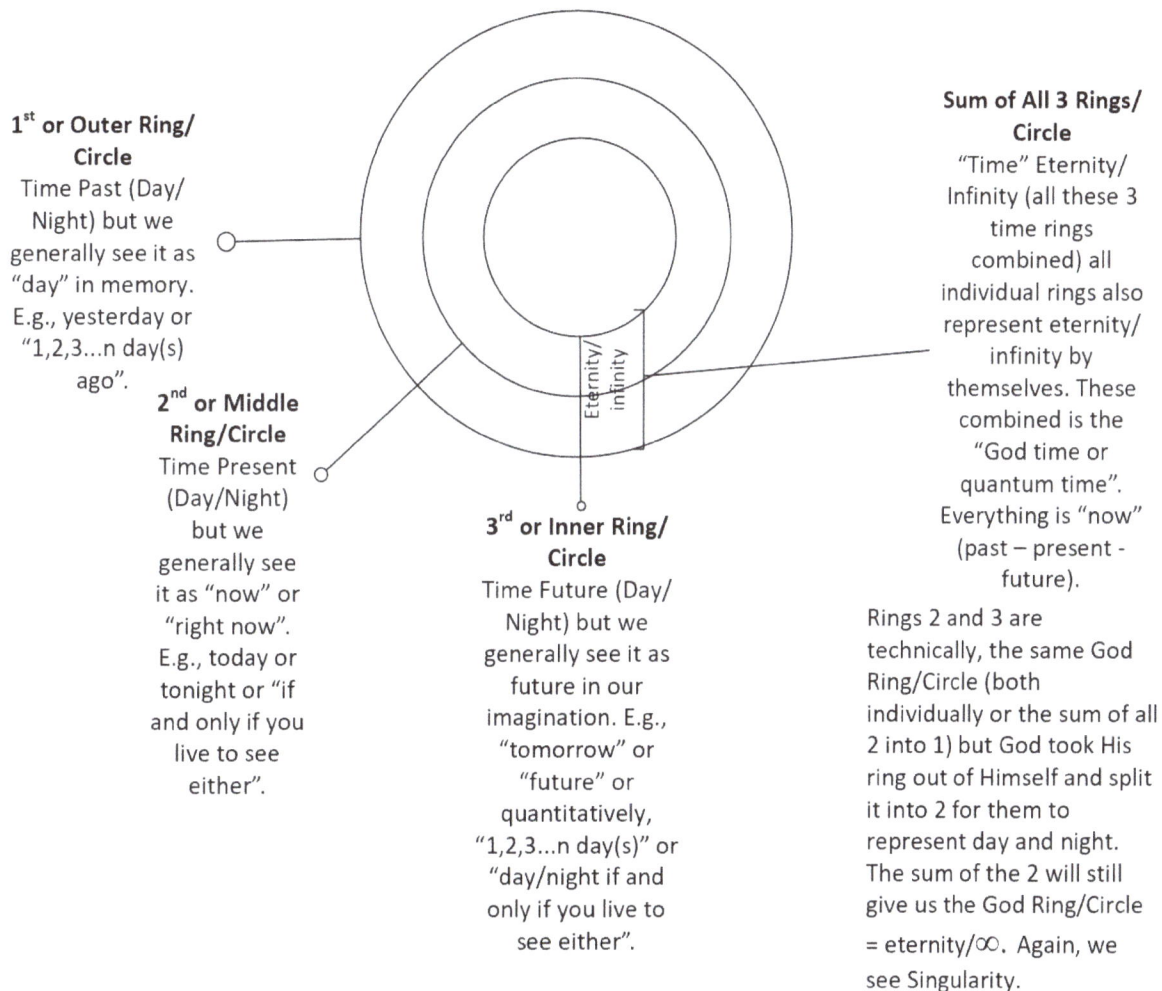

1st or Outer Ring/Circle
Time Past (Day/Night) but we generally see it as "day" in memory. E.g., yesterday or "1,2,3...n day(s) ago".

2nd or Middle Ring/Circle
Time Present (Day/Night) but we generally see it as "now" or "right now". E.g., today or tonight or "if and only if you live to see either".

Eternity/infinity

3rd or Inner Ring/Circle
Time Future (Day/Night) but we generally see it as future in our imagination. E.g., "tomorrow" or "future" or quantitatively, "1,2,3...n day(s)" or "day/night if and only if you live to see either".

Sum of All 3 Rings/Circle
"Time" Eternity/Infinity (all these 3 time rings combined) all individual rings also represent eternity/infinity by themselves. These combined is the "God time or quantum time". Everything is "now" (past – present - future).

Rings 2 and 3 are technically, the same God Ring/Circle (both individually or the sum of all 2 into 1) but God took His ring out of Himself and split it into 2 for them to represent day and night. The sum of the 2 will still give us the God Ring/Circle = eternity/∞. Again, we see Singularity.

A representation of God's idea of time and eternity for Himself and for Man
Image Source – Revelation given to me by God

When you study the above diagram, you will understand why there is no time outside of God. For it is within Himself that He created time (day and night) and space. And there was evening, and there was morning on the first day. Are you still wondering why the first and original 24-hour clock is represented by a circle, starting at 0 and ending at 12 or 24 in military time? It is no accident or coincidence; time is basically endless (eternal). Until our clock batteries die, they go forever and if we had anything like never-dying batteries or power sources for these clocks, they would go forever and ever and never stop. God only divided eternity into time so that we can relate to it in this 3D world. The 3D physical body cannot handle eternity (eternity is a never-ending time).

In physical terms, the 3D world is like a 3D box and we and all of creation are in the box. All we see are the four sides of the box, the ground of the box and the top of the box, depending on how high and far we can see. Our 3D world is contained within the 4D world (the tiny 3D box within the tesseract) and held together in position by the bigger outer box. The outer 4D box is God's dimension (eternity) and it is encapsulating the 3D box and the 3D box is also encapsulating the 4D box. The inner 3D box is man's universe (night and day). Assuming there is an eagle far and high in the 4D box outside the 3D box, the eagle will see everything in the 3D box because it will have a wider and full view of it. But the eagle won't be able to see everything all at once from that view, no matter how high it goes. Think of the 3D box as a crystal (it is), which is transparent. Everything can be seen and there are technically no secrets in it when viewed from outside the 3D box. But there requires special access to view outside the 3D box from within the 3D box. And sight from within the 3D box is limited to how high you have risen in the 3D box; else sight is limited to a particular pointed view. It's like we are contained somewhere within God's dimension (eternity). When you rise to a higher dimension, it's like being on a higher altitude – you will have a broader view of what's below you. And even with that, you need a lot of eyes. And even with a lot of eyes, you can only see to some extent. So, physically this is not a possibility, but it will help you have an idea of what is being discussed here.

That is why death is inevitable for the physical body unless you tap into higher dimensions then you can ascend into those dimensions with your physical body – like Enoch and Elijah in the Bible. The current state of physics should be a wake-up call for humanity to arise, pick up the Bible and start serving the one and only true God – not the Islam Allah or God, not Buddha, not the Sun or the Moon or the Stars, not Krishna etc., but rather, the Lord God Almighty of the Heavens and the Earth, and the Father of our Lord Jesus Christ. Yes, He exists. Midnight is called 24:00 hours and is used to mean the end of the day and 00:00 hours is used to mean the beginning of the day. In actual sense, the hours of 6pm to 6am is night (evening) and the hours of 6am to 6pm is day (morning) – it's basically a reversal (12 hours x 2 = 24 hours). Below is an image as illustrated to me by God.

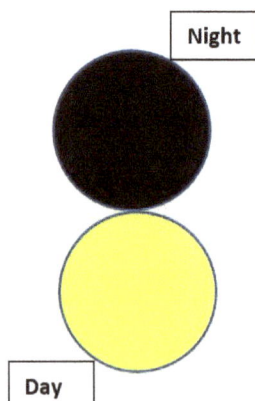

Representation of how spacetime functions
Image Source – Revelation given to me by God

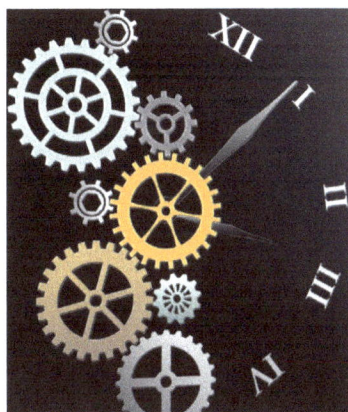

Image Source – Public Domain

Think of the night and day time circles like the gears in this watch – every two touching gears here represent the two circles of night and day. They always move in opposite directions. They are two circles of equal sizes, but they are completely asymmetrical (the lack of equality between them). This is because their attributes and what they offer are very different. While night moves in one direction, day moves in the opposite direction and vice versa. You can call this an illusion to help you better understand but this is how it works, and this is how space-time is supposed to function. This means that both are 12 hours each and it explains why time is basically a reversal. But they are the same thing if God removes the "night" and "day" division – then we will get eternity.

What Is the Origin of the Infinity Symbol?

Ancient Greek mathematicians and philosophers originally called the infinity symbol 'lemniscate' meaning 'ribbon. ' This notion strives from Ouroboros, an ancient symbol depicting a serpent biting its own tail. This symbol is representative of infinity, immortality, continuity, self-fertilization, and eternal return. This is the meaning of space-time or Earth time. If God decides to let the Earth continue without destroying it, we will always multiply on the surface of the Earth and continue to exist, if there is a male and a female. Take one side of this symbol to be day and another to be night – technically, it is the same circle and we have found ourselves in the center of it. That's why I say, illusion will help you understand it better. When we leave the Earth, we will go into a dimension where what you see ("time") won't be crossed to look like the number 8. Instead, it will untwine or untangle to give us what looks like the number 0, which is the symbol representing God and eternity.

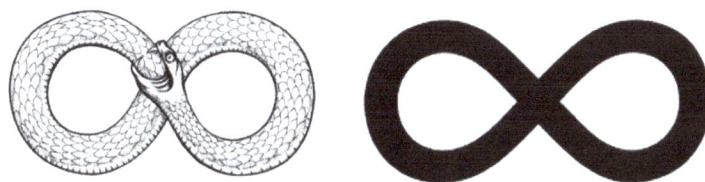

Image Source – Public Domain

In eternity, there is no time (past – present – future). Time is "now or present". Therefore, you don't have to commit a sin (the act) in eternity before it is considered a sin. Once you think about the sin, you have already committed it.

Isaiah 14:12-14

The Fall of Lucifer

[12] "How you are fallen from Heaven,
O Lucifer, son of the morning!
How you are cut down to the ground,
You who weakened the nations!
[13] For you have said in your heart:
'I will ascend into Heaven,
I will exalt my throne above the stars of God;
I will also sit on the mount of the congregation
On the farthest sides of the north;
[14] I will ascend above the heights of the clouds,
I will be like the Most High.'

This was what Satan (Lucifer then) did and he was casted out of Heaven. He said it in his heart/mind. Now you know the difference between eternity (Heaven's time) and Earth's time. God made it this way so that we can relate. That is why He gave Einstein the theory of relativity.

We can go on and on to break it down further into dusk, night, dawn, twilight etc. These periods together represent the complete God eternity circle. In other words, we are encapsulated in God and God encapsulated in us – He is within us, we are within Him, and He's everywhere. Nothing else exists outside of God. This again shows that what we call death is just a transition from body (matter) to spirit (antimatter). That's why spirit beings mostly see what we do but as humans, we need to be given access to the higher dimensions before we can see these spirits. Therefore, quantum physics at a physical 3D level is simply an impossibility. Therefore, after several experiments in quantum physics, below is what some of the physicists are saying in an article I read about the universe.

"At some point, you achieve energies, densities, and temperatures that are so large that the quantum uncertainty inherent to nature leads to consequences that make no sense. Quantum fluctuations would routinely create black holes that encompass the entire Universe. Probabilities, if you try to compute them, give answers that are either negative or greater than 1: both physical impossibilities. We know that gravity and quantum physics don't make sense at these extremes, and that's what a singularity is: a place where the laws of physics are no longer useful. Under these extreme conditions, it's possible that space and time themselves can emerge. This, originally, was the idea of the Big Bang: a birth to time and space themselves. "

Of course, so, they know that when they try to compute, they get answers that are either negative or greater than 1 (if you look at my illustration of time and eternity above, this is the infinity problem that they will never solve) – they also know that gravity and quantum physics don't make sense at these extremes, and that's what a singularity is: a place where the laws of physics are no longer useful (that's right because this is an answer that lies in a higher dimension). Spiritual things are supposed to not make sense to the carnally minded (physically minded) man.

Romans 8:6-11

[6] For to be carnally minded *is* death, but to be spiritually minded *is* life and peace. [7] Because the carnal mind *is* enmity against God; for it is not subject to the law of God, nor indeed can be. [8] So then, those who are in the flesh cannot please God.

[9] But you are not in the flesh but in the Spirit, if indeed the Spirit of God dwells in you. Now if anyone does not have the Spirit of Christ, he is not His. [10] And if Christ *is* in you, the body *is* dead because of sin, but the Spirit *is* life because of righteousness. [11] But if the Spirit of Him who raised Jesus from the dead dwells in you, He who raised Christ from the dead will also give life to your mortal bodies through His Spirit who dwells in you.

In the same article, the physicists also know that under these extreme conditions, it's possible that space and time themselves can emerge. This, originally, was the idea of the Big Bang: a birth to time and space themselves. That is exactly the answer to the source of the universe. The Big Bang is an accurate idea. God created everything in the beginning and again, this can be found in the first chapter of the book of Genesis. The scriptures below tell us a bit about how life is in the New Jerusalem – the city had no need of the lights from the Sun or the Moon. It is the glory of God that illuminated it. We can already see that there is nothing like "time" over there. It is eternity.

Revelation 21:22-25

The Glory of the New Jerusalem

[22] But I saw no temple in it, for the Lord God Almighty and the Lamb are its temple. [23] The city had no need of the Sun or of the Moon to shine in it, for the glory of God illuminated it. The Lamb *is* its light. [24] And the nations of those who are saved shall walk in its light, and the kings of the Earth bring their glory and honor into it. [25] Its gates shall not be shut at all by day (there shall be no night there).

The following image is another representation of the Big Bang, like the one we have already seen, and it has some interesting comments by the researchers. Here are the comments.

"Our entire cosmic history is theoretically well-understood, but only because we understand the theory of gravitation that underlies it, and because we know the Universe's present expansion rate and energy composition. Light will always continue to propagate through this expanding

Universe, and we will continue to receive that light arbitrarily far into the future, but it will be limited in time as far as what reaches us. We still have unanswered questions about our cosmic origins, but the age of the Universe is known."

Pay attention to "Light will always continue to propagate through this expanding Universe, and we will continue to receive that light arbitrarily far into the future, but it will be limited in time as far as what reaches us". They are talking about the end of this universe because surely that day will come since it is written in the Word of God. The dictionary defines the word "arbitrarily" as based on random choice or personal whim, rather than any reason or system. Or and without restraint in the use of authority; autocratically. This already is a very dangerous and alarming word being used here. The authority referred to here is God and He owes you absolutely no explanation as to why He will destroy the Earth when the time comes. Also, the unanswered question about our cosmic origin is in this writing. The unanswered question is God. The use of the word "questions" and the word "origins" in the last sentence are wrong because it's supposed to be referring to only one origin – and that origin is God; the one who dwells in unapproachable light. It is only the true Church and the true children of God who will ever be able to solve this most important mysterious question in the history of man – not physics. It had always been reserved for us (people of God) to reveal it to defy science and to show where science was birthed from. Remember, everything that is birthed, must surely die. This means that the day will surely come when physical science also dies. Physics and science in general MUST obey God and the spiritual realms – higher dimensions for in Him is our eternal dwelling place.

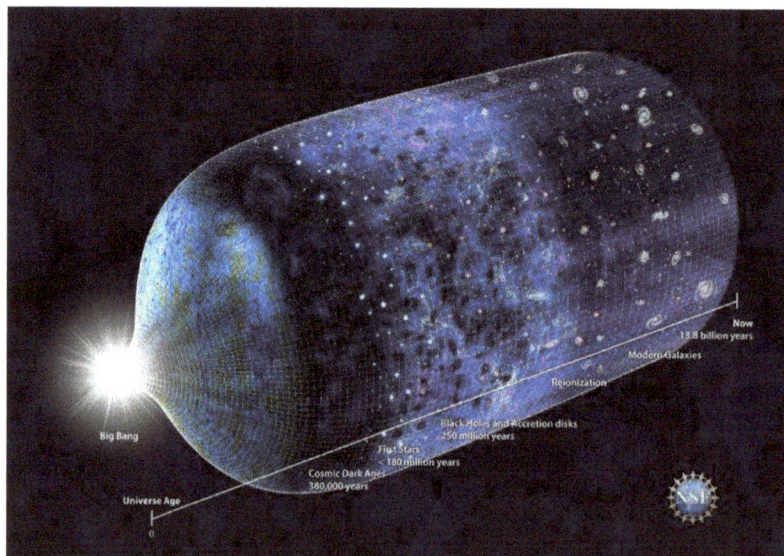

NSF Photo of the Bing Bang

Image Source – Public Domain

You hear and read humanity, especially those involved in natural science, saying that we can't prove God, but they can prove things with science. I challenge you – get a Bible and read it every day and do as the Bible teaches. Follow its teachings with diligence as you would with a scientific experimentation. That is the experiment that true Christians go through, and they see the results.

I am sure that for a science theory to be valid, whatever experiments are involved are carefully respected and followed accordingly because it is always a process. The same is true for true Christianity. This is my challenge to you. After you have done what I suggest to you, come back, and tell the world whether God is real or not. Physics have been struggling for decades to solve this mystery. I challenge you to be diligent in doing what the Bible says for only one month then tell the world your story on encounters.

I was reading another article that talked about exteroceptive and interoceptive senses that neuroscientists wrote on how they have discovered that humans have more than five sense. Science always proves how big and dominant the supernatural is. There are no limits in the realms of God and those that have believed in Him know these things. These extra senses have always been known and exercised by the people of God.

You don't examine evidence in Christianity. It is expected that you practice the "evidence". Christianity is a lifestyle – a way of living. It is not a scientific theory to be examined based on evidence. You also hear about all these skepticisms going around and how that's encouraged. In the life of a true Christian, you only become skeptical when you are well grounded in the Word of God and the things of the spirit – for example, your spiritual discernment is heightened. That's how you stand close to someone possessed by a demon and you know it's a demon. That's why you hear false teachings, and you know that it's the devil talking. That's why you hear physicists talking about the origin of the cosmos and all these higher dimensions and you laugh because they have no idea of what they are doing with respect to that topic. Why do I laugh? Because they are about to start believing what they have refused to believe for a very long time – the spiritual realm and God. Now, they have gone from physics to talking about topics like "What God, Quantum Mechanics, and Consciousness Have in Common". They are getting really close now. I encourage them to keep working hard and through this they will find God. You all write books and come on the radio or television and talk big scientific words, yet you don't even know where you fall in or your exact position in what you have labelled as "bubble in an oceanic multiverse". Little did you know that for decades you have been trying to prove "God" with physics. You are beginning to see His Supremacy. I thought physics was about physical theories and calculations but now you are all talking about consciousness – very interesting.

Again, I am not a physicist, but I know and say all these things by the Spirit of God. Don't doubt if you'll ever know if God exists – because He already exists and whether you choose to believe or not, doesn't change that reality and once you accept Him and start serving Him then you will truly experience Him and He will even start showing you what you don't know; the past, present, and the future. The more people know, the more they know that they don't know much. Very soon, you will know that God is truly the beginning and the end of everything, including science. The end of "quantum" science is here. Just don't die before you believe in God – that would be the worst thing for you because it would be too late. If you are a physicist looking into these areas of study to breakthrough, I'm doing you a big favor now – stop wasting your time. I know the things I speak and write. There are a lot of things that you will NEVER understand in this 3D world and that is why God made His word available to follow so that we can penetrate through the 3D world into higher dimensions with Him. This is a journey – life on Earth right now is like the transit you make at the airport to get to a destination. You are all about to learn soon that Christians are not crazy after all, and that the Bible is truly the Word of God and not some historical book or lies. Regarding the source of the universe, the area of emphasis in my revelation of the light (God) joining with the gas (spirit) here is internal energy. God is three persons (Father, Son, and the Holy Spirit) but still the same as one God. This is what we call in Christianity as the Holy Trinity. God is the purest light, and He dwells in unapproachable light. God is also spirit. That is why He says that those that serve Him must do so in spirit and in truth (truth is light).

1 Timothy 6:16

[16] who alone has immortality, dwelling in unapproachable light, whom no man has seen or can see, to whom *be* honor and everlasting power. Amen.

John 4:24

[24] God *is* Spirit, and those who worship Him must worship in spirit and truth."

Singularity is the keyword here and it had been the most probable point in the Big Bang theory for many years. Georges Lemaître was right to call it singularity because that is what it can be called in natural sciences, but I call it sovereignty – the Sovereignty of God is the accurate starting point of the theory. God was concentrated in Himself as a single point and singlehandedly created the universe – space and time. It is only when you worship Him in spirit and in truth that He shows you what happened before the universe was created. Physics alone cannot explain this without Christianity; spirituality – the duality of the body (matter) and the spirit (antimatter).

So, physicists believe that the Big Bang created and stretched space itself, expanding the universe – that is very accurate. This is because while an explosion of a man-made bomb expands through air, the Big Bang did not expand through anything. That's because there was no space to expand through at the beginning of time. Hence, the Big Bang is the mightiest type of nuclear explosion that you could ever imagine. Except that it wasn't meant for destruction. Instead, it was meant for creation. That's what blows the physical mind and physics can't explain the rest. I am validating what Georges Lemaître, the Belgian cosmologist and Catholic priest proposed in 1931 about the Big Bang theory without any physical scientific research or experimentation. This must have been revealed to him by God and God only. This is hidden knowledge and wisdom, so I believe without a tiny doubt that he tapped into a higher dimension of intelligence except that what happened prior to that wasn't revealed to him. We see in parts, and we prophecy in parts.

1 Corinthians 13:9-13

[9] For we know in part, and we prophesy in part. [10] But when that which is perfect has come, then that which is in part will be done away.

11 When I was a child, I spoke as a child, I understood as a child, I thought as a child; but when I became a man, I put away childish things. **12** For now we see in a mirror, dimly, but then face to face. Now I know in part, but then I shall know just as I also am known.

13 And now abide faith, hope, love, these three; but the greatest of these *is* love.

So, now that you know the truth, you can do away with all kinds of assumptions about how the universe came into being. The short answer is that it was created by God. There is nothing else to see after the realm or dimension of God. Physics cannot take you into the realm of God. The Holy Spirit is the Spirit of God – and spirits can't be seen with the physical eyes just like wind and or gas. You physicists believe in gas and wind, yet you doubt God and everything He says in His word about Himself and the Holy Trinity. If only you will open your eyes and spirits to humbly receive like ones who don't know anything, you will realize that everything you attempt to create is already in the Word of God, but you are like the scribes and the pharisees; too arrogant and prideful and too physically intellectual to accept truths for you to be able to receive.

Matthew 23:1-12

Woe to the Scribes and Pharisees

23 Then Jesus spoke to the multitudes and to His disciples, **2** saying: "The scribes and the Pharisees sit in Moses' seat. **3** Therefore whatever they tell you to observe, *that* observe and do, but do not do according to their works; for they say, and do not do. **4** For they bind heavy burdens, hard to bear, and lay *them* on men's shoulders; but they *themselves* will not move them with one of their fingers. **5** But all their works they do to be seen by men. They make their phylacteries broad and enlarge the borders of their garments. **6** They love the best places at feasts, the best seats in the synagogues, **7** greetings in the marketplaces, and to be called by men, 'Rabbi, Rabbi.' **8** But you, do not be called 'Rabbi'; for One is your Teacher, the Christ, and you are all brethren. **9** Do not call anyone on Earth your father; for One is your Father, He who is in Heaven. **10** And do not be called teachers; for One is your Teacher, the Christ. **11** But he who is greatest among you shall be your servant. **12** And whoever exalts himself will be humbled, and he who humbles himself will be exalted.

Scientists explain scientific theories, but little do they know that they are explaining the Word of God in other words. For example, we can't smell or see carbon monoxide, but it is deadly, that is why we have detectors for them. So, from this, we know that what we call spirit can't be seen but just like carbon monoxide (gas), we have the faith to believe that it could find itself into our environments, hence, put detectors around to detect its presence. Therefore, people are perishing but the unfortunate part is that most people will realize this after their souls permanently leave their bodies – death. That breath that leaves our bodies upon death is the Life of God. You can't see it, yet you breathe it. This is another proof that God is everywhere. Why do you still believe in the reality of the air or wind and breathe it while you can't see it? There is a prior story, which led God to divide the Earth from the Heavens. I write these revelations not to get the applauds or awards of men but because the Father in Heaven has burdened me with it to know, understand, and to share to save His people through His Son Jesus Christ. Science is supposed to be used to glorify the works of God. This should tell you that Heaven is the real place, not Earth. Earth is barely a fraction of the realities and possibilities in Heaven.

Hosea 4:6

[6] My people are destroyed for lack of knowledge.
Because you have rejected knowledge,
I also will reject you from being priest for Me;
Because you have forgotten the law of your God,
I also will forget your children.

John 3:12-17

[12] If I have told you Earthly things and you do not believe, how will you believe if I tell you Heavenly things? [13] No one has ascended to Heaven but He who came down from Heaven, *that is,* the Son of Man who is in Heaven. [14] And as Moses lifted up the serpent in the wilderness, even so must the Son of Man be lifted up, [15] that whoever believes in Him should not perish but have eternal life. [16] For God so loved the world that He gave His only begotten Son, that whoever believes in Him should not perish but have everlasting life. [17] For God did not send His Son into the world to condemn the world, but that the world through Him might be saved.

We can only know and understand spiritual things through a life in Jesus and maintaining a relationship with Him. Verse 17 in the above scriptures is a very dangerous one. It means that the whole world becoming saved is very conditional, hence, Jesus used the word "might" to show how tentative this is. It is only guaranteed and sealed for true Christians to inherit the kingdom of God and the rebellious ones shall perish but if the whole world can't be saved, that proves why the Earth is due for destruction at an appointed time no matter what – the same reason why there will be a new Heaven and a new Earth. You better pick up the Word of God and start believing and serving God in spirit and in truth. Don't let the final hour take you by surprise – you have been warned.

1 Thessalonians 4:16-18

[16] For the Lord Himself will descend from heaven with a shout, with the voice of an archangel, and with the trumpet of God. And the dead in Christ will rise first. [17] Then we who are alive *and* remain shall be caught up together with them in the clouds to meet the Lord in the air. And thus, we shall always be with the Lord. [18] Therefore comfort one another with these words.

It was after the interpretation of my vision from God and through research that I came across a lot of materials regarding the Venn diagram (Vesica Pisces) on the Internet. This image is popularly called the Sacred Geometry. It is being used all around you in plain sight. I have no doubt that some of our fathers of old received this same vision that I received from God and that was how geometry started – creation of all things. You will soon understand why God is full of power and how He exert it in the Vesica Pisces – creation of all things.

Physicists talk about the four forces of the universe, which are already being used in the Earth – gravitational force, electromagnetic force, weak nuclear force, and strong nuclear force. They work over different ranges and have different strengths. Gravity is the weakest, but it has an infinite range. Physicists have begun thinking and wondering whether there is a fifth force. Maybe there is (not a force though), and that may be when you are joined as one spirit with God – that equals Power. Power that is mightier than all the four forces combined in physics. Therefore, force and power can both be described and measured, but a force is an actual physical phenomenon, and power is not. The equation for power reveals that a powerful machine is both strong (big force) and fast (big velocity). A powerful car engine is strong and fast. Side note – any "Bible" or "Christian book" that calls the Spirit of God (Holy Spirit) or even the Power of God through the Holy Spirit as a "force" is in error (false teaching). Burn that book. All the four forces combined can't even be compared to the Power of God, let alone the Holy Spirit. If force is greater than power, then God did not create the universe. But if power is greater than force, and force is just one of the elements in the equation of power, that already should tell you that God created the universe. Power = Force * Velocity. If we need force inside the formula to derive power, then power is clearly mightier than force. So, the fifth "force" that physicists are wondering whether it exists is not force but power – the Power of God. Faith is the foundation of exercising the Power of God and that is through which the world was formed and held together. Everything in creation is an offspring of faith.

Hebrews 11:3

[3] By faith we understand that the worlds were framed by the word of God, so that the things which are seen were not made of things which are visible.

Power can also be defined as the rate of energy transfer when energy is transformed from one form to another. In a lightbulb, for example, the wattage refers to the rate at which the bulb can convert electrical energy to light. Therefore, power is not just a measurement of how much force that an object can exert, but a measurement of the rate at which the force can do work.

Force is a vector quantity – a quantity that has magnitude and acts in a particular direction is described as vector. It is measured in newtons (N).

Power is a scalar quantity – a quantity that has magnitude, but no direction is described as scalar. It is measured in watts (W).

Scalars and Vectors

NASA — Glenn Research Center

A scalar quantity has only magnitude.
A vector quantity has both magnitude and direction.

Scalar Quantities
length, area, volume
speed
mass, density
pressure
temperature
energy, entropy
work, power

Vector Quantities
displacement
velocity
acceleration
momentum
force
lift , drag , thrust
weight

volume

velocity

Image Source – Public Domain

Power as a scaler quantity explains why quantum mechanics is observed as very powerful, yet a very difficult to understand phenomenon. This is because when physical conditions such as temperature and pressure are applied to matter, a change of state occurs. A substance's state of matter is an extrinsic property, meaning it can be changed by its environment. Both temperature and pressure can be measured, and state changes can be observed. For example, when thermal energy is added to a substance, its temperature increases, which can change its state from solid to liquid (melting), liquid to gas (vaporization), or solid to gas (sublimation). When energy is removed, the opposite happens, decreasing the substance's temperature and turning it from liquid to solid (freezing), gas to solid (deposition), or from gas to liquid (condensation).

Regarding force, these scalar laws don't apply and that is why no matter how fast a supersonic jet flies or a rocket engine shoot to space, it does not change states. That is why no matter how fast engines ran, they can never take you into a higher dimension. You can never fly your way out of the 3D world into the 4D world no matter how fast you fly. How fast a bullet travels out of a gun will never change the state of that bullet. If this were true, then a bullet could never be used to kill a thing because it would change from say solid to gas by the time it hits a target. Rather, depending on how much pressure alone that you apply to a bullet, this will surely change the state of that bullet. The high pressure alone that sends the bullet out of the gun causes the bullet to change temperature. Therefore, a cartridge case (brass or steel) containing a bullet is very hot upon extraction and ejection of the actual bullet from a gun because of the amount of pressure applied to it by the firing pin. Also, that is why when you tap water is barely flowing, you complain about the pressure rather than the force. Therefore, we have pressure washers, and we all know how they work and depending on the amount of pressure applied, even the water can cut through a metal or concrete or kill you.

Therefore, a force can still make or allow an object to physically occupy space, initiate movement, increase its speed, maintain momentum, decrease its speed, and stop. So, the Holy Spirit is not a force because He's not limited to the few properties of force – He is God/Jesus Christ unlimited and can do even what you can never imagine or comprehend, including your very own existence. This will help you understand why thermal energy is the foundation of science that God used to create the universe and why the Bible uses the word power to describe God's ability in His people.

This is because what a scalar quantity can achieve is unlimited or infinite and it can accommodate the eternal nature of God. It is no surprise that scientists are struggling in this area of dealing with scalar quantities. It is the laws of power (scalar quantities) that apply to quantum mechanics. All the vector and scalar quantities can be found in power – power is a host of all of them although it is listed or known individually in science to be a scalar quantity.

Now you will understand why there are expressions like "the government in power" instead of "the government in force", or "the Earth's heat is powered by the Sun" instead of "the Earth's heat is forced by the Sun", or "the phone is powered by electricity" instead of "the phone is forced by electricity", or "the jet engine is powered by JP-8" instead of "the jet engine is forced by JP-8" etc. That is why the Bible only uses the word power to describe the capacity, or ability, or potential of God.

Ephesians 1:19-21

[19] and what *is* the exceeding greatness of His power toward us who believe, according to the working of His mighty power [20] which He worked in Christ when He raised Him from the dead and seated *Him* at His right hand in the Heavenly *places,* [21] far above all principality and power and might and dominion, and every name that is named, not only in this age but also in that which is to come.

The number 5 symbolizes God's grace, goodness and favor toward humans and is mentioned 318 times in scriptures. Five is the number of graces, and multiplied by itself, which is 25, is 'grace upon grace' (John 1:16). The Ten Commandments contain two sets of five commandments. The first five commandments are related to our treatment and relationship with God, and the last five concern our relationship with other humans. When you live a perfected Christian life as the Bible teaches, you host God, hence, you host the manifestation power of God. It is by this same grace that I can see what most people cannot see, feel, and speak what most people cannot speak.

In God, there are four dimensions of power – Dunamis, Exousia, Ischus, and Kratos. I'm sure you're wondering why there are mostly four fundamental forces in physics, even in aerodynamics. You have already read about those earlier in this writing. All these four dimensions of power in God together is what raised Christ from the dead. The following are the explanations of these powers.

Dunamis is the state of power – power of potential or ability. It can also mean inherent power or power residing in a thing by virtue of its nature to make it function in a particular way. Dunamis is the dynamic ability to cause changes based on your type of being. Tying all the meanings together, dunamis means the vested and inherent power of God in all of us. Our very lives are inherent because we get it from Jesus.

John 1:1-4

1 In the beginning was the Word, and the Word was with God, and the Word was God. ² He was in the beginning with God. ³ All things were made through Him, and without Him nothing was made that was made. ⁴ In Him was life, and the life was the light of men.

Ephesians 3:20

²⁰ Now to Him who is able to do exceedingly abundantly above all that we ask or think, according to the power that works in us,

Exousia is bearer of delegated power – bearer of ruling authority and the right to engage. Used in the human context, exousia means authority, official, and government. And used in the Christian faith context, exousia would mean God's priests, co-heirs with Christ, and ambassadors of Christ (which is who we are according to the Bible) – Rom 8:17, 2 Cor 5:20.

1 Peter 2:9

⁹ But you *are* a chosen generation, a royal priesthood, a holy nation, His own special people, that you may proclaim the praises of Him who called you out of darkness into His marvelous light;

Ischus is absolute or endowed power – potential or ability, and mighty strength. Coupled with dunamis and kratos, the word describes a powerful form of action such as the amount of power that can be used to do what ordinary men cannot do.

1 Kings 18:45-46

⁴⁵ Now it happened in the meantime that the sky became black with clouds and wind, and there was a heavy rain. So, Ahab rode away and went to Jezreel. ⁴⁶ Then the hand of the LORD came upon Elijah; and he girded up his loins and ran ahead of Ahab to the entrance of Jezreel.

Kratos is the action of power. It is rendered as 'mighty strength.' The Greek word used for this power is kratos, which means the ability to exhibit or express resident strength or might. While dunamis lies within and may not be readily visible, kratos is the exhibition or expression of that power through a form of visible dominion and ruling. So, kratos is demonstrative and eruptive and proves its supernatural nature. This is where we can physically see the laws of physics defied. Just like how Christ walked on water, and the biggest winning for the Body of Christ is the resurrection from the dead.

Romans 1:1-4

1 Paul, a bondservant of Jesus Christ, called *to be* an apostle, separated to the gospel of God ² which He promised before through His prophets in the Holy Scriptures, ³ concerning His Son Jesus Christ our Lord, who was born of the seed of David according to the flesh, ⁴ *and* declared *to*

be the Son of God with power according to the Spirit of holiness, by the resurrection from the dead.

So, we people of God can host and manifest all these powers from our Father in Heaven. The true Christian is a very high multidimensional supernatural being who is a custodian of the supernatural Power of God and can live in it perpetually and demonstrate it at will.

Towards the later parts of the year 2020, I was in the place of prayer in the night, and I had a vision of a perfect crystal cube which looked more complex than just a simple 3D cube.

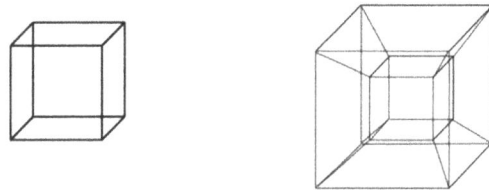

Left: Simple 3D Cube, Right: 4D or Tesseract
Image Source – Public Domain

I now understood where that perfect crystal cube came from. It looked more like a tesseract although I lack the details because it was a crystal and I had never seen anything like that before. It had two cables (wires) of yellow and black colors attached to it. In this earlier vision, I asked the Lord afterwards about the interpretation and He said, think of this perfect multidimensional cube as my dwelling place and the two cables as my wires connecting to you. This is how from now onwards; you will be downloading from me. The yellow color represents the glory presence and wisdom of God, and the black color represents the passion (deepest color of blood is black), death as in sacrificial repentance, and the hiding place of God. After my dream interpretation about the Venn diagram (Vesica Pisces), He instantly fitted into my spiritual eyes, the formula, where the perfect multidimensional cube belongs in this diagram – right within the intersection (Vesica Pisces). He said that out of Him came all things from His dwelling place – from His dimensions into creation. In other words, out of Him was, is, and will always be everything created, being created, and to be ever created.

John 1:1-5

The Eternal Word

1 In the beginning was the Word, and the Word was with God, and the Word was God. **2** He was in the beginning with God. **3** All things were made through Him, and without Him nothing was made that was made. **4** In Him was life, and the life was the light of men. **5** And the light shines in the darkness, and the darkness did not comprehend it.

Colossians 1:16

[16] For by him were all things created, that are in Heaven, and that are in Earth, visible and invisible, whether they be thrones, or dominions, or principalities, or powers: all things were created by him, and for him:

The dimensions issue that the physicists are struggling with is just like viewing a house. Depending on how far you are standing away from it, you may be looking at either a 1D, 2D, 3D etc., but you need to get closer, and or you must be graced with the all-seeing eyes of God then you can see even through darkness. You can see beyond your physical 3D. That is why we Christians can exercise our spiritual gifts. The same way by grace, I have been given this revelation. This is the same way our fathers of old were inspired by the Holy Spirit to write the Bible. Human beings, specifically scientists are too prideful and arrogant to accept God but the insight you are using now is His grace and intelligence and very soon you will all know how much you don't know.

Physicists keep trying to explain everything with physics. I wonder if they are all aware that their discussions about dimensions now isn't physics anymore. What is the physicist's proof that smoke permeates in all 3D but never disappears? Just because the physical eyes can't see it doesn't mean that what you think is correct. This is just like my earlier example with carbon monoxide. My incense I burn, my worship and praises, and my prayers all go to Heaven to God. And in fact, they are stored. This disproves your thought.

Revelation 5:8

Worthy Is the Lamb

[8] Now when He had taken the scroll, the four living creatures and the twenty-four elders fell down before the Lamb, each having a harp, and golden bowls full of incense, which are the prayers of the saints.

So, just because you don't see it with your eyes doesn't mean it doesn't exist. The following is an interview by Dr. Michio Kaku on – "Are there Extra Dimensions?" My comments will be after the interview. Pay attention while you read this and ask why he used the "fish" (Vesica Pisces/Ichthus/Jesus) in a "large pond" (the two intersecting circles), and finally a "crystal" for this illustration. Does he know something that you don't know? Or is it merely a coincidence.

Dr. Michio Kaku was interviewed about higher dimensions with regards to string theory. The interviewer started by saying, Michio, extra dimensions is front and center in the scientific world. It's no longer just science fiction. I want to know how it works in string theory, in fundamental physics, and then potentially in cosmology in large extra dimensions. How significant is this in our understanding?

Dr. Kaku responded and said, let me tell you a story. When I was a child growing up in San Francisco area, I used to visit the Japanese Tea Garden and visit the cap fish swimming in a 2D world (pond). I used to spend hours looking at them. They would swim forward and backward and left and right. They had eyes to their sides, and they couldn't see me. I was in the 3D, in hyperspace. They were totally unaware that there was a universe beyond their pond. And then I thought, what if I reached out and grab one of the fish, lift the fish up – maybe that fish was a scientist, and the scientist says there's no world of "up" – up does not exist. I would grab this scientist, lift them up into the world of "up" (hyperspace). What would he see? The scientist will see beings breathing without water – a new law of biology. Beings moving without fins – a new law of physics. And then I would put the being back into the pond. What kind of stories would the being tell? Well, today, we physicists believe – we cannot prove it yet, but we (humans) are the fish. We spend all our lives in 3D – forward, backwards, left, right, up, down, thinking that anything beyond our pond (little universe) is science fiction. We say impossible but we can't say that anymore because the concept of higher dimensions now is the "biggest game in town". You see, in 3D, there's not enough room to put all the laws of physics but when you go to the larger pond, this pond of hyperspace, then all the laws of physics just fit together like a jigsaw puzzle.

The interviewer added – in our 3D, the laws of physics are there, and we can explain things but there are lots of pieces that seem to be random that you must enter constants by hand, you might have two dozen thirty or so constants in physics and more in cosmology and they look like they all have nothing to do with one other.

Dr. Kaku responded – I like you to think of a crystal. A beautiful crystal shutters and lands on a tabletop and there are little insects like flat landers living on the tabletop and they say let us reassemble the crystal. They bring it together and they have one crystal – it's called the quantum theory. And they assemble other pieces of crystal – it's called relativity (the theory of space time) but then they try to bring these two chunks together, but they cannot, no matter how they bring these chunks together, they cannot. And then one day, someone says, let us go to the world of "up", let us move one crystal up and then fit it into the 3D and it would create a beautiful, unified crystal. That's where we are today with everything. We live in a 3D world. We see pieces, we see the electromagnetic force, we see gravity, we see nuclear force – little piece of this unified field theory. We bring them together and now have the theory of the quantum theory (everything) – the theory of the small (the theory of atoms), the theory of Einstein (the theory of space, time, relativity) but they don't fit together until you go into hyperspace and then they fit together beautifully.

The interviewer asked, so when they fit together, what does it mean? We now learn that we need 10 or 11 dimensions only, 3 of which, well 4 to include time that we have so there are many as 6 smaller dimensions and what's happening in those dimensions – why do you need 6 in the string theory?

Dr. Kaku answered, today we see the world as very broken – pieces of it. But at the beginning of time, when the universe was first created, that's when the crystal existed in its perfect form. We call it the superforce. A single superforce held this crystal together and then we had the Big Bang which shuttered this crystal, giving us the shuttered universe of today. When you look around you and you see the different forces – mountains, clouds, planets etc., it's broken. We live in a horribly broken world but at the instant of creation, there was perfection, there was perfection in a higher dimension. This perfection cannot exist in 3D. Now some people say, well, why 10, why 11?

He continued – it turns out that there are certain magic numbers in mathematics; numbers which have spectacular properties. It turns out that if you go to a 13D universe or 15D universe, it's unstable – particles will prefer to collapse down to 10 or 11 dimensions because the mathematics shows that self-consistency is important – they're unstable. Universes in 29D are simply unstable.

The interviewer added – and so, the mathematics have shown that we need 10 or 11D, including the 3 we see to make stability and so, the simplest forces or strings can then emerge in our 3D world in the particles and forces that we normally see.

Dr. Kaku responded – that's right. So, in this crystal, the crystal exists in a higher dimension, but it eventually cracked apart for reasons that we are still trying to understand. And the 3D world we see today is quite broken. Now, where are these higher dimensions? Look at smoke – smoke permeates throughout the room; smoke permeates in all 3D, but smoke never disappears. Smoke never floats into the 4D. Therefore, a 4th, 5th, 6th dimension must be smaller than smoke. But atoms also don't certainly drift away into hyperspace. Therefore, these higher dimensions must be smaller than an atom or else our universe will float away. So, you think that at the beginning of time, there was this perfection of 10 or 11D hyperspace but these other dimensions curled up, so small that atoms cannot lean into these higher dimensions.

The interviewer added, so, these are the kinds that when looked from a distance, look as if they are 1D but when you get very small on scales that are much smaller than an atom, they will curl around each other and be like a straw.

Dr. Kaku responded, that's right. So that the universe we see around us really is hyperdimensional, but we can't see it because these other dimensions are curled up – they are too small to be observed. The interviewer added – compactification is the word that I think string theorist use.

Dr. Kaku responded, that's right. If I have a tabletop – a tabletop exists in 2D, but I can roll it up like a cigarette, roll it up and then I see this 1D thing which is 2D if I get very close with a microscope. So, we think that these higher dimensions are all around you – all around you, in your body, in your living room, the pond touches the 3D at every point so if I have a pond and we (humans) are the fish swimming in the pond, and you ask the fish where is the 3D? The answer is "everywhere" – and both him and the interviewer smiled beautifully.

The interviewer asked – now we have that at the microscopic scale so what about large extra dimensions that seem to be talked about now in some theories of cosmology?

Dr. Kaku responded – well, strings can only vibrate in 10D but in the 90s there was a revolution that it turns out that if you add an 11D, one more dimension, then membranes can exist – not just little strings but beach balls and golf balls can vibrate and perhaps our universe is a membrane, in which case, perhaps some of these dimensions can be large. Perhaps, even infinite. So, once you go from the 10D world of strings, where these dimensions are very tiny and go to 11D then you are talking about a whole new picture, a picture whereby some of these dimensions can be huge and that may even explain why gravity is so weak. Gravity is a very weak force. Perhaps, gravity oozes – escapes into these higher dimensions and that's why gravity is so weak.

The interviewer said, this so-called hierarchy problem which gravity may be 10^{39} or 10^{40} time smaller than the electromagnetic force. Seems to me that two of these fundamental forces to have a vast difference in scale, doesn't seem to make sense.

Dr. Kaku responded, that's right – I can put pieces of paper on the table and comb my hair and we did this in elementary school – pick up the pieces of paper. Well, I just defied gravity. The Earth weighs 6 trillion, trillion kilograms – I defied 6 trillion, trillion kilograms with a comb by picking up pieces of paper with electrostatic force – that's how weak gravity is. And perhaps, these higher dimensions are due to the fact that space oozes, a gravity oozes into these higher dimensions.

The interviewer asked, now, if we look at the possibilities of these large extra dimensions, which you (Dr. Kaku) said might be infinite in size, are we limited to these extra 6 or 7 dimensions other than the 3 we see, or might there be a vast number of infinite number of dimensions as well, each one being infinite in size – how many infinities are we dealing with here?

Dr. Kaku responded – we think that 11 is the upper limit. Some people have looked at 12D. In 12D, we have two times but in 13D, the universe becomes unstable. I had looked at 13D and it's a horrible dimension to work with mathematically – they both laughed. 12D seems to be the limit and even in 12D you have double times. The interviewer said, he didn't know what to make of that.

Dr. Kaku continued – but one thing is maybe we can experimentally see some of these objects because if the universe is hovering just above you, it is invisible to you like that underneath and that may explain dark matter. Dark matter is invisible, it has gravity – Hubble space telescope has given us maps of this invisible matter – maybe it's nothing but an ordinary galaxy hovering just above us in another dimension. If you read H. G. Wells famous novel; The Invisible Man – he becomes invincible because he's blown into the 4th dimension. He's hovering just above us, like those underneath the invincible man but he can look down on us. So perhaps, dark matter which makes up most of the matter of the universe, is nothing but ordinary matter of a galaxy hovering in a parallel universe just above us.

The Interviewer added, under the thinking gravity then being the only kind of force that can transmit in some way between different dimensions – it's the one thing that different dimensions are permeable to, will be gravity, everything else can't penetrate it but gravity can.

Dr. Kaku responded, that's right. We are like flies on fly paper – the fly paper represents our universe. We are stuck – we can't get up but gravity oozes between fly papers and therefore, we can, perhaps, detect experimentally, the presence of alternate universes. This is not just science fiction. Perhaps, with our instruments, we can detect dark matter like objects from other universes hovering just above our universe because gravity oozes between dimensions. *End of interview.*

My Comments on the Interview

It is very clear that what is being used here for the illustration is the Vesica Pisces. The fish being used here is no coincidence because that's exactly what we are. That's why the Vesica Pisces is the Jesus/fish/gateway of creation and salvation etc. Don't be surprised the next time you see this symbol with Jesus or the Virgin Mary in it – now you know what it truly means.

Creation or the Earth specifically, is a 3D world where we can't see past our 3D environments unless you tap into a higher energy (Holy Spirit) to bring you up hither then you are graced with the all-seeing eyes of God. This is how certain spiritual gifts are demonstrated – visions, dreams (visions of the night), word of knowledge, prophecies etc.

He mentioned that today we see the world as very broken – pieces of it. That's exactly what it is because there is a story in the Bible that explains how that happened. "But at the beginning of time, when the universe was first created, that's when the crystal existed in its perfect form. He calls it the superforce. A single superforce held this crystal together and then we had the Big Bang which shuttered this crystal, giving us the shuttered universe of today. When you look around you and you see the different forces – mountains, clouds, planets etc., it's broken. We live in a horribly broken world but at the instant of creation, there was perfection, there was perfection in a higher dimension. This perfection cannot exist in 3D."

Indeed, we are aware of the crystal in Heaven in which God has mirrored Himself to dwell in but His fullness dwells in the unapproachable light. Also, the universe is like a giant puzzle like Dr. Kaku said, and we are a shuttered piece because of the war that happened in Heaven. It's interesting to hear a physicist know that the universe used to be a perfect crystal – that is true. There was perfection before the fall of man. So, when you finally repent and be born again and you press into the things of the spirit, then you move up from your 3D world into a higher dimension – this is purely spiritual. Your crystal would fit perfectly into the higher dimension, and you can be living on Earth and in Heaven at the same time and know things in the spirit. Do scientists really think they can fit all the pieces together to make the Heavens and the Earth a perfect crystal as it used to be before time? Impossible.

He added that the theory of quantum doesn't work until you go up into hyperspace. Einstein called this the God Equation which he couldn't solve for 30 years, and it still hasn't been solved practically yet, as far as I know. It is an unsolvable problem forever and ever. It is not given unto the natural man to figure these things out with mere intellect. God is not that cheap.

That single "superforce" is God – who these same physicists are refusing to accept. We can only attain the perfection in God through our Lord and Savior Jesus Christ.

"So, in this crystal, the crystal exists in a higher dimension, but it eventually cracked apart for reasons that they are still trying to understand. And the 3D world they see today is quite broken. Now, where are these higher dimensions? Look at smoke – smoke permeates throughout the room; smoke permeates in all 3D, but smoke never disappears. Smoke never floats into the 4D. Therefore, a 4th, 5th, 6th dimension must be smaller than smoke. But atoms also don't certainly drift away into hyperspace. Therefore, these higher dimensions have to be smaller than an atom or else our universe will float away."

That is correct except that the 4D is both very large and very small. The 4D is both around and within our bodies. Eternity is both outside and inside our bodies. A 6-foot-tall man is not more of a human being than a newborn baby. Eternity is in both. This implies that eternity is in even something as small as a droplet of sperm. So, this also means that before you were a sperm in your father, you were a sperm (an invisible matter) inside the sperm from your grandfather that produced your father. I use "invisible matter" here because if we had analyzed with science, your grandfather's sperm that produced your father, we couldn't have found anything that would have predicted your existence or birthing you along the way somewhere in time. Therefore, human beings are spirit beings – you existed even before you were conceived. You existed even before you became visible and were seen with the natural eyes. Did even your father know that you were inside of him? But God knew. This is mentioned in the Word of God. The scriptures below are some of the many proofs that unbelieving scientists will never have a practical theory of everything in their current state of the rejection of God.

Ecclesiastes 3:11

[11] He has made everything beautiful in its time. Also, He has put eternity in their hearts, except that no one can find out the work that God does from beginning to end.

Jeremiah 1:5

[5] "Before I formed you in the womb, I knew you;
Before you were born, I sanctified you;
I ordained you a prophet to the nations."

A human being is an eternal being and eternity is encapsulated both outside and inside this being. It is a mystery that as small as human beings look, eternity is within them. What can contain them is also trapped inside them. That's why God exists outside of time, yet He came into time as Jesus. Has science been able to figure out the entirety of the mystery of a person yet? If you want to be able to break through the dimension or quantum problem, first, completely answer this question: "What is man or a human being?". I challenge you – even you don't know who you truly are because you are an eternal being. Before you rebel against God and discredit His Supremacy, figure out if you could reverse the DNA testing process to predict who else will be conceived and born from the intercourse of a man and a woman in the future. Why? Because if you can test to confirm that a baby belongs to a particular man or woman, then you should scientifically be able to prove by the same DNA process on a sperm to predict with accuracy, the next human being from that sperm. Even that, science cannot do it, but God does it all the time because it's His technology. And I'm not talking about cloning. I'm talking about finding you from your father's or grandfather's sperm. There is no doubt that if you are here today then it means that you were inside of them even when you weren't on Earth yet.

Dr. Kaku contradicted himself unknowingly when he used the illustration of smoke. Think of smoke like the Holy Spirit. He can be everywhere in the room, in all 3D and smoke disappears. Matter of fact, you can even be breathing in this smoke. Just because you don't see the smoke getting into 4D doesn't mean that's not the case. We see this a lot even in burnt offerings.

Genesis 8:20-22

²⁰ Then Noah built an altar to the LORD, and took of every clean animal and of every clean bird, and offered burnt offerings on the altar. ²¹ And the LORD smelled a soothing aroma. Then the LORD said in His heart, "I will never again curse the ground for man's sake, although the imagination of man's heart *is* evil from his youth; nor will I again destroy every living thing as I have done.

4D is right around and within you because the Holy Spirit lives inside the believer – you are just a vessel. God still sits on His throne in His own realm. That's why we keep our bodies as living sacrifices, holy and acceptable to God as our reasonable act of worship.

Romans 12:1-2

Living Sacrifices to God

12 I beseech you therefore, brethren, by the mercies of God, that you present your bodies a living sacrifice, holy, acceptable to God, *which is* your reasonable service. ² And do not be conformed to this world, but be transformed by the renewing of your mind, that you may prove what *is* that good and acceptable and perfect will of God.

My comments are in bold.

"So, we (physicists) think that these higher dimensions are all around you – all around you, in your body, in your living room, the pond touches the 3D at every point so if I (**God/Jesus Christ/Holy Spirit**) have a pond (**Venn Diagram/Vesica Pisces**) and we (humans) are the fish (**Creation/Jesus/Mary**) swimming in the pond (**Venn Diagram/Vesica Pisces**), and you ask the fish (**Creation/Jesus/Mary**) where is the 3D? The answer is "everywhere" (literally means everywhere – **omnipotence, omnipresence, omniscience of God/Jesus Christ/Holy Spirit**)" – and both him and the interviewer smiled beautifully.

The Ichthus (It is not just a cool symbol somebody designed)

Image Source – Public Domain

This is my favorite part. I literally smiled too. If the physicists are now saying that the higher dimensions are all around us, in our bodies, in our living room, the pond touches the 3D everywhere, and the answer is everywhere, why then do they say that because you see smoke around you, it never disappears and doesn't access the higher dimensions? This is the contradiction that I spoke about earlier. So, when I use my relationship with God and my incense I burn for example, I am correct in saying that the incense goes into the higher dimension or realm, including my worship, praises, prayer etc., because God lives inside of me and He's also all around me. Of course, this happens because of knowledge and understanding of the mystery. When I claim that I sense the presence of God/Holy Spirit or Angels around me, it is very accurate because I can carry dimensions with me as I move around the Earth based on my relationship with God through Jesus Christ by the power of the Holy Spirit. When prophets say they are seeing a live vision and telling what they see, they are seeing into a higher dimension where the secrets lie. God is all around you, most importantly, inside of you but like physicists say about for example human beings being the fish in the pond, until you rise and live in a higher dimension, your vision is like that of the fish. They spend all their lives in 3D – forward, backwards, up, down, thinking that anything beyond their universe is science fiction. A lot of human beings live in 3D and die in 3D. It is only when they die (soul leaves body permanently) that they realize that Earth was only a transition but at that point you won't be able to come back to correct any mistakes or misbeliefs. Then right that moment, Heaven, and Hell become very real because they truly are, and you will be going to one of those two locations. They are like the country or town or village that you don't know about or seen before. Except that you have heard about them before – you just don't believe that they exist.

So, these scientists prove the Bible accurate every day, but I doubt that's their true intentions. And or maybe they know secrets that you don't know or maybe are blind to these secrets and truths. God only grants us the grace to tap into higher intelligence and wisdom. Every honest person will agree. As much as I believe in science and respect it a lot, I believe that scientists discredit God a lot. But as you can already see, everything comes from God, including science.

The interviewer asked, "now, if we look at the possibilities of these large extra dimensions, which you (Dr. Kaku) said might be infinite in size, are we limited to these extra 6 or 7 dimensions other than the 3 we see, or might there be a vast number of infinite number of dimensions as well as each one being infinite in size – how many infinities are we dealing with here? Dr. Kaku responded, we think that 11 is the upper limit – some people have looked at 12D. In 12D, we have double times but in 13D, the universe becomes unstable. I had looked at 13D and it's a horrible dimension to work with mathematically, they both laughed. 12D seems to be the limit and even in 12D you have double times etc."

God is an eternal God – He's Alpha Omega so the short answer here is that there is not a finite number of dimensions. God is infinite so the number of dimensions is infinite (infinity ∞ as we call in mathematics). The error in science is that scientists are separating God from it. Without the Venn diagram (Vesica Pisces), there would be no mathematics, science, or engineering of any sort today. And as we clearly know now, it came from God. The humans of old that we call geniuses would not admit it because they want to take the glory, but they encountered God and either did not know it or knew it but decided to get all the glory for themselves anyway instead of giving God all the glory. There is no other way I would have known this if not in a vision. Just like we have several books of the Bible taken out, I have no doubt that there are humans in very influential places who have historical records of when this vision first came to man from the light of God, but they hid it because secrets are very powerful.

Strings vibrating in ten dimensions is not exactly accurate. There is no limitation or finiteness in God and the vibrations in His dimensions or realms. Eternity (God) dwells and is trapped in man so if science can understand the totality of the being of man, then you can quantify dimensions in the universe. This also means that even the universe is trapped inside of man. Scientists in all honesty don't know what they're doing to achieve perfect Artificial Intelligence (AI) and Quantum because these problems are unsolvable. To some extent, it can help advance technology but not it's fullness or entirety as I know it to be. All these problems attempt to break into the sovereignty, supremacy, and divinity of God through mere science, which is impossible. Science comes from God, but science cannot create God.

Quantum Mechanics – How the Universe Works

Quantum mechanics is God's technology that makes up and govern the universe. Quantum – the change in the state of matter, medium, and position with a constant time – where the time can be past, present, or future or at best, all three combined (now or happening at the same time) as the Lord wills. Quantum mechanics is both classical and quantum, and the midpoint of both – it is first, quantum, second, the midpoint (bridge) of quantum and classical, and third, classical. This means that it is first a set of scalar quantities, and second, an intersection of scalar and vector quantities, and third, a set of vector quantities.

The intersection of the sets is the entanglement. Therefore, entanglement arises in situations where we have partial knowledge of the state of two or more systems, and each system can only be fully described with reference to the others. Therefore, the systems can't be described independent of each other. That is why most people have partial knowledge about God, and the Holy Spirit. The state of entanglement between the two is creation because we (humans) fall in the midpoint of the Godhead. That is why most people also have partial knowledge about creation because to understand creation, you first need to understand the entire Godhead (God the Father, God the Son, and God the Holy Spirit), the story before creation, and the story through the end of creation. The union of the sets is the superposition – the equilibrium of all three sets. In other words, quantum mechanics is the mystery in the triple point – equilibrium state of all three forms – solid, liquid, and gas.

There must be a third state and equilibrium (union and stability) must be maintained in all three states for quantum mechanics to maintain superposition. In physics or quantum computing, quantum bit, known as a qubit, can represent 0, 1, or a state that exists between both. In other words, while a bit, or binary digit, can have a value either 0 or 1, a qubit can have a value that is either 0, 1 or a quantum superposition of 0 and 1. This is wrong. It should be 0 and 1 and a state that exists before both. The mathematical operator needed is an 'and' rather than an 'or' – and all three states or bits must be true or on for it to work. Physically, perfect quantum is true if and only if there is an equilibrium state of all three states. In binary computers, this is 0 or 1 but we need another number before 0 and 1 because 0 is a neutral and transformational state number. Imagine the gear order of your car (reverse, neutral, drive) or the coordinate system. Perhaps, for example, something like -1, 0, 1. There must always be a representation of all three states (bits) – just like how 0 and 1 are already present in classical computers. If everything is done right, quantum computers will be able to run at room temperature just fine and be energy efficient. It will take high levels of *consciousness* in systems for them to be stable without the need for very close to absolute zero (-450 degrees Fahrenheit) in giant freezers to keep them working properly. Consciousness here means exactly what you are thinking – very intentional learning, knowing, and understanding by each individual state to always gain and maintain awareness on the state of all other states in individual systems, and or in all three systems progressively if it's a distributed or network of systems. Consciousness that enables the ability to maintain synchronicity among all three states or systems is a very fundamental requirement here. Our current binary sequence consists of only two numbers – 1 or 0 because it is derived from √2.

If scientists and engineers can use a ternary operation (using 3 as base) – √3, there will be great progress in quantum. This will mean using qutrit instead of qubit. Scientists should investigate three-phase electric power for ideas. This same technology can be applied to maintaining energy efficiency, stability, entanglement, superposition, and coherence. Research this area in depth and you will find solutions.

In electricity, the phase refers to the distribution of a load. Single-phase power is a two-wire alternating current (AC) power circuit. Typically, there is one power wire – the phase wire – and one neutral wire, with current flowing between the power wire (through the load) and the neutral wire. Three-phase power is a three-wire AC power circuit with each phase AC signal 120 electrical degrees apart.

One important difference between three-phase power versus single phase power is the consistency of the delivery of power. Because of the peaks and dips in voltage, a single-phase power supply simply does not offer the same consistency as a three-phase power supply. A three-phase power supply delivers power at a steady, constant rate. The keywords here are steady and constant.

Comparing single-phase versus three-phase power, three-phase power supplies are more efficient. A three-phase power supply can transmit three times as much power as a single-phase power supply, while only needing one additional wire (that is, three wires instead of two) because it is built using 3 as base – √3. Thus, three-phase power supplies, whether they have three wires or four, use less conductor material to transmit a set amount of electrical power than do single-phase, two-phase, or direct-current (DC) systems power supplies at the same voltage.

For quantum mechanics to function properly in physics, you need to have at the minimum, three (3) systems or states interacting. Not greater than three and not less than three systems. Three is the perfect number of systems needed in the interaction process to at least help advance quantum in our physical technologies. The first (Father) system will depend on the third (Holy Spirit) system, and the second or middle (Son) system will depend on the third (Holy Spirit) System. Altogether, they are one entangled state. This is the current order. All three systems or states can be called the same one or Godhead system because they all cannot exist independent of each other. There must always be entanglement and superposition for quantum to function properly. Anything that brings about independence of a state or system among the three destroys quantum.

God is the same yesterday, today, and forever. These states represent God's constant time and governance or mechanics. Scientist's already have mathematical problems with their so-called thirteen dimensions (13D) calculations since they claim it has double times. How then can they solve triple times working as one in an infinity dimension where all the times are joined together and working as a constant? Different states or systems control time, and all these states together is called time.

What is missing in the current quantum or string theory is the infinity variable, which scientists hate to encounter. The problem with infinity is that it is larger than any (finite) number you can think of, and it defies all intuition. Some interesting features of infinity are illustrated in a thought experiment presented by David Hilbert in 1924. I suggest to scientists currently working on quantum or string theory to get some advice from David Hilbert's experiment from 1924 – he called infinity a MESS. It isn't a mess – it is rather how God in His infinite wisdom does what He wants. Except that my God does not exist or is not the creator and master of the universe, then scientists will be able to solve this problem the current ways they are going about it with mere qubits. But if my God is still God, and out of Him came all things, this problem can never be solved by mere humans forever and ever, especially if the intent is for time travel etc., and for worldly lust and vain glory. There is nothing like physical time travel through mere scientific means in wormholes etc. Science is trying to go way too far while it still doesn't have the eyes to see or ears to hear. Humans have become 'too smart' for themselves. The current pursuit for a breakthrough in quantum computing is represented in the following image but this will never work.

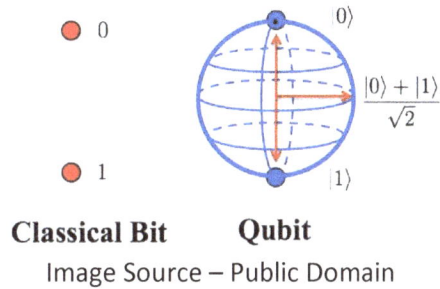

Classical Bit **Qubit**

Image Source – Public Domain

Using √3 for Quantum Computers

The ternary bit sequence will be as follows: 1, 3, 9, 27...

The goal is to achieve a balanced trinary (-1, ±0, +1). A n-qutrit system can be in superposition of all those 3^n states at a given time and it needs the value of coefficients of all the 3^n states basis to be fully recognized.

Because of this superposition in qutrit system, we can store 3^n bit information compared to n bit information in classical bit system or 2^n in qubit which is currently a struggle in science and engineering and will continue to be. Like I said earlier, quantum is a power (the set of scalar quantities) dimension and works like electricity. In simple terms, this is how the Power of God works – like high voltage electricity. Below is how we can go about it to get it to work.

$$^1/\sqrt{3}\ (|-1\rangle + |\pm 0\rangle + |1\rangle)$$

Then apply phase shift like it's done in three-phase power systems as in the images below.

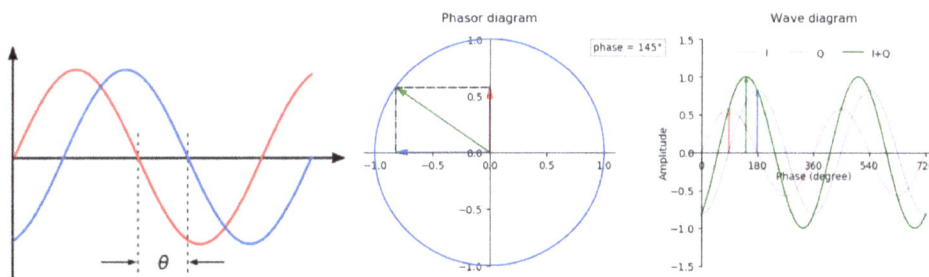

Image Source – Public Domain

In a three-phase system, there are three conductors that carry alternating current. These are called phases and are usually referred to as A, B and C. Each phase is set at the same frequency and voltage amplitude, but phase shifted by 120° allowing for constant power transfer during electrical cycles. For quantum computing to work, it must follow this formula and standard. The changes required for quantum computing to work are radical. If scientists and engineers do away with their classical prejudices, they will progress because quantum computing will be a whole new but most fundamental breed. Study the technology of three-phase electric power and learn how to apply it to quantum computing.

The current attempt to solve quantum computing with qutrit has three orthonormal basis states or vectors, often denoted $|1\rangle$, $|2\rangle$, $|3\rangle$ Ain Dirac or bra–ket notation. These are used to describe the qutrit as a superposition state vector in the form of a linear combination of the three orthonormal basis states:

$$|\Psi| = \alpha|0\rangle + \beta|1\rangle + \gamma|2\rangle$$

where the coefficients are complex probability amplitudes, such that the sum of their squares is unity (normalization):

$$|\alpha|^2 + |\beta|^2 + |\gamma|^2 = 1$$

This is wrong.

It must be three orthonormal basis states or vector, denoted by $|-1\rangle$, $|\pm 0\rangle$, $|1\rangle$ Ain Dirac or bra–ket notation. These are used to describe the qutrit as a superposition state vector in the form of a linear combination of the three orthonormal basis states:

$$|\Psi| = \alpha|-1\rangle + \beta|\pm 0\rangle + \gamma|1\rangle$$

where the coefficients are complex probability amplitudes, such that the sum of their squares is unity (normalization) and nondimensionalized:

$$|\alpha|^2 + |\beta|^2 + |\gamma|^2 = 0$$

We need a scalar result instead of a vector. Qutrits require a space of higher dimension (3D), and this is how quantum coherence can be maintained. The dimensionless quantity here is a quantity to which no physical dimension is assigned, also known as a bare, pure, or scalar quantity or a quantity of dimension one.

An important property of three-phase power is that the instantaneous power available to a resistive load is always constant – constant power transfer. In the formula for calculating this, there is a definition of a nondimensionalized power for intermediate calculations. This maintains consistency and that's key.

Unified Field Theory
The God Equation or the Theory of Everything

Qutrit State

$$R_{\mu vw} + R_{\mu vw} + R_{\mu vw} = 0$$

$$\mu = (-1, \pm 0, +1)$$

$$v = (-1, \pm 0, +1)$$

$$w = (-1, \pm 0, +1)$$

$$R_{\mu vw} + R_{\mu wv} + R_{v\mu w} = 0$$

Each subscript represents the three spatial dimensions – space or vacuum, gravity, and matter. It is very important to note that time gives expression to vacuum, and vacuum gives expression to matter through gravity working at different levels. This is because you can only calculate or measure what is called time when there is space or vacuum and matter occupying that space to serve as reference points. What works on matter within the space is gravity. Time gives expression to everything in a three-dimensional world. All three spatial dimensions represent the same thing and work together to give us time because it is the same underlying force of gravity that works at different levels to make it all happen. So, we form a 3 x 3 matrix from it by multiplying any one set by the two other sets. We can also safely call gravity, time since gravity controls time. Since matter was created first, and it was formless and empty (vacuum), we will multiply matter by space and gravity to get time. Time rules night and day, and the seasons, and years, and can be defined as the unit of destiny.

Genesis 1:1-2

1 In the beginning God created the heavens and the Earth. **²** Now the Earth was formless and empty, darkness was over the surface of the deep, and the Spirit of God was hovering over the waters.

First, we see the creation of the heavens and the Earth (matter), then second, we see it formless and empty (space or vacuum), and then third, we see the Spirit of God working as gravity. We are still working with the 3D here in a trinity or triune nature. A particle trapped in a 3D box in this coordinate system will have no external force acting on it inside the box. When the potential energy is infinite, then the wavefunction equals zero. We will come up with nine equations – nine states of entanglement when we perform the calculations.

A pure qutrit state is a coherent superposition of the basis states. This means that a single qutrit can be described by a linear combination of $|-1\rangle$ and $|\pm 0\rangle$ and $|+1\rangle$.

$$|\Psi| = \alpha|\text{-}1\rangle + \beta|\pm0\rangle + \gamma|\text{+}1\rangle$$

where α and β and γ are the probability amplitudes, that are all complex numbers.

When we measure this qutrit in the standard basis, according to the Born rule, the probability of outcome $|\text{-}1\rangle$ with value "-1" is $|\alpha|^2$, and the probability outcome $|\pm0\rangle$ with value "±0" is $|\beta|^2$ and the probability outcome $|\text{+}1\rangle$ with value "+1" is $|\gamma|^2$.

Because the absolute squares of the amplitudes equate to probabilities, it follows that α and β and γ must be constrained according to the second axiom of probability theory by the equation.

$$|\alpha|^2 + |\beta|^2 + |\gamma|^2 = 0$$

Qutrit Quantum Entanglement

$$\frac{1}{\sqrt{3}}(-1-1-1\rangle + |\pm0\pm0\pm0\rangle + |+1+1+1\rangle)$$

Below are the 9 states (modification of Bell states) or phase shifts entanglement operations.

$$|\Phi^-\rangle = \frac{1}{\sqrt{3}}(|-1\rangle_A \otimes |-1\rangle_B \otimes |-1\rangle_C - |-1\rangle_A \otimes |\pm0\rangle_B \otimes |\pm0\rangle_C - |-1\rangle_A \otimes |1\rangle_B$$
$$\otimes |1\rangle_C)\ (1)$$

$$|\Phi^\pm\rangle = \frac{1}{\sqrt{3}}(|-1\rangle_A \otimes |-1\rangle_B \otimes |-1\rangle_C \pm |-1\rangle_A \otimes |\pm0\rangle_B \otimes |\pm0\rangle_C \pm |-1\rangle_A \otimes |1\rangle_B$$
$$\otimes |1\rangle_C)\ (2)$$

$$|\Phi^+\rangle = \frac{1}{\sqrt{3}}(|-1\rangle_A \otimes |-1\rangle_B \otimes |-1\rangle_C + |-1\rangle_A \otimes |\pm0\rangle_B \otimes |\pm0\rangle_C + |-1\rangle_A \otimes |1\rangle_B$$
$$\otimes |1\rangle_C)\ (3)$$

$$|\Phi^-\rangle = \frac{1}{\sqrt{3}}(|\pm0\rangle_A \otimes |-1\rangle_B \otimes |-1\rangle_C - |\pm0\rangle_A \otimes |\pm0\rangle_B \otimes |\pm0\rangle_C - |\pm0\rangle_A \otimes |1\rangle_B$$
$$\otimes |1\rangle_C)\ (4)$$

$$|\Phi^\pm\rangle = \frac{1}{\sqrt{3}}(|\pm0\rangle_A \otimes |-1\rangle_B \otimes |-1\rangle_C \pm |\pm0\rangle_A \otimes |\pm0\rangle_B \otimes |\pm0\rangle_C \pm |\pm0\rangle_A \otimes |1\rangle_B$$
$$\otimes |1\rangle_C)\ (5)$$

$$|\Phi^+\rangle = \frac{1}{\sqrt{3}}(|\pm0\rangle_A \otimes |-1\rangle_B \otimes |-1\rangle_C + |\pm0\rangle_A \otimes |\pm0\rangle_B \otimes |\pm0\rangle_C + |\pm0\rangle_A \otimes |1\rangle_B$$
$$\otimes |1\rangle_C)\ (6)$$

$$|\Phi^-\rangle = \frac{1}{\sqrt{3}}(|1\rangle_A \otimes |-1\rangle_B \otimes |-1\rangle_C - |1\rangle_A \otimes |\pm0\rangle_B \otimes |\pm0\rangle_C - |1\rangle_A \otimes |1\rangle_B \otimes |1\rangle_C)\ (7)$$

$$|\Phi^\pm\rangle = \frac{1}{\sqrt{3}}(|1\rangle_A \otimes |-1\rangle_B \otimes |-1\rangle_C \pm |1\rangle_A \otimes |\pm0\rangle_B \otimes |\pm0\rangle_C \pm |1\rangle_A \otimes |1\rangle_B \otimes |1\rangle_C)\ (8)$$

$$|\Phi^+\rangle = \frac{1}{\sqrt{3}}(|1\rangle_A \otimes |-1\rangle_B \otimes |-1\rangle_C + |1\rangle_A \otimes |\pm0\rangle_B \otimes |\pm0\rangle_C + |1\rangle_A \otimes |1\rangle_B \otimes |1\rangle_C)\ (9)$$

Nine specific three-qutrit states with the maximal value of 3√3. They are known as the nine maximally entangled three-qutrit God (modified Bell) states and they form a maximally entangled basis, known as the modified Bell basis, of the three-dimensional space for three qutrits. They are in a superposition of -1 and ±0 and +1 – a linear combination of the three states.

Vector Representation of Three-Qutrits

The tensor product (or Kronecker product) is used to combine quantum states. The combined state of three qutrits is the tensor product of the three qutrits. The tensor product is denoted by the symbol $\otimes$.

$$|abc\rangle = |a\rangle \otimes |b\rangle \otimes |c\rangle$$

$$= V_{-1\text{-}1\text{-}1}|\text{-}1\text{-}1\text{-}1\rangle + V_{-1\pm0\pm0}|\text{-}1\pm0\pm0\rangle + V_{-1+1+1}|\text{-}1+1+1\rangle...$$

$$V_{+1\text{-}1\text{-}1}|+1\text{-}1\text{-}1\rangle + V_{+1\pm0\pm0}|+1\pm0\pm0\rangle + V_{+1+1+1}|+1+1+1\rangle$$

$V_{-1\text{-}1\text{-}1}$	$V_{-1\pm0\pm0}$	V_{-1+1+1}
$V_{\pm0\text{-}1\text{-}1}$	$V_{\pm0\pm0\pm0}$	$V_{\pm0+1+1}$
$V_{+1\text{-}1\text{-}1}$	$V_{+1\pm0\pm0}$	V_{+1+1+1}

Time

There are three dimensions of time (space, gravity, matter). Within each dimension, there are three dimensions of space, three dimensions of gravity, and three dimensions of matter. We can think of time as a trinity of several trinities just like everything else. We can represent time with the values -1, ±0, +1 for the three types of time, which are past, present, and future. Think of this as the gear of your car (R, N, D) for reverse (backward), neutral (static), and drive (forward).

Time = space + gravity + matter

If there is no space, and no matter, and gravity doesn't act within space in and around matter, there is no way we can measure time because there would be nothing to measure. So, time can only have expression when there is first, space, second, gravity, and third, matter. Matter exists because of space and gravity. When there is no matter within space to serve as reference points, time cannot be calculated because the distance between matter or the transformation effect that the different phases of gravity have on matter is what we call time. Gravity creates and controls matter in space – that process is what we call time. Physically, time is irreversible. Spiritually, one can travel into time past, time present, and time future. The Lord said to me that a treasure is compensated by time.

117

Relationship Between Time and Entropy

Entropy is a scientific concept as well as a measurable physical property that is most associated with a state of disorder, randomness, or uncertainty. As entropy increases, time increases. For instance, if we had no concept of time and we decide to count the number of visible stars in the sky, we would never finish counting. Assuming we had only a hundred stars in the sky, we would count one hundred stars. The distance and velocity between visibly or invisibly going or moving from one star unto the next star to count, is what we call time. In other words, the transition between the stars is what we count to represent time. Velocity rather than speed is appropriate in this context because time needs both rate or speed and direction of movement. Time becomes relative at this point because if we decide to be quick in counting the stars then we in a way reduce the distance between the stars with speed. But if we are slow then we in a way increase the distance between stars. This is where speed and energy through gravity come into the picture.

Therefore, the kinetic energy of an object is proportional to the square of its velocity. In other words, if there is a twofold increase in speed, the kinetic energy will increase by a factor of four. If there is a threefold increase in speed, the kinetic energy will increase by a factor of nine. This is how gravity works in our universe. Every object with mass free falls in the universe following this law. Gravity creates and controls time in space.

If nothing happens in the entire universe, and not even thoughts, and consciousness can exist, then time will cease to exist or time will not continue to move forward. It wouldn't mean that the invisible or eternity would cease to exist. Only the physical would cease to exist because the concept of time as we generally experience it exists because of the physical. Outside of the physical is eternity – where past, present, and future are all one. So, time is not external to the universe, and cannot be measured independently of the universe. Time is simply a slowed down version or slowed motion of eternity. This universe is time – time is the physical universe. Time would not continue if this universe were completely empty of all matter and objects. Imagine a universe like the Moon where the Moon doesn't even exist to stand upon, but you still have that kind of lunar gravity.

Although eternity would continue to exist. There is no day or night in eternity, so the concept of time is only applicable to the physical universe as we see it. Movement in eternity is instant. Matter and objects are time – time is matter and objects. Absolute or Newtonian time is in fact wrong. Newton would be right if he made the difference clear between eternity and time. Eternity is infinity but time is finite. So, for him to have said that time, in his conception of Newtonian time, was external to the universe was a big error and very misleading – unless he had said, "invisible time". Because even in eternity, time is not absolute – "time" in the invisible realm (heaven or hell) is still dependent on God. The heavens and the Earth were all created. Every creation depends on the creator. God dwells both outside and inside of heaven. You dwell outside of your children, but we can still find you inside of your children. Think about that. We can't do calculations in mathematics or physics with eternity (infinity) but at the physical level, eternity is divided or slowed down to give us what we call and can relate to as time (finite), which is dependent on our universe. The happenings in our universe are what measure time but the Sun, Earth, and Moon serve as our guide to adjust our clocks, which we can relate to better. Our clocks are only trackers, registers, or loggers – they are not time in themselves. That's why if you rely on just your clock, the world may be ending, and you would not know it.

The error with the current spacetime equations as proposed by Einstein is due to this separation of time from space, gravity, and matter, and for thinking that space is three-dimensional and time is a dimension all by itself, which gives us a four-dimension universe. This is wrong. So, the fourth dimension is the invisible or eternity. And it's inside and all around us – with things happening at like lightning speed. At a mere physical or visible level, our universe is three-dimensional. And this is what we need for any physical calculations. Einstein was trying to correct Newton with his relativistic time, but he also failed by adding time as one dimension of spacetime, making it four dimensions. Spacetime is three dimensional.

So, time is when the invisible is slowed down to become visible so that the visible can serve as reference to the invisible. Gravity creates and controls matter in space. Gravity creates and controls time. Time creates and controls entropy, and entropy creates and controls time. Therefore, time equals entropy, and entropy equals time. Gravity equals time, and time equals gravity. Our physical universe is time – time is the universe. They are symmetrical. Our universe is all symmetrical.

Gravity is what causes entropy through matter in space. The first condition is that there must be space available. Then the entropy causes time. The time causes entropy. The entropy causes gravity. It's a cycle.

I listened to Arvin Ash's extrapolation on Lee Smolin's paper. Lee Smolin suggests in a 2021 paper that what distinguishes the past from the present is a kind of knowledge that is gained once indeterminate quantum events consisting of only probabilities in the present become a classical definite past. According to Smolin the past is completely classical – they are no longer probabilities – they are definite. They have already happened. They cannot unhappen. However, the future is quantum, it consists of probabilities – it is still unfolding.

So, what seems to separate the past from the present is whether it is knowable or not. Whether it has become actual knowledge. Something for which we can say, yeah, it was like this. So, according to the paper, the change from a quantum indefinite present to a classical definite past is what defines the arrow of time. This points always in the forward direction as the quantum present – constantly turns out a classical past. The future is also quantum according to Smolin. It consists of only possibilities. So, we are living constantly in the very moment when probabilities become actualized, and reality becomes imprinted in the past as actual knowledge.

Arvin said that although Smolin does not talk specifically about information in his paper, if one interprets actualized knowledge as a kind of information being added to the universe then perhaps, this is the link that connects entropy to time. If Smolin is correct, and the arrow of time is due to indeterminate quantum events becoming the classical past and this knowledge is leading to more information constantly being created then entropy is also increasing because of its link to information. And since the classical definite past becomes known and cannot go back to being unknown, time cannot be reversed, and entropy also cannot be decreased. They all go one way – quantum becomes classical, information increases, entropy increases, and time flows only forward. Finally, Arvin added that although it is established that information is related to entropy, both Smolin's paper and his extrapolation of Smolin's paper to information are not established theories but conjecture. So, you should take this as food for thought. And that they don't really know what time is, but they are quite sure that entropy is increasing in the universe and that it's getting increasingly disorder. That means that entropy must have been much lower earlier in time, especially near the big bang. So, how did the universe get to this low entropy super orderly state in the beginning? This is a mystery, but it brings a discussion of time to the scale of the universe and cosmic time. Will time continue to flow forward forever? Arvin ended here.

I like the lines along which Lee Smolin thinks. Well, this writing will help you answer all or most of those questions. At a physical level, yes, you can say that the past is completely classical, and the future is quantum with probabilities which are still unfolding. I'm sure by now you already know what time is. The universe got to this low super orderly state at the beginning near the big bang because of the universe's age. The second law of thermodynamics states that the entropy of any isolated system always increases. The Earth is an isolated system, just like your body. And no, time will not continue to flow forward forever. The physical concept of time has an expiry date. Below is the universe right from the big bang as relating to time and entropy. This is reality – don't be shocked. We will dive deeper into this as we go on.

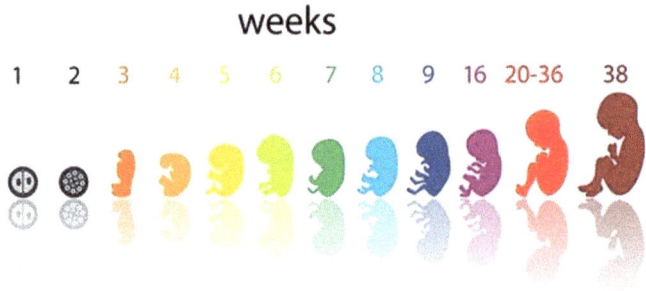

Image Source – Public Domain

Lee Smolin is mostly correct but not entirely. So, what seems to separate the past from the present is not whether it is knowable or not. In pure physical sense, we can say yes, but the reality which is the line along which we want to view things, no. Even in the physical, we don't always know what happened in the past. If we did then humanity would not be this messed up because the truth about life would be very clear and obvious everywhere. Most people still don't know what the past was like and knowledgeable about what happened, except in their own lives. And even that depends on when they became conscious and started knowing things. But the past can always be knowable depending on which realm you operate from. You can spiritually know the past, present, and the future accurately. Spiritually, these are never hidden to the sons of God.

Although according to Smolin, time points always in the forward direction, that applies at the physical level. Time can physically be viewed more accurately like a network rather than a line. Time is exactly how we are dispersed all around the world – it's not a straight line or arrow. Multiple events are happening at the same time, and all these events are relative. There are events that you can never run away from because they are in your network so you must go through them. You can call this predestination. That doesn't mean you can't wrongly veer into a network in which you don't belong. This is how people can even die untimely death. Yes, we won't relive the lives we have already lived. Time points in both and all directions but doesn't quite "flow" on like an arrow or straight line because everything is always happening in the network as the present. Time is "now" and works like the coordinate system and has inversion. Inversion because you could either become a policeman with integrity or a criminal. An inverse is defined as a reverse or direct opposite. So, the directions in time are either -, ±, +. And before you can travel to either side, you must go through the center – translation or transformation. Time is light or darkness, or truth or lies. Physically, time can't be traveled backwards through physics. Physics can only travel forward because of intuition. Supernaturally, we can travel or see in both and all directions as all events are in the present time in a network. The images below will help give you an idea.

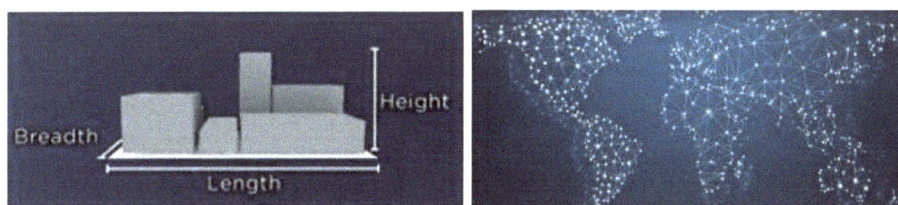

Left: 3D spacetime resulting from space, gravity, and matter, Right: Network of time

Since you are used to time as an arrow, think of it now as a network of arrows. Although Smolin thinks that we can't change the past, the past was once changeable before it became unchangeable. The past was once the future, then it became the present, and finally became the past. There's symmetry everywhere. Your decisions and choices for the future, modifies and controls your present and establishes your unchangeable past. That's why you need the guidance of the Holy Spirit to make better decisions and choices for your life. You can't say that your past is fixed or unchangeable when you had and continue to have multiple opportunities to make it a past that you wouldn't want to change anyway because it's a great and memorable past. So, the past is the present, and the future. You can write it in any order, and you will still see the symmetry.

Like Arvin's thought that if Smolin is correct, and the arrow of time is due to indeterminate quantum events becoming the classical past and this knowledge is leading to more information constantly being created, then it means that entropy is also increasing because of its link to information. Both entropy and information in this physical context are tricky. The knowledge has always been there, and the information have already been created. They are just the invisible coming into the visible. You can confidently say you plan to have a child or children in a year or two. Why are you so confident when you say that? Because that has always been there in the invisible until you bring it into the visible. For instance, the same information in your human anatomy right now had all existed even when you were merely a seed of a day old in your mother's womb. Even prior to becoming a seed, that information had always been available in the invisible. With knowledge and understanding, you already existed even before you entered your mother's womb, but we will focus on physics now. Although without the visible physical human features, you still were complete as a seed in the womb as a dot. If we know what to measure, we could measure a whole human being even when he or she is just a day old in the womb. If we measure entropy by visible features or information, we will be wrong, but if we measure entropy by the knowledge of what potentially exists in the invisible or space or object, then we will be right. This is gravity, and this is quantum mechanics.

We can only have an accurate measurement if we understand space, gravity, matter, and time. In information theory, these will be memory (bits or qubits or 1, 0), algorithm, data or information to be processed – then we will know the time it will take. We can in turn know how much time we will need to process some quantity or size of data. In other words, we will know the entropy from the time and the time from the entropy. Assuming we try to measure or solve a problem that goes into infinity because of an infinite number of possibilities, what would be the time and or entropy? In quantum computing, we require qutrits for memory and computation because our universe is three-dimensional. Our current classical computing is two-dimensional. This means that the current approach to quantum computing using qubits will never work.

Finally, Smolin is somewhat accurate in saying that time flows forward. Physically, it helps your intuition if you think about it this way, but you at least now understand that it's more like a network. This will help you understand why you cannot physically time travel through physics or wormholes – something that physicists need to stop worrying or talking about. The universe isn't designed like that.

If the present equals a classical definite past, and the future equals a classical indefinite present, then we can say that the past equals the present and the present equals the future, and the future equals the past. Mathematically, we can write this in any order – forward or reverse. This also means that the Bible is accurate in saying that God knew us before He created us and that He knows the end from the beginning and the beginning from the end. Therefore, the equation of quantum mechanics is generally time symmetric.

$$\hat{H}|\psi\rangle = E|\psi\rangle$$

Schrödinger Equation

It doesn't have a flow preference and some people will say that it's time agnostic. Therefore, the invisible equals the visible, and the visible equals the invisible. What happens in the invisible world, controls what happens in the visible world – they are symmetrical.

Time always exists in the seed, even when you decide to destroy the seed. Seed here can be a human, animal, or a plant seed. Everything grows based on its gravity or energy potential trapped or confined inside of it. Just like in an atomic clock, as anything grows upwards, sidewards, and or forward, the height, breadth, and or length changes and increases and it registers or logs that change itself. Unlike an atomic clock, you just don't physically see it written on the face of a human being or a plant or the Earth until you take a measurement. Like in Arvin's illustration, if we have two separate gases in a chamber separated by a partition, it becomes easy to identify which is which – i.e., it is half and half, which is 50/50. Together, they are 100. But when we decide to remove the partition and combine those two gases, then the entropy increases since it will take more information to describe it. This moves from a classical problem to a quantum problem since it would require using probabilities to find the different gases. This means that the probability of the individual gas particles of the two gases to be in either part of the chamber becomes 0% because the particles would be everywhere.

This means that a wave function becomes the ideal way to look for the particles in the chamber. Therefore, the result for a theory of everything or a unified field theory equals a scalar value of 0. We can apply the same to a human or plant seed. When the human or plant is grown, they will make visible the invisible features or information (entropy) that were always trapped inside them when they were just a seed. At this stage, they will still be quantum, but the visible features or information will make them appear more classical. This is gravity, this is time, and this is quantum mechanics.

We can turn a quantum wave diagram or a Feynman diagram either way on the coordinate system because it's symmetrical with time, so it doesn't matter which direction. The transition from time symmetry at the quantum level to time asymmetry at the macro level happens at the center of gravity (±0), which is the translation or transformation point through the different manifestations of the force of gravity. This is also the definition and measurement of time.

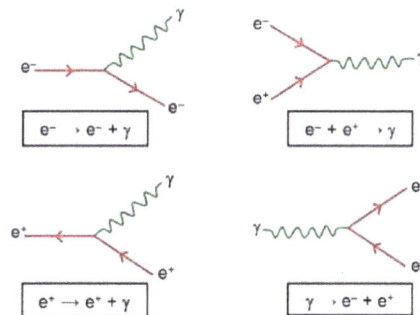

Image Source – Public Domain

Therefore, we have t-symmetry or time reversal symmetry, which is the theoretical symmetry of physical laws under the transformation of time reversal. If we reverse the manifestations of gravity or time of a human or plant, we will finally get to where they weren't even a seed.

$$T : t \mapsto -t.$$

Image Source – Public Domain

One definition of time in physics is the process that brings the unknown future into the recorded past, via the present. This can be modified to be the process that brings both the known and unknown future into the recorded past, via the present through the different manifestations of gravity in and around matter to cause change of state of matter in space.

In physics, time is also defined as a change, or the interval over which change occurs. It is impossible to know that time has passed unless something changes. The amount of time or change is calibrated by comparison with a standard. The SI unit for time is the second, abbreviated s.

It is possible to know that something has changed even if a visible manifestation has not occurred yet because not everything is visible to the eyes. Change does not always occur over time. Change can occur and defy what we call time at lightning speed. It is possible to know that time has passed even if something has not physically changed. How do you measure that change? For our physical concept of time to be measurable, there must be visible space, gravity, and matter.

Atomic Clocks and Time

The Earth is a gigantic atom, and the atomic clocks have electrons in them that react to the electrical/magnetic or electromagnetic field of the Earth to put the electrons in the atomic clock in excited states. This is how seconds are counted and time is tracked in the atomic clock. Don't be surprised to learn that when airplanes containing atomic clocks travel around the world, their times change from the time on the clock that's on Earth. Scientists have carried out several experiments on this.

Atomic clocks use lasers to control atoms and measure their oscillations. They are currently the most stable and accurate way to measure time intervals. At the heart of an atomic clock is a very stable oscillator – like a pendulum in an ancient or grandfather clock. Like in a regular clock, instead of having gears, levers, and springs etc., it's a series of lasers. The oscillator is the atom itself. Atoms trapped in an electric field receive a series of pulses, which aid in controlling and measuring their oscillations. Instead of one tick per second, these clocks oscillate or tick a million billion times per second, allowing for much more precision. They are so reliable that it will take about double the age of the universe (approximately 30 billion years) to drift by even a second. So, the higher the clock is from the ground, the faster it ticks.

Resonance

Everything in nature has a vibration, including the human body, and plants. Everything is made up of atoms, and these atoms are in a constant state of motion. And depending on the speed of these atoms, things can change or maintain states to either appear as a solid, liquid, or gas. Our thoughts are vibrations. Music or sound is also a vibration. Therefore, there is something called resonance in science.

Resonance is when one object vibrating at the same natural frequency of a second object forces that second object into vibrational motion. The word resonance comes from Latin, and it means to "resound" – to sound out together with a loud sound. Every manifestation in your life is resonant to the vibrations from your mind and thoughts. Every form or state of matter or manifestation in the universe has an underlying vibration. Everything in the universe is in constant motion. Vibrations express themselves in corresponding geometrical shapes or figures. You will learn more on music and sounds and how they are fundamental to our being and why there is what is called the Star of David in the Bible – Jesus Christ, the tree and the fruit of life.

Revelation 2:7

[7] "He who has an ear, let him hear what the Spirit says to the Churches. To him who overcomes I will give to eat from the tree of life, which is in the midst of the Paradise of God.'"

Revelation 22:14-16

[14] Blessed *are* those who do His commandments, that they may have the right to the tree of life and may enter through the gates into the city. [15] But outside *are* dogs and sorcerers and sexually immoral and murderers and idolaters, and whoever loves and practices a lie.

[16] "I, Jesus, have sent My angel to testify to you these things in the Churches. I am the Root and the Offspring of David, the Bright and Morning Star."

Resonance and vibration are being introduced here to help you understand that the higher you lift any object or atomic clocks, the more energy you must spend. Again, this goes back to gravitation or electric potential. The taller you grow, the more energy you must spend. The higher you lift a metal ball, the more energy you must spend. This is what registers on the atomic clocks as fast ticking. If a human being or plant had a digital screen, you would see the same readings whenever they go higher or grow taller. The gravitational or electric potential energy of an object or a body is what causes the atoms in the atomic clock to vibrate faster the higher it is lifter in space. All bodies go through this – you just don't see the vibrations. For example, you only see physical growth in humans, and plants and a physical increase in features or parts or entropy. These are the different manifestations of gravity, and this is what we call time. Atomic clocks ticking faster at higher heights isn't magic. Your body goes through the same thing.

If the Sun does not rise and set, we cannot mark Sunrise and Sunset, which are both frames of reference when it comes to measuring time. If the Moon does not go through the different phases, we cannot mark the times of the month, which represent frames of reference when it comes to measuring time. If the Sun, Earth, and Moon do not go through their orderly rotations and revolutions, which most people call "dance", we will not be able to have any frame of reference when it comes to knowing and registering the seasons, which overall gives us the years etc., because they would not even exist. These are all markers of time and together, they create time.

Do we have any other external or isolated time device outside of these three bodies that tells us the different seasons, and when it's maybe summer or winter etc.? I don't think we do. When the Sun and Moon change their courses according to the different seasons, we also change our clocks on Earth. We have what we call daylight saving time. Is that correct? Daylight Saving Time is the practice of setting the clocks one hour ahead of standard time to make use of more Sunlight in the spring, summer, and fall evenings. If clocks or time were "fixed", why do we use the amount of Sunlight we have to update our clock settings? So, man-made clocks can never replace the Sun, Earth, and Moon and how they control the seasons. These are fundamental to creating and measuring time in the universe. They are the bigger atoms at the cosmic level, just like the atomic clock, and they are the reason why the atomic clock even functions. They are the reason why our bodies function.

So, you see, time as we know and measure it, does not exist outside of space, gravity, and matter. Space and all the different bodies in the solar system help us to measure time based on orderly movements and positioning through the force of gravity. The Sun, Earth, and Moon are time. Together, space, gravity, and matter, are time. There would not be anything called time if not for these bodies in the universe.

Length Contraction and Time Dilation

In physics, length contraction is the phenomenon that a moving object's length is measured to be shorter than its proper length, which is the length as measured in the object's own rest frame. It is also known as Lorentz contraction or Lorentz–FitzGerald contraction (after Hendrik Lorentz and George Francis FitzGerald) and is usually only noticeable at a substantial fraction of the speed of light. Length contraction is only in the direction in which the body is traveling. For standard objects, this effect is negligible at everyday speeds, and can be ignored for all regular purposes, only becoming significant as the object approaches the speed of light relative to the observer.

In special relativity, the rest frame of a particle is the coordinate system (frame of reference) in which the particle is at rest. The rest frame of compound objects (such as a fluid, or a solid made of many vibrating atoms) is taken to be the frame of reference in which the average momentum of the particles which make up the substance is zero (the particles may individually have momentum, but collectively have no net momentum). The rest frame of a container of gas, for example, would be the rest frame of the container itself, in which the gas molecules are not at rest, but are no more likely to be traveling in one direction than another. This is like the seed of a plant. The seed's coat is like the container and the inner parts of the seed are like the gas molecules, which will eventually germinate and grow into a big plant by breaking loose from the rest frame. Same with a baby in the womb – the mother may be the rest frame, but the baby still vibrates in the womb until eventually the force of gravity brings that baby out and that same gravitational or electric potential energy contained in the child will make him or her grow towards the sky. The rest frame of a river would be the frame of an unpowered boat, in which the mean velocity of the water is zero. This frame is also called the center-of-mass frame, or center-of-momentum frame.

In physics, the center of mass of a distribution of mass in space (sometimes referred to as the balance point) is the unique point where the weighted relative position of the distributed mass sums to zero. This is the point to which a force may be applied to cause a linear acceleration without an angular acceleration.

In other words, the center of mass is a position defined relative to an object or system of objects. It is the average position of all the parts of the system, weighted according to their masses. Below is the center of mass for some simple geometric shapes.

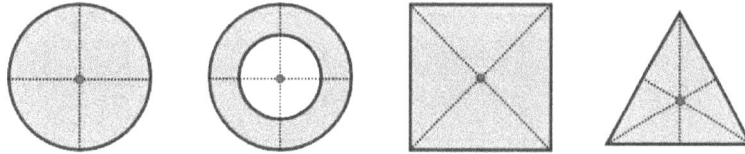

Image Source – Public Domain

The center of gravity is the point through which the force of gravity acts on an object or system. You will understand why the waist area of a normal or healthy human body keeps a uniformity or balance for the whole body between the upper and lower torsos to give the body the desirable dimensions of parts. In most problems in mechanics, the gravitational field is assumed to be uniform. The center of gravity is then in the same position as the center of mass. The terms center of gravity and center of mass tend to be often used interchangeably since they are often at the same location.

It is said in physics that the idea of time dilation by going into deeper gravitational fields is accurate. In physics and relativity, time dilation is the difference in the elapsed time as measured by two clocks. It is either due to a relative velocity between them (special relativistic "kinetic" time dilation) or to a difference in gravitational potential between their locations (general relativistic gravitational time dilation). When unspecified, "time dilation" usually refers to the effect due to velocity.

This was first theorized by Einstein in his theory of relativity. People think that it's a very bizarre thing because when you are in a place where gravity is stronger, time moves more slowly. Another way that it occurs is through your relative movement through space. If you have two observers that have clocks that tick at the same rate, and one of those observers moves away at a very high speed, the moving observer's clock will tick more slowly – their time will literally pass slower. And it is said that some people are confused and think that it's a clock mechanical issue but it's not – it's time. It doesn't matter what the clock is – it could be a clock, it could be your heartbeat, it could be a count – it's time. So, we can agree that a clock is not necessarily what time is. Time is independent of a physical clock. Time is the measurement of the speed at which a distance is covered within space.

This is also even true for someone who is walking, compared to someone who is sitting at a table. Time moves slower for the person who is walking. Similarly, for gravitational time dilation, someone who is at sea level, compared to someone who is at a mountain, will also experience time at a slower rate. That is because gravity is stronger when you are closer to the Earth center of mass. The Earth's core is a nucleus (protons and neutrons). But in these examples, the amount of time dilation is so miniscule that it's totally unnoticeable. Apart from a few examples, humans don't typically deal with fast enough speeds or enough gravity to experience a significant amount of time dilation. But is has been experimented that atomic clocks are reaching a sensitivity that can measure even the tiniest amount of time dilation. This is because atomic clocks are made up of the same elements that in our real world, create and control time. So, the atomic clocks are sensitive and react to these elements. All these elements together are called gravity.

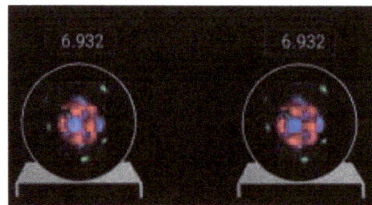

Image Source – Public Domain

In 2010, two ultra-precise synchronized atomic clocks were placed next to each other. They were so precise that they would lose about 1 second over the history of the entire Earth. Then one of them was raised about 33 cm. The result was that the clock that was higher up began to tick faster.

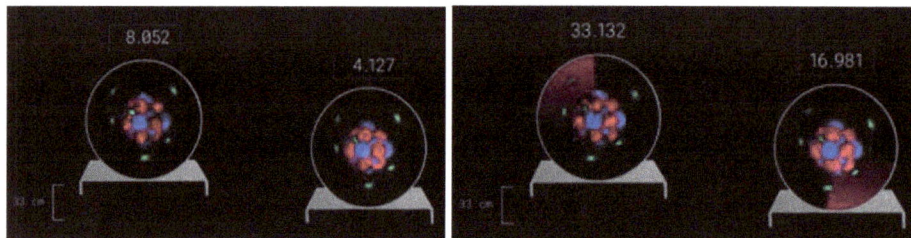

Image Source – Public Domain

Nothing was wrong with the clocks. It was rather time that sped up for the higher clock relative to the lower clock due to the tiniest decrease in gravity as the clock moved higher up. Scientists flew atomic clocks on airplanes around the world and compared the time before and after and what they found, confirmed their predictions. Time slowed down for the moving clocks. The technology then became integral to what we depend on every day like the GPS. One scientist said he thinks of the atomic clocks as constantly working in the background – you don't see it, but they are important to have the whole thing run. The universe is an atomic clock. You are an atomic clock. Space, gravity, and matter make up the atomic clocks in the universe.

The reason why length contraction is only in the direction in which the body is traveling and can be ignored for standard objects at everyday speeds, and can be ignored for all regular purposes, and only become significant as the object approaches the speed of light relative to the observer is because the direction of travel and the speed of travel are the true measurements of time. Like I said earlier, if you have objects or matter in space, then you have position and direction. The objects traveling close to the speed of light become "shorter" because of how fast they are moving. When they reach the speed of light, they become invisible. Does that mean there is no object traveling? No. It just means that they are traveling at lightning speed. If you are in an airplane traveling at such speed, you will not be able to observe anything on the ground or through the window as they will all be invisible as if they don't exist. The same applies to when you observe from the ground – you will not be able to see a moving airplane. Maybe you might hear the sound.

A simple physical example is a sonic boom jet – it travels faster than the speed of sound. Sonic boom is an impulsive noise like thunder. It is caused by an object moving faster than sound – about 750 miles per hour at sea level. Research on your own to get a detailed explanation. Lightning heats the air and causes shock waves. These in turn cause sonic booms – but you know them better as thunder.

Lightning and thunder happen at the same time. But you see lightning before you hear thunder because light, which travels a million times faster than sound, arrives almost instantly. Sound, on the other hand, takes about five seconds to travel one mile. You can measure how far away lightning is by counting the number of seconds between seeing the flash and hearing the thunder. For example, if you count ten seconds between the lightning and the thunder, the lightning is about 2 miles away.

If the lightening were to be a solid object that's not made of light but traveling at the speed of light, will you physically see it traveling or moving? The answer is no because not only will the object's length "shorten" to the observer, but the object will also become invisible due to how fast it will be traveling. Will that mean that the object does not exist? No, the object will still exist, but your physical senses or eyes are too slow to capture its movement at the speed of light.

A supernatural example is how fast a being like an angel of the Lord travels. Below is how Satan fell from heaven.

Luke 10:17-18

[17] The seventy-two returned with joy and said, "Lord, even the demons submit to us in your name."

[18] He replied, "I saw Satan fall like lightning from heaven.

This is how fast angels move from place to place. So, next time you doubt that angels exist, think again. Just because you can't see them don't mean they don't exist.

Hebrews 2:6-7

[6] But one testified in a certain place, saying:

"What is man that You are mindful of him,
Or the son of man that You take care of him?

7 You have made him a little lower than the angels;
You have crowned him with glory and honor,
And set him over the works of Your hands.

Physically, man is made a little lower than the angels but in the order of glory and honor, man is next to God in the hierarchy. A man surrendered to the Holy Spirit is literally God walking in human flesh because God dwells in him. So, with knowledge and understanding, man is a god. Don't think the Bible is full of crazy stories. That's why unbelieving scientists are so lost. If you say there was nothing before the big bang, think again. Even at this low physical level, is there nothing before the sonic boom? Think again. You may hear the sound late and never see a jet pass by – would it mean that no jet flew by over your head? Think again.

So, length contraction is like when you speed up in your car and you are pulled backwards tightly into your seat. This is because as the car speeds up very fast, it's as if it removes space from around you. When any object moves very fast close to or at the speed of light, space or distance in a sense ceases to exist for that object. When you are in such an object, you won't be able to move forward or backward. You can only move in the direction of the object unwillingly. Assuming your body is the ticking clock, and the car or jet accelerates very fast, although there is room in your car or jet, you may not be able to move fast or even at all towards the front of the car depending on the speed, but you may without effort be able to move freely to the back if there's space behind you and depending on the speed of travel.

Just like an atomic clocks experiment, we can read the ticks moving faster because it's "alive" in a sense. The same may happen to your heartbeat if you decide to count. The jet might arrive before it even beats once. Time is determined by space, gravity, and matter.

We know that length contraction and time dilation are all due to gravitational or electric potential. In physics, the gravitational potential at a location is equal to the work (energy transferred) per unit mass that would be needed to move an object to that location from a fixed reference location. It is analogous to the electric potential with mass playing the role of charge. The reference location, where the potential is zero, is by convention infinitely far away from any mass, resulting in a negative potential at any finite distance.

Another way to look at time dilation is that every object in theory ticks faster when you elevate it because the higher it gets, the bigger the negative value between that object and the ground because of space and gravity. You technically give the object more weight when you elevate it. The added weight in increments is the fast ticking which gives the high tick value that we see based on the height.

It simply means that you create a negative charge between the ground and the object going up to the high altitude or height. The ground remains neutral or positively charged and the object high above automatically gets a negative charge. If not supported or held up and dropped, it will drop very fast because of the "attraction" between both masses (the ground and the high object). At this point, it has gained more mass and will accelerate very fast to the ground because of weight, which is how we can measure the amount of downwards force that gravity exerts on that object. So, when it hits the ground, it will be a much bigger collision because of the opposite signs involved (–+) – like an attraction between a proton and an electron. The space between the ground and the high object is the theater for gravity to perform. If there is no space between the ground and the object, and if you can support the object the higher you lift it, it doesn't mean that the object is not adding more mass. The support just keeps the mass unchanged. The mass and weight aren't felt because of the support underneath it. If it's not an atomic clock, it won't register any value(s) for every change in height but technically, these values are added to the object being lifted weather you see it ticking faster and adding numbers or not.

That is why a 20 pounds metal ball may not kill you when dropped from one meter above your head, but it will crush your head and kill you if it's dropped from a height of 100 meters above your head. That's also why a watermelon may not crush when you lift and drop it from a height of one meter but when you drop it from a height of maybe 10 meters above the ground, it will crush into pieces. Therefore, a parachute gives you a safe landing but a free fall from an airplane will kill you. The distance between the ground and any object with mass at a high altitude automatically becomes added weight to the weight of that object and the fall accelerates. The fall distance will be traveled at an accelerated speed that is directly proportional to the square of the measurement that it takes to hit the ground. That measurement is called time. This is how gravitational potential and electric potential work. Just like Galileo, if you perform this same experiment on the Moon, the 20 pounds metal ball will not kill you if dropped from 100 meters above your head, and the watermelon won't crush if dropped from 10 plus meters above the ground. Assuming we can rotate the plane on which an object on the ground and an object that is high above the ground sit, without changing the positions of those two objects, they will simply swap places instantly as inverses. The two objects will perform an addition and subtraction operation instantly. That which was above will immediately become the object which was below or on the ground and vice versa in terms of height readings and weight. The object closer to the ground or on the ground has sort of almost no weight because of the support of the ground or it has a little weight because of the short distance between it and the ground.

Again, space gives room for gravity to have expression. Gravity creates and acts in and around matter within space to cause a change of state or position of matter. So together, space, gravity, and matter, give expression to time. Finally, this is to say that, if you drop an object in space where the force of gravity exists, the speed it takes for that object to cover the distance between its frame of reference and another object of interest frame of reference is called time. If the speed is instant, that is your time. If the speed can be counted, whatever value you get is your time. The measurement is dependent on the moving body, and not on an external clock or object.

Relativity is true because it depends on position, direction, speed, and overall perception. But there is truly, nothing like length contraction and time dilation. The reason why it seems that there is a concept like that or why Einstein thought along these lines is because he did not fully understand how the universe works. He did not understand the fullness of space, gravity, and matter. Most importantly, he did not understand spiritual things and the possibilities in that realm. That is why I say that science is merely a way or attempt to physically manifest spiritual laws. Therefore, science has a limit (time). The supernatural is limitless (eternity). If an angel travels from Mars to Earth instantly, it doesn't change the fact that the distance from Mars to Earth is still a minimum of about 33.9 million miles. In the angel's world, it's instant – everything is now but in our physical world, it is the hardest journey. That's why angels are constantly executing assignments for the Lord because they travel that fast.

It seems as if length contraction and time dilation are true because the object in motion is not independent of time. The object in motion is time. The real clock is the object in motion. There's change when an object is in motion – so, a higher speed equals slower time or slower clock. I used how we can count the stars or any object in space for illustration earlier. The faster you count, the less time you use to count. The slower you count, the more time you use to count. If you don't count at all while you are supposed to count, we will say that the more time you spend doing nothing but truly time is neutral or zero at this point because time has not started for that person yet for that activity since time is not independent of the count activity. The motionless object is a static or neutral clock – so, there's no change over a distance.

Real time is an object's speed of travel or change over a distance. You don't say you are ten years old because somebody else is twenty years old. Your age and the speed at which you grow is a unique timeline to only you. You are your own time or timeline. That's why you don't die because somebody else dies or died.

Time moves slower for a moving clock because a moving clock is the real time. In other words, the moving object in which the clock is traveling, is the true measurement of time for that object and for the clock which is inside that object. Time can't be measured outside or external of that object. So, the faster moving objects go, the slower the time they take to cover a distance. The slower moving objects go, the longer they take to cover a distance. The object is the clock. You are the clock. Your speed is time. How fast or slow you grow, or move is time. How fast or slow a body travel, is what we call time – the speed is the time. So, there is a relationship between speed and time, which means physically, there is a relationship between energy and time.

In everyday language, when you see someone who suddenly looks or appears to be old, while you know from their true age that they are young, you say that the person has aged very fast when they may not have lived very long from what you already know about them. But you make your conclusion based on the physical events or changes or manifestations that have taken place on the person's body. Why do you say that the person has "aged"? You say that because you compare that person to people in that age group or to people who are older and have similar manifestations. You use prior knowledge, the looks, and interval or distance between the person's date of birth (a frame of reference) to the current date or age of the person (another frame of reference), and to other young people in the same age group and their looks (a frame of reference), and to much older people and their looks (another frame of reference). You don't necessarily justify their age with somebody else's age or looks but it at least gives you a frame of reference to take measurements. So, the person may be 30 years old but may be looking like 60 years old. That old physical appearance will be independent of other people who are 30 years old. You don't measure time, or your age based on how long the Sun, Earth, and Moon have been around although they help us keep track of time through seasons. That's why we give an age to the Earth which is independent of our own age or vice versa because time for anybody in the universe is measured by that same body – not by something outside of that body. We are all individual universes or time moving around in space.

There is no universal time or what Newton would call "absolute time". If time were a different dimension external or outside of space, then time everywhere on the globe would all be synchronized and register the same values. But time is relative, like Einstein proposed, except that he made a mistake to read time in space as a dimension on its own. Frame of reference and interval speed to or from one reference to another is how we count time. The distance from Seattle to London is about 4781 miles. If an airplane travels that distance in an hour, it doesn't mean that the distance has shortened. If that same airplane travels that distance in twenty hours, we cannot say that the distance has been extended or is longer than 4781 miles. The distance remains the same regardless because of space and matter. Physically, the determining factor is the speed that the airplane uses to cover the distance, which is based on the energy that it uses to travel that fast or slow. This is real time. What we have as time here on Earth in our clocks are just there to help us have several frames of reference that we can relate to. So, the closer a frame of reference is to you, the closer or similarity of your time zones because of the distance and speed required to cover that distance. For example, Seattle and Oregon or Los Angeles are on the same time zone (Pacific Time) because of the distance among those cities as individual frames of reference. Compared to traveling from any of these places to London, now you understand why the time zones are very different. The distance among places may be absolute but the position, direction, and speed of travel for bodies make time relative. Our bodies may individually be viewed as absolute because all humans should follow the same biological design but when we are born and how we grow through gravity, are relative. Life in general may be absolute because all humans eat etc., but how we individually live it every day are relative. If you view it this way, then both Newton and Einstein will be partially correct.

This is time. This is how it works. The determining factor is the force of gravity that exist between the Sun, Earth, and Moon to regulate our seasons. Therefore, physically, time is relative. Even in eternity, it's still relative in a sense. The only thing is that God has made it absolute in terms of how fast a being travels – lightning speed. So, if you travel at lightning speed, you just will arrive almost instantly – you will not travel into the future or the past. You will only arrive quicker or instantly. So, we can say that time is both absolute and relative.

Time is like an elastic band. The elastic band is a body. When you stretch the elastic band, the measurement of the length is time. Time is a dynamic body. When you stretch it, you increase the range of motion, and when you don't stretch it, the length remains the same. The elastic band initially has an absolute length but over time, the absolute length increases the more you use or stretch it, and it weakens overall in resistance. Gravity does both the stretching and contraction.

Space

Space is the boundless three-dimensional extent in which objects and events have relative position and direction. So, space is made up of objects and events, position, and direction. We can represent space with the values, −1, ±0, +1. There is no position or direction in space if and only if there is no matter in space to activate gravity or if gravity has not created any matter. The moment space is occupied by matter or objects then we can have events happening in and around those objects. The objects and events serve as our frame of reference for position and direction. And time becomes the distance between two objects or reference points or events and the speed at which the distance is covered, or the events happen.

If one can cover any distance between reference points in space at lightning speed, then the travel becomes instant, and the concept of "time" wouldn't apply. This is how things are in eternity or the spiritual realm. This has been the physicist's confusion with time travel but the act of travel (motion or gravity) itself is what we call time. Therefore, Newton would be correct to say that time is absolute in that sense, but God divided eternity into time for us to slow things down so that we can relate. So, a theory of relativity is more accurate to describe time in the physical since although there is space, gravity, and matter everywhere, their interactions to give us the result of time are different everywhere you go. Your body grows through gravity in space, and that represents time. Age is time. Time is derived from space, gravity, and matter, which are the same three things that give us our seasons. This is how the Earth also grows – through seasons. Seasons are the distance and speed measurements that give a result of time (age) for the Earth. Time is not a separate dimension outside of space, gravity, and matter. All these together is time. We are time.

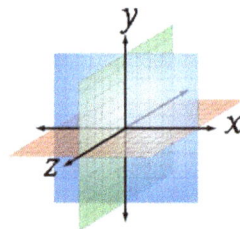

A 3D Cartesian coordinate system used to indicate positions in space

Image Source – Public Domain

Gravity

Gravity or gravitation is a natural phenomenon by which all things with mass or energy – including planets, stars, galaxies, and even light are attracted to (or gravitate toward) one another. So, gravity is made up of weak nuclear force, strong nuclear force, and electromagnetic force. These are the three types of gravity. It starts as neutral, but neutrality is not a force. An object is neutral when it is not positively or negatively charged. In physics, we know that a force is an influence that can change the motion of an object. Force can also be described intuitively as a push or a pull.

134

Gravity is either a weak or strong push or a weak or strong pull depending on the type of interaction taking place and the sides or faces or elements of matter interacting. For example, a proton and an electron attract each other. And a proton and proton or an electron and electron repel each other. Another way of saying this is that the same or 'like' charges repel (push) one another and opposite charges attract (pull) one another. Since opposite charges attract each other, the negatively charged electrons are attracted to the positively charged protons.

Neutral objects don't move, hence can't be considered as force by themselves. An example are neutrons because they have no charge. Although all objects that gravitate start by initially being in a neutral state or position. All atoms are neutral. This is because they contain equal numbers of positive protons and negative electrons. These opposite charges cancel each other out making the atom neutral. We can represent gravity with the values -1, ±0, +1. This force of gravity is the same phenomenon that works in and outside our bodies, and the universe at large.

Matter

Matter is any substance that has mass and takes up space by having volume. There are three types or states of matter – gas, solid, liquid. At low temperatures (below 0°C), it is a solid. When at "normal" temperatures (between 0°C and 100°C), it is a liquid. While at temperatures above 100°C, water is a gas (steam). But for example, an element like helium has a boiling point of -458°F (-272.2°C) and becomes liquid at −268.9°C (−452 °F). At room temperature helium is an odorless, tasteless, colorless gas. It has very low boiling and melting points, meaning that it is generally found in the gas phase except under the most extreme of conditions. We have ±0 as the determinant of the state of matter. Again, we can represent the three states of matter with the values, −1, ±0, +1. Everything is a cycle.

We have a two-dimensional coordinate system (space and matter) that is controlled by a third dimension called gravity (acting within space in and around matter) to give us time as a result. We can see from the above descriptions that for most things in the universe the transformation or translation is determined by ±0, so, that is our center of gravity (present or now) and that is where a pull or push is used to decide the state of matter on an even surface. The whole coordinate system moves together as one whole body, which is controlled from the origin or center of mass or center of gravity in space and on matter to regulate time. Together, these form a 3D system of our universe. I'm sorry to disappoint you but spacetime is 3D. Space, gravity, and matter work together to regulate time. The 4D is the spiritual or invisible realm. Together as one body, the whole coordinate system moves as time. This applies to the human body as well. Anytime you move from one position to another or perform an act, after that movement or act, it will become something considered as of the past while you move into the future and remaining in the present, and the present instantly becomes the past. So, time is really "now" or "present". You already know this now. And if you want to do anything that has not happened yet, you will be looking forward to that in the future.

Life to me is the journey of an invisible being (–), coming into the visible (+) to have duality of being in both the invisible and visible at the same time (±), and finally going back into the invisible. The entirety of life sits on these three symbols or signs.

Galileo Galilei on Gravity, Distance, and Time

Galileo's discovery which was experimented on both the Earth and Moon proved that two falling objects will land at the same **time** (result) regardless of weight and or size. Dropping hammers versus feathers will be misleading due to air resistance. A fact demonstrated on the Moon, where there is no air, in 1971 during the Apollo 15 mission. If you take the air out of the equation, everything falls at the same rate. The result of the experiment was time. Time is calculated throughout the experiment from start to finish or beginning to end. In space, gravity acted among matter and the result was time. So, space + gravity + matter = time.

Galileo found out that an object dropped at one height did not take twice as long to drop from twice as high – it accelerated. It's hard to measure that because everything is happening so fast.

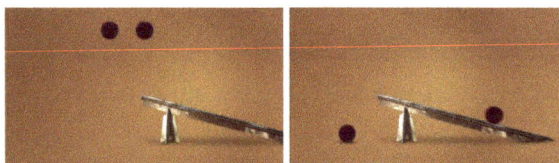

Image Source – Public Domain

In a reproduced experimentation by some recent scientists, for time, an arbitrary unit was used – Galileo. In one Galileo, it traveled one unit (1 gal = 1 unit). So, 1 Galileo equal to 1 unit or 1 second equals 1 unit. This can also be represented as 1 unit of distance in 1 unit of time. In 2 units of time, the ball rolls 4 units of distance. In 3 units of time, the ball had gone 9 units of distance. The conclusion was that there is a mathematical relationship between time and distance. So, the space between matter is called distance.

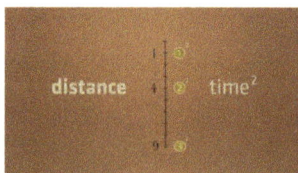

Image Source – Public Domain

Galileo's inspired idea to use a ramp showed that fallen objects follow mathematical laws. He came up with a genius solution. He built a ramp – an inclined plane to slow the falling object and motion down so that he could measure. He wanted to find a relationship between time and distance. The distance the ball traveled is directly proportional to the square of the time. The

136

mathematical expression that was observed is the mathematical expression of our universe. Galileo's centuries old observations about falling objects remain valid today.

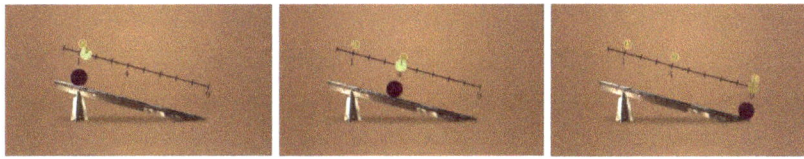

Image Source – Public Domain

It's the same mathematical expression that we can use to understand how objects might fall here on Earth; roll down a ramp. The discovery was profound. He later wrote that "the universe is written in the language of mathematics". These laws have been applied to most things in our world through the laws of science. Mathematics can be used to uncover and discover the hidden rules of our universe and existence through God.

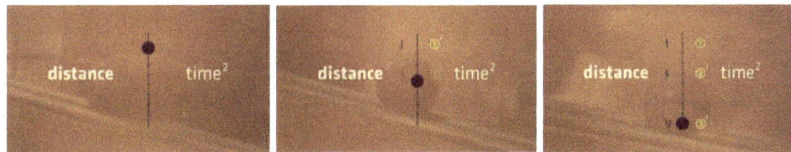

Image Source – Public Domain

It is important to note that the result of the experiment was time, and the balls were the first masses, and the Earth or ground was the second mass. The vacuum through which they fell to the ground represents the space. And gravity is activated throughout the motion of the balls from the sky to the ground, up until if the balls roll on the ground until they come to a complete stop or neutral. The neutral position is where they won't move again until another force is exerted on them.

In this experiment, we first see **space** that gives expression to **gravity**. We see **gravity** that acts within the space, around, and between **matter** (distance between the balls and ground) because of their masses. And at the end, we measure **time**. We can also choose to measure it at any point. So, time is truly when it is measured or the moment a measurement is taken.

Mass is a measurement of an object's tendency to resist changing its state of motion, known as inertia. In other words, mass is a measure of the amount of matter in a substance or an object. Left to its own devices, an object will stay put (± or neutral) or move in a straight line (– or +). Mass is a measure of how much force it will take to change the path or direction of an object. Mass depends on how much matter – atoms and so on – there is in an object; more mass means more inertia. Inertia is the resistance of any physical object to any change in its velocity. In other words, this is a tendency to do nothing or to remain unchanged. Or a property of matter by which it continues in its existing state of rest (neutral) or uniform motion in a straight line (– or +) unless that state is changed by an external force.

Therefore, where there is space, gravity, and matter, the four forces of aerodynamics are required to act on mass. The four forces are lift (+), thrust (+), drag (−), and weight (−). Weight is a measure of the amount of downwards force that gravity exerts on an object. There are up and down, and front and back directions in space. More mass means more inertia if and only if there is no space or is space but the object between the space is sitting on a flat, even, or neutral surface, plane, or coordinate. If space exists and the direction of space is up but the object is sitting on a neutral ground, the object will not move, although gravity still exists inside, and around the object. The object will only move if the positions of space and the object are flipped or when a force is applied underneath the object to push it upwards towards space.

In this experiment, gravity exists both inside (−, ±, +), and around (−, ±, +) the balls. Therefore, we have a magnetic moment between the balls and the ground. The space between the balls in an up (+) position and the ground in a down (−) position becomes a free fall area because below the balls are the balls negative or down (−) position being enforced by weight (−), and the surface of the ground is the ground's positive (+) position. So, if we want to go in the opposite direction then we will need to apply lift (+) between the ground and the balls towards the up position. This can be achieved by applying the like-charge or pole against the mass (+) of the balls. The force between the ground and the balls will generate an electric or magnetic field of two positives (++), which in science, we know, repel each other. We know that the force that acts between space and matter is gravity, and gravity exists in (−, ±, +). When the positive electric charge or gravity is generated between the ground and the balls, the effect will be a lift (+) or up (+) or push (+) and the balls will move towards their opposite end of space if the right amount of gravitational force is applied. But if the force applied is weaker than what can lift the balls, then there may be little or no change in the states of the balls. It would either be a weak push or neutral. If a stronger gravitational force is applied, then there will be a successful lift.

When there is space or opening around an object, it automatically gives the object the potential to behave according to these universal charges (−, ±, +). But if there is no space or no opening around the object, or if any opening is closed, then the object may still have potential but won't be able to move in any direction. It could still be very charged, but all that energy will be contained in the closed area or system. This is generally how gravity works – how magnetism works – and how electricity works. They are the same thing.

Just as the positive (+) and negative (−) electrical charges attract each other, the north (N) and south (S) poles of a magnet attract each other. In electricity, like charges repel, and in magnetism like poles repel. We see the symmetry here. That's why they are manifestations of the same phenomenon, which is gravity. An example of the open or closed space is a valence electron. An atom with a closed shell of valence electrons (corresponding to a noble gas configuration) tends to be chemically inert. The tendency for non-reactivity is due to the valence. The word valence universally has the same meaning, no matter what field it's used in. In linguistics, it's the number of grammatical elements with which a particular word, especially a verb, combines in a sentence. In science, it relates to or denotes electrons involved in or available for chemical bond formation. And a bond can be formed if and only if there is space or room for two or more objects or elements to interact and a compatibility among them to fit together. So, if there is space inside, around, or

138

between objects, then gravity as we know it can have expression. And when there is space with objects or matter in it, that's the only way we can measure time using the distance between the objects or the change of state of either or both objects. Therefore, God uses the space and interactions between the Sun, Earth, and Moon to control time and help us to measure time. This is generally how gravity works. It is only one force governing the universe at different levels and in different ways. The laws of gravity or aerodynamics can all be represented with our coordinate system. It is fundamental.

Galileo was followed by Newton. And Newton's groundbreaking insight was that the same force that took the comet around the Sun was the same force that brings cannon balls back to Earth. It was the same force behind Galileo's law of falling objects or bodies and even held the planets in their orbits. Newton called the force, gravity and he described it precisely in a surprisingly simple equation that explains how masses attract each other, whether here on Earth or in space. It surprises, impresses, and is dramatic to the science world that such a simple equation and law will allow you to move throughout the universe.

Gravity in and around the Sun, Earth, and Moon

Image Source – Public Domain

Isaac Newton on Gravity

Newton's law of universal gravitation is usually stated as that every particle attracts every other particle in the universe with a force that is directly proportional to the product of their masses and inversely proportional to the square of the distance between their centers.

Maybe modify and redefine gravity and its equation? Gravity is neutral, a push or a pull, or a combination of all – and it depends on which particles or charges are interacting then there is either an attraction and or repulsion, or no attraction and or repulsion.

James Maxwell on Electricity and Magnetism

Electricity and magnetism are related (James Maxwell) – each could generate the other. It was also discovered that both merged, travel as waves of energy at the speed of light – electromagnetic waves.

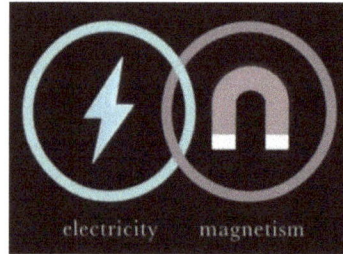

Image Source – Public Domain

When we study the history of science, we can see some errors. Gravity is faster than the speed of light because gravity is what produces light. Gravity is responsible for both magnetism and electromagnetism. Maxwell was right in his theory of electromagnetic radiation describing electricity, magnetism, and light as different manifestations of the same phenomenon for the first time. I add to it that the same phenomenon he was referring to is gravity.

Before light can travel, there must be space or vacuum. And the moment there is space, gravity already exist by default in any state that it wants to. So, before light can appear, first, there must be gravity (−, ±, +) already in space to interact with itself to generate the light, and there must be space to give expression to that light. Just like there should be darkness to truly experience light. Without space, there's no light. If there was no space, we couldn't see the Sun, Moon, Stars, a laser, or a torchlight or flashlight. And the space we have in the universe is all darkness because the Earth dwells in darkness. The Word of God mentions this.

Psalm 82:5

[5] They do not know, nor do they understand;
They walk about in darkness;
All the foundations of the Earth are unstable.

The answer, that is the light to this darkness, is Jesus Christ. Just because you have electricity and bright lights don't mean you are living in light. You don't know.

John 1:1-9

The Eternal Word

1 In the beginning was the Word, and the Word was with God, and the Word was God. [2] He was in the beginning with God. [3] All things were made through Him, and without Him nothing was made that was made. [4] In Him was life, and the life was the light of men. [5] And the light shines in the darkness, and the darkness did not comprehend it.

John's Witness: The True Light

[6] There was a man sent from God, whose name *was* John. [7] This man came for a witness, to bear witness of the Light, that all through him might believe. [8] He was not that Light but *was sent* to bear witness of that Light. [9] That was the true Light which gives light to every man coming into the world.

Take a piece of wood or any solid object for instance, you don't expect to find light inside of it when you break it open. But you'll still find the fundamental particles in that object even in the absence of light. Therefore, the opposite is also true that as soon as protons, neutrons, and electrons start interacting, a fundamental of gravity (magnetism) starts happening. It is first neutral, weak, strong, and magnetic/electromagnetic. That's why the center of gravity is the translation point. Gravity is symmetrical (−, ±, +). Therefore, magnetism creates electricity and electricity creates magnetism. This is the reason why matter attracts matter but not every matter attracts every matter, and not every matter repels every matter. Already embedded in matter is gravity or one half or part of it. If there is space among matter, then gravity can have effect – the space will give expression to gravity among matter and gravity will have effect on matter and matter will have expression in space. It's a cycle. This same gravity is responsible to create and expand or grow matter, and it is also responsible to decay matter. We call the process and measurement, time. And if gravity didn't work in this manner, then your house could not fit into the ground and be permanent until it's brought down or demolished. The foundation is the negative or down part (−), the part that connects the foundation to the structure above the surface of the ground (footing) is the neutral part or center of gravity (±), and the structure above the ground in which we live is the positive or up part (+). This same effect is also why a tree grows both downwards and upwards and there's a clear separation between what's underground and what above ground. The connection point between underground and the surface structure is the center of gravity for that tree. Hence, the tree can grow but remains in the same spot on the ground. Also, our bodies are intact and not broken down into smaller particles and as we grow normally, there is a calculated distance and balance made by God from your waist area down to your feet (lower torso) and from the waist area up to your head (upper torso). This is gravity.

Now you will understand why the currently known forces of nature do have quarks, leptons, and bosons as elementary particles. The atom has a nucleus made up of protons and neutrons, surrounded by electrons. The protons and neutrons are made up of different groups of quarks. The electrons are a type of leptons. The quarks in protons and neutrons are either '**up**' (+) or '**down**' (−) quarks – so, we can represent this by '**neutral**' (±) because it can be either or both. The universe is all about these three charges.

In beta decay, a down quark changes to an up quark, turning a neutron into a proton. The nucleus is the center of gravity for any atom, and this is where translation or transformation happens as we have learned until this point in this writing. As weak as you would think that 'neutral' is, without it, there would be no transformation, growth, decay etc. This is where and how gravity starts working and progresses through different stages. Again, therefore in humans, even the reproductive organs and sexual intercourse happens at the center of gravity (waist area). It's not an accident or coincidence. It has been known that particle physics is full of 'conservation laws': when any particles interact with each other, quantities like the total energy and momentum must be the same before and after. It's not just in particle physics. The same science applies to all levels – subatomic, atomic, molecular, and whatever else is there. God is consistent – He never changes on us. That's why His promises are true and hold from everlasting to everlasting. This scripture below is very short but it has profound meanings. I want you to decipher it and apply the meaning to the point I'm making here.

Hebrews 13:8

[8] Jesus Christ *is* the same yesterday, today, and forever.

In physics, the conservation law states that a particular measurable property of an isolated physical system does not change as the system evolves over time. If you understand this well, you will know that this is quantum mechanics and that has always been the foundation of the universe, including your body. In simple terms, as you grow, your head does not transform to become a leg and vice versa, your ears do not transform to become your eyes and vice versa etc. You get the idea now. This is how your body works because you are a universe, and this is how everything else works in the universe. As we grow, our physical measurable properties don't change or evolve over time. Now, you will know that Darwinism is a bunch of nonsense. You can see Darwinism in the image below and you'll know that it's not correct. Life or nature doesn't work that way. God did not make it this way – this is very misleading. Stop teaching it in schools.

Darwinism

Image Source – Public Domain

The ape did not evolve to become human and will never evolve to become a human someday. The cat will not evolve to become a Leopard someday. There is evolution by means of a hybrid. For example, in humans, when the white race meets with the black race to make a baby, we see the result. The result is still a human being with perfect human features. When the watchers (fallen angels) took the form of humans, married, and had sexual intercourse with humans, the result can be found in the following scriptures. The image will help give you an idea. Even they, still had human forms but were evil giants. If we ever merge a human and an ape, the product would be an abominable creature that would violate God's laws. Don't even imagine or think about it.

Genesis 6:4-5

[4] There were giants on the Earth in those days, and also afterward, when the sons of God came into the daughters of men, and they bore *children* to them. Those *were* the mighty men who *were* of old, men of renown.

[5] Then the LORD saw that the wickedness of man *was* great in the Earth, and *that* every intent of the thoughts of his heart *was* only evil continually.

Average Man versus a Nephilim

Image Source – Public Domain

The dragonfly for example, goes through transformation or metamorphosis. Scientists' studies found out that dragonflies undergo incomplete metamorphosis; unlike other winged insects, such as butterflies, dragonflies do not have a pupal stage and transition straight from a larva to an adult. This transition, the final larval moult, takes place out of water. This metamorphosis is triggered by day length and temperature, and is synchronized in some species, such as Emperor Dragonfly. The most important thing to note here is how day length and temperature power this process. Day length and temperature result to time. This is the 'evolution' or transformation or the different phases of gravity in the life of dragonflies – this is quantum mechanics. Every physical object goes through quantum mechanics, which is powered by the power of God through gravity. Research to learn more on this on your own. Just know and understand that when you isolate or remove God from everything and start thinking that it's always just mere science or being intellectual, you are a very lost being. The images and description show only the 'emergence' phase of the life of the dragonfly. There is always an underlying process, whether you visible or invisible, in everything or 'emergence'. Nothing just happens randomly or magically. The dragonfly came out in whole, so it did not just 'emerge'. This is like how gravity works generally and why scientists think it's different from the other forces of nature, but it is the same gravity, working and taking different forms.

Image Source – Public Domain

We must understand universal symbols because we obviously are a lost generation because we have veered away from the ways of God. There is also a reason why the multiplication symbol is called 'time'. The multiplication sign, also known as the 'times' sign or the dimension sign, is the symbol ×, used in mathematics to denote the multiplication operation and its resulting product. In mathematics, a product is the result of multiplication, or an expression that identifies factors to be multiplied. While like a lowercase X (x), the form is properly a four-fold rotationally symmetric saltire. This is the universal symbol representing 'time'. We have already seen the definition of time and how it is derived. The unit of life on Earth is time. The answers to the questions we have in life are encoded in ancient symbols all around us in plain sight. You need God to decode and understand. The mathematical symbols have deeper meanings, and that's why we use them. They were discovered from the meaning of nature. These are the foundations of our spacetime.

1st (left): Crucifixion of Jesus Christ, 2nd: Times or spacetime symbol, 3rd: Hourglass, and 4th: Infinity symbol, and 5th: Number eight (8)

Image Source – Public Domain

You should be able to identify this symbol by now as first, the crucifix of Jesus Christ, and second, our space time curvature, which also is the inspiration or meaning behind the hourglass design. In all the symbols, the middle parts (center of gravity) are very significant. Eight is a symbol of infinity and a constant flow of energy and power. A simple quantum bit could be designed to achieve basic entanglement using the idea or design of the crucifix of Jesus Christ, which looks like the plus or times symbol. But qubits are still not recommended.

All the above were to help you understand the conservation law. In physics, charge conservation is the principle that the total electric charge in an isolated system never changes. The net quantity of electric charge, the amount of positive charge minus the amount of negative charge in the universe, is always conserved. This applies to human bodies because we are the universe. Charge conservation, considered as a physical conservation law, implies that the change in the amount of electric charge in any volume of space is exactly equal to the amount of charge flowing into the volume minus the amount of charge flowing out of the volume.

The three-phase power arrangements supply puts greater sums of power – 1.732 times the single phase on the same current. Most industrial plants throughout the United States use three-phase, four-wire power setups, as this arrangement – 480Y / 277V – is the densest and most powerful. In comparison to the 208V three phase, the 480V three phase offers a considerably greater power supply with either the same current or with 43% reduced current. The benefits of this setup are as follows. Lower costs for construction, because of the smaller electrical devices and circuitry required. Lower costs on energy, due to the conservation of electrical currents, which get transformed into heat instead of being lost. Below is an example circuitry diagram. The neutral (±) wire carries the circuit back to the original power source. Again, a normal quantum computer can be built on this type of architecture to become energy efficient so that it will also not need the crazy low temperatures to maintain coherence. Study beta decay and conservation of charge some more and you will understand even better.

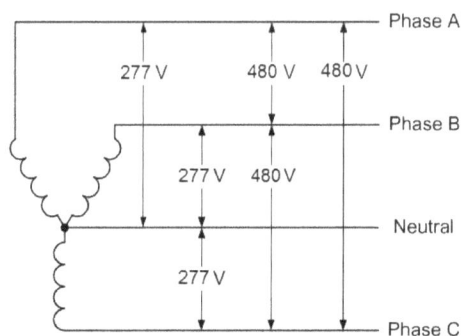

United States three-phase, four-wire power setup – 480Y / 277V

Image Source – Public Domain

Therefore, you don't want an all-male or all-female workforce. You need to have a balance of the two genders or all electrical charges (–, ±, +) to have true dynamics. It all goes back to the cross, the cartesian coordinate system and all that are being said here repeatedly. Therefore, all the world leaders are being warned right now, especially on the issue of homosexuality, to fix it immediately because judgement is coming from God, and it's coming very fast. This starts from the home (smaller government), the society or company (local or medium government), and the country at large (large government). If you can't put your house in order, you have no business being in any other leadership positions. Don't satisfy your children, families, friends, governments, and citizens by conforming to their ideas to sign abominable and demonic bills into laws, just to make them happy people or for you to be seen or perceived as a good person or leader. You shall be judged, and you will face the bigger judgement. This is not just about homosexuality but all other sins too, including wickedness, abortions, surrogacy, corruption, greed, selfishness etc. Teachers in the following scriptures include all leaders.

James 3:1-2

The Untamable Tongue

3 My brethren, let not many of you become teachers, knowing that we shall receive a stricter judgment. **2** For we all stumble in many things. If anyone does not stumble in word, he *is* a perfect man, able also to bridle the whole body.

You shall face the judgement of God, and you shall face it as an individual, not as a group or with your family or friends or citizens. Heaven or Earth is an individual affair. You who collects or takes bribe for the job you must do, you are warned. You who sleeps with the individual before you have to offer help such as a job etc., you are warned. You who sleeps with animals, you are warned. You who alters your body or looks, even to the point of trying to look like an animal, you are warned. Scan your life and know what to change. What you are getting "pleasure" doing or believing that it's alright to do is killing several people and sinning against God. You who corrupts the electoral system to win elections, you are warned. You who has taken it upon yourself to be a terrorist who through suicide missions, all in the name of killing people to make some "God" somewhere happy and that you will go to heaven when you do that, you are warned. Repent and don't compromise. All these above are not the nature of the one and only true God of the heavens and the Earth. Judgement is here and justice shall prevail.

Without the space between the Sun and the Moon, the Moon would never be able to store and use the light of the Sun. Without space, there would be annihilation of the three bodies and the entire solar system. This annihilation already happens among other particles in the universe when particles collide with their respective antiparticle to produce other particles, but that physical annihilation is not supposed to happen between the Sun, Earth, and Moon because their existence control time and their current relationship is how things are supposed to be while we live in time.

God divided eternity into two to create time so that we can relate to the physical world in our fallen nature. The result is a 3 x 3 matrix (3 rows and 3 columns). Time (space, gravity, matter) is the determinant of time and it's controlled in the origin by gravity as in the following images. The three parts or types of time (past, present, future) all move together as one body. Real time is "present" or "now". The following images are some representations. The image to the right is a good one because it depicts our current universe very well. Inside the 3D box are space, gravity, and matter, and together, they give us the measurement or result of time.

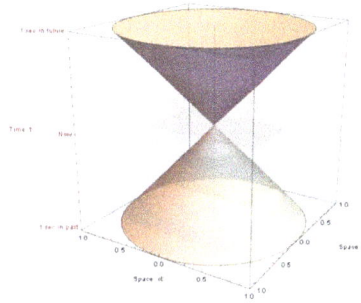

Origin
(or "Pole")

Polar axis

Image Source – Public Domain

In the matrix below, blue represents the three dimensions of gravity. Red represents three dimensions each for space and matter. And green represents the three dimensions result of time. We can see the symmetry. This is how much force of gravity is being applied (pressure). For example, pressure exerted by ideal gases in confined containers is due to the average number of collisions of gas molecules with the container walls per unit time. As such, pressure depends on the amount of gas (in number of molecules), its temperature, and the volume of the container. In this context, the amount of gas is the volume of matter, the temperature is gravity, and the volume of the container is space. All three of them together equal to time. We are multiplying gravity by space and by matter to get time. Or even better, essentially, we are multiplying time by itself. Time requires space, gravity, and matter to find expression. If there is no space, there is no matter. If there is no space and matter, there is no gravity. And if there is no space, matter, and gravity, there is no time. If there is no time, there is no physics or physical world.

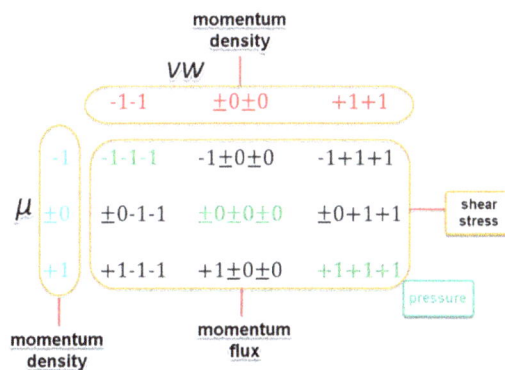

The curvature of spacetime is always in one position and not in multiple locations at the same time. Any particle can always be found within these coordinates in the tensor.

The action of the gate on a specific quantum state is found by multiplying the vector $|\Psi_1\rangle$ which represents the state, by the vector or matrix U representing the gate. The result is a new quantum state $|\Psi_2\rangle$:

$$U|\Psi_1\rangle = |\Psi_2\rangle$$

147

God (Modification to Hadamard) Gate Operations

This gate is a one-qutrit rotation, mapping the qutrit-basis states $|-1\rangle$ and $|\pm 0\rangle$ and $|+1\rangle$ to three superposition states with equal weight of the computational basis states $|-1\rangle$ and $|\pm 0\rangle$ and $|+1\rangle$. The phases are chosen so that:

$$G = \frac{|-1\rangle - |\pm 0\rangle - |+1\rangle}{\sqrt{3}}\langle -1| + \frac{|-1\rangle \pm |\pm 0\rangle \pm |+1\rangle}{\sqrt{3}}\langle \pm 0| + \frac{|-1\rangle + |\pm 0\rangle + |+1\rangle}{\sqrt{3}}\langle +1|$$

The God transform G_m is a $3^m \times 3^m$ matrix.

V_{-1-1-1}	$V_{-1\pm 0\pm 0}$	V_{-1+1+1}
$V_{\pm 0-1-1}$	$V_{\pm 0\pm 0\pm 0}$	$V_{\pm 0+1+1}$
V_{+1-1-1}	$V_{+1\pm 0\pm 0}$	V_{+1+1+1}

The gate operations will look like this and give us these three different states upon completion. The expansion steps in-between is skipped for the sake of brevity. We will jump straight into the solution. In mathematical formulas, the $\pm$ symbol may be used to indicate a symbol that may be replaced by either the plus and minus signs ($+$ or $-$), allowing the formula to represent two values or two equations. It is important to note that ± 0 can be written in two forms to simplify calculations: $+0$ and -0. Hence, we will have two parts to the equation or logic wherever we see this sign.

$$G((|-1\rangle) = \frac{1}{\sqrt{3}}(|-1\rangle - \frac{1}{\sqrt{3}}|\pm 0\rangle - \frac{1}{\sqrt{3}}|1\rangle) =: |-\rangle$$

$$G((|\pm 0\rangle) = \frac{1}{\sqrt{3}}(|-1\rangle \pm \frac{1}{\sqrt{3}}|\pm 0\rangle \pm \frac{1}{\sqrt{3}}|1\rangle) =: |\pm\rangle$$

$$G((|1\rangle) = \frac{1}{\sqrt{3}}(|-1\rangle + \frac{1}{\sqrt{3}}|\pm 0\rangle + \frac{1}{\sqrt{3}}|1\rangle) =: |+\rangle$$

1.

$$G\left(\frac{1}{\sqrt{3}}|-1\rangle - \frac{1}{\sqrt{3}}|\pm 0\rangle - \frac{1}{\sqrt{3}}|1\rangle\right)$$
$$= \frac{1}{3}(|-1\rangle - |\pm 0\rangle - |1\rangle) - \frac{1}{3}(|-1\rangle \pm |\pm 0\rangle \pm |1\rangle) - \frac{1}{3}(|-1\rangle + |\pm 0\rangle + |1\rangle)$$

We will simplify the calculations above and solve them in parts.

For the first part of the equation:

$$\frac{1}{3}(|-1\rangle - |\pm0\rangle - |1\rangle) = t \leq 0, t > 0:$$

$$\frac{1}{3}(|-1\rangle - |-0\rangle - |1\rangle) = 0$$

$$\frac{1}{3}(|-1\rangle - |+0\rangle - |1\rangle) = 0$$

For the middle part of the equation:

$$\frac{1}{3}(|-1\rangle \pm |\pm0\rangle \pm |1\rangle) = t \leq 0, t > 0:$$

$$\frac{1}{3}(|-1\rangle - |-0\rangle - |1\rangle) = 0$$

$$\frac{1}{3}(|-1\rangle - |-0\rangle + |1\rangle) = \frac{2e|k||t|}{3}$$

$$\frac{1}{3}(|-1\rangle - |+0\rangle - |1\rangle) = 0$$

$$\frac{1}{3}(|-1\rangle - |+0\rangle + |1\rangle) = \frac{2e|k||t|}{3}$$

$$\frac{1}{3}(|-1\rangle + |+0\rangle - |1\rangle) = 0$$

$$\frac{1}{3}(|-1\rangle + |-0\rangle + |1\rangle) = \frac{2e|k||t|}{3}$$

$$\frac{1}{3}(|-1\rangle + |-0\rangle - |1\rangle) = 0$$

$$\frac{1}{3}(|-1\rangle + |+0\rangle + |1\rangle) = \frac{2e|k||t|}{3}$$

For the third part of the equation:

$$\frac{1}{3}(|-1\rangle + |\pm0\rangle + |1\rangle) = t \leq 0, t > 0:$$

$$\frac{1}{3}(|-1\rangle + |-0\rangle + |1\rangle) = \frac{2e|k||t|}{3}$$

$$\frac{1}{3}(|-1\rangle + |+0\rangle + |1\rangle) = \frac{2e|k||t|}{3}$$

Finally, we can join all parts together and the result will be:

$$= 0 - \frac{2e|k||t|}{3} = -\frac{2e|k||t|}{3}$$

2.

$$G\left(\frac{1}{\sqrt{3}}|-1\rangle \pm \frac{1}{\sqrt{3}}|\pm0\rangle \pm \frac{1}{\sqrt{3}}|1\rangle\right)$$

$$= \frac{1}{3}(|-1\rangle - |\pm0\rangle - |1\rangle) \pm \frac{1}{3}(|-1\rangle \pm |\pm0\rangle \pm |1\rangle) \pm \frac{1}{3}(|-1\rangle + |\pm0\rangle + |1\rangle)$$

Finally, we can simplify it as:

$$= 0 \pm \frac{2e|k||t|}{3} = 0$$

$$= 0 - \frac{2e|k||t|}{3} = -\frac{2e|k||t|}{3}$$

$$= 0 + \frac{2e|k||t|}{3} = \frac{2e|k||t|}{3}$$

$$= -\frac{2e|k||t|}{3} + \frac{2e|k||t|}{3} = 0$$

$$= t < 0, t \geq 0$$

3.

$$G\left(\frac{1}{\sqrt{3}}|-1\rangle + \frac{1}{\sqrt{3}}|\pm0\rangle + \frac{1}{\sqrt{3}}|1\rangle\right)$$

$$= \frac{1}{3}(|-1\rangle - |\pm0\rangle - |1\rangle) + \frac{1}{3}(|-1\rangle \pm |\pm0\rangle \pm |1\rangle) + \frac{1}{3}(|-1\rangle + |\pm0\rangle + |1\rangle)$$

Note: calculation steps have been skipped because this is an inverse of the answer in equation #1. Finally, when we join all parts together, the result will be:

$$\frac{1}{3}(|-1\rangle + |\pm0\rangle + |1\rangle) = t < 0, t \geq 0$$

$$= 0 + \frac{2e|k||t|}{3} = \frac{2e|k||t|}{3}$$

So, altogether, we will have:

$$= -\frac{2e|k||t|}{3}, 0, t < 0, t \geq 0, and + \frac{2e|k||t|}{3}$$

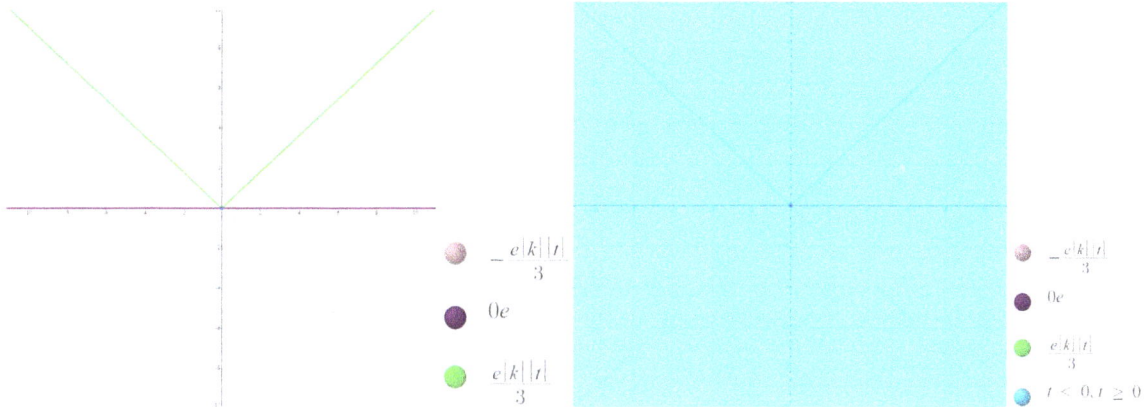

The graph representations

Left: without positive and negative intervals, Right: with positive and negative intervals

If we do away with the ± sign and use just the value 0 for calculations as in classical physics, we get these graph as shown below. Just from these basic calculations above and plotting on the graphs above and below, you should see entanglement and superposition.

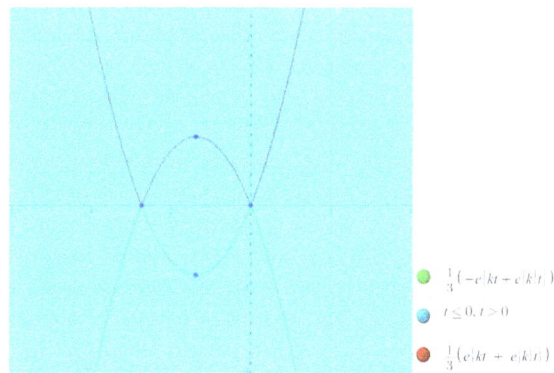

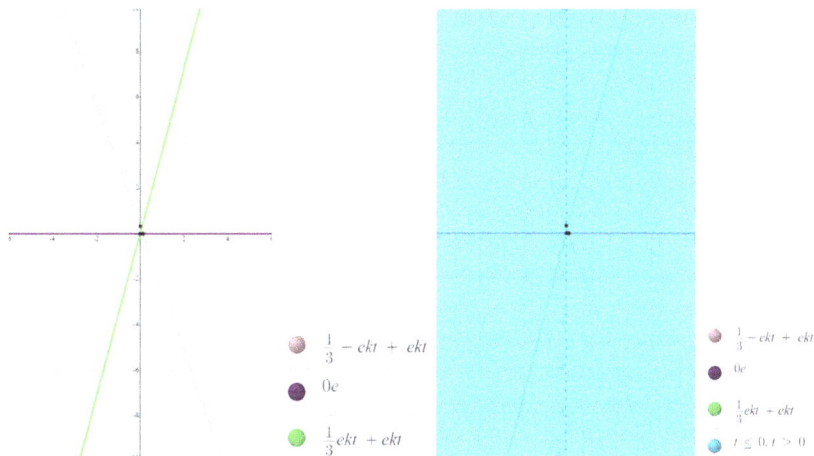

Left: without positive and negative intervals, Right and up: with positive and negative intervals

We want to get a perfect hexagon from our calculations and graph but the seventh point in the center is key. I will talk to you below in geometry – with a smiley face. I hope you will get it.

Quantum Mechanics Described in Geometry

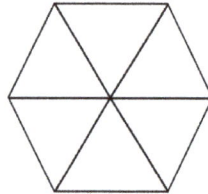

A Hexagon – **3rd** Grade Math 😊

It is a hexagon (6 points or faces) but the 7th point in the middle or center is the difference. The number 7 is God's number for completion and perfection.

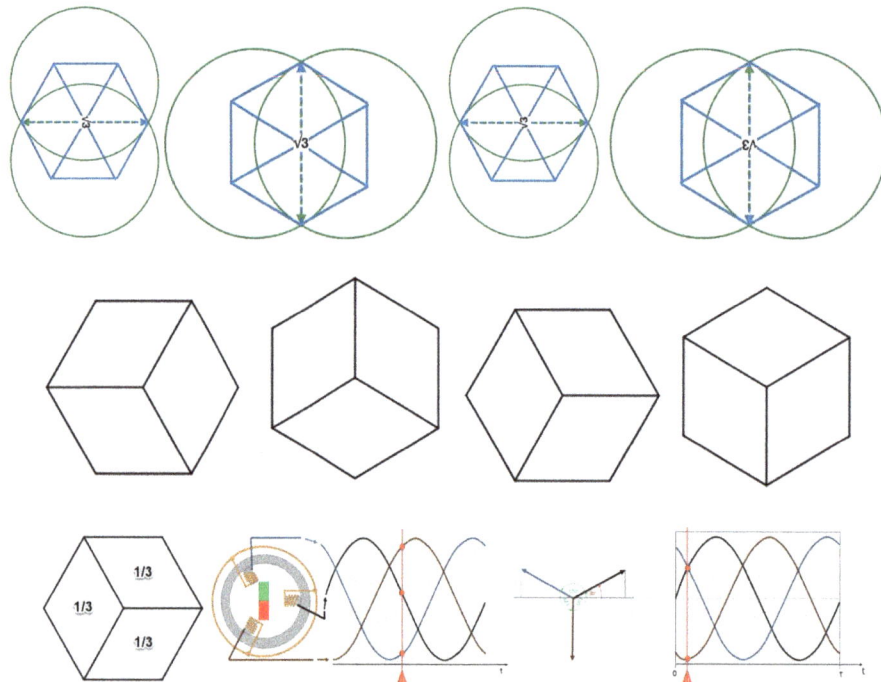

Image Source – Public Domain

This is the fundamental of the universe and everything else that's in it, including our existence. This is quantum mechanics. This will help in information processing that offer better performance and lower energy consumption. Apply this design to any quantum system, including quantum computing and you will succeed.

Nothing is invented by man in the universe – everything is discovered and applied. Look around you and study nature and you will know that everything can be learned from what God has already created. Everything has a meaning, and everything depend on everything else. You can't isolate or make independent any of God's creation. We can learn a lot from even spider webs to discover important technologies such as very closed and centralized network sensors. The same storage capacity, energy conservation and efficiency that can be found in the honeycomb applies to three-way electric power in a sense among other things. Our job here on Earth is to figure out who we truly are and what we came here to do and where we will be going after here. That will make our discoveries here very well applicable in the next dimensions. Man should learn to worship and glorify God. If we are humble and submit ourselves to the Holy Spirit of God, He will guide us into all truth and teach us everything we need to make life very easy and fulfilling for us.

John 16:12-15

[12] "I still have many things to say to you, but you cannot bear *them* now. [13] However, when He, the Spirit of truth, has come, He will guide you into all truth; for He will not speak on His own *authority,* but whatever He hears He will speak; and He will tell you things to come. [14] He will glorify Me, for He will take of what is Mine and declare *it* to you. [15] All things that the Father has are Mine. Therefore, I said that He will take of Mine and declare *it* to you.

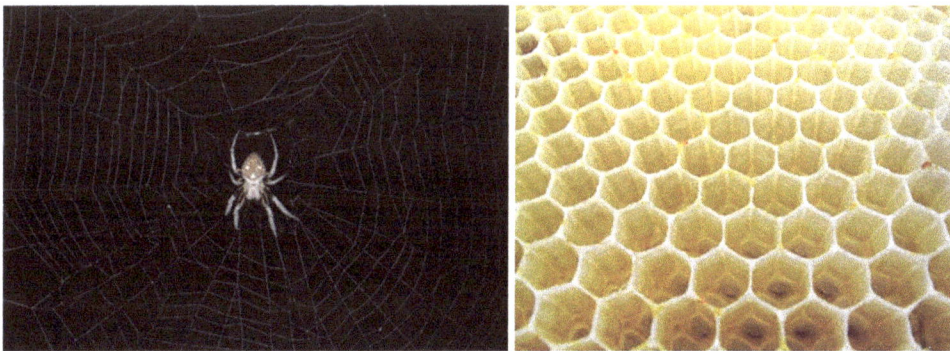

Left: Spider Web, and Right: Bee Honeycomb

Image Source – Public Domain

But some scientists and engineers will make others feel stupid and less important so that they (scientists and engineers) can appear as geniuses. Nobody is stupid and nobody is less important. Also, nobody is ugly – everybody is very infinitely smart and beautiful. For all these, you just need to get the right knowledge and understanding that will put you in the right environment, and you shall truly experience your infinite or limitless nature or self. We are all equal and very important. If it's mere creativity and physics that shows how much of a genius someone is, then we can all agree that even the spider and the bees are the real geniuses. Look at what they can create with such perfection and excellence – even the birds too. Think about how they weave their nests. Who taught them? How does even a baby of either a human or another living being learn how to feed immediately after birth or through any other form of delivery into the world? It is all the wisdom of God, people. In fact, God is like the spider who built the web (Earth). The spider sits in a position where it sees and hears everything happening inside that web and that's how it catches and eats its preys. This is only to boost your understanding – **God is not a spider,** but He has put His essence in the form of a dimension into even all these little creatures. If only we are humble, we are limitless just like God. He is a good and unselfish God.

The attitude of unbelievers bothered me so much and I asked God that why can't they even apply common sense so that they will believe in His existence and understand? God said, what we call common sense is very uncommon sense. I realized how true His statement is and I'm astonished at God and His ways even the more. If common sense is common, then we wouldn't have our supposed leaders to agree and even write and pass it as a legal law for a man to sleep with or marry another man, and a woman to sleep with or marry another woman. We would also truly know that life in this world is temporal and not supposed to be a competition. Rather, we should live it in love to truly experience why we are here on Earth in our journey of eternity. Even a spider or a bee or a bird can live and do these things without human help or what we call "money", yet scientists who don't believe in God go about stealing ideas from these creatures while we humans are supposed to be the ideas because the Architect and Creator has hidden Himself inside us. The sad part is that we even go as far as patenting these ideas to protect them as "our" intellectual properties. They will say that they got inspired by a spider web or some other creature in nature to come up with the idea or technology. Yet, they say God doesn't exist. If that's the case, then they are idiots or foolish because even these small organisms are smarter than they. Shame on the hypocritical unbelieving scientists.

Everything humanity need is in the Word of God. The foolish and wicked humans have also removed parts of these knowledge from the Bible and when you start talking about these other books now, some immature Christians will start calling your doctrine heresy. Humanity has a very big problem that only the Wisdom of God can solve. The scriptures below should prove to you why although you may even be very wealthy on Earth or a scientist with a thousand publications, you may in fact still be very foolish. If you worship God, then you are truly wise and wealthy. To me, below are two MOST important scriptures in the Bible. The wicked editors forgot to remove them. Every word of God is a gate or door into a dimension in the spirit so the satanic scheme to remove parts and some very important books from the Bible didn't help the enemy. In fact, it has fired up the People of God and the world is about to be shaken like never. Watch it unfold. Let these be your starting point to seek the Lord your God because you will need Him forever.

Proverbs 9:10

[10] "The fear of the Lord *is* the beginning of wisdom,
And the knowledge of the Holy One *is* understanding.

Hosea 4:6

[6] My people are destroyed for lack of knowledge.
Because you have rejected knowledge,
I also will reject you from being priest for Me;

Because you have forgotten the law of your God,
I also will forget your children.

Recently, a team of scientists from Germany, Sweden, and China discovered what they called a "new physical phenomenon: complex braided structures made of tiny magnetic vortices known as skyrmions." It is a great discovery, like most things in science but it is not new – when you study the images above and the content of this writing, you will understand why I say this. Skyrmions influence the magnetoresistive and thermodynamic properties of a material.

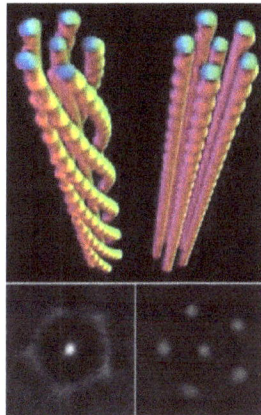

Complex Braided Structures Made of Skyrmions

Image Source – Public Domain

Study how the threads can in fact twist together to varying degrees, and how these complex shapes stabilize the magnetic structures, making them particularly interesting for use in a range of applications, and apply it the best way possible to quantum computing. It is true that these types of structures inside magnetic solids have unique electrical and magnetic properties. It will help in information processing that offer better performance and lower energy consumption. This is quantum mechanics. God and the crucifix cannot be excluded from quantum mechanics because God is the power and logic behind the technology of the universe. You can think of it as God is the two 'qubits' and He is still the third qubit in the middle who will hold the two qubits together – so, three qubits total. But qubits are not recommended. Use qutrit – trinary.

This final theory doesn't mean the end of science. This is only a revolution and a revival. Without God, you are nothing and you shall perish forever and ever. Without God, humanity will waste centuries after centuries and in the end, perish or go to hell. If only you had given your lives to Christ, you would understand the ways of God. Although the end is very near, this is only the beginning. You may now know the truth, but it still doesn't mean you know everything. Commit your life to God and journey in Him to find yourself. There are depths of Him that even in eternity, we can never exhaust. Learn and experience Him, for this is the purpose of your life. Therefore, you were created. You don't belong to yourself. You belong to God. You are His temple and a witness. The God you don't believe in because you see "no evidence" of Him, is already inside of you. Once you accept Him and confess that Jesus Christ is your Lord, you will activate God inside

155

of you. He is already hidden inside of you – and that happened after He formed you with His own hands and breathed Himself into you. God is to be experienced and manifested through your life. That can only be achieved through having a relationship with Him.

Significance of the Number Seven

Genesis 2:2-3

The Garden of Eden

2 Thus the heavens and the Earth, and all the host of them, were finished. **2** And on the seventh day God ended His work which He had done, and He rested on the seventh day from all His work which He had done. **3** Then God blessed the seventh day and sanctified it, because in it He rested from all His work which God had created and made.

Jesus spoke in a grouping of seven when He used seven metaphors to describe Himself as the path to salvation, the perfect reward for a good and faithful servant. Jesus tells us He is:

The bread of life

John 6:35

35 And Jesus said to them, "I am the bread of life. He who comes to Me shall never hunger, and he who believes in Me shall never thirst.

The light of the world

John 8:12

12 Then Jesus spoke to them again, saying, "I am the light of the world. He who follows Me shall not walk in darkness but have the light of life."

The gate to salvation

John 10:9

9 I am the door. If anyone enters by Me, he will be saved, and will go in and out and find pasture.

The good shepherd

John 10:11

11 "I am the good shepherd. The good shepherd gives His life for the sheep.

The resurrection and the life

John 11:25-26

25 Jesus said to her, "I am the resurrection and the life. He who believes in Me, though he may die, he shall live. 26 And whoever lives and believes in Me shall never die. Do you believe this?"

The way, the truth, and the life

John 14:6

6 Jesus said to him, "I am the way, the truth, and the life. No one comes to the Father except through Me.

The vine

John 15:5

5 "I am the vine; you *are* the branches. He who abides in Me, and I in him, bears much fruit; for without Me you can do nothing.

The Seven Spirits of God

Isaiah 11:2-3

2 The **Spirit of the Lord** shall rest upon Him,
The Spirit of **wisdom** and **understanding**,
The Spirit of **counsel** and **might**,
The Spirit of **knowledge** and of the **fear of the Lord**.

3 His delight *is* in the fear of the Lord,
And He shall not judge by the sight of His eyes,
Nor decide by the hearing of His ears;

Revelation 4:5-7

5 From the throne came flashes of lightning, rumblings and peals of thunder. In front of the throne, seven lamps were blazing. These are the seven spirits of God. 6 Also in front of the throne there was what looked like a sea of glass, clear as crystal.

In the center, around the throne, were four living creatures, and they were covered with eyes, in front and in back. 7 The first living creature was like a lion, the second was like an ox, the third had a face like a man, the fourth was like a flying eagle.

Revelation 5:5-7

[5] Then one of the elders said to me, "Do not weep! See, the Lion of the tribe of Judah, the Root of David, has triumphed. He is able to open the scroll and its seven seals."

[6] Then I saw a Lamb, looking as if it had been slain, standing at the center of the throne, encircled by the four living creatures and the elders. The Lamb had seven horns and seven eyes, which are the seven spirits of God sent out into all the Earth. [7] He went and took the scroll from the right hand of him who sat on the throne.

Of course, there is a lot more you may read in this writing. You can also research and read later.

Fibonacci Sequence – The Symmetry of Life

In mathematics, the Fibonacci numbers, commonly denoted F_n, form a sequence, called the Fibonacci sequence, such that each number is the sum of the two preceding ones, starting from 0 and 1. This is a series of numbers discovered by a 13th century mathematician. These numbers occur everywhere in nature.

We first have 0 + 1 = 1. The order then starts with the numbers 0 1 1 and you keep adding the last two numbers to continue.

0 1 1 2 3 5 8 13 21 34 55 89 144 233….

This sequence is in petal count, especially in daisy flowers. Pay attention to the flower with three (3) petals. We will come back to it later.

Image Source – Public Domain

Statistically, this sequence have been observed a lot in botany. If you look at the bottom of pine cones, there are spirals in their scales and if you count forward or backwards, you will find a Fibonacci number.

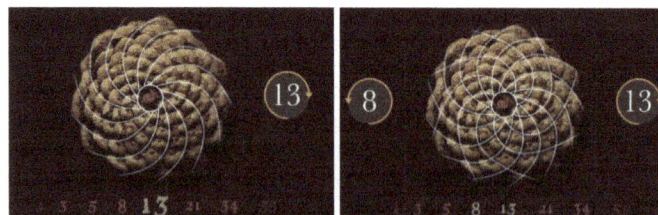

Image Source – Public Domain

158

This is true for Sunflower head – two sets of spirals, which when you count in each direction, both are Fibonacci numbers.

Image Source – Public Domain

In a simple geometric way, everything in creation follows the same fundamentals according to God's programming. Take the Fibonacci sequence and divide each number into the one that follows it. Here is what you get:

1/1 = 1; 2/1 = 2; 3/2 = 1.5; 5/3 = 1.666 … ; 8/5 = 1.6; 13/8 = 1.625; 21/13 = 1.615 … ; 34/21 = 1.619 … ; 55/34 = 1.6176 … ; 89/55 = 1.6181 …

This is what science calls the golden ratio and it is not an accident.

The Golden Ratio

The Fibonacci sequence and golden ration are interconnected. If you take any two successive (one after the other) Fibonacci numbers, their ratio is very close to the Golden Ratio (Φ) which is approximately 1.618034…

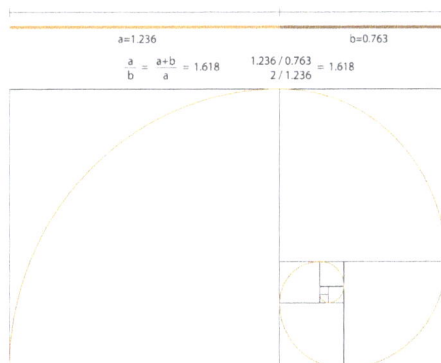

Image Source – Public Domain

We will go over this in depth later but this is just to help you understand the Fibonacci sequence and how it is interconnected to the entire universe. It has the hidden code of the universe or life inside of the sequence. And of course, it has the foundation of mathematics inside of it. We can see this in the proportions of man as drawn by Leonardo Da Vinci. Everything perfectly made or built is based on the proportions of man since man is perfectly made.

Image Source – Public Domain

The First Law of Thermodynamics, also known as the Law of Conservation of Energy, states that energy cannot be created or destroyed in an isolated system – it can only change form. Everything in the universe is part of thermodynamics, including you the reader. Therefore, you will live forever and ever. You have been changing form since the beginning of time. You are like the primordial energy that moves at the speed of light from the embryonic singularity like the big bang. You are an entire universe who goes through the entire process of life just like everything else in nature. The energy bound up in you is the same energy that started and exploded at the big bang.

When you study the flower and petals in the Fibonacci sequence, you will see that first, there is nothing then there is something or zero (0) or neutral. This is very important. In the context of human conception and birth, you are one-dimensional, then two-dimensional, and then three-dimensional. The fourth dimension is not visibly in the sequence but it's still there invisibly. So, your life goes through these stages until you become an adult.

We were created by God, who is made up of three persons (Father, Son, Holy Spirit), and He created us in His image, so we have His triune nature. The physique of God in the flesh looks just like us. We are made up of a spirit, soul, and body. The universe was created by God in His three persons (blessed trinity). We live in the 3D world, and the root or foundation of our existence is three (3) because of the triune nature of the Creator. Deep inside of you is this Creator (God) – science can call Him a quantum singularity so that they can relate, whose goal is to discover Himself to become aware or conscious of Himself and all His glory. You are the entire universe, and the entire universe is locked inside of you. The only way you can know who you truly are is to pray consistently and have communion, fellowship, and relationship with God. Then you will truly know who you are and where you came from and what your mission is on Earth and in eternity. You can never be destroyed – you can only metamorphose or change forms. The reality of this involves consciousness.

Time is only applied at this stage of the metamorphosis to help you relate to the invisible realm in visible form. When you follow the principles (Word of God or Bible) that's our guide for this

160

metamorphosis then you truly will live and understand the following stages in the invisible when you get there else you shall surely be lost when you cease to live in the body and exist fully as a spirit. It is a process and a journey. Your current experience as a human being and all the stages you are going through is exactly the universe playing its process and journey. You don't need physical technologies to study or learn about the universe because you are the universe. We are not independent but dependent on each other – everything in the universe. Science have arrived here and have been confused for decades – they call it quantum mechanics.

I will go over a secret with you that unlocks the mystery of the universe as hidden by God in the Fibonacci sequence, which is all connected to the purpose of this writing; to help you understand God and how quantum mechanics is all connected to Him. The biggest secret in the Christian faith is the triune nature of God, which is the doctrine of the trinity – God as Father, God as Son, and God as Holy Spirit. Three persons but the same God. When you finally understand this, it will change your life. This doctrine had caused tensions in the past especially when it had revealed to the world that the Christian faith is the one and only true faith, which worships the one and only true God. Prior to Christianity, there were several other existing religions and practices but eventually, the truth was revealed about what is supposed to be the one and only true religion.

I suggest the same to you in this writing to turn to the one and true God, who is three persons in a blessed trinity. The same revolution and persecutions that happened when the Christians as a new religious group were coming out of Judaism claimed and still claiming that we have the one and only true faith and serve the one and only true God – the one true way of understanding the world, the universe, and what's going to happen to everyone in the journey of life or existence, will happen again. But Jesus Christ always wins, and He has won already. Get on the winning side. This writing will challenge several doctrines or beliefs, but no matter how hard it may seem or be for you because you have lived your entire life believing something else, please believe in God through Jesus Christ, by the power of the Holy Spirit that He truly is the one and only true God of the heavens and the Earth.

We currently are the Christ on Earth. Jesus Christ is our Lord, Savior, King, and High Priest, and He has given us His Power of Attorney. When you pray, you don't pray with the word "I". When you live, you must understand that you represent one part of this trinity. i.e., the Son. Therefore, Jesus thought the disciples to pray in this manner – "Our Father…".

Matthew 6:9-13

[9] In this manner, therefore, pray:

Our Father in heaven,
Hallowed be Your name.
[10] Your kingdom come.
Your will be done
On Earth as *it is* in heaven.
[11] Give us this day our daily bread.

¹² And forgive us our debts,
As we forgive our debtors.
¹³ And do not lead us into temptation,
But deliver us from the evil one.
For Yours is the kingdom and the power and the glory forever. Amen.

When you engage the Lord in prayer, you must have the understanding that you are a part of the trinity that makes it complete and not a foreign part that is coming into the fellowship as a fourth person. This is a very powerful revelation. When you know this, you will see yourself joined with any other human being on Earth as one being. So, when you live, you live as part of a bigger body. The Word of God calls this the Body of Christ. You are basically in essence, like an ear, or an eye, or a mouth, or a nose, or a finger etc., tied to the bigger body. The problem with the world right now and why chaos and much wickedness and sin still go on is because we are all not on the same page on this. So, you are a part (1/3) of the Godhead, and you are also a god (1).

Psalm 82:6

⁶ I said, "You *are* gods,
And all of you *are* children of the Most High.

Therefore, you function both as a part and a whole. If you separate this, it loses essence and there is no revelation or power. Doctrine is extremely important because this universe or our existence is powered and controlled by truths (light). If you don't have the information, then you don't have knowledge. If you have the information, then now you are informed but what kind of knowledge do you have about the information – good or bad knowledge? That is, true knowledge or false knowledge? If you have false knowledge, then it is even worse than no knowledge at all. But if you have true knowledge or if you have the information so that you know about it but do not understand, then you are still in darkness. For example, even the weakest virus can still kill you if you don't know about the existence of the virus. This is lack of knowledge. If you know about the existence of the virus but you don't understand how it behaves, it can still kill you because there is a lack of understanding. But if you know about the existence of the virus and how it behaves, you can overcome it. This is called revelation because you have both the true knowledge and understanding.

Significance of the Number Three – God's Holy Trinity

You are now familiar with the Fibonacci sequence and golden ratio. Again, this is how the sequence goes: 0 1 1 2 3 5 8 13 21 34 55 89 144 233....

Image Source – Public Domain

It has already been proposed in this writing as revealed by God to use the base or root of three to solve the problem in quantum mechanics, including quantum computing, and to help you better understand His creation. When we look at the purple daisy flower above, we see a shape that everybody must be interested in if you want to understand God and life – or in science, quantum mechanics. This is the secret code to unlocking the universe. Each part of the petal represents one part of the trinity – Father, Son, Holy Spirit. This is the nature of God – three in one.

Working Out the Symmetry of Life - Fibonacci Sequence

We won't solve all of it because we will get into eternity or infinity. We will start by adding the unique numbers in the sequence in multiples of 3 based on the revelation of the root of 3 as the number representing the different persons of the Godhead.

$$0 + 0 + 0 = 0$$
$$1 + 1 + 1 = 3$$
$$2 + 2 + 2 = 6$$
$$3 + 3 + 3 = 9$$
$$= 18$$

$$= 18 + 78 = 96.\ 96 - 30 = 66$$

$$5 + 5 + 5 = 15$$
$$8 + 8 + 8 = 24$$
$$13 + 13 + 13 = 39$$
$$= 78$$

$$= 426.\ 426 - 30 = 396$$

$$21 + 21 + 21 = 63$$
$$34 + 34 + 34 = 102$$
$$55 + 55 + 55 = 165$$
$$= 330$$

$$= 1824$$

$$89 + 89 + 89 = 267$$
$$144 + 144 + 144 = 432$$
$$233 + 233 + 233 = 699$$
$$= 1398$$

For the simple addition and subtraction in the simple math above, we start with a root or base of 3. We have the Father, the Son, and the Holy Spirit (Godhead), who are represented by the number 3 here, but they are still individually God (1), and altogether God (1+1+1). You can represent the Godhead by the number 0 or 1 as the same God or 3 when you refer to the individual personalities of the Godhead. We will add the numbers in the Fibonacci sequence starting from the unique numbers. When we add them in multiples of 3 as we have above, we will start the sequence with the numbers 3, 6, and 9. From that point forward, you can either add or subtract any of those three numbers in any order or amplifying them with a 0 – 0, 03, 06, 09, 30, 60, 90, 33, 36, 39, 63, 66, 69, 93, 96, 99, 369, 396, 639, 693, 936, 963, and you will always arrive at a smaller number which could be broken down further by one of these numbers and finally arrive at 0. Everything started, develops, progresses, grows, expands, transforms, or evolves with God, and everything will end with God. The unity in the Godhead is why everything is created, exists, and goes through the process of life and the reason why the Church or Body of Christ stands. This symmetry also applies in the negative. The numbers 3, 6, and 9 are very powerful numbers in creation. Praying at 3, 6, 9, and 12 are important for these reasons and because they also represent the cross. These are divine times for reset and restoration.

The Mystery of Methuselah

If you understand the secrets of the numbers 3, 6, and 9, you will surely understand the mystery of Methuselah. He was the oldest man that ever lived on the Earth.

Genesis 5:25-27

[25] Methuselah lived one hundred and eighty-seven years, and begot Lamech. [26] After he begot Lamech, Methuselah lived seven hundred and eighty-two years, and had sons and daughters. [27] So all the days of Methuselah were nine hundred and sixty-nine years; and he died.

The meaning of the name Methuselah is "His death shall send" or "Man of the Javelin" or "Death of Sword". Have you ever investigated it or wondered why? God used him as a symbol for His love, mercy, grace, long-suffering, patience etc., as a signal for destroying the Earth at an appointed time.

Methuselah lived 969 years. If you follow the basic mathematics, we did earlier in the Fibonacci Sequence above, 969 is a number in this sequence when you calculate with 3, 6, and 9. In the year that Methuselah died, God sent the flood in the days of Noah.

Methuselah's age at the birth of Lamech:	187	(Genesis 5:25)
Lamech's age at the birth of Noah	182	(Genesis 5:28)
Noah's age at the beginning of the Flood	600	(Genesis 7:6)
Total	969 =	Methuselah's age at death (Gen 5:27).

So, Methuselah died in the year of the Flood. Again, both Methuselah's and Noah's ages at death, fall within the Fibonacci Sequence calculations using the numbers 3, 6, and 9 as we have seen earlier. The number 120 also falls in this sequence. Noah used 120 years to build the ark.

The Pattern of Prophecy in Relation to the Great Acts of God in History

← Great Acts of God →	FLOOD		EXODUS	RETURN From EXILE	MESSIAH'S 1ST ADVENT	MESSIAH'S 2ND ADVENT
Time Periods →	Methuselah's lifetime	120 years	430, 400 years 1875/1845 BC – 1445 BC	70 years, 605-536 BC	70 weeks of years = 490 years; 457 BC – AD 34	2300 years 457 BC [-456] to 1844
Predicting Prophet(s) →	Enoch Genesis 5:21-27; 7:6 Jude 14	Noah Genesis 6:3	Abraham Exodus 12:40-41, Galatians 3:17 (430); Genesis 15:13, Acts 7:6 (400)	Jeremiah, Isaiah Jeremiah 25:11-12; Isaiah 7:14; 2 Chronicles 36:19-23	Daniel Daniel 9:24-27; Ezra 7:1, 8, 9; Luke 3:1; 4:21; Mark 1:14-15 2 Thessalonians 2:1-8	Daniel Daniel 7:9-14; 8:14,23-24; 9:24-27, etc.; Leviticus 23; Hebrews 8 & 9 1 Thessalonians 5:9-11; 4:13-18; 1:9-10; Luke 21:34-36
Fulfilling Prophet(s) →	Noah Genesis 6:3, 7, 8, 17; 7:4		Moses	Daniel 9:2; Ezra, Nehemiah, Haggai, Zechariah	John the Baptist, Jesus Christ (Messiah) Mark 11:7-11; Luke 24:19; Acts 2; 6:8 – 8:1, 4, 5, 26-27	Joel Joel 2:28-32; Ephesians 4:11-13; John 16:13-14; Revelation 20:4; 13:5-8; 12:17; 14:12; 19:10; 22:9; 1:9-10
Elements of Delay →	7 days, 40 days Genesis 7:4, 10-12		40 years in the wilderness Numbers 14:34	Returned on time, but full rebuilding took much longer. Daniel 9:25; Ezra 7:25-26; Nehemiah 6:15	3 ½ years intervals between Jesus' anointing, crucifixion, and Gospel to the Gentiles at end of the 70th week. Daniel 9:24-27	The Cosmic War won't be over until it's won. Matthew 24:14, 36; Mark 4:26-29
Movement →	Those saved in the Ark		Nation of Israel	Israel Restored **This is where we are in History... Restoring**	Christ Established the Christian Church **The Repeat will be the Rapture of the Body of Christ**	Advent Movement **The Repeat will be the Great Tribulation**

The Lord has said these words to me repeatedly this year (2021) – **judgment, salvation, righteousness, and equity**. We will see these playing out wonderfully and globally in 2022 and beyond.

History is repeating itself but with new prophets (vessels) and the same old systems or spirits of God. I know this because the Lord has told me Himself, and the spirit He has put inside of me. It has already begun. And there will be a restoration of the Body of Christ with a great harvest. Then Jesus Christ will privately return for His bride (rapture), and afterwards, there will be the great tribulation. He will then return for the second time during the tribulation where He will be seen by everybody. Time is extremely short. I perceive the coming of the Lord as if it's happening right now.

The Return of the Lord Jesus Christ

Remember, Jesus Christ descended by becoming sin through becoming a man born of a woman, and then died on the cross because He had become sin, after which he descended into Hell and then ascended back onto the Earth and then into Heaven. For proof and for day like this where humanity have fallen away from the ways of God, Jesus Christ showed Himself to at least one person on each account. First, most men saw Him before He was crucified. Second, Mary Magdalene saw Him after He had gone into Hell. Third, Jesus Christ ascended into Heaven. We count three (3) different realms. We can represent these three realms with the signs or symbols –, ±, +. Hell is –, where evil exists. Earth is ±, where both good and evil exists. And heaven is +, where only holiness and light exist. At a physical level, we can use our own bodies to represent these three states. Death is exponential decay which has the sign –. Life on Earth in the human body is a neutral ground which has the sign ±. And finally, Heaven is a realm with only positivity which can be represented by the symbol +. When someone is alive, he or she can make things right to either grow or die. When you are nourished, you grow. When you are malnourished, you die. This is the same thing. Our spiritual lives (true selves) and what can become of these selves can all be seen here in the physical. But in the spiritual, you will not have the chance to make things right anymore. The center of gravity (point of change or translation) is Earth. The proof of all these realms as mentioned earlier are in the following. Jesus Christ made sure that He was seen.

John 20:11-18

Mary Magdalene Sees the Risen Lord

[11] But Mary stood outside by the tomb weeping, and as she wept, she stooped down *and looked* into the tomb. [12] And she saw two angels in white sitting, one at the head and the other at the feet, where the body of Jesus had lain. [13] Then they said to her, "Woman, why are you weeping?"

She said to them, "Because they have taken away my Lord, and I do not know where they have laid Him."

¹⁴ Now when she had said this, she turned around and saw Jesus standing *there,* and did not know that it was Jesus. ¹⁵ Jesus said to her, "Woman, why are you weeping? Whom are you seeking?"

She, supposing Him to be the gardener, said to Him, "Sir, if You have carried Him away, tell me where You have laid Him, and I will take Him away."

¹⁶ Jesus said to her, "Mary!"

She turned and said to Him, "Rabboni!" (which is to say, Teacher).

¹⁷ Jesus said to her, "Do not cling to Me, for I have not yet ascended to My Father; but go to My brethren and say to them, 'I am ascending to My Father and your Father, and *to* My God and your God.'"

¹⁸ Mary Magdalene came and told the disciples that she had seen the Lord, and *that* He had spoken these things to her.

Ephesians 4:9

⁸ Therefore He says:

"When He ascended on high,
He led captivity captive,
And gave gifts to men."

⁹ (Now this, "He ascended"—what does it mean but that He also first descended into the lower parts of the earth? ¹⁰ He who descended is also the One who ascended far above all the heavens, that He might fill all things.)

1 Peter 3:18-22

Christ's Suffering and Ours

¹⁸ For Christ also suffered once for sins, the just for the unjust, that He might bring [f]us to God, being put to death in the flesh but made alive by the Spirit, ¹⁹ by whom also He went and preached to the spirits in prison, ²⁰ who formerly were disobedient, [g]when once the Divine longsuffering waited in the days of Noah, while *the* ark was being prepared, in which a few, that is, eight souls, were saved through water. ²¹ There is also an antitype which now saves us— baptism (not the removal of the filth of the flesh, but the answer of a good conscience toward God), through the resurrection of Jesus Christ, ²² who has gone into heaven and is at the right hand of God, angels and authorities and powers having been made subject to Him.

My point for referencing these scriptures is to help you understand that everything that have been said in the Word of God will happen – and it will be history repeating itself as showed in the table earlier. Jesus Christ has already our savior now so no need for His death again. He showed us the way so when believers die, they go to Heaven. But the events of the last days will follow the same pattern as in the days of Noah and as in the days of Jesus Christ when He came as a man through the womb of a woman – this is marked in the table as the Messiah's 1st advent.

Before Jesus Christ's wrath or tribulation, He will first come privately for His people and take them to Heaven to be with Him – this will be the repeat of the Messiah's 1st advent in a different fashion. **Remember, just like the first one, this will be private too and ONLY His bride (Body of Christ) shall see Him and leave the Earth with Him – just like only Mary Magdalene saw Him as mentioned in John 20:17**. This statement is bolded because it is **extremely** important. Therefore, Mary is considered as the "bride" of Jesus. Believers call this the rapture and ONLY true believers shall witness this event and leave the Earth suddenly. This will be a glorious event for believers.

Luke 17:34-37

34 I tell you, in that night there will be two *men* in one bed: the one will be taken and the other will be left. 35 Two *women* will be grinding together: the one will be taken and the other left. 36 Two *men* will be in the field: the one will be taken and the other left."

37 And they answered and said to Him, "Where, Lord?"

So, He said to them, "Wherever the body is, there the eagles will be gathered together."

After this event or rapture, we will be at the marriage supper with the Lamb for seven (7) years in Heaven. Then Jesus Christ will return the second time during the tribulation together with His bride (Body of Christ) that He took away in His private first return – this is marked in the past-present-future table I showed earlier as the Messiah's 2nd advent. You should understand why I call it a past-present-future table. If not, then think about it.

Revelation 19:9

9 Then he said to me, "Write: 'Blessed *are* those who are called to the marriage supper of the Lamb!'" And he said to me, "These are the true sayings of God."

In this final return (second coming), everybody will see Him, not only believers. Every eye will see the Lord. Take note that there was a 3 ½ years intervals between Jesus' anointing, crucifixion, and Gospel to the Gentiles at the end of the 70th week as we see in Daniel 9:24-27. The 70 weeks in these scriptures in the book of Daniel is like the days of the seventy that were sent out in Luke 10. In the following image, which was well developed by Jimmy Evans according to the Word of God, we see that while we are in Heaven for seven years, the world will be going through a tribulation – a period broken into 3 ½ years each. The second coming is a horrific event.

Timeline of the End Times

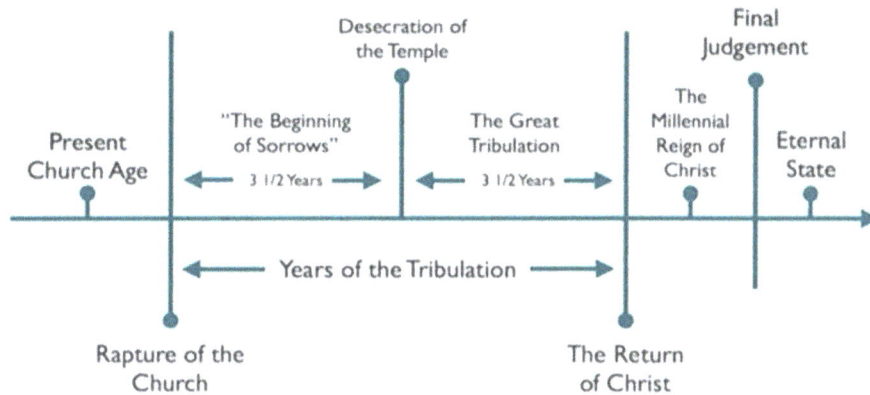

Image Source – Public Domain

Jesus mentions in Matthew 24 that the second half of the tribulation will be the worst time in the history of the world. So, the rapture of the Body of Christ is seven years before the tribulation and the second coming in which we come with Jesus will be seven years after the tribulation.

If you don't believe in the Word of God, think again. This is a warning. You won't have an excuse that the Word didn't get to you. Read from Luke 10, what will happen to you.

Luke 10:10-12

[10] But whatever city you enter, and they do not receive you, go out into its streets and say, [11] 'The very dust of your city which clings to us we wipe off against you. Nevertheless, know this, that the kingdom of God has come near you.' [12] But I say to you that it will be more tolerable in that Day for Sodom than for that city.

But to those who heed to this warning, read below.

1 Thessalonians 1:9-10

[9] For they themselves declare concerning us what manner of entry we had to you, and how you turned to God from idols to serve the living and true God, [10] and to wait for His Son from heaven, whom He raised from the dead, *even* Jesus who delivers us from the wrath to come.

1 Thessalonians 4:13-18

The Comfort of Christ's Coming

¹³ But I do not want you to be ignorant, brethren, concerning those who have fallen asleep, lest you sorrow as others who have no hope. ¹⁴ For if we believe that Jesus died and rose again, even so God will bring with Him those who sleep in Jesus.

¹⁵ For this we say to you by the word of the Lord, that we who are alive *and* remain until the coming of the Lord will by no means precede those who are asleep. ¹⁶ For the Lord Himself will descend from heaven with a shout, with the voice of an archangel, and with the trumpet of God. And the dead in Christ will rise first. ¹⁷ Then we who are alive *and* remain shall be caught up together with them in the clouds to meet the Lord in the air. And thus, we shall always be with the Lord. ¹⁸ Therefore comfort one another with these words.

1 Thessalonians 5:9-11

⁹ For God did not appoint us to wrath, but to obtain salvation through our Lord Jesus Christ, ¹⁰ who died for us, that whether we wake or sleep, we should live together with Him.

¹¹ Therefore comfort each other and edify one another, just as you also are doing.

Luke 21:34-36

The Importance of Watching

³⁴ "But take heed to yourselves, lest your hearts be weighed down with carousing, drunkenness, and cares of this life, and that Day come on you unexpectedly. ³⁵ For it will come as a snare on all those who dwell on the face of the whole earth. ³⁶ Watch therefore, and pray always that you may be counted worthy to escape all these things that will come to pass, and to stand before the Son of Man."

2 Thessalonians 2:1-8

The Great Apostasy

2 Now, brethren, concerning the coming of our Lord Jesus Christ and our gathering together to Him, we ask you, ² not to be soon shaken in mind or troubled, either by spirit or by word or by letter, as if from us, as though the day of Christ had come. ³ Let no one deceive you by any means; for *that Day will not come* unless the falling away comes first, and the man of sin is revealed, the son of perdition, ⁴ who opposes and exalts himself above all that is called God or that is worshiped, so that he sits as God in the temple of God, showing himself that he is God.

[5] Do you not remember that when I was still with you, I told you these things? [6] And now you know what is restraining, that he may be revealed in his own time. [7] For the mystery of lawlessness is already at work; **only He who now restrains** *will do so* **until He is taken out of the way**. [8] And then the lawless one will be revealed, whom the Lord will consume with the breath of His mouth and destroy with the brightness of His coming.

References from these five scriptures confirm that Jesus Christ will come for His bride first for departure at the beginning of the tribulation and then the Holy Spirit and the Body of Christ will be taken out of the way. Only then shall the great tribulation start. The antichrist spirit is already on the Earth but because there will be a second coming of Jesus Christ with His Army for

The Great Tribulation

Revelation 13:5-8

The Beast from the Sea

13 Then I stood on the sand of the sea. And I saw a beast rising up out of the sea, having seven heads and ten horns, and on his horns ten crowns, and on his heads a blasphemous name. [2] Now the beast which I saw was like a leopard, his feet were like *the feet of* a bear, and his mouth like the mouth of a lion. The dragon gave him his power, his throne, and great authority. [3] And I saw one of his heads as if it had been mortally wounded, and his deadly wound was healed. And all the world marveled and followed the beast. [4] So they worshiped the dragon who gave authority to the beast; and they worshiped the beast, saying, "Who *is* like the beast? Who is able to make war with him?"

[5] And he was given a mouth speaking great things and blasphemies, and he was given authority to continue for forty-two months. [6] Then he opened his mouth in blasphemy against God, to blaspheme His name, His tabernacle, and those who dwell in heaven. [7] It was granted to him to make war with the saints and to overcome them. And authority was given him over every tribe, tongue, and nation. [8] All who dwell on the earth will worship him, whose names have not been written in the Book of Life of the Lamb slain from the foundation of the world.

[9] If anyone has an ear, let him hear. [10] He who leads into captivity shall go into captivity; he who kills with the sword must be killed with the sword. Here is the patience and the faith of the saints.

Daniel 8:23-24

[23] "And in the latter time of their kingdom,
When the transgressors have reached their fullness,
A king shall arise,
Having fierce features,
Who understands sinister schemes.
[24] His power shall be mighty, but not by his own power;

He shall destroy fearfully,
And shall prosper and thrive;
He shall destroy the mighty, and *also* the holy people.

The Beast from the Earth

11 Then I saw another beast coming up out of the earth, and he had two horns like a lamb and spoke like a dragon. **12** And he exercises all the authority of the first beast in his presence and causes the earth and those who dwell in it to worship the first beast, whose deadly wound was healed. **13** He performs great signs, so that he even makes fire come down from heaven on the earth in the sight of men. **14** And he deceives those who dwell on the earth by those signs which he was granted to do in the sight of the beast, telling those who dwell on the earth to make an image to the beast who was wounded by the sword and lived. **15** He was granted *power* to give breath to the image of the beast, that the image of the beast should both speak and cause as many as would not worship the image of the beast to be killed. **16** He causes all, both small and great, rich and poor, free and slave, to receive a mark on their right hand or on their foreheads, **17** and that no one may buy or sell except one who has the mark or the name of the beast, or the number of his name.

18 Here is wisdom. Let him who has understanding calculate the number of the beast, for it is the number of a man: His number *is* 666.

Revelation 20:4

The Saints Reign with Christ 1,000 Years

4 And I saw thrones, and they sat on them, and judgment was committed to them. Then *I saw* the souls of those who had been beheaded for their witness to Jesus and for the word of God, who had not worshiped the beast or his image, and had not received *his* mark on their foreheads or on their hands. And they lived and reigned with Christ for a thousand years.

Daniel 11:32-35

32 Those who do wickedly against the covenant he shall corrupt with flattery; but the people who know their God shall be strong and carry out *great exploits.* **33** And those of the people who understand shall instruct many; yet *for many* days they shall fall by sword and flame, by captivity and plundering. **34** Now when they fall, they shall be aided with a little help; but many shall join with them by intrigue. **35** And *some* of those of understanding shall fall, to refine them, purify *them,* and make *them* white, *until* the time of the end, because *it is* still for the appointed time.

This first coming or rapture will be a glorious event for God's people but a tough one for the ones who will be left behind although they will still have another opportunity to make it right. That experience will still be a horrible one. The second coming will also be a horrific one.

Genesis 7:6

6 Noah *was* six hundred years old when the floodwaters were on the earth.

You can start reading the story of the flood from Genesis 6. Moses died at the age of 120. There were about 120 in the disciples quorum in the upper room. The number 120 is the desirable distance used in three-phase electric power. So, we see the significance of this number too.

God is using the Holy Spirit in our times as this symbol and signal. The day the Holy Spirit leaves the earth is the day the earth gets destroyed like in the days of Noah.

2 Thessalonians 2:6-7

6 And now you know what is restraining, that he may be revealed in his own time. **7** For the mystery of lawlessness is already at work; only He who now restrains *will do so* until He is taken out of the way.

The day the Holy Spirit leaves the Earth is the day the earth gets destroyed. The Holy Spirit and the Body of Christ is God's restraining power in our world right now. Just like it was in the days of Noah – that symbol (restrainer) was Methuselah. You can read how this same event played out in what you will call the past or history in the days of Noah and the flood.

Genesis 6

The Wickedness and Judgment of Man

6 Now it came to pass, when men began to multiply on the face of the earth, and daughters were born to them, **2** that the sons of God saw the daughters of men, that they *were* beautiful; and they took wives for themselves of all whom they chose.

3 And the Lord said, "My Spirit shall not strive with man forever, for he *is* indeed flesh; yet his days shall be one hundred and twenty years." **4** There were giants on the earth in those days, and also afterward, when the sons of God came into the daughters of men, and they bore *children* to them. Those *were* the mighty men who *were* of old, men of renown.

5 Then the Lord saw that the wickedness of man *was* great in the earth, and *that* every intent of the thoughts of his heart *was* only evil continually. **6** And the Lord was sorry that He had made man on the earth, and He was grieved in His heart. **7** So the Lord said, "I will destroy man whom I have created from the face of the earth, both man and beast, creeping thing and birds of the air, for I am sorry that I have made them." **8** But Noah found grace in the eyes of the Lord.

Noah Pleases God

9 This is the genealogy of Noah. Noah was a just man, perfect in his generations. Noah walked with God. **10** And Noah begot three sons: Shem, Ham, and Japheth.

11 The earth also was corrupt before God, and the earth was filled with violence. **12** So God looked upon the earth, and indeed it was corrupt; for all flesh had corrupted their way on the earth.

The Ark Prepared

13 And God said to Noah, "The end of all flesh has come before Me, for the earth is filled with violence through them; and behold, I will destroy them with the earth. **14** Make yourself an ark of gopherwood; make rooms in the ark and cover it inside and outside with pitch. **15** And this is how you shall make it: The length of the ark *shall be* three hundred cubits, its width fifty cubits, and its height thirty cubits. **16** You shall make a window for the ark, and you shall finish it to a cubit from above; and set the door of the ark in its side. You shall make it *with* lower, second, and third *decks.* **17** And behold, I Myself am bringing floodwaters on the earth, to destroy from under heaven all flesh in which *is* the breath of life; everything that *is* on the earth shall die. **18** But I will establish My covenant with you; and you shall go into the ark—you, your sons, your wife, and your sons' wives with you. **19** And of every living thing of all flesh you shall bring two of every *sort* into the ark, to keep *them* alive with you; they shall be male and female. **20** Of the birds after their kind, of animals after their kind, and of every creeping thing of the earth after its kind, two of every *kind* will come to you to keep *them* alive. **21** And you shall take for yourself of all food that is eaten, and you shall gather *it* to yourself; and it shall be food for you and for them."

22 Thus Noah did; according to all that God commanded him, so he did.

1 Peter 3:19-20

19 by whom also He went and preached to the spirits in prison, **20** who formerly were disobedient, when once the Divine longsuffering waited in the days of Noah, while *the* ark was being prepared, in which a few, that is, eight souls, were saved through water.

2 Peter 2:5

5 and did not spare the ancient world, but saved Noah, *one of* eight *people*, a preacher of righteousness, bringing in the flood on the world of the ungodly;

Hebrews 11:7

7 By faith Noah, being divinely warned of things not yet seen, moved with godly fear, prepared an ark for the saving of his household, by which he condemned the world and became heir of the righteousness which is according to faith.

Luke 17:26-27

[26] And as it was in the days of Noah, so it will be also in the days of the Son of Man: [27] They ate, they drank, they married wives, they were given in marriage, until the day that Noah entered the ark, and the flood came and destroyed them all.

Matthew 24:36-39

No One Knows the Day or Hour

[36] "But of that day and hour no one knows, not even the angels of heaven, but My Father only. [37] But as the days of Noah *were,* so also will the coming of the Son of Man be. [38] For as in the days before the flood, they were eating and drinking, marrying and giving in marriage, until the day that Noah entered the ark, [39] and did not know until the flood came and took them all away, so also will the coming of the Son of Man be.

After reading these stories and prophecies, you should know why the governments will attempt to close all Churches but leave the clubs, bars etc., open – you will understand why they will also try so hard to censor the truth to leave you in darkness. You will understand why they will encourage same sex sexual relationships among many other things. The world is coming to an end very soon. Let your eyes be open so you can see. There is still hope for you.

Ephesians 2:8-9

[8] For by grace you have been saved through faith, and that not of yourselves; *it is* the gift of God, [9] not of works, lest anyone should boast.

Romans 10:13

[13] For "whoever calls on the name of the LORD shall be saved."

The good news is that Jesus Christ is our Ark of Salvation today. He is the way, the truth, and the life. This was still true in the days of Noah because his ark was three stories, one window, and one door. Jesus is the only door – hop in before He shuts the door.

John 10:9

[9] I am the door. If anyone enters by Me, he will be saved, and will go in and out and find pasture.

Genesis 7:16

[16] So those that entered, male and female of all flesh, went in as God had commanded him; and the LORD shut him in.

God had been gracious enough to repeat or play the last days in very different ways although the theme is the same. This again is just like gravity – same theme with different levels of manifestation. Time was created by God as a slowed-motion version of eternity so that we can learn and correct our mistakes. If you never knew this, now you know so decide as quickly as possible to come to Jesus Christ because in the next second, you could leave the Earth. Don't waste any time. He couldn't make His message and warning to you any clearer than this.

The Secret Code of Life Is Love

Genesis 1:26

[26] Then God said, "**Let Us make man** in Our image, according to Our likeness; let them have dominion over the fish of the sea, over the birds of the air, and over the cattle, over [a]all the earth and over every creeping thing that creeps on the earth."

Genesis 6:16

[16] You shall make a window for the ark, and you shall finish it to a cubit from above; and set the door of the ark in its side. You shall make it *with* **lower, second,** and **third** *decks.*

Right from the beginning, the Godhead have remained in perfect holy unity (blessed trinity). When there is no love or unity, everything breaks apart. This is the secret code of life and why even our bodies are not disintegrated but all the parts are held together. This is the force that holds everything together. This is how God, and His power is physically demonstrated in the universe through the force of gravity, right from the subatomic level, the atomic level, the molecular level, through the spiritual levels or dimensions. Gravity is therefore, one force with three different manifestations, where the next manifestation is a combination or unity of the two previous manifestations, and the last manifestation is a combination of all earlier or previous manifestations. This is how the force of gravity is amplified in nature.

Every problem in the universe has a solution. That solution sits on love. All the issues in relationships, right from our homes, the communities, governments, or individual nations throughout all nations in the world can be solved with love. When there is love, there is obedience, and the right thing(s) will always be done. When there is love, there is no cause to hate or do what is inappropriate. When there is love, two political parties in the parliament or congress will always do the right thing and sign the right bills into laws, no matter what side they are on. It won't be a matter of following or agreeing with who is in the same party as you, you will always agree on what is right regardless. When there is love, two or more nations will have peace regardless of whatever problems that they may be facing. There will always be diplomacy enough to meet in the middle (neutral) where a decision on the right thing or course shall be made. And when you meet at the neutral point or the center of gravity (±), you have only one of two mirrored or symmetrical directions to go. You can either go up (+) or down (–), or forward (+) or backward (–).

When you love, there is always a positive atmosphere and positive energies are very powerful. When you love, you care and take care of the problems of others. You seek for good things in your personal life towards the good of the immediate home, community, the nation, and the world at large. When there is love, you don't call your sister or brother next to you as white or black person or whatever skin color only to be racist, but you will rather reference their complexion to be in awe about God and His perfect and beautiful creation. You will identify your family and friends and people around the world with their unique complexions to show or point out to them or others how you appreciate their uniqueness. When you love, you will truly know that we are all one, regardless of where you come from or your race. When you love then you won't even have anything as a major or minor race anymore. Instead, you will judge or evaluate all based on their individual uniqueness or talents or gifts or skills. When there is love, you won't keep piling up the money in your account or wherever you keep it while there is a human being somewhere suffering and hurting and dying from poverty. The true reason why you were saving the money is to take care of others in need. When you love, you won't be squandering the country's money while citizens are suffering and dying. That is not love – that is wickedness.

Matthew 22:36-40

36 "Teacher, which *is* the great commandment in the law?"

37 Jesus said to him, "'You shall love the LORD your God with all your heart, with all your soul, and with all your mind.' 38 This is *the* first and great commandment. 39 And *the* second *is* like it: 'You shall love your neighbor as yourself.' 40 On these two commandments hang all the Law and the Prophets."

1 John 4:20

Obedience by Faith

20 If someone says, "I love God," and hates his brother, he is a liar; for he who does not love his brother whom he has seen, how can he love God whom he has not seen?

God has hidden Himself in all of us, but you must seek Him to understand. When you ask, who is God? Look in the mirror and you will see God. Look right next to who's beside you, and you will see God in them.

When you study the secret code of life as you have right now, you will surely understand that unity is indeed strength. And unity is love. And love only brings about development or positive progression or great or glorious evolution or transformation. **This is the secret of life**. This is the universe. Therefore, the word is 'universe', which means 'unity' or 'combined into one or whole'. This is the force of gravity, and gravity is quantum mechanics. Gravity is life. **Quantum mechanics is life**. Love or unity keeps all the elementary particles together. So now, do you truly mean it when you say, 'I love you'? Read the following scriptures – base or root 3.

1 Corinthians 13:13

13 And now abide **faith**, **hope**, **love**, these **three**; but the greatest of these *is* **love**.

1 John 4:7-11

Knowing God Through Love

7 Beloved, let us love one another, for love is of God; and everyone who loves is born of God and knows God. **8** He who does not love does not know God, for God is love. **9** In this the love of God was manifested toward us, that God has sent His only begotten Son into the world, that we might live through Him. **10** In this is love, not that we loved God, but that He loved us and sent His Son *to be* the propitiation for our sins. **11** Beloved, if God so loved us, we also ought to love one another.

Polar Graph

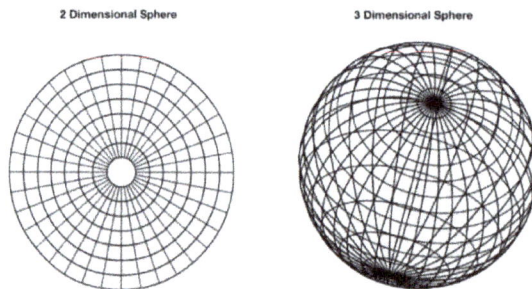

Image Source – Public Domain

The 2D polar graph is a shadow of the 3D sphere or Earth. It is made from 36 radial lines in 10-degree increments representing the 360 degrees then concentric circles are drawn each with the same distance away as the last, creating each equal demarcation as the one before counting the inside circle as one. It's called the shadow form when the 3D sphere is projected unto a flat surface and casting shadows is a sacred and good way to obtain information.

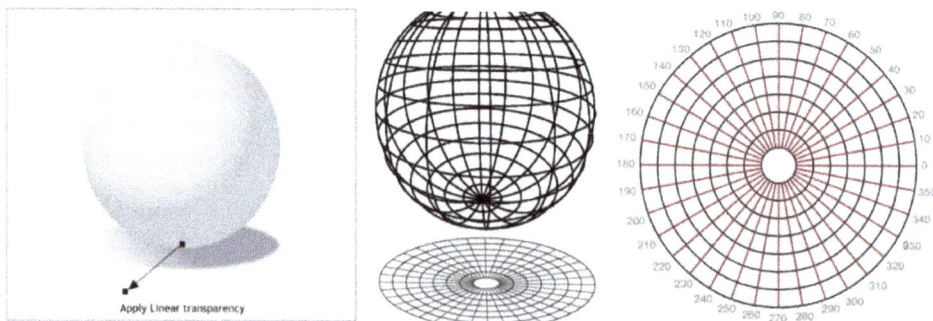

Image Source – Public Domain

A polar graph also has both straight male lines and circular female lines – with both the male and female energies interacting at once.

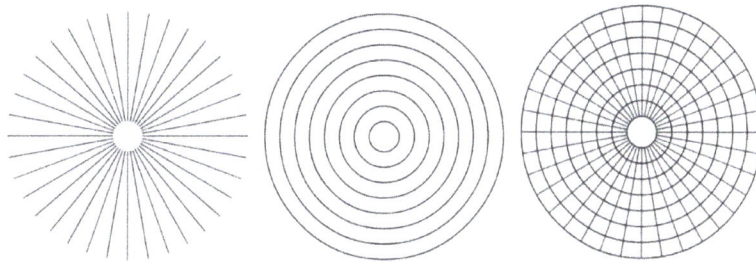

Left: male, Middle: female, and Right: union

If you plot a golden mean spiral at zero degrees on the polar graph, it will loop all the way around before hitting zero again exactly at the eighth circle. You will find that this golden mean line crosses five specific places as it goes out. These specific places are where the female circular lines meet the male lines.

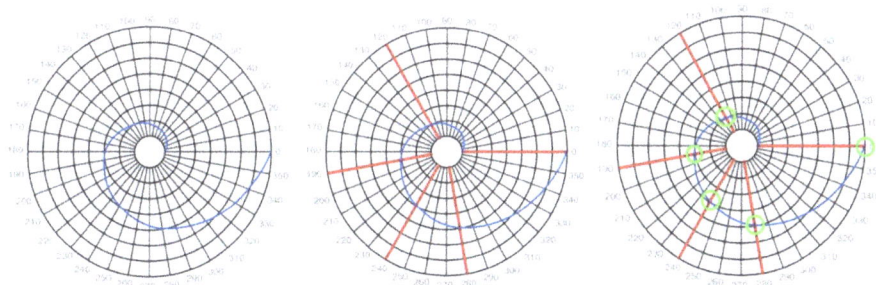

Blue: golden mean spiral, Red: female meets male, Green: union

It crosses at 120 degrees, 190 degrees, 240 degrees, to 80 degrees and then it jumps to 360 degrees or back at 0 degrees, depending on how you look at it. What's interesting about this is that it creates both a binary and a Fibonacci sequence looking at the radial increments. From the center, it crosses at 1, 2, 3, 5, and 8. That's Fibonacci sequence.

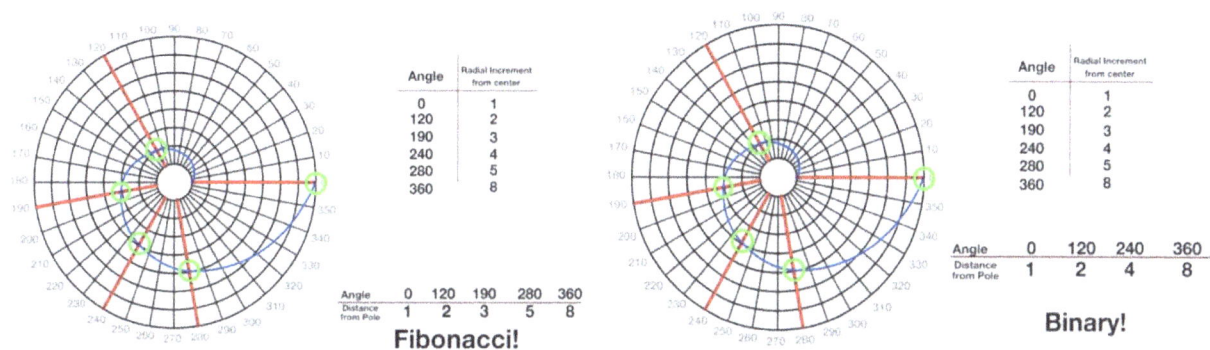

Angle	Radial Increment from center
0	1
120	2
190	3
240	4
280	5
360	8

Angle	0	120	190	280	360
Distance from Pole	1	2	3	5	8

Fibonacci!

Angle	Radial Increment from center
0	1
120	2
190	3
240	4
280	5
360	8

Angle	0	120	240	360
Distance from Pole	1	2	4	8

Binary!

Left: Fibonacci, and Right: Binary

179

But it also crosses at 2, 4, and 8, and that's binary sequence. When we look at the binary sequence, you will find out that if you draw lines from the outermost circles on the lines where the binary sequence was formed, you will get this equilateral triangle. And if you continue the spiral outward, it will continue to hit these exact same places and continue to form larger equilateral triangles.

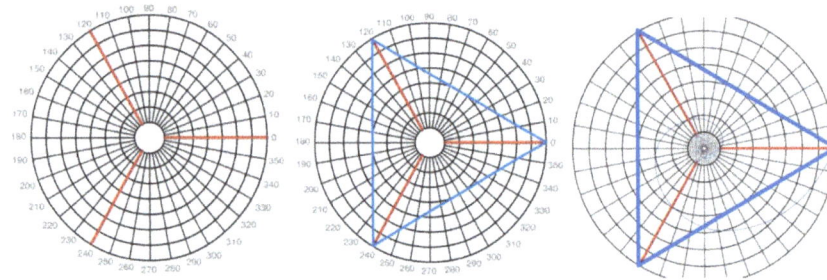

Image Source – Public Domain

The Sequences in Nature and Their Relationship to Music

There was a man named Keith Critchlow, who discovered something very important to understanding the geometry of music. First, he drew a straight line through an equilateral triangle and then he measured from the middle of the center line and drew a straight line up to the top edge and back down to the bottom corner then he did the same but passed through the center line of the top and back down again. He did it again on the other side as well by drawing this the funny little form. He discovered something of great importance.

He wrote that continuing in this way, each successive proportion will be the harmonic mean between the previous proportion and the total length and all these proportions will be musically significant 1/2 being the octave, 2/3 being the 5th, 4/5 being the major 3rd, 8/9 being the major toner step, and 16/17 being the halftone step. In other words, he discovered the geometries of music or at least one aspect of them.

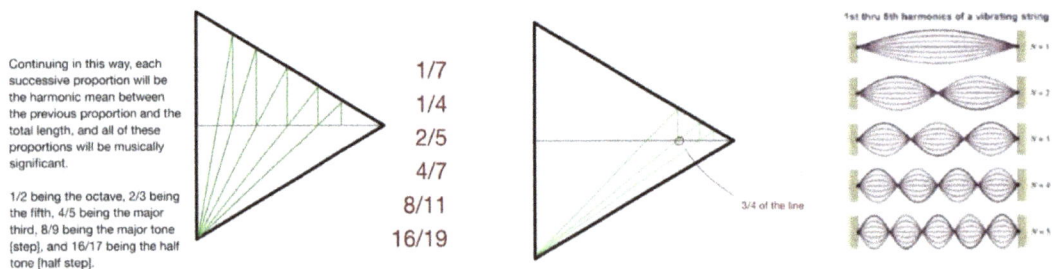

Image Source – Public Domain

Then he tried measuring it in a different way, starting at a different point in the center line. At ¾, he found the measurements for 1/7, ¼, 2/5, 4/7, 8/11, and 16/19. All these numbers are musically significant. This is very interesting and significant because it means that the harmonics of music

180

are related to the proportions of the central line moving through a tetrahedron. I'm sure you are still tracking that the central line is root of 3.

Back to the polar graph, we can see that this drawing has a much greater value suddenly. Not only that – it becomes even easier to make measurements. You can just draw a straight line through the polar graph, and it will give you the center line. This information has been taken light-years beyond what can be showed you.

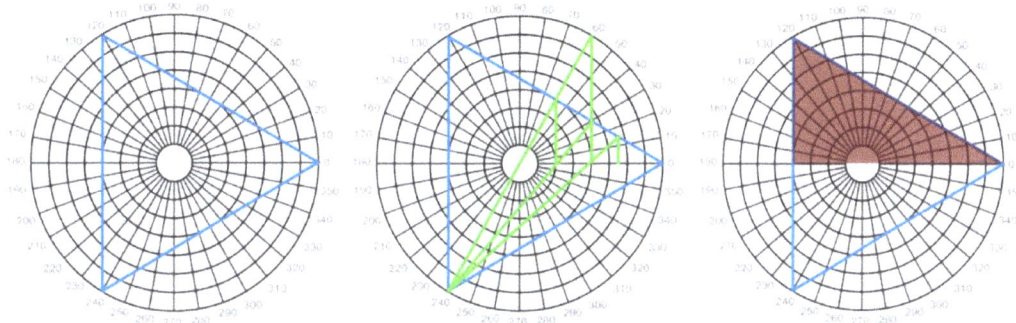

Image Source – Public Domain

Though a research team found out that you can draw these lines, not only from the center but from any nodal points inside the upper half of the triangle and you will come up with all known harmonics in existence. Basically, this means that anywhere the straight line and curved lines on the polar graph cross from 0 to 120 degrees and start making a pattern, you will come up with all known harmonic systems.

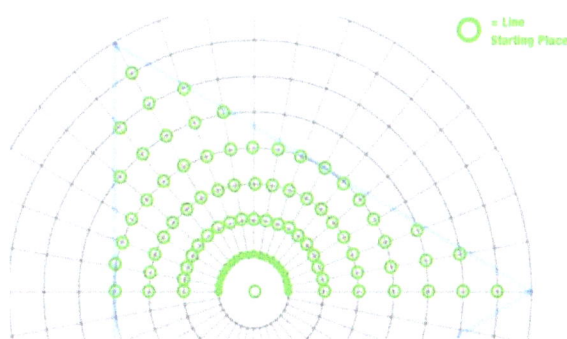

Image Source – Public Domain

Not only the Western keyboard but the Eastern and even many unknown systems that have never been used. Now that musicians understand the power of the square root of 3, let's see how far they can take this.

We talked about spirals in nature, and they often travel in twos. Usually, these are male and female, so, on the polar graph if you are going to copy nature, you must plot two spirals. When you do that, it gives you the image of a star tetrahedron inside of a sphere.

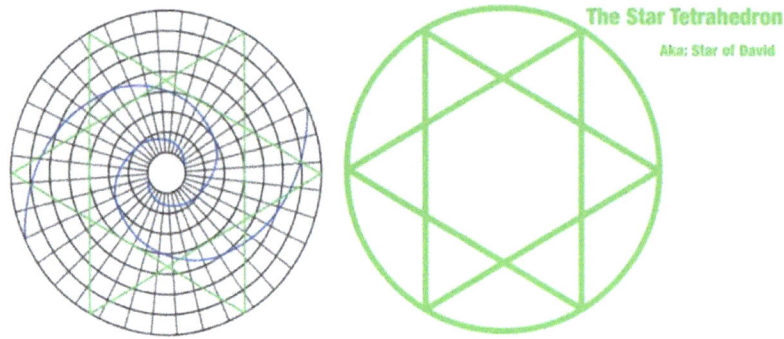

Image Source – Public Domain

This is commonly known as the Star of David. David was a King, Priest, Prophet, and a Psalmist in the Bible. This is the meaning of the symbol in the Flag of Israel. Nothing is without meaning.

Image Source – Public Domain

Christianity existed several centuries before Islam, yet we see the Star of David and other sacred geometrical symbols being used in Islam as Islamic symbols or patterns. These are all errors and a very dangerous deviation from the truth that sends them to hell every day and every second. Now you know the truth. Turn back to Jesus Christ and serve the true God of the heavens and the Earth. For the Muslims, when you come to Jesus, study the true teachings of the Bible, get rid of anything or idol Islam, and change the names of your different prayers but keep up with your consistency in prayer and maintain the prayer schedule and your fasting lifestyle. Fast intentionally but do not intentionally eat heavy to go through a fast. When you convert, you will learn. For the other religions, now you also know the truth so decide now before it's too late.

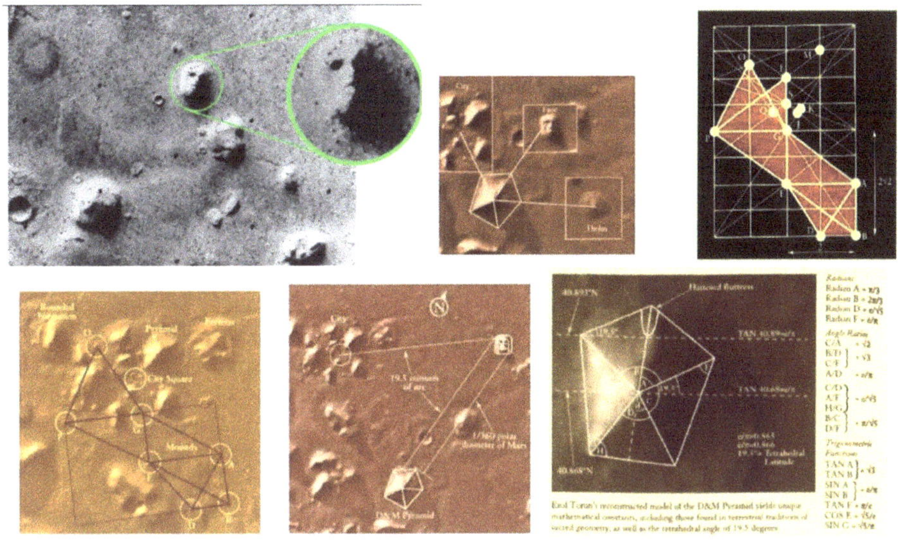

Image Source – Public Domain

A face was found on Mars and NASA tells the story that it's just a random formation on the surface of the planet but right next to the face are a few pyramids and other anthropomorphic structures. Richard Hoagland and his colleagues spent a long time researching and deciphering a message on the surface of the red planet (Mars). The message was a star tetrahedron inscribed in a sphere.

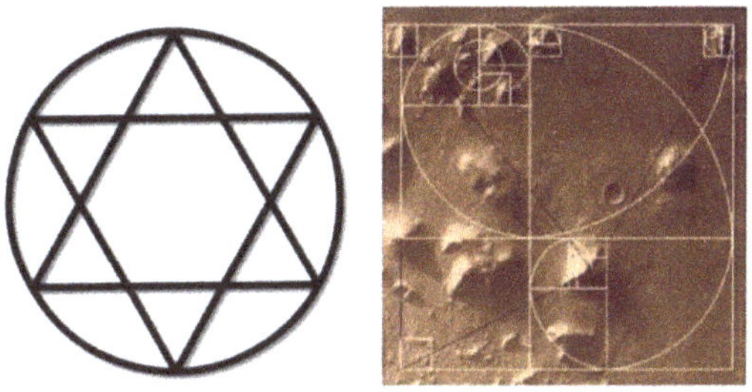

Image Source – Public Domain

Inside the star tetrahedron, another one fits perfectly. We can continue to put more and more star tetrahedron inside or outside of the other star tetrahedron – the same way the golden mean spiral can wrap around the polar graph infinitely big or small.

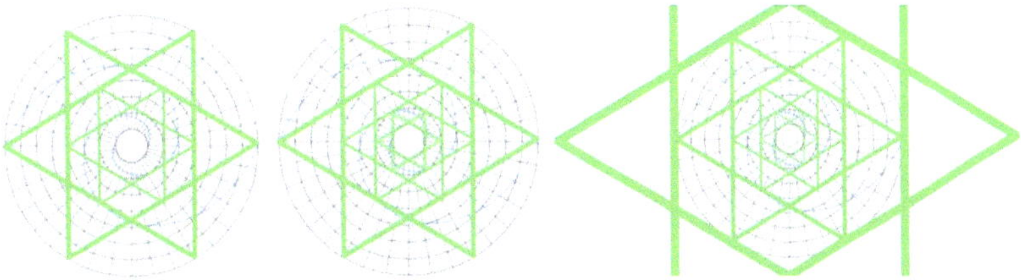

Image Source – Public Domain

The smaller tetrahedron also happens to fit perfectly around the sphere. If you put the same size sphere centered on the point of every single star tetrahedral point, it reveals the Fruit of Life.

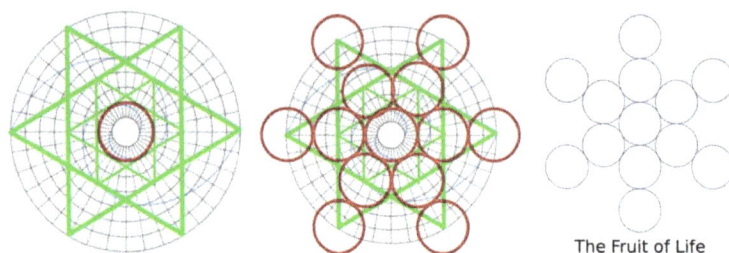

The Fruit of Life

Image Source – Public Domain

The Fruit of Life is the blueprint of the universe, containing the basis for the design of every atom, molecular structure, life form, and everything in existence. If you will pay attention, it looks just like the graphs that we derived from our earlier calculations. It also represents our spacetime curvature. This is the universe, this is life, and this is quantum mechanics. Now, you will also have a better understanding of why Jesus Christ was crucified on a cross.

The Tree of Life and the Fruit of Life

God created man because He wanted to create Himself. The fruit of life is the life of Jesus. The same fruit that Adam and Eve didn't get a chance to eat before they sinned by eating of the tree of the knowledge of good and evil in the Garden of Eden. The tree of life is the tree that bears the fruit of life.

Genesis 3:22-23

22 Then the LORD God said, "Behold, the man has become like one of Us, to know good and evil. And now, lest he put out his hand and take also of the tree of life, and eat, and live forever"— 23 therefore the LORD God sent him out of the garden of Eden to till the ground from which he was taken.

When you accept Jesus Christ and maintain a consistent relationship, communion, and fellowship with the Holy Spirit, He gives you encounters, and through the life of Christ, you eat of the fruit of life then you become a god like we were supposed to be in the Garden of Eden before the fall. God is the master strategist and cryptographer. Even you, a mere scientist and engineer, you think you know cryptography. The strategy for Jesus Christ was the cross – tree of life, which bears the fruit of life.

John 15:5

5 "I am the vine; you *are* the branches. He who abides in Me, and I in him, bears much fruit; for without Me you can do nothing.

God encoded the fruit of life in Jesus Christ so that the kingdom of darkness would not know. That's why the devil killed Jesus before he realized that Jesus is our fruit of life – salvation. That's the same reason why he had caused Adam and Eve to sin against God so we would never get to eat of it. But you can freely eat of the fruit if life now even without the true revelation of it. But when you have the revelation then it's even more powerful. The Bible makes us understand that Adam and Eve were drove out of the Garden of Eden and then God guarded the entrance with Cherubim and the way to the tree of life with a flaming sword.

Genesis 3:24

²⁴ So He drove out the man; and He placed cherubim at the east of the garden of Eden, and a flaming sword which turned every way, to guard the way to the tree of life.

That's very true. To Satan, we lost access, but God encrypted the tree of life in the ark of the covenant. That's why we have two cherubim spreading their wings over the mercy seat, which represents the east gate or entrance to the Garden of Eden. As we are crucified with Christ, He is the vine of the tree of life and we are the branches, like you read in the scripture above. And together with Him, we bear and eat the fruit of life, through which we live forever and ever.

Galatians 2:20

²⁰ I have been crucified with Christ; it is no longer I who live, but Christ lives in me; and the *life* which I now live in the flesh I live by faith in the Son of God, who loved me and gave Himself for me.

Now, mathematically and physically, we know that the fruit of life came from the Vesica Pisces or sacred geometry – the unity of the Father, Son, and the Holy Spirit. We are one with Christ, so we are the sons and daughters and the Holy Spirit lives in us, so God lives in us. That's why this is our foundational geometry from which every physical thing is built. These are the secrets and mysteries of the ark of the covenant, the crucifix of Christ, the coordinate system, the Vesica Pisces, and the tree and fruit of life.

These are also the secrets of the Sun, Earth, and Moon, and everything else created as part of the universe as programmed by God. With knowledge and understanding, we also identify this as the Venn diagram or Vesica Pisces or the Cartesian coordinate system. It's important to note that neither the Sun nor the Moon is God. This is where the error started, and humans started worshipping other creations in the universe as their God. This same error is why there is Astrology, Divination, Spirit Mediums, Magic, Wizardry, and Necromancy. Astrology for example, was taught as forbidden knowledge by the falling angels to men. Part of why they are fallen until this day.

Numerology as a religion or isolated practice is bad if the definition is associated with the paranormal, alongside astrology and like divinatory arts. But there is a way God uses numbers to communicate to His people and to achieve His purposes. A common and physical example is in mathematics. We study the patterns or sequences in numbers all the time to reveal their meaning and to build things. We measure and count in numbers. There are also specific spiritual ways that God uses numbers to communicate to His people. The spiritual knowledge and understanding of numbers are valid. That, when done according to the revelations of God, is not bad but those doing this without the worship and power of God are inspired by the devil. We see God giving instructions to His people in the scriptures using numbers repeatedly – from dimensions of tabernacles or temples, ark, lampstand etc. When he was recruiting His disciples, He looked for a specific number. God also specifically talks to His people in numbers to conceal His message if He knows that He has given them the grace to decode it. If this is not well understood and talked about, it may be perceived as heresy. This is a lecture for another day.

Finally, below is the union between the Sun, Earth, and Moon and the geometries that can be formed from their daily assignments as given to them by God. This is gravity – this is quantum mechanics, and this is how life and time are controlled in the universe.

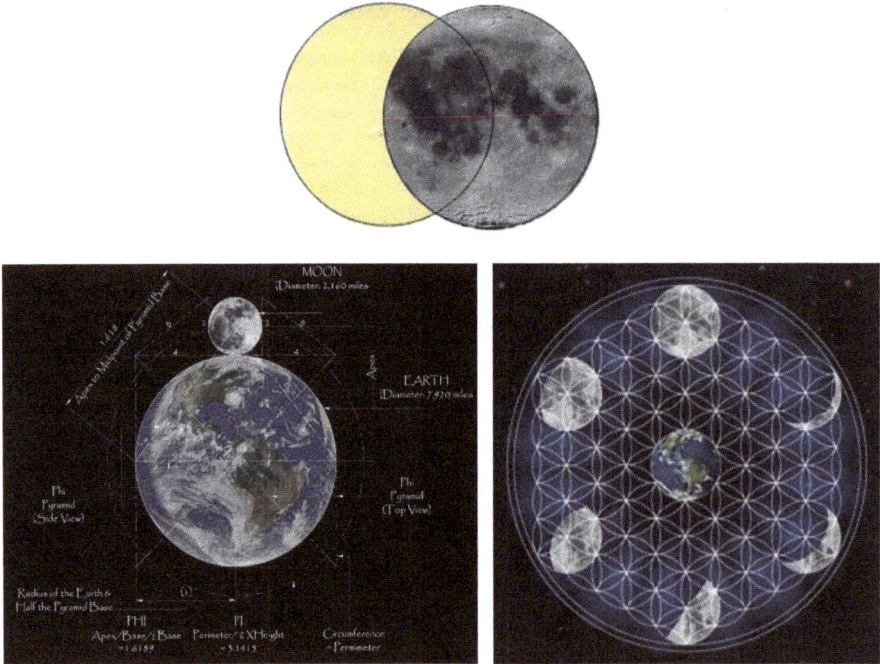

Image Source – Public Domain

By now you should know that God created everything with His power and underneath it is mathematics. God talks a lot in numbers but those who don't understand this or worship God and deal with Him in this manner are worshipping the devil. Every power in the heavens and the Earth belongs to God, including the powers that are used to do evil. The problem and the error are how you channel that power. Good examples are the several Egyptian so-called deities like Amun Ra etc. They did not understand the true source of these living creations, so they worshipped the Sun, Moon, air, water, etc., as their gods. These were like in the days of Pharoah and when God wanted to deliver the Israelites from it, He sent Moses to be the deliverer in whom He could perform His works.

When God appoints and anoints deliverers, then it is always a signal that humanity has gone wayward due to sin that result from many things, including false doctrines and teachings, and idolatry.

Ancient Egyptian gods

AMUN-RA: The Hidden One, MUT: The Mother Goddess, OSIRIS: The King of the Living, ANUBIS: The Divine Embalmer, RA: God of the Sun and Radiance, HORUS: God of Vengeance, THOTH: God of Knowledge and Wisdom, HATHOR: Goddess of Motherhood etc.

Is God Almighty the Hidden One? Yes, He is hidden inside of you. Is God Almighty the Mother Goddess? Yes. Is God Almighty the King of the Living? Yes. Is God Almighty the Divine Embalmer – anointer, preserver? Yes. Is God Almighty God of the Sun and everything else in the universe etc.? Yes. Is God Almighty God of Vengeance? Yes. Is God Almighty God of Knowledge and Wisdom? Yes, He created all things. Is God Almighty God of Motherhood etc.? Yes. Our God Almighty is a God of Everything, including you. This is the God of the heavens and the Earth. In other countries or traditions, God is referred to as Zeus etc., and worshipped the wrong way. It's all idolatry. All these are errors and sin. They all want to worship God but do not understand who this God truly is. I hereby present to you in this writing, the true God of the heavens and the Earth. You don't have any excuse now that the gospel did not reach you. Repent.

The ancient Egyptians experienced His manifestations but channeled the worship towards the wrong 'God' – things created by God. But Satan likes error because he creates it and he will manifest through covetousness, the powers of God Almighty as given to him at the time of his creation by God. And the gifts of God are without repentance. If God revokes His gifts, then He will cease to be God because He couldn't manifest Himself or His powers in any human being.

Romans 11:29

²⁹ For the gifts and the calling of God *are* irrevocable.

Satan still has all the powers that were given to him at the time of his creation, but he doesn't have any authority anymore because of the sacrifice of Jesus Christ, which took that authority back and has been given to man. Now, the Body of Christ (Church) has that authority in the name of Jesus. Satan is still a legal holder of his powers given to him by God and there's nothing even God can do about it. He can only with His sovereign power if He wills but again, that will make His Word full of lies and doubtful and unsure, or uncertain. Hence, He would cease to be God.

Romans 3:4

⁴ Certainly not! Indeed, let God be true but every man a liar. As it is written:

"That You may be justified in Your words,
And may overcome when You are judged."

Therefore, it is very dangerous for any human being; a man or woman of God to possess and demonstrate the Power of God even when that person lives in sin or iniquity (perpetual sin) because when the day of judgement comes, he or she will not make it to the promise land. Satan is using all the Power of God made available to him but God is Just so He will do nothing about it. The only punishment is the eternal judgment which awaits Satan and his followers.

Matthew 7:22-23

22 Many will say to Me in that day, 'Lord, Lord, have we not prophesied in Your name, cast out demons in Your name, and done many wonders in Your name?' 23 And then I will declare to them, 'I never knew you; depart from Me, you who practice lawlessness!'

Don't go about worshipping creations and numbers. Those are all tools and ways that God can use to talk to us if you know and understand. Many things shall be left for teaching and discussion in the future when the Body of Christ or the world truly matures in the things or mysteries of God. Again, some things, if or when discussed now, will be called heresy while they are not. The things of God are very deep and eternal – some are very easy to behold and some, very strange and fearful. When you worship God, He will give you access to the legal ways of using all His powers that have been made available to His sons through the sacrifice of Jesus Christ. Can you command the creations in the universe like the Sun, Moon, stars etc., to obey you or to carry out an assignment for you as quickened or commanded by the Spirit of God in you or at your own will? Yes, and they will obey if you know what to do or when they know whence you speak. Are you serving the one and only true God being talked about here? If not, now you know so repent very fast and come to Jesus because judgement is here. Do not wait or continue in your erroneous and sinful ways because you shall perish forever and ever.

This applies to you who worships Buddha, Krishna, the Islam Allah or God etc., including Atheists etc. It even applies to you who intentionally erroneously teach the Word of God such as the Watchtower, Mormon, Seventh Day Adventist etc. Judgement is here. The Hand of God is upon the Earth, and He shall truly be known as He is – the One and only Supreme God. If you don't repent, you shall see and experience His wrath mercilessly. Ignorance, false doctrines, and the truth obscured or bent in any way are very dangerous things when it comes to the destinies of humans because we are all eternal spirits. We never die. Your decision today will determine where you will spend eternity – whether in heaven or in hell.

The Gold Lampstand and Base 3

Exodus 25:31-40

31 "You shall also make a lampstand of pure gold; the lampstand shall be of hammered work. Its shaft, its branches, its bowls, its *ornamental* knobs, and flowers shall be *of one piece.* 32 And six branches shall come out of its sides: three branches of the lampstand out of one side, and three branches of the lampstand out of the other side. 33 Three bowls *shall be* made like almond *blossoms* on one branch, *with* an *ornamental* knob and a flower, and three bowls made

like almond *blossoms* on the other branch, *with* an *ornamental* knob and a flower—and so for the six branches that come out of the lampstand. [34] On the lampstand itself four bowls *shall be* made like almond *blossoms, each with* its *ornamental* knob and flower. [35] And *there shall be a* knob under the *first* two branches of the same, a knob under the *second* two branches of the same, and a knob under the *third* two branches of the same, according to the six branches that extend from the lampstand. [36] Their knobs and their branches *shall be of one piece;* all of it *shall be* one hammered piece of pure gold. [37] You shall make seven lamps for it, and they shall arrange its lamps so that they give light in front of it. [38] And its wick-trimmers and their trays *shall be* of pure gold. [39] It shall be made of a talent of pure gold, with all these utensils. [40] And see to it that you make *them* according to the pattern which was shown you on the mountain.

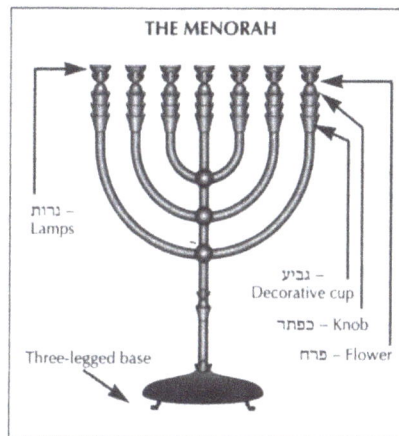

Image Source – Public Domain

A Quick Review of the Standard Model

Looking back at our calculations and graphs, we notice that all values are consistent – they just take different states as needed. All three numbers (−1, ±0, +1) are very important. The most important changing value is the ±1 at the ends of the linear equation. It is the differential value. But the ±0 is the translational or transformational value which gives the differential value the ability to become a multiplier and or take different forms. That is, an exponential growth or decay.

At the end of this reading, you will understand why the weak nuclear force is the only one among the three forces of nature that acts on all particles. It is the only force that neutrinos feel.

You will also understand the Higgs field, which is something like cosmic molasses, spreading across the universe and trapping matter particles as they travel through space and giving them a mass. This can also be represented by the $t < 0, t \geq 0$ interval. The state of matter changes over time. The principle of the mass of matter in a closed system is that mass will always be the same no matter what type of change happens to the matter. Whether it's a change in state, or dissolving, or a chemical reaction, or any combination of these, the amount of mass will not change.

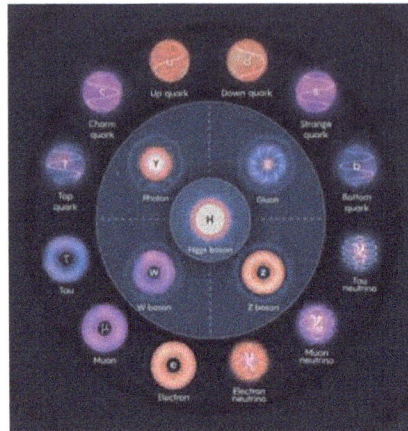

The standard model

Image Source – Public Domain

The twelve matter particles (twelve disciples of Christ) interacting with three forces (Father, Son, Holy Spirit) or the Godhead or God in three persons (blessed trinity), and a Higgs field (God or Elohim), is not an accident. Physicists have found all the subatomic particles in the universe. Any new discovery will only be a variant or behavior of the same particles.

The three fundamental (gravitational) force carrier particles

Image Source – Public Domain

There is an open-ended question about the standard model of whether the three fundamental forces are different, or whether they are a manifestation of a single all-encompassing force. **The answer is yes, they are a manifestation of a single all-encompassing force of gravity**.

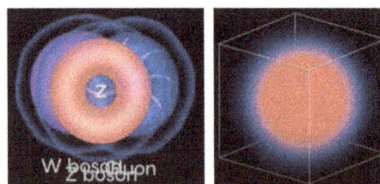

Unification of the three fundamental forces

Image Source – Public Domain

Continuing the Unified Field Theory explanation – this is an isolated or closed (loop) quantum system. The net external force acting on the system is zero – just like the human body. This is what Albert Einstein attempted to solve and called it the Unified Field Theory. In this writing, we unify the general theory of relativity with electromagnetism. In this solution, the three spatial dimensions are space, gravity, and matter as one body in a 3D universe, and the result is time. We also know that gravity is the only force in the universe with different manifestations.

Electromagnetism is a branch of physics involving the study of the electromagnetic force, a type of physical interaction that occurs between electrically charged particles. Electric charge can be positive or negative. Electric charge is a conserved property; the net charge of an isolated system – the amount of positive charge minus the amount of negative charge, cannot change.

The most important thing to note is that gravity is what makes electromagnetism and all the other forces possible. Gravity is both the fundamental and advanced force. You already know this now and you will continue to understand better as you read on. Quantum mechanics is both fundamental and advanced. Let's study the diagram below.

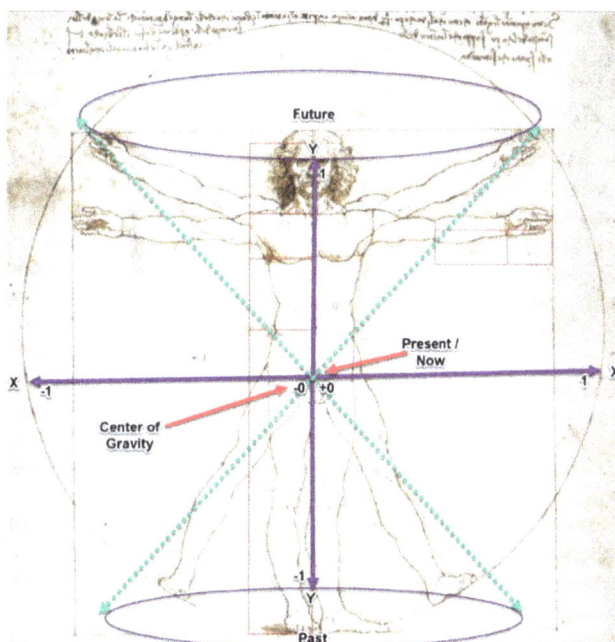

Leonardo da Vinci *Vitruvian Man* and Albert Einstein's General theory of Relativity spacetime cone or the hourglass or the image from the graph plotting from our previous calculations

Unifying modified general theory of relativity and quantum gravity

Unification Image Source – Revelation given to me by God

It is important to note that God is both male and female – those are two dimensions of Him but before He created the female, He was first a male, and He rules as a male. So, the foundation of human is first a male. Therefore, the Y chromosome is present in males, who have one X and one

Y chromosome, while females have two X chromosomes. These are the negative and positive values that are presented in the image above because that is how it works. God created man in His image so before everything can be or have meaning in the Earth, there must be man because man is the reason why the Earth exists. A man's chromosome decides what the gender of a baby would be. Without man, there is no time. And without time in this realm, there is no continuity.

Therefore, both a male and female can come out of a male. Man is the determinant or causal factor of time and able to do that only because God dwells in him. In our physical world and in mathematics, man is a scalar quantity derived from a matrix giving the volume scaling of the matrix or the Earth. In science, a male can be represented by -+ and a woman --. This physical definition of scalars, in classical theories, like Newtonian mechanics, means that rotations or reflections preserve scalars, while in relativistic theories, Lorentz transformations or spacetime translations preserve scalars.

Genesis 1:26-28

[26] Then God said, "Let Us make man in Our image, according to Our likeness; let them have dominion over the fish of the sea, over the birds of the air, and over the cattle, over all the Earth and over every creeping thing that creeps on the Earth." [27] So God created man in His *own* image; in the image of God, He created him; male and female He created them. [28] Then God blessed them, and God said to them, "Be fruitful and multiply; fill the Earth and subdue it; have dominion over the fish of the sea, over the birds of the air, and over every living thing that moves on the Earth."

God created a woman from a man because of time, which is a result of the fallen nature of man – when man sinned in the Garden of Eden.

Genesis 2

The Garden of Eden

2 Thus the heavens and the Earth, and all the host of them, were finished. [2] And on the seventh day God ended His work which He had done, and He rested on the seventh day from all His work which He had done. [3] Then God blessed the seventh day and sanctified it, because in it He rested from all His work which God had created and made.

[4] This *is* the history of the heavens and the Earth when they were created, in the day that the LORD God made the Earth and the heavens, [5] before any plant of the field was in the Earth and before any herb of the field had grown. For the LORD God had not caused it to rain on the Earth, and *there was* no man to till the ground; [6] but a mist went up from the Earth and watered the whole face of the ground.

[7] And the LORD God formed man *of* the dust of the ground and breathed into his nostrils the breath of life; and man became a living being.

Life in God's Garden

8 The LORD God planted a garden eastward in Eden, and there He put the man whom He had formed. **9** And out of the ground the LORD God made every tree grow that is pleasant to the sight and good for food. The tree of life *was* also in the midst of the garden, and the tree of the knowledge of good and evil.

10 Now a river went out of Eden to water the garden, and from there it parted and became four riverheads. **11** The name of the first *is* Pishon; it *is* the one which skirts the whole land of Havilah, where *there is* gold. **12** And the gold of that land *is* good. Bdellium and the onyx stone *are* there. **13** The name of the second river *is* Gihon; it *is* the one which goes around the whole land of Cush. **14** The name of the third river *is* Hiddekel; it *is* the one which goes toward the east of Assyria. The fourth river *is* the Euphrates.

15 Then the LORD God took the man and put him in the garden of Eden to tend and keep it. **16** And the LORD God commanded the man, saying, "Of every tree of the garden you may freely eat; **17** but of the tree of the knowledge of good and evil you shall not eat, for in the day that you eat of it you shall surely die."

18 And the LORD God said, "*It is* not good that man should be alone; I will make him a helper comparable to him." **19** Out of the ground the LORD God formed every beast of the field and every bird of the air and brought *them* to Adam to see what he would call them. And whatever Adam called each living creature, that *was* its name. **20** So Adam gave names to all cattle, to the birds of the air, and to every beast of the field. But for Adam there was not found a helper comparable to him.

21 And the LORD God caused a deep sleep to fall on Adam, and he slept; and He took one of his ribs and closed up the flesh in its place. **22** Then the rib which the LORD God had taken from man He made into a woman, and He brought her to the man.

23 And Adam said:

"This *is* now bone of my bones
And flesh of my flesh;
She shall be called Woman,
Because she was taken out of Man."

24 Therefore a man shall leave his father and mother and be joined to his wife, and they shall become one flesh.

25 And they were both naked, the man and his wife, and were not ashamed.

Genesis 3

The Temptation and Fall of Man

3 Now the serpent was more cunning than any beast of the field which the Lord God had made. And he said to the woman, "Has God indeed said, 'You shall not eat of every tree of the garden'?"

2 And the woman said to the serpent, "We may eat the fruit of the trees of the garden; **3** but of the fruit of the tree, which *is* in the midst of the garden, God has said, 'You shall not eat it, nor shall you touch it, lest you die.'"

4 Then the serpent said to the woman, "You will not surely die. **5** For God knows that in the day you eat of it your eyes will be opened, and you will be like God, knowing good and evil."

6 So when the woman saw that the tree *was* good for food, that it *was* pleasant to the eyes, and a tree desirable to make *one* wise, she took of its fruit and ate. She also gave to her husband with her, and he ate. **7** Then the eyes of both of them were opened, and they knew that they *were* naked; and they sewed fig leaves together and made themselves coverings.

8 And they heard the sound of the Lord God walking in the garden in the cool of the day, and Adam and his wife hid themselves from the presence of the Lord God among the trees of the garden.

9 Then the Lord God called to Adam and said to him, "Where *are* you?"

10 So he said, "I heard Your voice in the garden, and I was afraid because I was naked; and I hid myself."

11 And He said, "Who told you that you *were* naked? Have you eaten from the tree of which I commanded you that you should not eat?"

12 Then the man said, "The woman whom You gave *to be* with me, she gave me of the tree, and I ate."

13 And the Lord God said to the woman, "What *is* this you have done?"

The woman said, "The serpent deceived me, and I ate."

14 So the Lord God said to the serpent:

"Because you have done this,
You *are* cursed more than all cattle,
And more than every beast of the field;
On your belly you shall go,

And you shall eat dust
All the days of your life.
15 And I will put enmity
Between you and the woman,
And between your seed and her Seed;
He shall bruise your head,
And you shall bruise His heel."

16 To the woman He said:

"I will greatly multiply your sorrow and your conception;
In pain you shall bring forth children;
Your desire *shall be* for your husband,
And he shall rule over you."

17 Then to Adam He said, "Because you have heeded the voice of your wife, and have eaten from the tree of which I commanded you, saying, 'You shall not eat of it':

"Cursed *is* the ground for your sake;
In toil you shall eat *of* it
All the days of your life.
18 Both thorns and thistles it shall bring forth for you,
And you shall eat the herb of the field.
19 In the sweat of your face you shall eat bread
Till you return to the ground,
For out of it you were taken;
For dust you *are,*
And to dust you shall return."

20 And Adam called his wife's name Eve, because she was the mother of all living.

21 Also for Adam and his wife the Lord God made tunics of skin and clothed them.

22 Then the Lord God said, "Behold, the man has become like one of Us, to know good and evil. And now, lest he put out his hand and take also of the tree of life, and eat, and live forever"— **23** therefore the Lord God sent him out of the garden of Eden to till the ground from which he was taken. **24** So He drove out the man; and He placed cherubim at the east of the garden of Eden, and a flaming sword which turned every way, to guard the way to the tree of life.

Revelation 12

The Woman, the Child, and the Dragon

12 Now a great sign appeared in heaven: a woman clothed with the Sun, with the Moon under her feet, and on her head a garland of twelve stars. **2** Then being with child, she cried out in labor and in pain to give birth.

3 And another sign appeared in heaven: behold, a great, fiery red dragon having seven heads and ten horns, and seven diadems on his heads. **4** His tail drew a third of the stars of heaven and threw them to the Earth. And the dragon stood before the woman who was ready to give birth, to devour her Child as soon as it was born. **5** She bore a male Child who was to rule all nations with a rod of iron. And her Child was caught up to God and His throne. **6** Then the woman fled into the wilderness, where she has a place prepared by God, that they should feed her there one thousand two hundred and sixty days.

Satan Thrown Out of Heaven

7 And war broke out in heaven: Michael and his angels fought with the dragon; and the dragon and his angels fought, **8** but they did not prevail, nor was a place found for them in heaven any longer. **9** So the great dragon was cast out, that serpent of old, called the Devil and Satan, who deceives the whole world; he was cast to the Earth, and his angels were cast out with him.

10 Then I heard a loud voice saying in heaven, "Now salvation, and strength, and the kingdom of our God, and the power of His Christ have come, for the accuser of our brethren, who accused them before our God day and night, has been cast down. **11** And they overcame him by the blood of the Lamb and by the word of their testimony, and they did not love their lives to the death. **12** Therefore rejoice, O heavens, and you who dwell in them! Woe to the inhabitants of the Earth and the sea! For the devil has come down to you, having great wrath, because he knows that he has a short time."

The Woman Persecuted

13 Now when the dragon saw that he had been cast to the Earth, he persecuted the woman who gave birth to the male *Child.* **14** But the woman was given two wings of a great eagle, that she might fly into the wilderness to her place, where she is nourished for a time and times and half a time, from the presence of the serpent. **15** So the serpent spewed water out of his mouth like a flood after the woman, that he might cause her to be carried away by the flood. **16** But the Earth helped the woman, and the Earth opened its mouth and swallowed up the flood which the dragon had spewed out of his mouth. **17** And the dragon was enraged with the woman, and he went to make war with the rest of her offspring, who keep the commandments of God and have the testimony of Jesus Christ.

Note in verse 16 of the above scriptures that the Earth is also a living thing like you and me. Therefore, it opened its mouth and swallowed up the flood. This is not the first time in scriptures that the Earth opened its mouth to swallow something. I'm pointing this out again so that you will know truly that nothing is a non-living thing in the universe.

God knew before the foundations of the Earth that everything happening now would happen and that is why He created a woman to be part of a man for continuity within time and for the kingdom of God to prevail against Satan and his devils.

In the new heaven and the new Earth, there shall be no male or female – just like the angels.

Matthew 22:23-33

The Sadducees: What About the Resurrection?

23 The same day the Sadducees, who say there is no resurrection, came to Him and asked Him, **24** saying: "Teacher, Moses said that if a man dies, having no children, his brother shall marry his wife and raise up offspring for his brother. **25** Now there were with us seven brothers. The first died after he had married, and having no offspring, left his wife to his brother. **26** Likewise the second also, and the third, even to the seventh. **27** Last of all the woman died also. **28** Therefore, in the resurrection, whose wife of the seven will she be? For they all had her."

29 Jesus answered and said to them, "You are mistaken, not knowing the Scriptures nor the power of God. **30** For in the resurrection they neither marry nor are given in marriage but are like angels of God in heaven. **31** But concerning the resurrection of the dead, have you not read what was spoken to you by God, saying, **32** 'I am the God of Abraham, the God of Isaac, and the God of Jacob'? God is not the God of the dead, but of the living." **33** And when the multitudes heard *this,* they were astonished at His teaching.

Now that you have a foundational understanding of the creation of man and the universe, lets continue with the unification of the theory of relativity and quantum mechanics.

Unifying General Theory of Relativity and Quantum Mechanics

After a century of work by the greatest minds in all of physics, the union of these two theories still elude humanity. The first few decades of the 20th century were a time of miracles for physics. First, Einstein's relativity utterly changed the way humanity think about space, time, motion, and gravity. Then the quantum revolution of the '20s and '30s overturned all of humanity intuitions about the subatomic world. Together, general relativity and quantum mechanics have allowed humanity to explain nearly every fundamental phenomenon observed. And they have predicted many unexpected phenomena that have since been verified. And yet to the science world, these two theories contradict each other in fundamental ways.

In the century since that "golden era of physics", scientists have been trying to reconcile the two without success. In this writing, we present to you the theory of quantum gravity. That is, the theory of every known physical thing. Below are the current positions of both theories in terms of a union because they don't fit together. But they are perfectly unified in this writing.

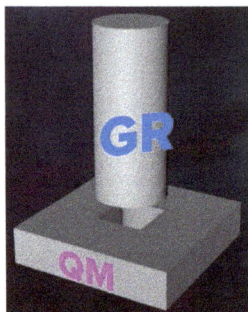

Image Source – Public Domain

You will also understand black holes, dark matter, and dark energy. Currently, scientists think that there is something called black hole information paradox – the black holes of pure general relativity swallow information in a way that can remove it completely from the universe, especially when the black holes evaporate via Hawking radiation. Well, this is not entirely accurate. Others think that's a big conflict with the quantum theory, which tells us that information should never be destroyed. If that thought is to support how the universe will end someday then it's on the right track to being accurate. Else, it's not quite accurate. If any object in space gets into the Earth's event horizon and that object falls on the Earth, would we say from the Moon or from any other planet that, that object evaporated? The object is still in the universe if you know and understand where it went and how to find it – so, the information never gets destroyed. The Earth is in a black hole so I will let you think about the rest to answer yourself. What I say is that just because you don't know it to understand it, or you don't see it or refuse to see it doesn't mean that it's not there. This is the same case with those who have chosen not to believe in the existence of God. This is what makes it very dangerous because you think that everything is mere science. The information that science has been looking for are always there and available to the people of God. Without God, mere science will always find itself in this uncertainty predicament. What should take a day to do would take you centuries.

Following the work of Hawking, Jacob Bekeinstein, Hooft and others, it has become clear that information swallowed by black holes can be radiated back out into the universe via their Hawking radiation. In a sense, both the source and the solution to the information paradox came from the discovery of Hawking radiation. The Hawking radiation – an attempt to unify the general relativity and quantum field theory was approximate and incomplete. The science world calls it a brilliant hack. Scientists think that it's very possible to shoehorn the curved geometry of general relativity into the way quantum field theory deals with space and time. But that approach completely fails when you have strong gravitational effects on the small scales of space and time, like the central singularity of the black hole or at the instant of the Big Bang. For that, you need a true quantum theory of gravity. And you will find that in this writing.

Hawking focused on how quantum mechanics affected the vicinity of a black hole but that not being the entire story, quantum mechanics doesn't include the force of gravity, and a complete description of what's going on near event horizons will have to include quantum gravity, or a description of how strong gravity acts at teeny tiny scales. My hope and belief are that after going through the calculations and explanations in this writing, you will know and understand that quantum mechanics include the force of gravity and that has always been the driving force – you just must know and understand well how quantum mechanics works then it will all make sense. Physicists will understand the full theory of quantum gravity and, how very powerful it is.

I read in a recent article how Xavier Calmet, a professor of physics at the University of Sussex in England explained that "if you consider black holes within only general relativity, one can show that they have a singularity in their centers where the laws of physics as we know them must breakdown. It is hoped that when quantum field theory is incorporated into general relativity, we might be able to find a new description of black holes." This is very accurate, and I hope that this writing will help him and colleagues to understand these areas of quantum mechanics much better, including the ± pressure exerted by the black hole that is found in their studies.

Their studies model weak quantum gravity and neglects strong gravity. If they use the model in this writing, it will help them explain black holes. This is because their result extends the idea of black holes as thermodynamic entities that have not just temperature and entropy, but also pressure. This is accurate – I had pointed out earlier how what makes quantum what it is are the scalar quantities. Again, this confirms how the Big Bang started with thermodynamics.

Researchers at NASA think that black holes "eat" stars i.e., cause a tidal disruption flare. A black hole is an area of such immense gravity that nothing – not even light – can escape from it. In other words, it is a place in space where gravity pulls so much that even light cannot get out. The gravity is so strong because matter has been squeezed into a tiny space.

NASA/Caltech

Image Source – Public Domain

"Whenever a star comes too close to a black hole, it is ripped apart into a streak of gases by gravitational forces, causing a tidal disruption event. During this process, high amount of energy is released" – scientists at the University of Arizona Steward Observatory revealed in this recent rendition.

I won't get into all the details but another hint to biologists is, think about the science surrounding the human sperm (activated motility and hyperactivated motility) and the making of babies – investigate flagellum. Study the two diagrams that are merged to form the unified field theory for hints. You will discover and learn very new important things.

What is a Tensor?

The result for quantum is a scalar value and quantum is derived from a tensor. A tensor is a mathematical representation of a scalar (tensor of rank 0), a vector (rank 1), a dyad (rank 2), a triad (rank 3) etc.

The rank (or order) of a tensor is defined by the number of directions (and hence the dimensionality of the array) required to describe it. For example, properties that require one direction (first rank) can be fully described by a 3×1 column vector, and properties that require two directions (second rank tensors), can be described by 9 numbers, as a 3×3 matrix. As such, in general an nth rank tensor can be described by 3^n coefficients.

Scalar has magnitude, and no direction. Number of components is 1 (3^0). Vector has magnitude and direction. Number of components is 3 (3^1). Dyad has magnitude in each direction x, y, and z, and the direction is expressed as the sum of three components, i.e., 3x3. Number of components is 9 (3^2). And a triad has magnitude and 3x3x3 dimensions. Number of components 27 (3^3).

The need for second rank tensors (dyad) comes when we need to consider more than one direction to describe one of these physical properties. A good example of this is if we need to describe electrical conductivity. Below are some examples to help visualize the differences.

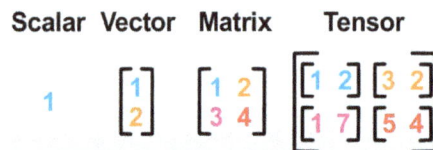

Image Source – Public Domain

An example is the Cauchy stress tensor. In continuum mechanics, the Cauchy stress tensor σ, true stress tensor, or simply called the stress tensor is a second order tensor named after Augustin-Louis Cauchy. The tensor consists of nine components σ_{ij} that completely define the state of stress at a point inside a material in the deformed state, placement, or configuration. The tensor relates a unit-length direction vector **n** to the traction vector $T^{(n)}$ across an imaginary surface perpendicular to **n**:

$$\mathbf{T^{(n)}} = \mathbf{n} \cdot \boldsymbol{\sigma} \quad \text{or} \quad T_j^{(n)} = \sigma_{ij} n_i,$$

or

$$\begin{bmatrix} T_1^{(n)} & T_2^{(n)} & T_3^{(n)} \end{bmatrix} = \begin{bmatrix} n_1 & n_2 & n_3 \end{bmatrix} \cdot \begin{bmatrix} \sigma_{11} & \sigma_{12} & \sigma_{13} \\ \sigma_{21} & \sigma_{22} & \sigma_{23} \\ \sigma_{31} & \sigma_{32} & \sigma_{33} \end{bmatrix}.$$

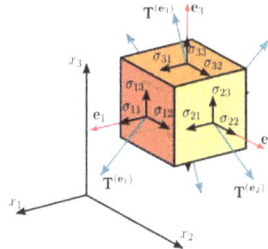

Image Source – Public Domain

The SI units of both stress tensor and traction vector are N/m^2, corresponding to the stress scalar. The unit vector is dimensionless. In dimensional analysis, a dimensionless quantity is a quantity to which no physical dimension is assigned, also known as a bare, pure, or scalar quantity or a quantity of dimension one, with a corresponding unit of measurement in the SI of the unit one (or 1), which is not explicitly shown.

In this solution, we will use the Ricci Tensor. In differential geometry, the Ricci curvature tensor, named after Gregorio Ricci-Curbastro, is a geometric object which is determined by a choice of Riemannian or pseudo-Riemannian metric on a manifold. It can be considered, broadly, as a measure of the degree to which the geometry of a given metric tensor differs locally from that of ordinary Euclidean space or pseudo-Euclidean space.

In differential geometry, a pseudo-Riemannian manifold, also called a semi-Riemannian manifold, is a differentiable manifold with a metric tensor that is everywhere nondegenerate. This is a generalization of a Riemannian manifold in which the requirement of positive definiteness is relaxed.

In mathematics, a definite quadratic form is a quadratic form over some real vector space V that has the same sign (always positive or always negative) for every nonzero vector of V. According to that sign, the quadratic form is called positive-definite or negative-definite. The zero vector of V is indefinite and can take on both positive and negative values.

For example, the quadratic form $p(x, y) = x^2 + y^2$ is positive definite.

201

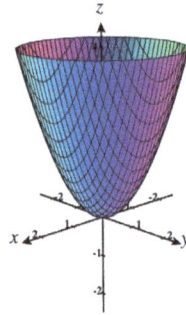

Paraboloid

Image Source – Public Domain

For example, the quadratic form $p(x, y) = -x^2 - y^2$ is negative definite.

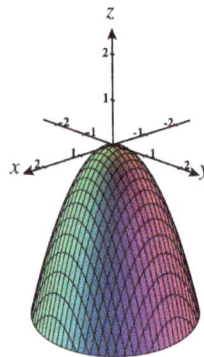

Paraboloid

Image Source – Public Domain

For example, the quadratic form $p(x, y) = x^2 - y^2$ is indefinite.

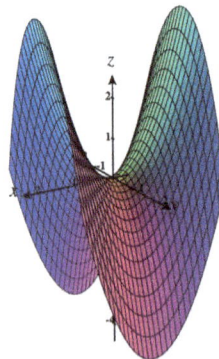

Hyperbolic Paraboloid

Image Source – Public Domain

All these three combined is our spacetime curvature. Therefore, the Ricci tensor is ideal.

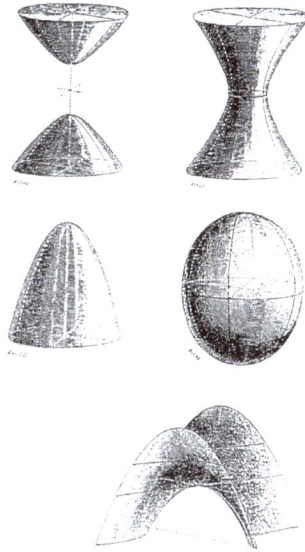

Quadrics: hyperboloids, paraboloid, ellipsoid, hyperbolic paraboloid

Image Source – Public Domain

You can see the different quadrics in parts or pieces above. A quadric is a curve or surface whose equation (in Cartesian coordinates) is of the second degree. Some examples of second rank tensors include electric susceptibility, thermal conductivity, stress and strain. They typically relate a vector to another vector, or another second rank tensor to a scalar. For our universe, we will be looking at what seems like this – a hyperboloid. This is our spacetime curvature.

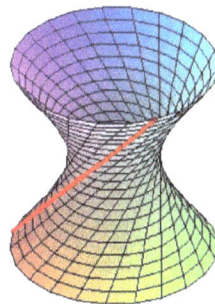

Hyperboloid

Image Source – Public Domain

We can see the same type of curvature and supernatural coding in our DNA sequencing. That's an entirely whole subject so research that when you can. You will know that truly, we are fearfully and wonderfully made.

Psalm 139:14

[14] I will praise You, for I am fearfully *and* wonderfully made;
Marvelous are Your works,
And *that* my soul knows very well.

The Ricci tensor is defined by

$$R_{\mu\kappa} \equiv R^{\lambda}{}_{\mu\lambda\kappa},$$

where $R^{\lambda}{}_{\mu\lambda\kappa}$ is the Riemann tensor. Instead of the four dimensions used in general relativity by Einstein, we will use three dimensions (space or vacuum, gravity, matter). Our result will be time. In three dimensions, we will make use of the symmetry relations,

$$R_{\mu vw} = R_{\mu wv} = R_{v\mu w}$$

$$\mu = (-1, \pm0, +1)$$

$$v = (-1, \pm0, +1)$$

$$w = (-1, \pm0, +1)$$

$$-1, \pm0, +1 = -1, +1, \pm0, = \pm0, -1, +1$$

Therefore, the equation can be defined as,

$$R_{\mu vw} + R_{\mu wv} + R_{v\mu w} = 0$$

Einstein got close enough but missed it because to fully understand science and the laws of the cosmos together, being a scientist or physicist alone isn't enough. You need to have a relationship with God to understand spiritual things and by His grace, He will teach you, His secrets. Then your true dual nature as both a spiritual and physical being will manifest. Below is the theory that Einstein published on 30th March 1953. This was his attempt at the Unified Field Theory.

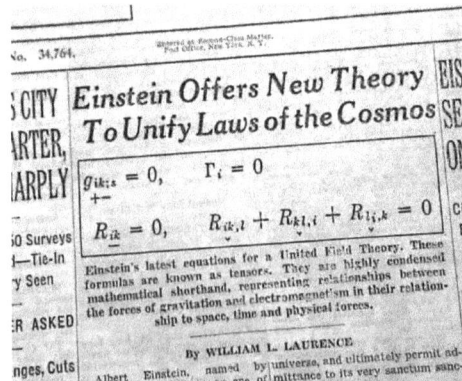

Image Source – Public Domain

Again, below is a recap of what God revealed to me as the unified field theory, which has already been presented and proposed in this writing.

$$R_{\mu v w} + R_{\mu w v} + R_{v \mu w} = 0$$

$$|\Psi| = \alpha|-1\rangle + \beta|\pm 0\rangle + \gamma|1\rangle$$

$$|\alpha|^2 + |\beta|^2 + |\gamma|^2 = 0$$

The quantum entanglement is derived from the below.

$$\frac{1}{\sqrt{3}}(-1-1-1\rangle + |\pm 0 \pm 0 \pm 0\rangle + |+1+1+1\rangle)$$

Use the vector representation of three-qutrits with the formula below to derive the magnetic flux needed for entanglement.

$$|abc\rangle = |a\rangle \otimes |b\rangle \otimes |c\rangle$$

The first three rounds (phase shifts) of the God (modification of Bell states) state operations will look like this.

$$|\Phi^-\rangle = \frac{1}{\sqrt{3}}(|-1\rangle_A \otimes |-1\rangle_B \otimes |-1\rangle_C - |-1\rangle_A \otimes |\pm 0\rangle_B \otimes |\pm 0\rangle_C - |-1\rangle_A \otimes |1\rangle_B \otimes |1\rangle_C\ ) \ (1)$$

$$|\Phi^\pm\rangle = \frac{1}{\sqrt{3}}(|-1\rangle_A \otimes |-1\rangle_B \otimes |-1\rangle_C \pm |-1\rangle_A \otimes |\pm 0\rangle_B \otimes |\pm 0\rangle_C \pm |-1\rangle_A \otimes |1\rangle_B \otimes |1\rangle_C\ ) \ (2)$$

$$|\Phi^+\rangle = \frac{1}{\sqrt{3}}(|-1\rangle_A \otimes |-1\rangle_B \otimes |-1\rangle_C + |-1\rangle_A \otimes |\pm 0\rangle_B \otimes |\pm 0\rangle_C + |-1\rangle_A \otimes |1\rangle_B \otimes |1\rangle_C\ ) \ (3)$$

The entanglement operations complete after 9 states or phase shifts.

Use the God gate (modification to Hadamard gate) to perform gate operations.

$$G = \frac{|-1\rangle - |\pm 0\rangle - |+1\rangle}{\sqrt{3}}\langle -1| + \frac{|-1\rangle \pm |\pm 0\rangle \pm |+1\rangle}{\sqrt{3}}\langle \pm 0| + \frac{|-1\rangle + |\pm 0\rangle + |+1\rangle}{\sqrt{3}}\langle +1|$$

The God transform G_m is a 3^m x 3^m matrix.

$$V_{\text{-1-1-1}} \qquad V_{\text{-1}\pm0\pm0} \qquad V_{\text{-1+1+1}}$$

$$V_{\pm\text{0-1-1}} \qquad V_{\pm\text{0}\pm0\pm0} \qquad V_{\pm\text{0+1+1}}$$

$$V_{\text{+1-1-1}} \qquad V_{\text{+1}\pm0\pm0} \qquad V_{\text{+1+1+1}}$$

The God gate operations will look like this upon completion.

$$G((|-1\rangle) = \frac{1}{\sqrt{3}}(|-1\rangle - \frac{1}{\sqrt{3}}|\pm0\rangle - \frac{1}{\sqrt{3}}|1\rangle) =: |-\rangle$$

$$G((|\pm0\rangle) = \frac{1}{\sqrt{3}}(|-1\rangle \pm \frac{1}{\sqrt{3}}|\pm0\rangle \pm \frac{1}{\sqrt{3}}|1\rangle) =: |\pm\rangle$$

$$G((|1\rangle) = \frac{1}{\sqrt{3}}(|-1\rangle + \frac{1}{\sqrt{3}}|\pm0\rangle + \frac{1}{\sqrt{3}}|1\rangle) =: |+\rangle$$

1.

$$G\left(\frac{1}{\sqrt{3}}|-1\rangle - \frac{1}{\sqrt{3}}|\pm0\rangle - \frac{1}{\sqrt{3}}|1\rangle\right)$$
$$= \frac{1}{3}(|-1\rangle - |\pm0\rangle - |1\rangle) - \frac{1}{3}(|-1\rangle \pm |\pm0\rangle \pm |1\rangle) - \frac{1}{3}(|-1\rangle + |\pm0\rangle + |1\rangle)$$

$$= 0 - \frac{2e|k||t|}{3} = -\frac{2e|k||t|}{3}$$

2.

$$G\left(\frac{1}{\sqrt{3}}|-1\rangle \pm \frac{1}{\sqrt{3}}|\pm0\rangle \pm \frac{1}{\sqrt{3}}|1\rangle\right)$$
$$= \frac{1}{3}(|-1\rangle - |\pm0\rangle - |1\rangle) \pm \frac{1}{3}(|-1\rangle \pm |\pm0\rangle \pm |1\rangle) \pm \frac{1}{3}(|-1\rangle + |\pm0\rangle + |1\rangle)$$

$$= 0 \pm \frac{2e|k||t|}{3} = 0$$

$$= 0 - \frac{2e|k||t|}{3} = -\frac{2e|k||t|}{3}$$

$$= 0 + \frac{2e|k||t|}{3} = \frac{2e|k||t|}{3}$$

$$= -\frac{2e|k||t|}{3} + \frac{2e|k||t|}{3} = 0$$

$$= t < 0, t \geq 0$$

3.

$$G\left(\frac{1}{\sqrt{3}}|-1\rangle + \frac{1}{\sqrt{3}}|\pm 0\rangle + \frac{1}{\sqrt{3}}|1\rangle\right)$$

$$= \frac{1}{3}(|-1\rangle - |\pm 0\rangle - |1\rangle) + \frac{1}{3}(|-1\rangle \pm |\pm 0\rangle \pm |1\rangle) + \frac{1}{3}(|-1\rangle + |\pm 0\rangle + |1\rangle)$$

$$= 0 + \frac{2e|k||t|}{3} = \frac{2e|k||t|}{3}$$

Don't let the conciseness and beauty of the unified field theory equation confuse you. It is not supposed to look scary, yet it is very deep and doesn't require physical intellect to know and understand. It is God that gives to man by grace and mercy. Don't be too physically intellectual. Depend on God. Therefore, the Word of God says,

Matthew 18:2-4

[2] Then Jesus called a little child to Him, set him in the midst of them, [3] and said, "Assuredly, I say to you, unless you are converted and become as little children, you will by no means enter the kingdom of heaven. [4] Therefore whoever humbles himself as this little child is the greatest in the kingdom of heaven.

Matthew 19:14

[14] But Jesus said, "Let the little children come to Me, and do not forbid them; for of such is the kingdom of heaven."

Ephesians 5:1

Walk in Love

5 Therefore be imitators of God as dear children. [2] And walk in love, as Christ also has loved us and given Himself for us, an offering, and a sacrifice to God for a sweet-smelling aroma.

To better understand the entanglement states, consider the unified field theory image from earlier as a depiction of time – well, it is time. This means that it will move in a clockwise direction but, it has a reversal ability. This happens when our clocks or time seems like it has reset. The simple linear calculation of $|-1\rangle$ and $|\pm 0\rangle$ and $|+1\rangle$ will yield a result of 0. Now, the unified images independently represent time if you know and understand. Dependently, they still represent time.

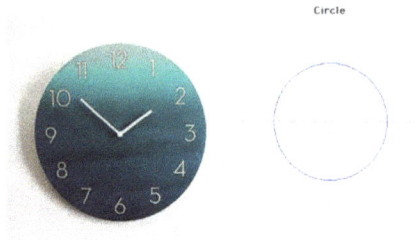

Image Source – Public Domain

The above images both represent time. When we can get the unified field theory result of 0, it means that no matter what direction you will go, you can still arrive back at your starting point, whether you know it or not. If you take the clock for example, no matter what direction you go (clockwise or anticlockwise), you will meet or pass through the same numbers in a reverse order. This explains the spacetime illustration from earlier that God gave to me. This is how time operates.

When it's midnight, the clock reads 00:00. If we have the number one or 1, it represents "something" in every language on the Earth. If we have the number zero or 0, it represents both "nothing" and "something" in every language on the Earth because it starts, resets, and amplifies. It makes sense to have something as the opposite of nothing. Therefore, in our daily languages, we have antonyms and synonyms. There is an inverse to any state. When you are traveling, no matter how far the journey is, you eventually arrive at a destination. When you begin counting, you have the most minimum value that you start counting from. We always tend to ignore the number zero, but it is the most significant number because it not only amplifies any number, but it also starts or resets every numbering system because it is our beginning and our end. How would we start anything or reset if zero didn't exist? We see this everywhere, and even in our current binary computer systems. We will see it even bigger in the trinary quantum systems.

Assuming you want to build a house, if you don't prepare the land, how would you build what you want to build? Clearing and preparing the land is like resetting the land to neutral to make it ready for suitable use. Think about it. Journeying in time in an airplane, we start at neutral, then start moving, then increase speed until we lift and maintain momentum, then finally, we arrive by reversing the starting process. If you don't take any measurements of any of these four states, the entire process of travel can be seen as once and we can just say, we traveled for an hour. But if you want to know how long it took from taxing, through landing at the destination, then the whole process breaks down. The underlying mechanics for our existence and daily lives is quantum. I can give several examples, but these are enough for now.

Why do I use these illustrations and explanations? Let's look at the two golden rules of quantum mechanics.

The first rule is superposition – it states that a quantum object can be in a superposition of multiple states at once. The whole house or the footing (center of gravity) is in a superposition of the foundation, the footing (itself), and rest of the house, including the roofing, all at once.

The second rule is measurement – it states that rule number one works if you don't look! The act of measuring the superposition will collapse it and change the state. From the previous rule, all the different parts of the house are entangled. If you choose to measure just the foundation, the entire house breaks down into their separate parts. But if you don't measure any part of the house then what you have is a house and all the different parts that make a house are still in the house.

I use this basic illustration because again, there is non-locality and entanglement in quantum mechanics. In all the current theories that scientists have tried to solve, they use two rules as basis. This will help you to better understand it. I am a universe, and you can call me a man and address me as a man but when I go to the hospital and a nurse chooses to take any kind of measurement on my body, my body breaks down. For example, I then become an eye (vision 20/20), a temperature (37 degrees Celsius), a weight (150 lbs.) etc. Or even better, my body breaks down into the different parts i.e., a head, left arm, right arm etc. This is nature – this is quantum mechanics.

Regarding the first rule, when we consider A and B as particles for instance, a quantum state can make definite only half the information needed to completely describe them. But in this case that half could describe relationships between the two particles that are definite, without either of them individually having any definite properties.

The second and the contrary is that pick any property and measure it on both A and B. Then the outcome on A will always be the opposite of the outcome on B. But when considered individually all the outcomes are random. Again, when you choose to measure a property like one of my legs, then the outcome on the left leg will always be the opposite of the right leg and vice versa. When you consider them individually, left will always be left and right will always be right regardless of body type, race, ethnicity, location on the Earth etc. It's simpler than you thought.

Both conditions are met in the calculations above and the image illustrations. It doesn't matter how far a point is in or on the circle's line of circumference – if it is part of the circle, the status or point of the particle can be known no matter which direction and distance you go or whichever point you take the measurement from because it is enclosed or part of the circle or system if it is not outside the circle or system. Nothing gets lost inside the coordinate system. You can even locate things outside the coordinate system. This is what physicists call Loop Quantum Gravity – which works by the law of conservation of charge or energy.

In string theory, a type of background independence emerges in an abstract space of moving strings and with that comes a gravitational field. But for that to work, first you need those strings to exist – and the science world don't know if they do. Loop quantum gravity tries to quantize general relativity with no strings attached, while preserving the background independence already inherent to general relativity.

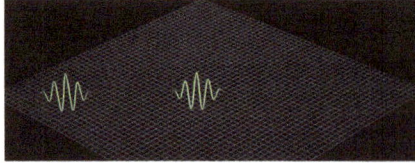

Image Source – Public Domain

The equations of quantum mechanics let you calculate changing properties of a particle – like its position or momentum – relative to the background coordinate system.

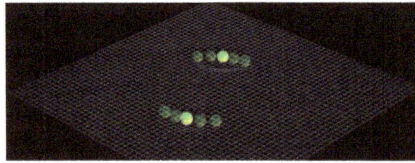

Image Source – Public Domain

The equations of general relativity let you calculate the changing shape of the coordinate system itself, encapsulated in the metric.

Loop quantum gravity (LQG) is a theory of quantum gravity, which aims to merge quantum mechanics and general relativity, incorporating matter of the Standard Model into the framework established for the pure quantum gravity case. In this writing, you see a solution to this problem.

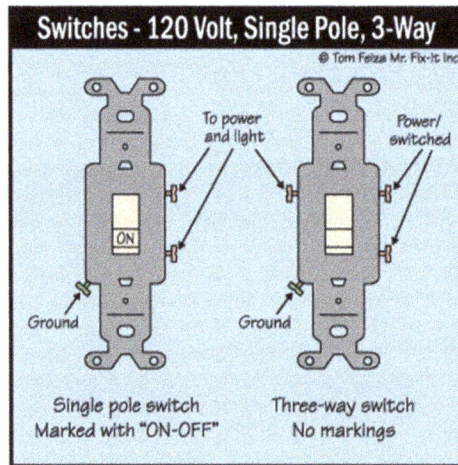

Image Source – Public Domain

Study the image above. A three-way switch has no marking (on-off) because there is no consistent on or off position. The on-off can change depending on the position of the second three-way switch. Any of the points within the powerline (circuit) always knows the state of the other points regardless of their positions or individual states. No matter how big this powerline grows, any three-way switch within the network will always know the states of other three-way

210

switches in the network. This is how quantum states truly work – it's a trinity; three-way or three-phase. It is used especially in large areas – then it even becomes a trinity of trinities.

On the other hand, single pole switches, with one switch controlling one light, are marked with an "on" and "off" position. Classical computers using two bits (1 or 0), including the so-called quantum computers using qubits (1 and 0, and a superposition of the two) are like single pole switches. The current approach in the science and engineering world to quantum computing will not work. Consider the ideas in this writing and you will make great progress.

That was a quick review of the entire calculations again as presented earlier. You will say that you have seen a lot of ideas and calculations so what makes them correct? I will tell you.

First, it is correct because God told me, and He has appointed me to teach His word. He will never tell me to publish what is not true. On September 22, 2021, the Lord showed me in a vision, a multicolored (blue and green as dominant colors) beautiful pyramid. When I asked Him the meaning of that, He said to me that He has opened me to ancient ideas, higher understanding, and a deeper meaning of life. And that I will be able to interpret ancient symbols. I am telling you this because it ties into how I believe with all my heart that the calculations and any following explanations are correct. God is indeed Elohim. God is truly my Creator. God is my Revealer, Interpreter, and my Teacher. He is the Life that keeps me alive and complete.

The value ±0 is the midpoint and considered as the center of gravity because it stabilizes and brings all movements or calculations back to normal no matter how extremely negative or positive, they go. In other words, it maintains the gravity that will pull all calculations back to normalcy even when they seem to veer into infinity minus or infinity plus (-∞ or +∞). You can call this the magnetic field or force that pulls everything together or maintain everything in their desirable controllable course or state. When we consider equilibrium, the center of gravity is the single point of concentration – weight is evenly dispersed, and all sides are in balance. The entire weight of the body will be concentrated at this point and if supported, we can maintain equilibrium at all points or states throughout the body. This applies to quantum computing and the entire universe.

Quantum computing needs a center of gravity (a magnetic field) among the number of bits that it uses so that it can hold (entangle) all other bits together to maintain a superposition for coherence. Gravity is not a weak force as physics think it is. Gravity holds the Earth together. An object in space rotates about its center of gravity.

In the movement of the Earth -1 is past, ±0 is present, and 1 is future. Assuming we're looking at the clock, the hands that tell the present time (now) are controlled from the center. If we put a set of eyes in the center, they will see and know all present activities happening in the past, present, and future – all at the same time but if we put them on the line of the circle or the circumference, they can only tell what happened in the past if they travel backward (downward) or tell the future if they travel forward (upward). But there is a control point you will have to go through to either go forward or backward – that point is God, who is right in the middle (present) of both the past and the future.

I call the clock, the Hand of God. Just like the clock, let's just say that God is in the center, so He doesn't have to travel backward or forward to know events – He sees everything as present (now) because He's the controlling arm of the clock right from the center. He has another arm that is always pointing to the opposite direction, but this is not built into clocks. One arm points to the past and the other points to the future. So, the same time He knows what's happening in the present time, He also knows both the past and future times. He can see the future time from the past time and vice versa. All of these, He does from one reference point: the present time. Therefore, He knows and sees everything. This is how Quantum can be built – using three points representing the Father, the Son, and the Holy Spirit. All of them together are one God and individually, each one of them is still God.

Regarding Einstein's spacetime diagram, there need to be some modifications. The moving observer is like the tip of the clock that points to what we call the present time (hour). The tip of the clock has an origin or reference point, which is the middle of the clock or circle, and that origin is God. He's the source that controls you or time. We all represent time. For some people, He's the source that's supposed to control them. A living and moving observer will always move on the circumference of the circle, like time, where it says future – from the center of the circle with limits to the boundaries of +0. The observer can't see anything in the -0 area. Be mindful that a person standing in the +0 towards 1 in the x, y axes is standing in a present time and looking into the future. It is the opposite with a person standing in the -0 towards -1 in the x, y axes – this person will be standing in the present time and looking into the past. The points from -1 and ±0 and to 1 represent the hand of the clock (God) or man so, as the hand moves, time moves. Think of this as the image of the man, which represent both the arms of time with God in the center, all move together at the same time, but the center (God) never changes. He's the same yesterday, today and forever.

Hebrews 13:8

[8] Jesus Christ *is* the same yesterday, today, and forever.

Like the illustration I gave earlier, the time will reset when it hits 24:00 hours and so becomes what seems like a reversal and repeat of the entire process all over again and again. So, the past, present, and future, all move at the same time, but the present always stays at the same place. The present is the center of gravity and a constant. Although we call past events as past and future events as the future, they all move concurrently based on the present time. The past is only past because of the present and so it the future – it is only the future because of the present. That is why "time" is simply an illusion made by God so that we can relate in our fallen form.

There are two legal ways to go or travel or see into the past (memory or imagination of past event) and the future (imagination) when standing in the present time. If you want to have an experience of what truly happens in both times (past and future) then you need to go through the center (God). At a physical level, the first would be like reversing the arms of the clock backwards on the circumference of the circle – moving anticlockwise. You can already tell that this is physically impossible. But the right and legal way is by going through the reference point or center (God) into either the past or the future – this is reality. Physical time travel through machines is an impossibility. It will never happen so scientists and engineers should stop wasting their time.

The past is not static, and so is the future. But the present is always static. Your past is someone else's future, and your future is someone else's past. But the present is always the present. In spiritual terms, all time is present (now) but in physical terms, we can base time on the theory of relativity and so if the present time must change, it falls into one of two categories: the past or the future. The reference point (God) never changes. The position of the two ends of spacetime will also change as the hand of God (time) moves but the position of the center of gravity never changes. It only transforms or translates. Everything moves when God moves while He's still standing or not moving.

Both halves of the graph represent the two dimensions or energies of God (male and female). That is why we see both positive and negative parts in the coordinate system. The center which represents God and or man is where sexual intercourse between a male and a female takes place and reproduction occurs. This is our God-like creative ability to bring forth offspring into the universe. Time travel into the past only means that one would have to literally travel even through his or her parents' private organs. Think about it – that was your initial passage. So, you can only go into the past backward or downward even until you enter the womb again. And you can travel into the future by going forward or upward since we grow in that direction. This is because time as we know, is a process or a set of events over a period and to physically time travel means there should be a reversal in that exact process. Your only possible, legal, and shortcut way is through the aid of a spirit. I suggest the Holy Spirit to you.

The reason why it is physically impossible by science or physics to time travel into either the past or the future is that the legal way to do this is through the center (God). He is the only portal into the past and future and higher dimensions. He is our legal access into the 4D. There is no other mere physical way with time machines. That will continue to be science fiction forever and ever. The portals to travel into time are already opened but you just don't do it physically – you do it spiritually. Those who know and use it, understand this.

The human being is a universe all by him or herself. Therefore, God says that He has hidden eternity in us. This modified image which forms the unified field theory that you saw is the reason why quantum always exists in three states – nothing more and nothing less. Once you can maintain equilibrium in all the three states then you can maintain coherence. When you achieve perfect quantum, in a Bloch sphere, you should get an image that looks just like the Venn diagram (Vesica Pisces) that follows.

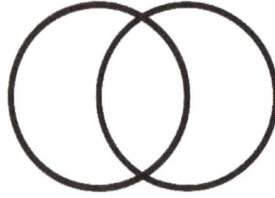

Venn Diagram (Vesica Pisces)

Image Source – Public Domain

How fast the universe is expanding can all be told or explained from this writing. Current methods for measuring the expansion rate are a problem.

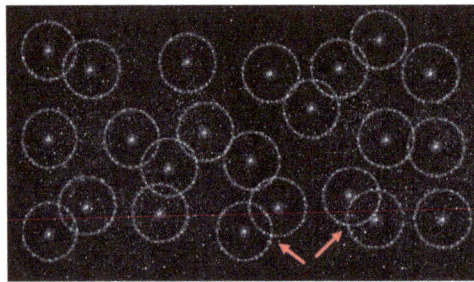

Image Source – Public Domain

Currently, the closest that scientists have gotten to regarding measuring the expansion of the universe is through what is called Baryon acoustic oscillations – which is represented in the image above. The first thing you should notice are the Venn diagrams (Vesica Pisces). This pattern printed on the fabric of spacetime is not an accident and I'm sure that at this point in this writing, you already understand why. The Vesica Pisces is the birthplace of the universe and everything else in it. This is the foundation or fundamental of creation, including science. This is how black holes, dark matter, and dark energy are formed.

Black Holes, Dark Energy, and Dark Matter

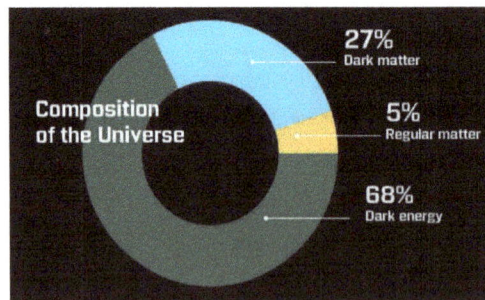

Image Source – Public Domain

This image from an article in 2017 shows the composition of the universe. Though we can't see or touch it, most astronomers say that most of the cosmos consists of dark matter and dark energy. Dark matter slows down the expansion of the universe, while dark energy speeds it up.

Dark energy is the far more dominant force of the two, accounting for roughly 68 percent of the universe's total mass and energy. Dark matter makes up 27 percent. And the rest – a measly 5 percent – is all the regular matter we see and interact with every day. Physicists and Astronomers had found more evidence that some invisible form of matter is apparently holding the universe together.

It is widely accepted that dark matter works like an attractive force – a kind of cosmic cement that holds our universe together. This is because dark matter does interact with gravity, but it doesn't reflect, absorb, or emit light. Meanwhile, dark energy is a repulsive force – a sort of anti-gravity – that drives the universe's ever-accelerating expansion. Well, black hole, dark matter, and dark energy are all related. These three things are all manifestations of gravity in our universe. This is how gravity becomes electricity, or magnetism, or electromagnetism and the effects are the strong gravitational fields that appear in these forms. Electrons and protons carry electrical charges of equal strength. The electricity generation sequence involves taking charge from the Earth, doing work on it to give it energy (expressed in terms of voltage), transporting the energy via a distribution system, using the energy, and dumping the spent charge back to the Earth. This is the inspiration behind three-phase electric power. There are three types of equilibrium: stable, unstable, and neutral. We can confirm this in our Cartesian coordinate system. Together, all three maintain balance in the universe.

When they say that information does not escape from a black hole, it is true because we can already see the cycle here. The Earth is very old or ancient. We drink the same water that our great grandfathers and grandmothers drank. We eat the same food they ate. The same water we drink and use, evaporates and forms clouds in the sky and pours back down as rain. The same seeds from the fruits they ate fell back into the ground and germinated to grow and produced more fruits. The same offspring, they brought forth reproduced and still reproducing to bring forth other offspring. The information never leaves the black hole (Earth). It's a cycle to ensure continuity, growth, and balance.

Dark matter is a positive mass (++). Black hole is a mass with all stages of gravity (–, ±, +). Dark energy is a negative mass (--). Therefore, spacetime has the shape it has – it works like a magnetic quadrupole.

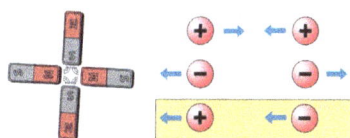

Left: a magnetic quadrupole, Right: the signed illustration – runaway motions (yellow)

Image Source – Public Domain

A quadrupole or quadrapole is one of a sequence of configurations of things like electric charge or current, or gravitational mass that can exist in ideal form, but it is usually just part of a multipole expansion of a more complex structure reflecting various orders of complexity. Study the mathematical definition or formula for this to enhance your understanding of quantum gravity. You will also understand why the crucifix of Jesus Christ in the Bible is not just a historical artifact or story. The cross has a very deep mystery and revelation.

For two positive masses, nothing changes and there is a gravitational pull on each other causing an attraction. Two negative masses would repel because of their negative inertial masses. For different signs however, there is a push that repels the positive mass from the negative mass, and a pull that attracts the negative mass towards the positive one at the same time.

The negative regions of our coordinate system are where all the negative pressure associated with dark energy come from and it is so large that it overcomes the positive (attractive) impulse of the energy itself, so the net effect is a push rather than a pull. Therefore, dark energy speeds up expansion of the universe. Negative mass repels both other negative masses and positive masses.

We have a strong magnetic field on Earth extending into outer space due to several of these natural magnetic dipoles, which attract and repel each other. These are all a result of the different transformations or phases that the force of gravity goes through from being neutral through electromagnetism. The attraction form what they call dark matter, which slows down the expansion of the universe. And the repulsion creates what they call dark energy, which accelerates the expansion of the universe. The magnetic moment is the magnetic strength and orientation of a magnet or other object that produces a magnetic field. Black holes, dark matter, and dark energy are all by-products of gravity.

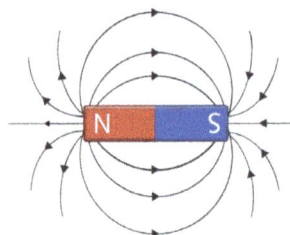

Image Source – Public Domain

When you study the image of the unified field theory in this writing, you will understand why even in humans, we grow upwards and not downwards or sideways – same concept. We (humans) are both individually and collectively like the entire universe. That is why our bodies are a temple of God because it has the capacities of an entire universe so He can dwell in us. Therefore, He often speaks from within us.

1 Corinthians 6:19

[19] Or do you not know that your body is the temple of the Holy Spirit *who is* in you, whom you have from God, and you are not your own?

Matthew 10:19-20

[19] But when they deliver you up, do not worry about how or what you should speak. For it will be given to you in that hour what you should speak; [20] for it is not you who speak, but the Spirit of your Father who speaks in you.

John 10:27

[27] My sheep hear My voice, and I know them, and they follow Me.

Therefore, galaxies are birthed just like humans, and they live and grow upward and bigger just like us with life in them, and when they run out of that life or energy, they die just like humans or all living things die. Naturally, we should be close to death when we lose our center of gravity or when it gets weakened. You can see this in our old families and friends – very old grandparents etc. You start losing your natural center of gravity as you grow and eventually you will start walking and supporting your body with a walking stick or aid. That walking stick or aid becomes your center of gravity. Study the image below to help your understanding.

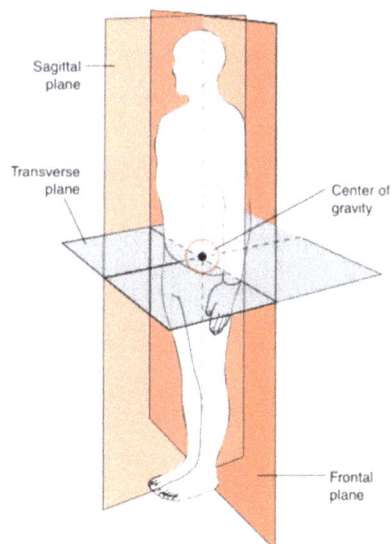

The center of gravity is the point at which three cardinal planes intersect

Image Source – Public Domain

You can study the entire universe by studying the human being. You can understand a human being better by studying God. Someday, the Earth will die just like human beings die. Everything

217

is alive and has its own type of consciousness. The best way to study the universe, is to study your life as given by God and how life operates in general. The best way to study quantum is to study God and you can study God through the life of man because He created us in His image, and He lives inside of us. You can also study Him through all His creations. The best way is to study Him through the Holy Spirit because He's our helper and our guide – and the Holy Spirit or the Spirit of God is God Himself. Jesus Christ is also God Himself who came to save us in human form. Therefore, God says that we are gods because we are the third person of the godhead.

Psalm 82:6

[6] I said, "You *are* gods,
And all of you *are* children of the Most High.

Therefore, positive, and negative electric currents can exist in batteries, human bodies, all living organisms, the ground, the ocean, the sky (ionosphere), mercury and solder, ion-based smoke detectors, air cleaners, and the vertical "sky current" in the atmosphere, among others. Because the Moon has its own laws, that is why humans don't exert the luxury of moving freely like you do on Earth according to the laws of gravity governing Earth.

Dark matter and regular matter represent the (++) and (-+) regions on the coordinate system. Positive mass attracts both other positive masses and negative masses. Dark matter slows down the expansion of the universe and helps the growth of inhabitants of the universe at the same time. Dark energy represents the (--) regions on the coordinate system and pushes out to expand from the bottom and inside out, and dark matter regulates that expansion by keeping all the elements together to prevent abnormalities. For both the male and female energy signs (-, +), there is a push that repels the positive mass from the negative mass, and a pull that attracts the negative mass towards the positive mass at the same time. This is the same way that male and female human beings are naturally and normally attracted to each other, and it points humanity in the direction of reproduction (continuity) and growth at the same time.

There are several issues with science at the very fundamental level and that is why quantum mechanics and especially quantum gravity has been a tough nut to crack. For example, the correct quantum harmonic oscillator should be defined by

$$E = \frac{1}{3}hv$$

When you study this carefully, you will know and understand why some definitions and values need to be changed at the very fundamental level of science. The calculations in quantum mechanics require the use of three states using base or root of three. Vacuum energy and quantum vacuum are all due to the force of gravity. The effects of gravity are the underlying energies.

Vacuum energy is an underlying background energy that exists in space throughout the entire universe. In quantum field theory, the quantum vacuum state (also called the quantum vacuum or vacuum state) is the quantum state with the lowest possible energy.

That is why my definition of quantum is the change in the state of matter, medium, and position with a constant time – where the time can be past, present, or future or at best, all three combined (now or happening at the same time) as God wills. Equilibrium in all three states must be achieved and maintained for it to function properly.

Without what scientists call black holes, dark matter, and dark energy, you cannot understand the universe's birth and evolution and how everything is the way it is, including the human body. For decades, physicists all over the world have employed increasingly high-tech instruments to try and detect dark matter. So far, they've found no signs of it.

What is called black hole, dark matter, and dark energy is just a gigantic electromagnetic field. The rotating black hole drags space around with it. Two black holes merged or overlapped together in 2D is the shape of our spacetime curvature and a Venn diagram (Vesica Pisces). Right in the center of one such black hole is Earth.

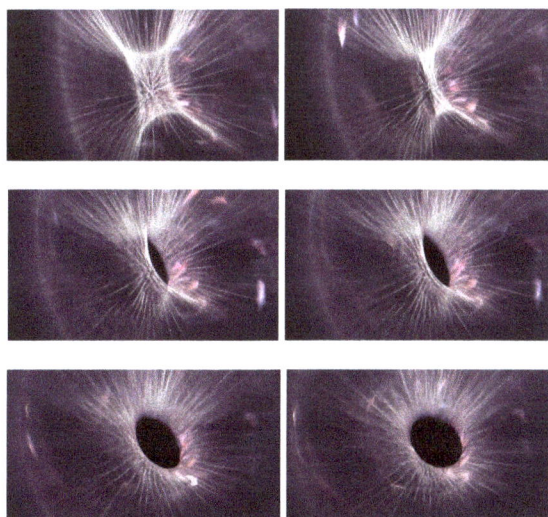

3D image of spacetime curvature/black hole – forms a 2D Venn diagram (Vesica Pisces)

Image Source – Public Domain

The problem of quantum mechanics is at the fundamental level, and it all started with the misunderstanding of particles. We will talk about the Bosons (e.g., Higgs boson) and Fermions (e.g., electron). The error was made at the basic level. That error was that physicists made quantum systems two-particle systems. But quantum systems are three-particle systems with the following charges, −, ±, +. They require operations using the √3 and a spin of $\frac{1}{3}$. In other words, a simple way will be the third turn, $\frac{1}{3}$ revolutions, 120 degrees, and $\frac{2\pi}{3}$ radians. At this very fundamental level too, all three particles or states can be considered as one. We have already gone over these many times. I'm sure you get the idea now.

The wave function is a mathematical description of everything we know about the quantum system.

Quantum Electrodynamics and G-Factor

In particle physics, quantum electrodynamics (QED) is the relativistic quantum field theory of electrodynamics. In essence, it describes how light, and matter interact and is the first theory where full agreement between quantum mechanics and special relativity is achieved.

Paul Dirac proposed g_e = 2. Also, the conventional definition of the spin quantum number is $s = \frac{n}{2}$. These are wrong.

In this writing, we propose g_e = 3 and spin quantum number is $s = \frac{n}{3}$. In atomic physics, the electron magnetic moment, or more specifically the electron magnetic dipole moment, is the magnetic moment of an electron caused by its intrinsic properties of spin and electric charge.

The spin angular momentum of an electron is $\frac{1}{3}\hbar$. The electron spin g-factor, a factor relating spin angular momentum to corresponding magnetic moment of a particle, is three. That is, g_e = 3.

If the electron is visualized as a quantum charged particle rotating about an axis with angular momentum S, its magnetic dipole moment μ is given by:

$$\mu_e = g\frac{e}{3m_e}S$$

A g-factor (also called g value or dimensionless magnetic moment) is a dimensionless quantity that characterizes the magnetic moment and angular momentum of an atom, a particle, or the nucleus. It is essentially a proportionality constant that relates the different observed magnetic moments μ of a particle to their angular momentum quantum numbers and a unit of magnetic moment (to make it dimensionless), usually the Bohr magneton or nuclear magneton.

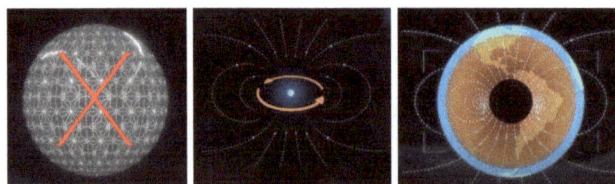

Image Source – Public Domain

Every particle with electric charge also has quantum spin. This is not the same thing as just a simple rotation but particles with quantum spin do generate a magnetic field – same as if you send electric charge around a looped wire or have electrical currents in the Earth's spinning core. The result is a dipole magnetic moment with a north and a south pole.

Image Source – Public Domain

Place an object with such a field inside a second magnetic field and the object will turn to rotate to align with that field.

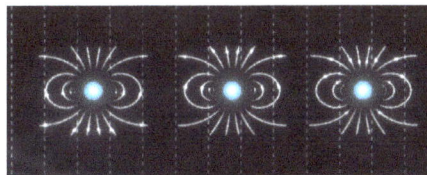

Image Source – Public Domain

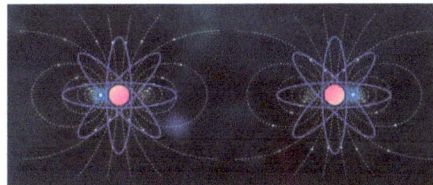

Image Source – Public Domain

The strength of that rotational pull or the torque is defined by the object's dipole moment. For a rotating charge, that depends on the object's right or left momentum or angular momentum, its charge, and its mass.

Physicists call the source of the magnetic field of the Earth, weirder. They say that it mostly comes from the summed dipole magnetic fields of individual electrons in the outer shells of its atoms and those electron dipole fields are indeed very weird. The nature is predicted by quantum theory, measure electromagnetic moments and you verify your quantum picture of reality.

The Earth is indeed like a big atom which is already residing in a black hole. Your simple proofs are the Sun and the Moon – to provide light to the Earth. Therefore, within a certain altitude, if you are dropped, you can only come down or fall back to Earth but after a certain altitude – in what we call space, you can float around just like another galaxy. That is also why for humans to be able to fly or go to space, they must apply the four forces of aerodynamics in spacecrafts. You don't need to travel into another black hole to learn how things work in there because you are already in a black hole. Each time astronauts take off to space they use the laws of aerodynamics to push out of the black hole (Earth) and defy the laws of gravity to escape the Earth's event horizon. That is why the farther you are in space, the less gravity you encounter. In other words, gravity becomes weaker with distance, but small amount of gravity can still be found everywhere in space. On your return from space to Earth, once you hit the event horizon again, you start facing the force of gravity. If the laws of aerodynamics are not put into effect, you will just keep dropping or free falling like how Newton observed the apple falling from the tree and then crash.

This explains why when anything gets closer to a black hole event horizon, it is sucked into it until it goes through the singularity. The Earth is a singularity – that is why it is round like a huge ball. It started very small like a baby and then grew up as a living thing. There is only one physical way to travel through the Earth in the opposite direction of space, and that is death. So, if you think that physical time travel is a possibility through time machines, think again. Don't let string theory fool you. It can only be possible with the help of a spirit. The spirit that I suggest to you to know and work with is the Holy Spirit of God. There is no other physical means other than death.

If you could go underneath the Earth, there are the laws of aerodynamics working to keep it floating and moving in orbit for several reasons. Again, this can be found in the Bible.

Revelation 7:1

The Sealed of Israel

7 After these things I saw four angels standing at the four corners of the Earth, holding the four winds of the Earth, that the wind should not blow on the Earth, on the sea, or on any tree.

The same laws applied to our aircrafts and rockets are applied at the four corners of the Earth in the spiritual realm. There are four angels on perpetual duty until this Earth is destroyed to keep up with this assignment. Therefore, the laws of aerodynamics, collectively are strong enough to keep our aircrafts and rockets in the air and even go in space.

What we currently call gravity simply starts as a neutral force then progresses from being a weak force to becoming the electromagnetic force. It is the same force at different levels. If you shift the gear of a car to neutral on a flat surface, it stays there until you push or apply force to it, and it moves easily either forward or backward. Gravity is not the cause of the curvature of spacetime. It is the curvature of spacetime. This is the same way gravity is not the cause of the shape of your waistline area (center of gravity). Gravity is the shape of your waistline area.

Therefore, the Earth is perfectly sitting in the center of our coordinate system – right in the middle of spacetime (black hole) where it is perfectly aligned and suspended in a uniform electric field. This can be represented by (−, ±0, +). This means that everything on either side of the spacetime curvature must surely go through or interact with this neutral point one way or the other. Therefore, it is the unifier of general relativity and quantum mechanics. We have only one force, and that is gravity. Gravity starts as the only force of the overall quantum gravity or loop quantum gravity process – it is the only force that is needed to make it perfect through evolution or transformation in a process. It is the only fundamental and central force. Again, I want you to think about the collision of the sperm and egg and how a human being starts as a fetus in the womb through birth and then to adulthood. This is the same human being going through a process. You also went through this same process and so did the Earth and every living thing. This is gravity starting at its earliest stage to becoming a very strong force. There are three forces, but they are all one, just like God is three persons but the same God. Just like in the Fibonacci sequence, you must add the previous weeks right from conception to arrive at the final week. This is gravity – this is quantum mechanics.

weeks

Image Source – Public Domain

I hope this image above will help your understanding of quantum gravity. Now, let's get back to reviewing the four forces of nature and I will show you why what have been said so far are true.

Fundamental Force Particles

Force	Particles Experiencing	Force Carrier Particle	Range	Relative Strength*
Gravity acts between objects with mass	all particles with mass	graviton (not yet observed)	infinity	much weaker
Weak Force governs particle decay	quarks and leptons	W^+, W^-, Z^0 (W and Z)	short range	
Electromagnetism acts between electrically charged particles	electrically charged	γ (photon)	infinity	
Strong Force** binds quarks together	quarks and gluons	g (gluon)	short range	much stronger

The "four" fundamental forces of nature

Image Source – Public Domain

Redefinition of Gravity

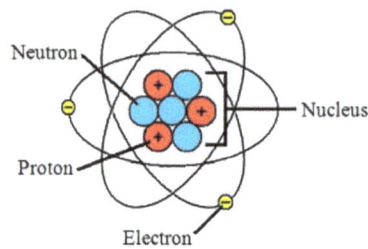

An Atom

Image Source – Public Domain

The Earth is a giant atom and can be represented by an atom of any size. An atom is made up of protons, neutrons, and electrons. Protons have a positive electric charge (+), a mass of one (1), and located in the nucleus. Neutrons have a neutral charge (0), a mass of one (1), and located in the nucleus. Electrons have a negative charge (-), a mass of zero (0), and are in the orbitals.

A nucleus is made up of protons and neutrons. The combination of the two is what forms the nucleus. The overall charge of a nucleus is positive (+).

Gravity is a nucleus. Protons plus neutrons equals the balanced and stable force of gravity. The strong nuclear force pulls together protons and neutrons in the nucleus. Scientists currently believe that at very "small" distances only, such as those inside the nucleus, this strong force overcomes the electromagnetic force, and prevents the electrical repulsion of protons from blowing the nucleus apart. This is not exactly true.

Now that you understand that the Earth is a giant atom, you also understand that there is a gigantic nucleus in the core of the Earth. This nucleus is what gives the spacetime curvature as described in general relativity. Not only is it seen there but when you study the image of the atom above, you will understand that this is the natural curvature indeed. This again confirms the three dimensions of space or vacuum, gravity, and matter, which give us what we call time. Together, these make up our 3D universe, which is governed by their result, time. That is, space + gravity + matter = time.

The abilities of the force in the nucleus (gravity) are the reasons why the electrons move around the Earth in the manner they do. Gravity is so strong that electromagnetism cannot break it apart. Electromagnetism is just another phase of gravity. The protons are perpetually stuck to the neutrons because of the strong nuclear force which gives "gravity" a hybrid ability to make it even more powerful than the electromagnetic force. The attraction between the protons and the orbital electrons is very strong but the force of gravity as a hybrid force prevents the electrical repulsion of protons from blowing apart the nucleus. Hence, the Earth is dragged by the hybrid force of gravity to orbit constantly. We can say that the Earth is dragged by another phase of gravity to orbit constantly.

What we call gravity at that level is a strong unification of protons and neutrons to form a nucleus, and an attraction to the orbital electrons with a repulsion of protons from blowing the nucleus apart. Therefore, gravity becomes a unification of three different forces – the weak force, the electromagnetic force, and the strong force. These are three forces working as one gravitational force at different levels and strengths. It's not a coincidence because it is God the Father, God the Son, and God the Holy Spirit, and they are one, so the work is divided among them, and the calculations are done with √3 or a qutrit. The base of everything quantum in the universe is a trinity.

So, gravity with a charge carrier graviton still has an infinite range with a charge of 0e. This charge is the reason why scientists have thought of gravity as a very weak force, but it isn't. This charge of 0e is just the neutral phase of gravity. The weak force is just one phase of gravity. The confusion about gravity in science currently is first because of identifying or counting gravity as a force on its own, i.e., one of the four forces of nature. And second, thinking and seeing the neutral phase of gravity as gravity. There is only one force of nature and that is gravity. Gravity needs to be redefined. We can say that gravity, as currently understood in science to be a very strong force and keeping everything together in the universe, is the unification of all that are currently the "three forces of nature", i.e., weak force, electromagnetic force, and strong force. This has been the paradox – scientists think gravity is very strong, yet it is also very weak. This is the reason why no force carrier particle has been found for gravity yet. There is only one force of nature called gravity, which is made up of neutral, weak nuclear force, electromagnetic force, and the strong nuclear force. This is gravity – this is quantum mechanics.

As the attraction between the protons in the nucleus and the electrons keep happening but are unable to get attached to each other because of the strong nuclear force that keeps the nucleus intact, stronger magnetic fields are formed, which propels the Earth in orbit. This is electromagnetism and how that force comes into being. Magnetic fields have a specific orientation or direction; this orientation is called the atom's (Earth's) magnetic moment. When all or most of these moments align in the same direction, the entire atom has a net magnetization and creates a magnetic field around itself. Again, these are the mysteries behind black holes, dark matter, and dark energy.

A Revision of the Four Forces of Nature

Now you know that there is only one force of nature, and that force is gravity. But when we look at the current "four forces of nature" and we study the particle composition of each one of them, we can see the following.

The Weak Force

First, the weak force – governs particle decay and the particles experiencing this force are quarks and leptons. We see in science and currently observed that the weak force has three carrier particles, which are W^+, W^-, and Z^0 (W and Z). The quarks are composed of six types of elementary particles (up, down, strange, charm, bottom, and top) and have an electric charge of $+\frac{2}{3}e$, $-\frac{1}{3}e$. And the leptons are composed of six types of elementary particles (electron, electron neutrino, muon, muon neutrino, tau, tau neutrino) with electric charge of +1e, 0e, −1e.

The Electromagnetic Force

Second, the electromagnetic force – acts between electrically charged particles and so the particles experiencing this force are electrically charged. The force carrier of this force is a photon and has no electric charge (0). Currently observed, photons are massless, so they always move at the speed of light in vacuum and belongs to the class of bosons.

The Strong Force

Third, the strong force – binds quarks together and the particles experiencing this force are quarks and gluons. The force carrier of this force is a gluon, and it has an electric charge of 0e. The gluon is an elementary particle that acts as the exchange particle (or gauge boson) for the strong force between quarks. It is analogous to the exchange of photons in the electromagnetic force between two charged particles. Gluons bind quarks together, forming hadrons such as protons and neutrons (nucleus). So, we can agree that a nucleus is a hadron.

In this writing, you have already seen the power of the numbers 3, 6, and 9. You continue to see them in the number of the types of elementary particles.

A Revision of the Elementary Particles

Start with this basic image and research on your own in detail for a better understanding on how everything looks in picture form.

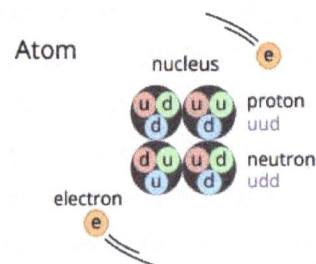

Atom
nucleus e
u d u u proton uud
d d
d u u d neutron udd
u d
electron
e

Image Source – Public Domain

It all starts with a neutron (0). This neutron somehow can attract protons (+) and together, they form a nucleus (hadron). The force that binds them together is so strong that it overcomes electromagnetism and the resultant effect of both the attraction between the proton and the orbiting electrons generates motion, which is how the Earth moves in orbit (spacetime). The net electric charge of a hadron is simply the sum of the electric charges of the quarks or antiquarks of which it is composed. The net charge of a hadron is therefore always a whole number, even though the quarks themselves have a non-whole number electric charge.

The Neutron

The neutron has no electric charge. The nucleus is held together by the strong nuclear force. The strong force counteracts the tendency of the positively charged protons to repel each other. It also holds together the quarks that make up the protons and neutrons. Neutrons contain one up quark and two down quarks, giving a net charge of $+\frac{2}{3} - \frac{1}{3} - \frac{1}{3} = 0e$.

The Proton

The proton has a positive electric charge of +1e. The proton is a baryon, so it is composed of three quarks, and it is composed of up and down quarks only. The only way that three up or down quarks can be combined to make this net charge is by combining two up quarks with a down quark. So, the quark content of a proton is (uud), giving a net charge of $+\frac{2}{3}e - \frac{1}{3}e - \frac{e}{3} = +1e$. Each proton and each neutron contain three quarks. The number three is not an accident. Each up quark has a charge of $+\frac{2}{3}$. Each down quark has a charge of $-\frac{1}{3}$. A quark is a fast-moving point of energy. Each up quark has a charge of $+\frac{2}{3}$.

The Electron

Then finally, we have the electron. The negative electric charge carried by a single electron is −1e. This is the opposite of a proton.

If we group the electric charges of these particles from left to right, we will have -1e, 0e, +1e and since the neutron is caught up in the interactions of a proton, neutron, and the electron, we finally have -1e, ±0e, +1e. This is the overall composition of the atom (Earth and the human body alike) – the universe at large.

Composite Particles – Hadrons

Composite particles are composed of two or more elementary particles. This shows some of the hundreds of known composite particles.

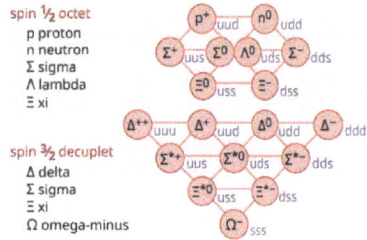

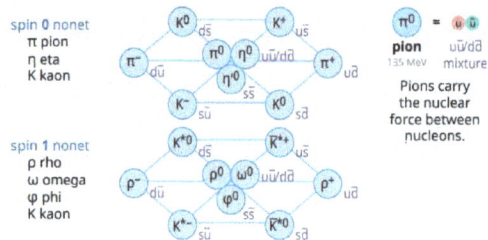

Image Source – Public Domain

Quarks and antiquarks only occur bound together inside hadrons; they have never been observed in isolation. While it may seem like the process of 'building' a hadron would be something very complicated (and yes, the underlying physics is indeed complex), there are in fact 3 simple 'recipes' to remember.

A hadron can consist of three quarks (in which case it is called a baryon). Three antiquarks (in which case it is called an antibaryon). One quark and one antiquark (in which case it is called a meson).

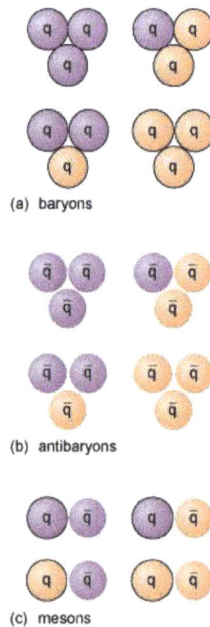

Image Source – Public Domain

The Pions

Finally, we have Pions. Pions are not produced in radioactive decay, but commonly are in high-energy collisions between hadrons. Pions also result from some matter–antimatter annihilation events. In particle physics, annihilation is the process that occurs when a subatomic particle collides with its respective antiparticle to produce other particles, such as an electron colliding with a positron to produce two photons. The total energy and momentum of the initial pair are conserved in the process and distributed among a set of other particles in the final state. In particle physics, a pion (or a pi meson, denoted with the Greek letter pi: π) is any of three subatomic particles: π^0, π^+, and π^-. The composition is π^+: ud, π^0: uu or dd, π^-: du. The antiparticles are π^+: π^-, π^0: self.

The electric charge of pions can also be represented like this — $\pi^\pm$: ±1e, π^0: 0e. Pions have hypercharge (0), parity (-1), and C parity (+1).

The quark structure of the positively charged pion

Image Source – Public Domain

Hypercharge

In particle physics, the hypercharge (a portmanteau of hyperonic and charge) Y of a particle is a quantum number conserved under the strong interaction. The concept of hypercharge provides a single charge operator that accounts for properties of isospin, electric charge, and flavor. The hypercharge is useful to classify hadrons; the similarly named weak hypercharge has an analogous role in the electroweak interaction.

Parity Transformation or P-Symmetry

In quantum mechanics, a parity transformation (also called parity inversion) is the flip in the sign of one spatial coordinate. In three dimensions, it can also refer to the simultaneous flip in the sign of all three spatial coordinates (a point reflection or inversion):

$$\mathbf{P} : \begin{pmatrix} x \\ y \\ z \end{pmatrix} \mapsto \begin{pmatrix} -x \\ -y \\ -z \end{pmatrix}$$

Image Source – Public Domain

229

C Parity

In physics, the C parity or charge parity is a multiplicative quantum number of some particles that describes their behavior under the symmetry operation of charge conjugation.

C-Symmetry

In physics, charge conjugation is a transformation that switches all particles with their corresponding antiparticles, thus changing the sign of all charges: not only electric charge but also the charges relevant to other forces. The term C-symmetry is an abbreviation of the phrase "charge conjugation symmetry" and is used in discussions of the symmetry of physical laws under charge-conjugation. Other important discrete symmetries are P-symmetry (parity) and T-symmetry (time reversal).

Charge conjugation changes the sign of all quantum charges (that is, additive quantum numbers), including the electrical charge, baryon number and lepton number, and the flavor charges strangeness, charm, bottomness, topness and Isospin (I_3). In contrast, it doesn't affect the mass, linear momentum, or spin of a particle.

T-Symmetry

T-symmetry or time reversal symmetry is the theoretical symmetry of physical laws under the transformation of time reversal,

$$T : t \mapsto -t.$$

Image Source – Public Domain

This is how what we call time in our universe works. The entire universe is a representation of time.

Polarization

Photon polarization is the quantum mechanical description of the classical polarized sinusoidal plane electromagnetic wave. In a vacuum, a photon has two possible polarization states. An individual photon can be described as having right or left circular polarization, or a superposition of the two. Equivalently, a photon can be described as having horizontal or vertical linear polarization, or a superposition of the two.

When a photon of light reaches a glass, it either passes through, or it doesn't. And whether it passes through is effectively a measurement of whether that photon is polarized in each direction. The following is an experiment by some physicists using two polarized glasses. Hint – Vesica Pisces.

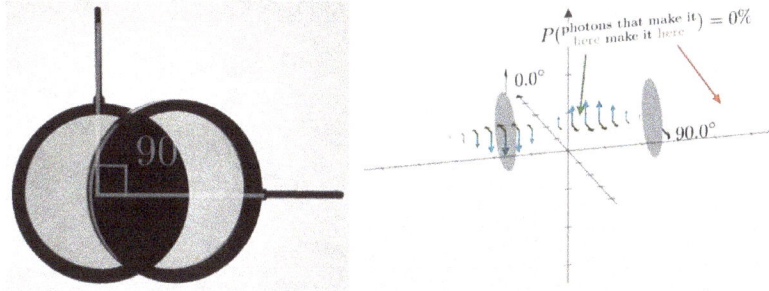

Image Source – Public Domain

Two sets of Sunglasses were held at some light source, like a lamp, and as the second polarizing filter is overlapped and rotated on the first one, it starts getting darker and darker and the lamp will look lighter and darker. It should look darkest when the second filter is oriented 90 degrees off from the first one. This is because the photons with polarization that allows them to pass through a filter on one axis have a much lower probability of passing through a second filter along a perpendicular axis – in principle 0%. This illustration was used to explain the Bell's theorem in what is called the quantum Venn diagram paradox. Except that only two filters are needed for the experiment to make it perfect just like in the image above instead of the three or more used in that experiment. The center of the intersection should be considered as the third part (superposition).

I added this piece to help you understand the nature of quantum – entanglement, superposition, time, black holes, dark matter, and dark energy. This is the explanation to your mystery of black holes and how not even light can escape from it. Inside the black hole are the "hidden variables". What you see is the same Venn diagram (Vesica Pisces) – the birthplace of the universe, which is a major part of this writing and the underlying geometry. Most importantly, they all came from God, and He is the foundation of everything.

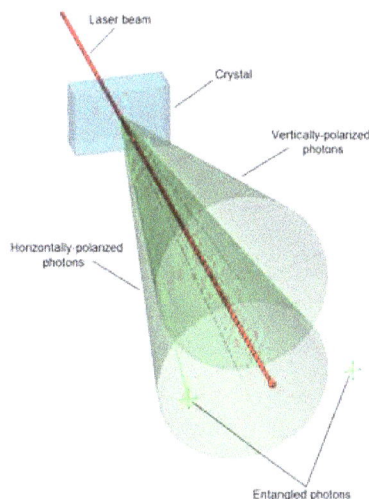

Image Source – Public Domain

The image above is from the Spontaneous parametric down-conversion experiment. It is a nonlinear instant optical process that converts one photon of higher energy (namely, a pump photon), into a pair of photons (namely, a signal photon, and an idler photon) of lower energy, in accordance with the law of conservation of energy and law of conservation of momentum. It is an important process in quantum optics, for the generation of entangled photon pairs, and of single photons. It will be even more important in quantum optics if the ideas given in this writing are followed.

The process seems right except that there is a missing value or point. That point is the pump or laser beam point, which can be found as the point between the two entangled photons where the red point is at (intersection of the coordinate system). Right now, only two points are being used but use all three points – the square root of 3.

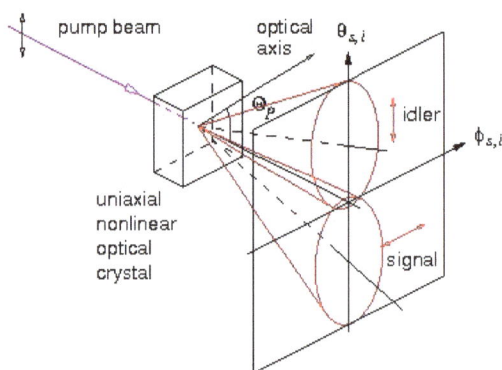

Image Source – Public Domain

Like in the image above, the center point where the coordinate system intersects is the missing point (±0). This coordinate system part of the image is our current world or universe. It clearly has one source (singularity), and that is God. It also represents spacetime as one body together with the coordinate system, which again represents the unified image of the Vitruvian Man by Leonardo da Vinci and General Relativity spacetime curvature by Albert Einstein with some modifications to spacetime. The resulting polarized photons (entangled images) move together as time – space, gravity, and matter. So, imagine the whole square moving as a clock or time. I hope you understand better now. This modification can also be made in quantum optics to make the technology better.

This is the birthplace of our universe and how it came into being. You can see that God is attached to every bit of information – you cannot isolate Him. Oh my God, He loves us too much. He's the 'pump' light (the Word) that goes through the crystal (Holy Spirit) and then gave birth to the universe. We are all beings of light. God dwells in unapproachable light, and He created us with His substance in His own image. This is the same entanglement we have with God the Father, God the Son, and God the Holy Spirit. We are in the Vesica Pisces, and that itself still has the tripartite nature of God. It is a continuous cycle of a duplication of Himself forever and ever. This is the Godhead (Father, Son, Holy Spirit), in case you needed a spiritual plus scientific proof of that. Hence, our duality nature to be able to walk in both the spiritual and physical realms at the same time. The reason why scientists struggle a lot and have struggled a whole lot with quantum mechanics is because they have decided to isolate themselves from God, their Creator. This is how lost you will all continue to be if you don't repent and come to the Lord God of the Heavens and the Earth. He is strong and mighty and holy. So, you are the 'hidden variable' that has always been hidden to you in quantum mechanics. Be humble and find out who you (human) truly are.

If you want to truly understand what God will look like in His form, look for the brightest pure light. If you can look at that light or see it and live, then it's not God because His true light is unapproachable. He functions like electricity, and we wouldn't have electricity if He didn't reveal Himself through it to us. Then surely, the whole world would be in darkness on top of the darkness that we already live in. What happens in one part of the world can truly affect what happens far away. It is a huge, interconnected network. By now you should know and understand who man truly is.

This is currently the scientific world understanding of quantum mechanics. The quantum phenomenon known as entanglement, in which two particles that we would normally think of as distinct entities lose their independence is true. This is how the people of God are connected or entangled with Him. In quantum mechanics, a particle's location, polarization, and other properties can be indefinite until the moment they are measured. Yet measuring the properties of entangled particles yields results that are strongly correlated, even when the particles are far apart and measured nearly simultaneously. The unpredictable outcome of one measurement appears to instantly affect the outcome of the other, regardless of the distance between them – a gross violation of locality.

To understand entanglement more precisely, consider a property of electrons and most other quantum particles called spin. Particles with spin behave somewhat like tiny magnets. When, for instance, an electron passes through a magnetic field created by a pair of north and south magnetic poles, it gets deflected by a fixed amount toward one pole or the other. This shows that the electron's spin is a quantity that can have only one of two values: "up" for an electron deflected toward the north pole, and "down" for an electron deflected toward the south pole.

Imagine an electron passing through a region with the north pole directly above it and the south pole directly below. Measuring its deflection will reveal whether the electron's spin is "up" or "down" along the vertical axis. Now rotate the axis between the magnet poles away from vertical, and measure deflection along this new axis. Again, the electron will always deflect by the same amount toward one of the poles. You'll always measure a binary spin value – either up or down – along any axis.

It turns out it's not possible to build any detector that can measure a particle's spin along multiple axes at the same time. Quantum theory asserts that this property of spin detectors is a property of spin itself: If an electron has a definite spin along one axis, its spin along any other axis is undefined. The axes together are one body and that's what makes a spin possible. You can't separate the axes of the coordinate system and measure past one dimension. Quantum mechanics at a physical level is three-dimensional.

I believe that from this writing, scientists will know why this is the case. First, the binary spin value is always going to be two values. In quantum, this is the first mistake – it is supposed to be a trinary spin value. In spacetime, the axes of the coordinate system can't be isolated or separated from time because the whole body together is what we call time.

The center (nucleus) is the center of gravity. That is what holds the entire system together and that is the reason why there is a curvature because spacetime naturally has that curvature. Think of it as the waist area of a human being – same thing. That is the center of gravity and that is the main point that coordinates movement of the entire human body. That is the major joint. One cannot naturally move in the expected or normal manner from one point to the other without moving the entire body and the point or center of gravity behind that movement which makes it possible is the wait area. The main body parts (upper and lower) are joined by the waist. When you want to move any of those parts, the main pivot or movement area is the waist. It is impossible to make a major turn of the body occurring at the waist area without turning the whole body because it is a coordinate system. The human body is a whole universe.

I use this illustration because it is the same as our universe because we humans are universes by ourselves. When you separate space from time and all that then you have a problem. The reason why it has been impossible to build any device that can measure a particle's spin along multiple axes at the same time is that the whole coordinate system moves together as one body so it doesn't matter whether you turn it upside down or left or right – you will always get the same readings or values. For example, when you turn a human being upside down and you want to find the positioning of the head, the waist, the arms, and the legs, you will always find these parts in the same areas. First, the entire body will read three values according to the coordinate system, i.e., minus, minus plus, and plus. The left arm and leg for example, will always have the sign +1, the right arm and leg will always have the sign -1, and the waist (center) will always have the sign ±0. The body is basically divided into two parts, and we also count where they join – so, we will have three parts in total. If the person changes the standing position and face the north, south, east, or west, these values will never change. This is quantum mechanics.

When you call somebody in another village, town, city, or country and ask the person, what is the positioning or location of your right or left arm, leg, eye etc., they will always give you a value that correlates to the positioning of that same part on your own body. This will never change. This is quantum mechanics.

This tells you that whether you believe in God or not, doesn't change the fact that He exists. Whether you believe in Heaven and Hell or not, it doesn't change the fact that those locations exist. Whether you believe in the spiritual realm or not, doesn't change the fact that they exist. You can choose to face north, south, east, or west, and it wouldn't change your right hand to become left and vice versa etc. Therefore, it seems like engineers are unable to build any detectors for measuring quantum bits. The reason is because they don't understand quantum mechanics. They don't understand that this is the foundational work of God in the creation of the Earth and everything that's in it. There are spiritual laws and if you don't understand these laws, how then do you build something based on those laws? Again, everything physical has a spiritual foundation. Matter has an antimatter foundation. The visible has an invisible foundation. That's the truth but you don't have to believe it if you don't want to. Your choice doesn't change or alter the truth.

Hidden Variables in Quantum Mechanics

The result of measurements depends on predetermined "hidden variables". The state of the particles being measured contains some hidden variables, whose values effectively determine, right from the moment of separation, what the outcomes of the spin measurements are going to be. This would mean that each particle carries all the required information with it, and nothing needs to be transmitted from one particle to the other at the time of measurement. My example in the previous paragraph explains this.

It is also said about quantum mechanics that armed with this understanding of spin, we can devise a thought experiment that we can use to prove Bell's theorem. Consider a specific example of an entangled state: a pair of electrons whose total spin is zero, meaning measurements of their spins along any given axis will always yield opposite results. What's remarkable about this entangled state is that, although the total spin has this definite value along all axes, each electron's individual spin is indefinite.

Suppose these entangled electrons are separated and transported to distant laboratories, and that teams of scientists in these labs can rotate the magnets of their respective detectors any way they like when performing spin measurements.

When both teams measure along the same axis, they obtain opposite results 100% of the time. But is this evidence of nonlocality? Not necessarily.

It is known and said that alternatively, Einstein proposed, each pair of electrons could come with an associated set of "hidden variables" specifying the particles' spins along all axes simultaneously. These hidden variables are absent from the quantum description of the entangled state, but quantum mechanics may not be telling the whole story.

Hidden variable theories can explain why same-axis measurements always yield opposite results without any violation of locality: A measurement of one electron doesn't affect the other but merely reveals the preexisting value of a hidden variable.

Bell proved that you could rule out local hidden variable theories, and indeed rule out locality altogether, by measuring entangled particles' spins along different axes.

This is because the result is linear. Quantum mechanics should be built on ternary instead of binary – and that will mean using qutrit instead of qubit. Using all the pointers that have been given in this writing and following the three-phase power design for electricity is the way to go. When the three points or systems are all even as far apart as possible – that is, all 120 degrees apart, as in the Mercedes logo – all systems involved will obtain the same result. This will exceed Bell's upper bound of 67%.

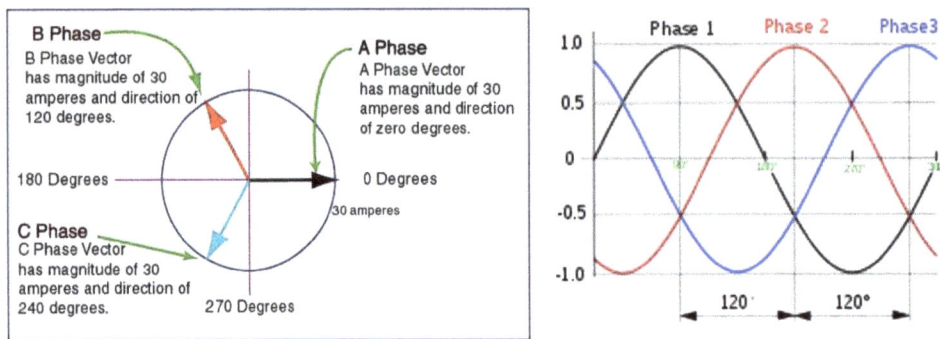

Image Source – Public Domain

120 Degrees Representation

We have already seen several scriptures and examples when we were looking at the mystery of Methuselah with relation to the end times. When there's 120° between phases, the sum of the voltages at any time will be zero. Being 120 degrees apart makes the phases balanced such that power transfer at any instant is a constant. This can be achieved by using the square root of 3 instead of 2. You can find the significance of the number 120 in the Bible – below are two examples. A good example is how God reset life on Earth due to sin in the days of Noah with the flood after 120 years of building the ark.

Genesis 6:3

[3] And the LORD said, "My Spirit shall not strive with man forever, for he *is* indeed flesh; yet his days shall be one hundred and twenty years."

2 Chronicles 5:12

[12] and the Levites *who were* the singers, all those of Asaph and Heman and Jeduthun, with their sons and their brethren, stood at the east end of the altar, clothed in white linen, having cymbals, stringed instruments, and harps, and with them one hundred and twenty priests sounding with trumpets—

Acts 1:15

[15] And in those days, Peter stood up in the midst of the disciples (altogether the number of names was about a hundred and twenty), and said,

The Word of God is not just a historical or made-up book and the numbers in there are not abstract or random. Everything in the Bible has a very deep meaning. Christianity is the ONLY truth and the ONLY valid way of life to eternal life through Jesus Christ by the Power of the Holy Spirit. Christianity may be used interchangeably with religion, but it is not a religion. And if only humanity will pay attention to the true Bible (not the Watchtower's, Mormon's, SDA's, and their associated false "Bible" and false teachings etc.), we won't stay or remain this far behind and messed up all over the world. But of course, there are very intentional satanic schemes to falsify and hide the truth, but they can NEVER hide light. They have failed. Get out and or stay away from any kind of secret societies or cults like the Freemasons, "New Age" beliefs etc. Run very fast for your soul. Most symbols and secrets they use are for Christians, but most Christians are so very lazy and ignorant that they don't even know what belongs to them in Jesus Christ. Christians alongside everybody else in the world truly need to WAKE UP! Pursue God intentionally and diligently and break through the spiritual veil so that you can see reality and your heritage.

If Satan can do all that he does and his powers were given to him by God, think about what you can do in Christ Jesus – who is the source of all power, including Satan's. Most of you have been brainwashed and blinded, and unfortunately, most of you will die in deception and go to Hell. Don't be one of those people.

Predetermination or Predestination
2 Chronicles 3:15-17

[15] Also he made in front of the temple two pillars thirty-five cubits high, and the capital that *was* on the top of each of *them* was five cubits. [16] He made wreaths of chainwork, as in the inner sanctuary, and put *them* on top of the pillars; and he made one hundred pomegranates and put *them* on the wreaths of chainwork. [17] Then he set up the pillars before the temple, one on the right hand and the other on the left; he called the name of the one on the right hand Jachin, and the name of the one on the left Boaz.

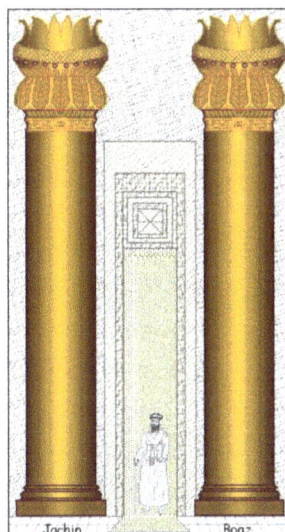

Image Source – Public Domain

237

What we read in the scriptures above are related to all that are being said in this writing. Solomon did not just name two pillars for naming's sake. The two pillars also represented the male and female dimensions (energies) of God and the pathway in between as the beginning of creation or man. The wreath of chainwork is how interconnected those three pillars are even when they are not seen from the ground when you look directly at the pillars. Man is the middle and third pillar and a bridge between the natural and supernatural who is still interconnected to the two pillars, which is signified by the wreath chainwork although he is not visibly attached to it. This is also the duality of man. We can see how even this harmony and balance can be found in the lives of the Sun (male) and the Moon (female) and man and woman.

The Vesica Pisces, just like the two pillars in front of Solomon's temple are portals – the equilibrium of two opposite divine energies of God with a third (middle) pillar that represents the product of the two pillars (man). The man has duality of being. That is, man is both a natural and supernatural being. The way between the two pillars or the Vesica Pisces is a reminder that God is spirit, and He's also both male and female (having human qualities). Human equilibrium requires two feet, the world gravitates by two forces and generations need two sexes to continue. Just like the Vesica Pisces, when the two pillars find equilibrium, it generates a third pillar, one in the middle, which esoterically represents man or mankind. This mankind can be both a natural and supernatural being. This is man. And this is how God dwells in man and predestines a man even before he or she is born. You are already connected to the wreath network. These names of the pillars have purpose – they contain the key to the entire Bible and to the whole order of nature.

The name Jachin means "He will establish". The name Boaz means "in Him is strength". Put together, the names are a reminder of the strength and stability of God's promise of a kingdom that will last forever through His son Jesus Christ. Jesus Christ purchased us back with His precious blood that was spilled on the Cross of Calvary. Boaz exercised the right to purchase back property to return it to the family it once belonged to. Boaz represented Jesus Christ in his days.

Ruth 4:1-4

Boaz Redeems Ruth

4 Now Boaz went up to the gate and sat down there; and behold, the close relative of whom Boaz had spoken came by. So, Boaz said, "Come aside, friend, sit down here." So, he came aside and sat down. **²** And he took ten men of the elders of the city, and said, "Sit down here." So, they sat down. **³** Then he said to the close relative, "Naomi, who has come back from the country of Moab, sold the piece of land which *belonged* to our brother Elimelech. **⁴** And I thought to inform you, saying, 'Buy *it* back in the presence of the inhabitants and the elders of my people. If you will redeem *it,* redeem *it;* but if you will not redeem *it, then* tell me, that I may know; for *there is* no one but you to redeem *it,* and I *am* next after you.'"

And he said, "I will redeem *it.*"

Read the Book of Ruth and learn the character of Boaz and you will understand this better. Thus, the two pillars typify unity and the redeeming power of love through our Lord Jesus Christ. This is Christ's bond of love and perfection in everything with us. We are truly joint heirs. Although Solomon's temple was physically destroyed, the spiritual hidden meaning still lives and we see it in the Vesica Pisces, which can be seen all around us in space and has been the source of our geometry and the birthplace of this entire universe.

Proverbs 25:2

[2] *It is* the glory of God to conceal a matter,
But the glory of kings *is* to search out a matter.

We are the kings and priests, and it is our duty to search out a matter because Jesus and deep mysteries are concealed all over in the Bible. We are kings and priests after the order of Jesus (Melchizedek). When you study the topology of Boaz and Jachin in the Bible, you will understand. The pillars have a dual purpose, just as the Venn diagram (Vesica Pisces).

The Power of God in the Similitude of Electricity

Electricity and magnetism are related, and their theories were unified: wherever charges are in motion electric current results, and magnetism is due to electric current. The source for electric field is electric charge, whereas that for magnetic field is electric current (charges in motion).

Electric charge is the physical property of matter that causes it to experience a force when placed in an electromagnetic field. Electric charge can be positive or negative (commonly carried by protons and electrons respectively). Like charges repel each other and unlike charges attract each other. An object with an absence of net charge is referred to as neutral. In ordinary matter, negative charge is carried by electrons, and positive charge is carried by the protons in the nuclei of atoms. If there are more electrons than protons in a piece of matter, it will have a negative charge, if there are fewer it will have a positive charge, and if there are equal numbers it will be neutral.

An electromagnetic field is a classical (i.e., non-quantum) field produced by accelerating electric charges.

Tesla's biggest contribution to the world was his innovations in alternating current (AC) technology, that allowed electrical power transmission over long distances, and the invention of the AC motor that allowed this AC power to be used by factories and businesses. The adoption of this technology was an uphill battle because Thomas Edison's direct current (DC) systems had been the standard early on. AC eventually won because the underlying truth about the superiority of any technology lies in the science.

Some Basics of Electricity

All materials are made up of atoms. Atoms have a positively charged nucleus and negatively charged electrons surrounding the nucleus. Think about the Earth or human body while you read on. These electrons are bound to the nucleus due to charged electrons surrounding the nucleus. These electrons are bound to the nucleus due to their electromagnetic attraction to the oppositely charged nucleus.

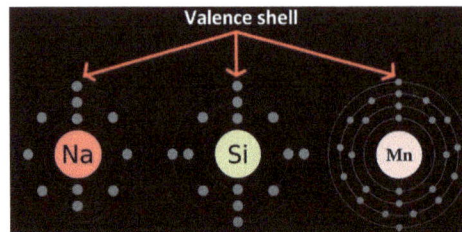

Image Source – Public Domain

Electrons in the outermost shell, called the valence shell, can sometimes become free due to external forces. These electrons that escape from the valence shell are called free electrons. And they can move from one atom to another.

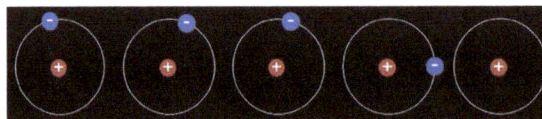

Image Source – Public Domain

This is what can cause a movement of charge. And this flow of electric charge is what electricity is all about. Materials that allow many electrons to move freely are called conductors. Examples of such materials are steel, silver, gold, seawater, copper, etc.

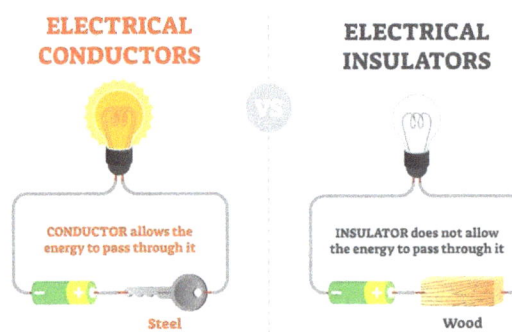

Image Source – Public Domain

And materials that don't allow much free movement of electrons are called insulators. Examples of such materials are wood, glass, rubber, plastic, oil etc.

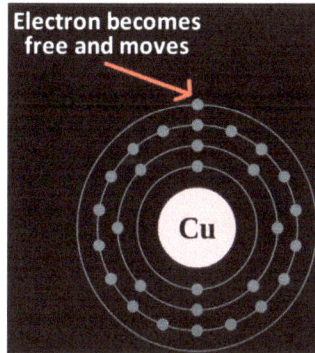

Image Source – Public Domain

For example, if you look at copper, you will notice that it has one electron in its outermost or valence shell. This can quite readily become a free electron. That's why copper is a great conductor. If we force this electron to move, we create electricity. An electrical current is the flow of free electrons from one atom to another.

There are three concepts you should understand if you want to understand electricity. And these are current, voltage, and resistance. The number three here is not a coincidence – God the Father, the Son, and the Holy Spirit. This is exactly how the power of God works and in the lives of the people of God. We (humans) are like the resistor or resistance.

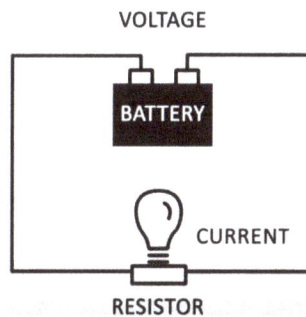

Image Source – Public Domain

All three are connected. If you change one, the others will change too. What you do in your daily life as a Christian is what determines how much you can be a conductor or conduit to manifest the power of God. The relationship between these three properties is described by Ohm's law – named after the German physicist Georg Ohm (1789 – 1854).

Voltage = Current x Resistance

These are not easy to visualize because you can't see them – they are invisible but very powerful. This is the same with the presence and power of God. It's invisible but very powerful and tangible. An analogy that scientists use is to think of this as a water tank, with a hose attached to the bottom. Current is the flow of water from the hose. It is measured in amps and is the rate at which charges flow.

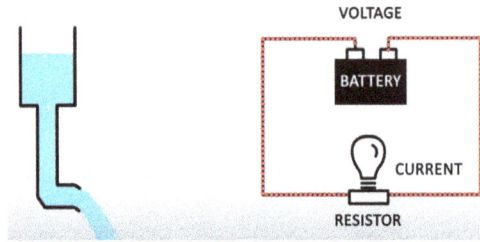

Image Source – Public Domain

It is analogous to the rate of flow of the water at the end of the hose. This is like the life of God or the Holy Spirit or Jesus Christ.

Voltage is like pressure

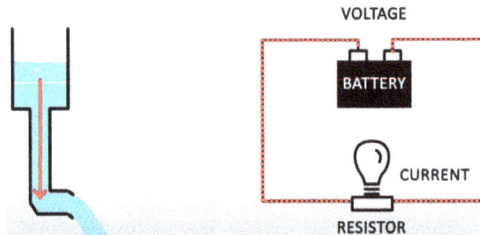

Image Source – Public Domain

Voltage, measured in volts, is the force required to make the current flow. It is analogous to the water pressure in the hose. This also is like the life of God or the Holy Spirit or Jesus.

Resistance is a material's tendency to resist the flow of charge. Think of resistance as the diameter of the hose. The smaller the hose, the higher the resistance.

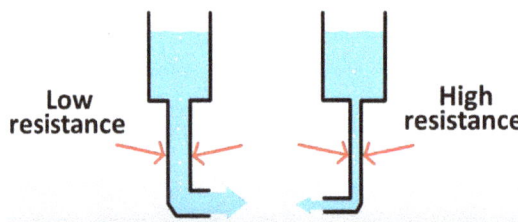

Image Source – Public Domain

So, if you have two tanks with the same amount of water, but one has a smaller hose than the other, or higher resistance, it will have a lower flow, given the same pressure. Similarly, a circuit with higher resistance, a constant voltage, will have a lower current.

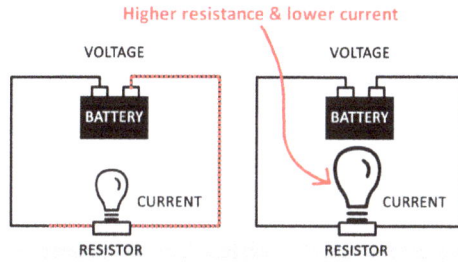

Image Source – Public Domain

But if water flow from the tank is constant, but the diameter is smaller, then pressure will increase. Similarly, if current is constant in a circuit, then a higher resistance will result in a higher voltage. If you live a genuine life of a Christian, this is how the manifestation of the Holy Spirit is in your life. Your consistency in maintaining a life of the secret place and in prayer (priesthood), and holy living will enable you to build and maintain a capacity that hosts the fullness of God, and you will continue to shine brighter and brighter and be a true witness of His word through the manifestation power of God as demonstrated and seen in the Bible.

Image Source – Public Domain

How does this water analogy relate to direct current and alternating current? Direct current is like the normal flow of water through the hose like we see below.

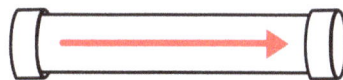

Image Source – Public Domain

The water flows in one direction. In this scenario, current flows at a constant rate over time. This was championed by Thomas Edison in the famous current wars that pit him against Nikola Tesla, who championed alternating current.

Alternating current is like water flowing back and forth within the hose 50 or 60 times per second.

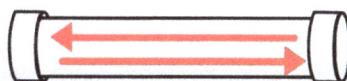

Image Source – Public Domain

This is called the frequency and is designated as either 50 Hertz (50 Hz) or 60 Hertz (60 Hz) and depends on the electric system of the country. The water analogy is not so great in this example because water does not flow in two directions or back and forth in a hose. But alternating current does. Alternating current is easily created by industrial electric generators and is now the world standard for transmission of electricity.

This technology won over direct current because of efficiency and power delivery. Power is like the volume or amount of water coming out of the hose. The same can be said about the power of God through an individual because we (humans) are the hose in this scenario.

Image Source – Public Domain

The reason electricity is generated is to send power to homes and factories. The mathematical formula for power equals the current times voltage.

Power = Current x Voltage

The greater the current and the greater the voltage in the transmission lines, the more power that is available to be delivered. Using the formula P = I x V, you can see that the same amount of power can be transmitted either at high current and low voltage, or low current and high voltage. But one is better than the other.

The power cables used to transmit electricity have a certain amount of resistance per meter of distance. The longer this cable is, the more resistance there is in the power line. When you follow the Word of God and do as the Bible instructs, you become efficient and effective rather than wasteful in manifesting the power of God. You wouldn't have to pray for hours to heal the sick or even cast out demons. It happens at the instant you speak the word, or you ask that devil to leave the person. Your presence is the difference – you don't even have to speak sometimes. You become a sign and a wonder and Mark 16:17 become a reality and you live the Bible experientially.

Mark 16:17

[17] And these signs will follow those who [a]believe: In My name they will cast out demons; they will speak with new tongues; [18] they[b] will take up serpents; and if they drink anything deadly, it will by no means hurt them; they will lay hands on the sick, and they will recover."

And any time you pass a current through resistance, you create heat, given by joule's equation for electric heat, where heat is equal to current squared times the resistance.

244

Joule's First Law

Heat loss = $I^2 \times R$ (per second)

Heat is wasted energy, because it essentially robs the grid of useful power that is not delivered to homes and businesses but is lost to the air. So, it is crucial to minimize this heat, otherwise much of the power that you want to deliver is going to get wasted. Since I = P/V from our power equation, if we substitute that back into the heat equation, we see that Heat equals Power squared times resistance R, divided by voltage V squared.

Heat loss = P^2R/V^2

Now we can see that to reduce heat, we want to maximize voltage V to deliver the same amount of power P because for any given power and resistance, the higher the voltage that we can create in the circuit, the lower the heat loss we will have while transmitting electricity. In modern electric power grids, electricity is routinely transmitted for hundreds of kilometers at hundreds of thousands of volts. But voltage cannot be this high when it arrives at your home because it would be very dangerous and could easily electrocute you. So, it must be stepped down before it gets to your house. This is done via a transformer which steps down the voltage from hundreds of thousands of volts to typically between 100 to 240 volts, which is the voltage of electrical outlets in most homes around the world. A true Son of God is a transformer to the Body of Christ because he steps up or steps down the Power of God and distribute it to the people. The people get transformed in the process.

Transformer

Image Source – Public Domain

This stepping up and stepping down of voltage is where alternating current shines in comparison to direct current. Direct current cannot easily be transformed from low to high voltage and vice versa. But this is quite easy to do with alternating current because when alternating current passes through a coil, it produces a constantly changing magnetic flux, per Maxwell's equations, that say that changing electric fields create magnetic fields. If we put a ring of iron through the coil, it can concentrate the changing magnetic flux within the ring. Now if we wind another coil around the other side of this ring, we can create electricity and induce voltage within the new coil because again, according to Maxwell's equations, a changing magnetic field creates a circulating electric field.

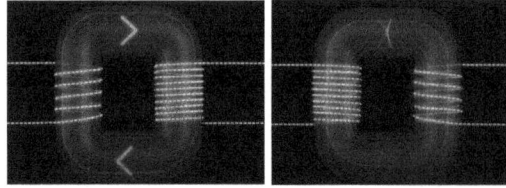

Left: Step-up, and Right: Step-down

Image Source – Public Domain

It so happens that the voltage we create in the second coil is proportional to the number of loops or turns we place around the iron ring. Using this method, we can create voltage that is much higher in the second loop than the original voltage in the first loop. This is very roughly how a transformer works, and this method is used to step up the voltage for transmission over vast distances to minimize energy loss. And we can use the same method to step down the voltage to a safer level, before it is delivered to your home by simply making a smaller number of turns in the step-down transformer. But as you can see, transformers like this require a time-varying voltage to function. And since direct current is constant, and only alternating current is time-varying, transformers like these only work with AC electricity. In Edison and Tesla's time, there was no easy way to transform voltage with direct current. And this is the primary reason Tesla's AC won out over Edison's DC in the early era of electrical transmission.

DC is still very important because many devices like light bulbs only require that the electrons move. They don't care if the electrons flow through the wire or simply move back and forth. So, a light bulb, for example, can typically be used with either AC or DC electricity. The fact that alternating current powers most of the modern industrial world has made Tesla the winner of the current wars.

DC isn't a losing concept long term because most high-tech appliances today that are powered by batteries, like laptops, cell phones, and tablets are all powered by direct current. In addition, in the late 20th century, engineers figured out a way to transmit electricity using high voltage direct current, or HVDC. It turns out that HVDC is more efficient than high voltage AC for transmitting electricity over extremely large distances of 1000 km or more.

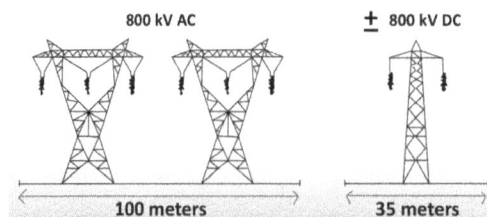

Image Source – Public Domain

This is because smaller, cheaper lines can be used to transmit the same amount of power using DC, and there is less induction loss because no changing magnetic field exists with DC, unlike with

AC. But the cost of DC transformers is huge, 10's of millions of dollars versus only thousands of dollars for AC transformers.

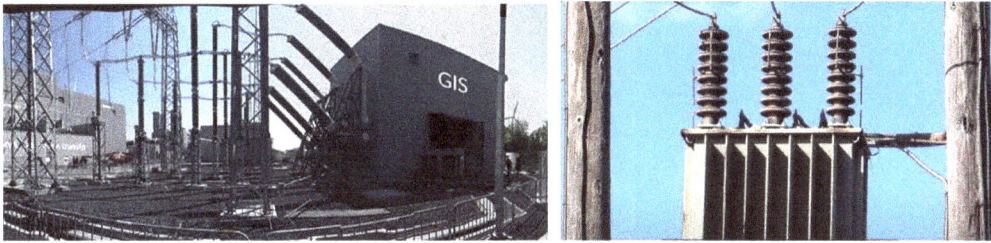

Left: DC converter station, Bruges, Belgium, and Right: AC transformer

Image Source – Public Domain

So, HVDC is only cost effective for very long transmission lines. In general terms, electricity flowing through a wire is just like the power of God and how humans are the conductors or conduits through which that power flows and is distributed for the works of God on the Earth.

Gravity and Seawater

There have been a lot of confusion in the scientific world regarding the explanations of tides and gravitational waves on the sea. Have you ever wondered why seawater is full of salt? Have you also wondered why we see tides heavily on the sea and not on rivers, lakes etc.?

The reason why seawater is a great conductor of electricity and a resource for renewable energy is that salt molecules are made up of sodium ions and chloride ions.

An ion is a particle, atom, or molecule with a net electrical charge. The charge of the electron is considered negative by convention. The negative charge of an electron is equal and opposite to charged proton(s) considered positive by convention. The net charge of an ion is not zero due to its total number of electrons being unequal to its total number of protons. So, an ion is an atom that has an electrical charge because it has either gained or lost an electron, also meaning it has a positive charge and a negative charge.

When you put salt in water, the water molecules pull the sodium and chlorine ions apart, so they are floating freely, increasing the conductivity. These ions are what carry electricity through the water with an electric current. In short, saltwater (water + sodium chloride) can help to produce electricity. Seawater or the ocean is a giant field of electrical conductor. This is the reason why it makes up about 71% of the Earth. It all has to do with powering the Earth in terms of the gravitational force that is used to propel the Earth in motion or orbit.

First, it is very important for you to know that without the sea or ocean, gravitation or electromagnetism would not be possible on the Earth.

Revelation 21:1

21 And I saw a new heaven and a new Earth: for the first heaven and the first Earth were passed away; and there was no more sea.

Therefore, there will be no more sea in the new heaven and the new Earth because the laws governing them will be different.

The Sun, the Moon, and the Tides

Below is a picture showing the Earth's magnetic field. In astronomy and planetary science, a magnetosphere is a region of space surrounding an astronomical object in which charged particles are affected by that object's magnetic field. It is created by a star or planet with an active interior dynamo.

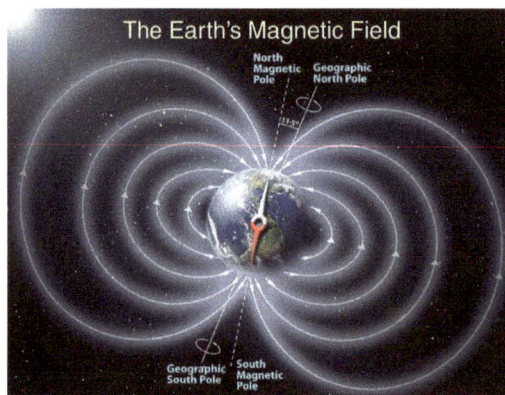

Image Source – Public Domain

This image will be your reference or reminder about the Earth's magnetic field while you read through these sections.

The Moon

I will start with the Moon since scientists have not dared to land on the Sun. The scientists' advantage has been powerful telescopes when it comes to matters of the Sun. The Moon doesn't have a magnetic field like the Earth or the Sun, and we all know how much gravity is on there – very little or low lunar gravity. If the Moon has no magnetosphere or lacks a magnetic field, why then do scientists say that the gravity of the Moon is part of what causes low and high tides? Also, note that there is no sea or ocean on the Moon.

The major difference between the Sun, Earth, and Moon is that the Earth is our habitat, and the major conductor of electricity is the sea or ocean. This is what makes gravity possible through electromagnetism to power and sustain (keep alive) the Earth and its inhabitants. This power is also what keeps it in constant motion in orbit.

The Moon was individually created as a light source (female) by God in the beginning. Again, you can reference this from the early parts of this writing. God calls the Moon a smaller light because it gets powered or energized by the Sun. This also gives the Moon the little bit of gravitational power that it has. This is mainly because of the force of attraction between the Moon and the Sun. This is because the Moon is a huge negatively charged electron and the Sun is a huge positively charged proton.

The Sun

The Sun is not a solid mass. It does not have easily identifiable boundaries like rocky planets like Earth. Instead, the Sun is composed of layers made up almost entirely of hydrogen and helium. These gases carry out different functions in each layer, and the Sun's layers are measured by their percentage of the Sun's total radius.

The Book of Enoch

Chapter 72:37

37 As he rises, so he sets and decreases not, and rests not, but runs day and night, and his light is sevenfold brighter than that of the Moon; but as regards size they are both equal.

The Sun's core, more than a thousand times the size of Earth and more than 10 times denser than lead, is a huge furnace. Temperatures in the core exceed 15.7 million kelvins (also 15.7 million degrees Celsius, or 28 million degrees Fahrenheit). The core extends to about 25% of the Sun's radius.

The core is the only place where nuclear fusion reactions can happen. The Sun's other layers are heated from the nuclear energy created there. Protons of hydrogen atoms violently collide and fuse, or join, to create a helium atom.

This process, known as a PP (proton-proton) chain reaction, emits an enormous amount of energy. The energy released during one second of solar fusion is far greater than that released in the explosion of hundreds of thousands of hydrogen bombs.

It takes the strong nuclear force to hold protons together and we see this in the formation of complex atomic nuclei. **Take note of the type of gravitational force at work here – strong interaction.**

During nuclear fusion in the core, two types of energy are released: photons and neutrinos. These particles carry and emit the light, heat, and energy of the Sun. Photons are the smallest particle of light and other forms of electromagnetic radiation. Neutrinos are more difficult to detect, and only account for about two percent of the Sun's total energy. The Sun emits both photons and neutrinos in all directions, all the time.

Remember that the photon is a type of elementary particle. It is the quantum of the electromagnetic field including electromagnetic radiation such as light and radio waves, and the force carrier for the electromagnetic force. It's massless and has an electric charge of 0.

And the neutrino is a fermion that interacts only via the weak gravity interaction. The neutrino is so named because it is electrically neutral and because its rest mass is so small that it was long thought to be zero. They have an electric charge of 0e. Neutrinos are created by various radioactive decays. **Again, notice the type of gravitational force here – weak interaction.**

Take note that gravity starts as a neutral force – then weak interaction force – then strong interaction force – then electromagnetic force – which then propels or puts objects or atoms in motion. Then the whole process starts all over again. This is very important because it is the redefinition of gravity. All the currently known forces of nature are one force – gravitational force operating at different levels.

We know the benefits of the energy of the Sun through several photosynthesis, fossil fuels, solar energy technology etc. Most importantly, to the human body we also know the heat or warmth we get from it and the vitamin D etc. Nothing in nature is an accident – everything was created for His pleasure and everything He created was good until sin kicked in.

Revelation 4:10-11

[10] the twenty-four elders fall down before Him who sits on the throne and worship Him who lives forever and ever, and cast their crowns before the throne, saying:

[11] "You are worthy, O Lord,
To receive glory and honor and power;
For You created all things,
And by Your will they exist and were created."

The galaxies, planets etc., are all products and producers of elementary particles at a cosmic scale. Everything is made from the same stuff – there are no surprises. You don't have to bring the whole Earth into a lab to be able to study it. You just need to know and understand nature through the power of God. The same experiments that are carried out by scientists in the labs are the same stuff happening at a much larger scale at the cosmic level. Hence, you can study the entire universe by studying a human being. If you want to understand who the human being is then you must study God. This means that if you want to have higher understanding of the universe, worship God because the true worshiping of God is the school of the Spirit of God – you will learn God experientially and won't require "scientific evidence" to prove His existence.

The Tides
The tidal bulges are a result of the complex movement or motion of the Sun, Earth, and Moon. The total effect is a push, rather than a pull of the Earth's seawater or ocean due to the rotation

and revolution of the three bodies in a balanced manner. Remember that the seawater is a great conductor of electricity. If it were a pull, then the seawater would be very close to the Sun and the Moon by now or the seawater would not return to its original position after some time because the fluctuations between low and high tide would mean the absence or stoppage of any form of gravitational interaction among the three bodies. We have already seen that there is a nuclear fusion (proton-proton) chain reaction that happens at the core of the Sun. Let's revisit our quadrupole illustration again.

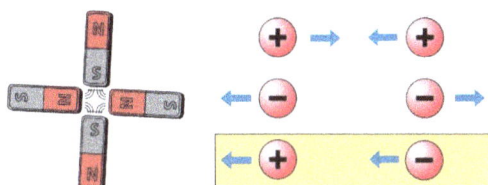

Left: a magnetic quadrupole, and Right: the signed illustration – runaway motions (yellow)

Image Source – Public Domain

The composition of the Sun is a positive electric charge. You can reference a recap on how interactions happen between particles from a few subsections below. The Sun all by himself is a giant positively charged body because of the proton-proton fusion.

The composition of the Moon is a negative electric charge. She gets energized by the Sun. The day side of the Moon becomes positively charged, as solar radiation knocks electrons from the surface. Meanwhile, electrons build up on the night side of the Moon and give the surface a negative charge. When a negative electron interacts with a positive proton, the electromagnetic force adds energy to the electron generating a photon. This is the generation of light by the Moon. An electron moving in a strong magnetic field will generate photons just from its acceleration. Also, energy from photons or light particles can be absorbed or released by electrons. When an electron absorbs a photon, the energy can free the electron to move around, or the electron can release the energy as another photon. This is how the Moon gets charged up and produce light from the Sun. Therefore, in the following images, even when the Moon is not directly interacting with the Sun, it still produces light according to the laws of God.

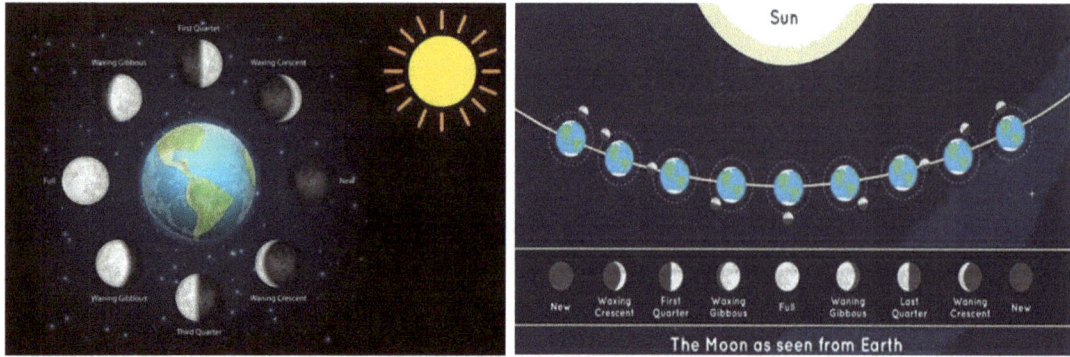

Lunar Phases

Image Source – Public Domain

The images above are the phases of the Moon as seen from the Earth. It is currently understood through several sources in science that the Moon appears to glow because it's bouncing off Sunlight from the day side of the Earth from where you are viewing it. And that the light reflects off old volcanoes, craters, and lava flows on the Moon's surface. How is this possible?

When we look at the full Moon, we see that it is on the other side of the Earth completely away from the Sun. If the current claim is true then it means that the full Moon shouldn't give the Earth any light at all because it is completely on the other side of the Earth away from the Sun where it doesn't get any Sunlight at all. How then does it produce this light – and not just partially but fully? Interestingly, when it is actually directly facing the Sun, the Earth doesn't get any light at all from it.

This should tell you that how the Moon produces light isn't just from mere reflection from the Sun as sicence claims. The Moon gets her light from the Sun in definite measure as written in the Word of God. Her full light amounts to the seventh part of the light of the Sun. You can read it below and make your own observations when the Moon starts appearing in the sky and compare it to the images above – count how many parts or phases that the Moon has.

The Book of Enoch

Chapter 73:1-8

1. And after this law I saw another law dealing with the smaller luminary, which is named the Moon. 2. And her circumference is like the circumference of the heaven, and her chariot in which she rides is driven by the wind, and light is given to her in (definite) measure. 3. And her rising and setting change every month: and her days are like the days of the Sun, and when her light is uniform (i.e., full) it amounts to the seventh part of the light of the Sun. 4. And thus, she rises. And her first phase in the east comes forth on the thirtieth morning: and on that day she becomes visible and constitutes for you the first phase of the Moon on the thirtieth day together with the Sun in the portal where the Sun rises. 5. And the one half of her goes forth by a seventh part, and

252

her whole circumference is empty, without light, except for one-seventh part of it, (and) the fourteenth part of her light. 6. And when she receives one-seventh part of the half of her light, her light amounts to one-seventh part and the half thereof. 7. And she sets with the Sun, and when the Sun rises the Moon rises with him and receives the half of one part of light, and in that night in the beginning of her morning [in the commencement of the lunar day] the Moon sets with the Sun and is invisible that night with the fourteen parts and the half of one of them. 8. And she rises on that day with exactly a seventh part and comes forth and recedes from the rising of the Sun, and in her remaining days she becomes bright in the (remaining) thirteen parts.

The older sections of the Book of Enoch (mainly in the Book of the Watchers) of the text are estimated to date from about 300–200 BC, and the latest part (Book of Parables) probably to 100 BC. Now you know the truth.

It is important to note that in Einstein's theory of relativity, he hypothesized that whenever matter or energy is present in space, it creates a curvature. There is an illustration with a trampoline with two types of masses: a heavy chunk of metal and a piece of marble. When the metal is placed on the trampoline, it bends it. Then the piece of marble is rolled on the surface. It orbits the heavy chunk of metal. In this scenario, the key point made is that there is "no force" acting on the marble but it still revolves around the heavy metal. Einstein went even further and said that the same thing happens when the Earth is orbiting the Sun. The Sun acts like a chunk of metal and creates a curvature in space and that the same can be applied to all objects in the universe. So, according to Einstein, matter, and energy warp spacetime, making nearby object to fall towards it.

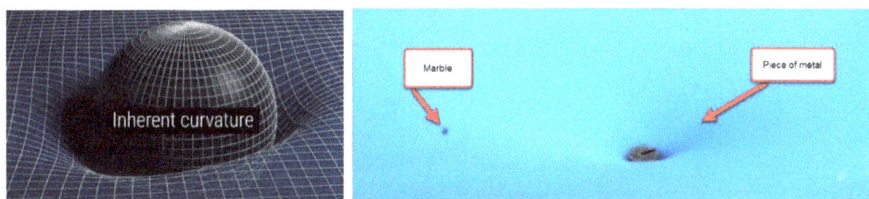

Image Source – Public Domain

It is also important to note that without any force acting between two revolving objects as seen in the image above, the smaller object will eventually fall on top of or collide with the bigger object around which it revolves – in this case the Sun, the Earth, and the Moon. What have kept them powered and in constant motion is because they are following specific strict laws given to them by God. This at our physical level is through the different phases of the gravitational force. The reason why a body like the Moon revolves around the Earth and both revolve around the Sun but never collide with each other is because of a level of gravity where electromagnetic suspension and revolution can be achieved and maintained. Study Faraday's rotation/revolution experiment. That is why Faraday used mercury (a very good conductor) to transform electrical energy into mechanical energy, creating the first electric motor. This technology and the attraction/repulsion ability in magnetism is how the revolutions happen between the three bodies.

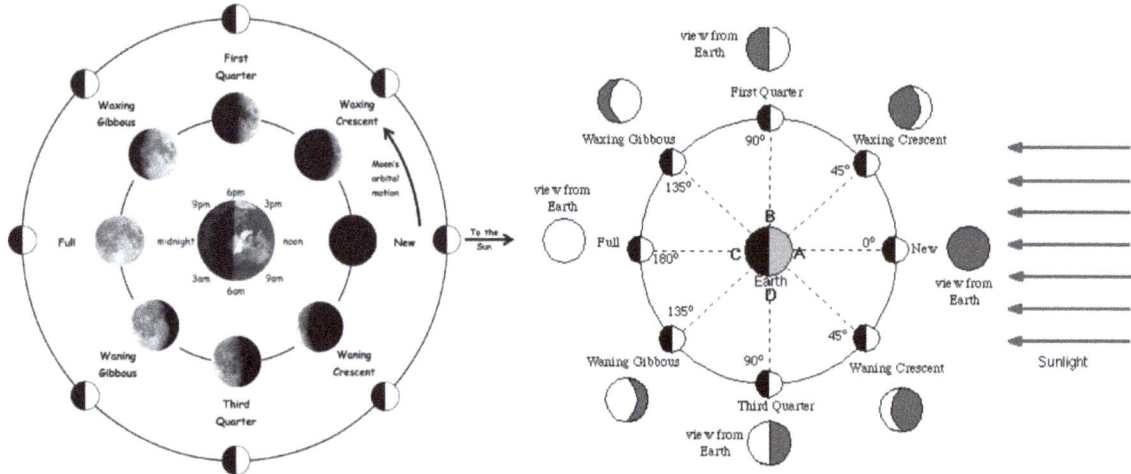

Lunar Phases (right image has degree measure of angles)

Image Source – Public Domain

Study the lunar phases again very carefully and take note of the angles and check out the movement of the three-phase electric power motor. This is what Tesla meant when he mentioned the power of the numbers 3, 6, and 9. The force interaction between the Earth and Moon is a bigger coordinate system although like the smaller version that governs just the Earth.

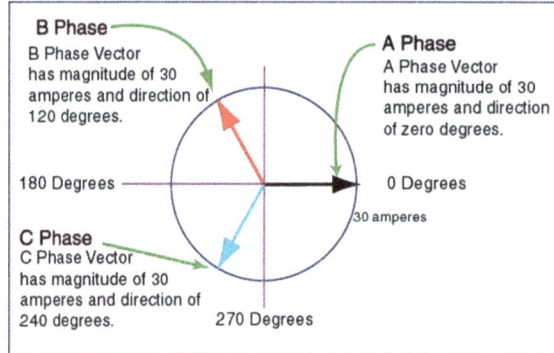

Three-phase electric power system

Image Source – Public Domain

The Sun, Earth, and Moon interact at a much bigger coordinate system, which is bigger than that of the Earth, and that of the Earth and the Moon. As you can see, the coordinate system is the same – it just keeps getting bigger. The coordinates never change. Just like the human body is built on this same foundation, this is also what is called quantum mechanics.

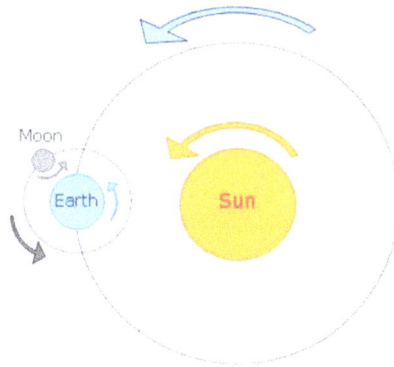

The Sun, Earth, Moon System

Image Source – Public Domain

It is no accident that the Earth is the third planet from the Sun. All the three bodies as shown above rotate on their axes. The Moon revolves around the Earth at the same time the Earth and the Moon together revolve around the Sun. This is how our night and day, seasons, and the whole year are given to us repeatedly in a uniform manner, following the laws of God. Altogether, this trinity represent what we call "time". Therefore, in the new heaven and the new Earth, we will have no Sun or Moon or seas. The glory of God will be our light forever and ever. If you isolate any of these three bodies from the system, it will collapse and wouldn't represent what we currently know them to represent. God uses His foundation in all His creation – Father, Son, and the Holy Spirit. He follows this order to make everything (quantum) work together in a trinity. And a bigger network is always a trinity of trinities.

Regarding quantum mechanics, when you study the phases of the Moon again, you will notice that whenever you take a measurement from any side of the Moon, you will always measure the inverse or opposite on the other side, no matter where you stand on Earth or the universe. The same applies to the human body like I mentioned earlier. No matter where you are in the world, when we ask you to tell us the position of you left hand, it will always be the left etc. This is quantum mechanics. And for this to be experimentally applied, it requires a base or root of three ($\sqrt{3}$). In quantum computing, this means using qutrits ($\sqrt{3}$) instead of qubits ($\sqrt{2}$).

The Earth's core is a nucleus (protons and neutrons), and the outer rings are made up of negative electrons. Since the outer rings of the Earth are made up of negatively charged electrons, i.e., seawater or ocean, it helps spin on its axis. The Earth has two types of motion – namely, rotation, and revolution. Rotation happens on the Earth's axis and that's what controls the 24-hour clock because that's how long it takes for a full rotation to complete. This is what controls night and day. The Sun exerts a gravitational pull on the Earth because it is positively charged. The Earth also both attracts and repels these electrons in its orbitals due to the nucleus at the center of gravity as we learned earlier. Therefore, there is both an attraction and repulsion going on between the magnetic fields of the Sun, the Earth, and the Moon. But as shown in the quadrupole diagram earlier, it is like a runaway motion between the Sun's positive electric charge and the Earth's surface negative electric charge. No matter how much the Earth is attracted to the Sun,

255

the Sun repels the Earth based of these magnetic or gravitational laws. Two objects of equal and opposite mass would produce a constant acceleration of the system towards the positive-mass object, an effect called "runaway motion".

Floating globe – magnetic levitation with a feedback loop

Image Source – Public Domain

It is this same gravity (attraction and repulsion) between the Sun and the Earth that propels the Earth into orbital motion around the Sun. The same technology propels the Moon in a revolution around the Earth. Reference the image above to help understand the concept. It is all electromagnetism, which is just another phase of gravity.

The Moon rotates on its axis and then revolves around the Earth and simultaneously, the Earth rotates on its axis constantly and then revolves simultaneously around the Sun. These are what control the seasons throughout the year and keep a good balanced set of seasons for all continents across the globe all year round.

Revelation 21:1

All Things Made New

21 Now I saw a new heaven and a new Earth, for the first heaven and the first Earth had passed away. Also, there was no more sea.

Revelation 22:5

[5] There shall be no night there: They need no lamp nor light of the Sun, for the Lord God gives them light. And they shall reign forever and ever.

When you read the two scriptures above, you will notice that there will be no more sea in the new heaven and the new Earth and, there shall be no night there so there will be no need for a lamp or light of the Sun. The reason for this is because we will be living in eternity like originally planned by God. The main reason why we have the Sun, Moon, and the Earth working in this manner as we have seen is to regulate times and seasons using the physical laws of God through the differential force of gravity.

How Seawater Affects Magnets

Freshwater is diamagnetic, which means that it exerts a weak magnetic field, and repels other magnetic fields. This means it creates a weak oppositional magnetic field to an applied magnetic field. If a magnet is suspended over water, the water's diamagnetism will repel the magnet.

However, when salt is added to water, it reduces the diamagnetism of the water. In addition, salt raises the freezing point and lowers the boiling point of water. Salt also strengthens the water's electrical conductivity. Due to these effects, magnets do not affect salt water the same way that they do to regular water.

Saltwater and Electromagnetism

Saltwater conducts electricity more efficiently than freshwater, and its conductive properties create a moving magnetic field when an electromagnet is placed nearby. Then, the saltwater creates an opposing magnetic field, causing turbulence (erratic changes in pressure and flow velocity) in the water. When a charged magnet meets saltwater, the ions flow through the metal to become stabilized, resulting in the electrical field.

The Earth's magnetic field started at the instance of creation when God made two great lights – the Sun and Moon to divide the day from the night; and to let them be for signs and seasons, and for days and years.

Genesis 1:1-19

1 In the beginning God created the heavens and the Earth. **2** The Earth was without form, and void; and darkness *was* on the face of the deep. And the Spirit of God was hovering over the face of the waters.

3 Then God said, "Let there be light"; and there was light. **4** And God saw the light, that *it was* good; and God divided the light from the darkness. **5** God called the light Day, and the darkness He called Night. So, the evening and the morning were the first day.

6 Then God said, "Let there be a firmament in the midst of the waters, and let it divide the waters from the waters." **7** Thus God made the firmament and divided the waters which *were* under the firmament from the waters which *were* above the firmament; and it was so. **8** And God called the firmament Heaven. So, the evening and the morning were the second day.

9 Then God said, "Let the waters under the heavens be gathered together into one place, and let the dry *land* appear"; and it was so. **10** And God called the dry *land* Earth, and the gathering together of the waters He called Seas. And God saw that *it was* good.

11 Then God said, "Let the Earth bring forth grass, the herb *that* yields seed, *and* the fruit tree *that* yields fruit according to its kind, whose seed *is* in itself, on the Earth"; and it was so. **12** And the Earth brought forth grass, the herb *that* yields seed according to its kind, and the tree *that* yields fruit, whose seed *is* in itself according to its kind. And God saw that *it was* good. **13** So the evening and the morning were the third day.

14 Then God said, "Let there be lights in the firmament of the heavens to divide the day from the night; and let them be for signs and seasons, and for days and years; **15** and let them be for lights in the firmament of the heavens to give light on the Earth"; and it was so. **16** Then God made two great lights: the greater light to rule the day, and the lesser light to rule the night. *He made* the stars also. **17** God set them in the firmament of the heavens to give light on the Earth, **18** and to rule over the day and over the night, and to divide the light from the darkness. And God saw that *it was* good. **19** So the evening and the morning were the fourth day.

On the first day of creation, God divided the light from darkness. The light was called day and the darkness was called night. It is very important to note that before one can make progress in life, one must first know the truth and that is why God divided light from darkness right after He commanded light into being. Truth is light and it gave God the ability to see clearly and to know what else to do after that.

On the third day, God gathered the waters in one place to have dry land appear and He called the dry land Earth and the waters Seas. After He had created plants, fruits etc., on the third day, He immediately followed that up with creating the Sun and Moon on the fourth day. Therefore, light is different from the Sun and Moon although they are all light sources. The confirmation for this is how it could be day in one country but night in another country. And wherever there is darkness, all you need is a good light source and there will be light. It could be day, yet it could be dark. You could have information, yet not have the right knowledge. And you could have knowledge, yet not have the right understanding.

The reason for referencing this is because the Earth's magnetic field has been a mystery to scientists. On the fourth day of creation, after the creation of the Sun and the Moon, was when the magnetic field was activated because that was when the rotations and revolutions started happening and everything was put into motion. All these mechanics had to be in place before living creatures could inhabit the Earth. Everything is in order – there's no trial and error. I don't need to explain why God started creating living creatures after this phase in the order of creation – you should know why by now.

Now, an important reason for the existence of seawater of that volume on the surface of the Earth is that first, it is a great conductor of electricity, which the electromagnetic force acts upon to accelerate the Earth's rotation on its axis and revolution around the Sun at the desirable constant speed. It also has a relationship with the low and high tides of the sea as well as the waves due to the gravitational force acting between the three bodies. If the seas were freshwater, then the diamagnetism of it would repel the magnetic field between the Sun, Earth, and Moon and cause a big imbalance especially for the Earth since the Earth's core is like a bar magnet with a uniformly distributed magnetic field. This imbalance would cause us to feel the motion of the Earth because it wouldn't be constant anymore. But since seawater conducts electricity better, the magnetic fields around it cause significant turbulence in the water, which are the waves we see but it maintains gravitational balance among the three bodies due to electromagnetism. The seawater does not repel the magnetic field – it conducts it rather. Therefore, the ocean can never be still and will always have currents. The salt in the sea is not random – God is not random. The seawater is why we can enjoy desirable climates all year round among many other things.

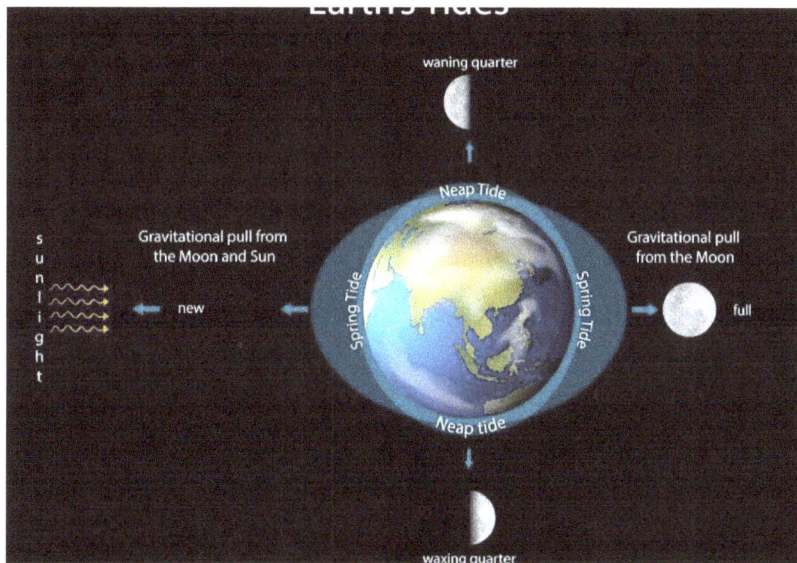

Image Source – Public Domain

When you take a measurement on the other side of the Earth for a particular tide, you will always notice that it happens on the four points on the coordinate system. Hence, we can measure a neap tide on the positive side when it is happening on the negative side and vice versa. We can say the same about spring tides. The interesting part of spring tide is the balance it brings and shows surrounding the union between the Sun, Earth, and the Moon. Spring tides truly show how the three bodies lie in a negative, neutral, and positive coordinate system. When the Sun and Moon are right angled, there is neap tide because the tides sort of cancel out each other. And when all three are linear, there is spring tide. This is called superposition in quantum mechanics. You can truly prove entanglement from this by taking a quantum measurement. One can choose to take this measurement even at the sea tide level or electric current on the Earth and not necessarily from the Sun or the Moon and still be accurate because when you know what you are measuring and you choose to do that from either the Sun or the Moon, they will all correlate, and you will still be accurate. You can be in either of the three places and be able to tell what the state is like on either of them. This is quantum mechanics.

Earth has one Moon, and this is because God wants to help you understand Him better. He wants us to understand why without any of His persons in the holy trinity, even the Christian is lost. Each one of them (Father, Son, and Holy Spirit) must be equally revered and worshiped as God because all three of them together is one God (Elohim) and individually, they are still God (Eloha). This does not mean that the Sun, Earth, and Moon or any other planet(s) is God. Again, some people make this mistake – don't be one of them. Knowing and understanding the truths about His creation helps you understand Him better and to know who He truly is because He has hidden dimensions of Himself in all His creation. Earth is the most balanced planet for this reason, and this is possible because of the Sun, Earth, and Moon (+, 0, -) working together as one body although you can still individually identify them. And, because it is the legal habitat for man. They all bring something unique to the party of life or existence. Remove one of them and see everything collapse, including all the other planets. Don't write off the other planets just yet because they all exist for a reason, and the very least is that they help us understand and appreciate Earth much better. But a day has been written where every member of the solar system will collapse or fall into a black hole one after the other and be destroyed forever and ever. I saw this in a vision.

Even when scientists try to explain nature to you, for example, regarding the Earth, they use a language and sentences like, "much of the water on Earth today may have been delivered by cometary and asteroidal bombardment several hundred million years after the planet formed. That includes the water in the atmosphere, the oceans, the polar caps and glaciers, in human bodies, and in all other living things in the biosphere." Disregard all these because it's a bunch of nonsense. If you want to learn how the universe was created in a truthful and orderly manner, read the Word of God (Bible). And don't read versions from like the Watchtower or Jehovah Witness', Mormon etc. We will discuss more on that later because even those so-called groups or organizations and what they teach is a bunch of nonsense (error and lies).

The Sun is a positively charged proton, and the Moon is a negatively charged electron. The Earth already has the nucleus (protons and neutrons) pulling the electrons in the outer rings in orbit. The whole Earth serves as the nucleus among the gravitational interactions between the Sun and the Moon.

The nucleus (Earth) in this trinity has the same effect on the whole Moon because it is a negatively charged electron. The result is the entire Moon orbiting the Earth just like how the electrons on the outer rings of the Earth orbiting and causing the Earth to spin through gravitation.

The reason why the Moon doesn't collide with the Sun is the negatively charged electrons of the Moon and that of the Earth's outer rings repelling each other. Opposite charges attract each other while same charges repel each other. The Moon orbits the Earth as a result because the Earth's nucleus still attracts the Moon since the Earth's nucleus is a positively charged proton.

The Sun then as a positively charged proton pulls on the negatively charged electron Moon but the Earth's electromagnetic field is so strong that it overpowers the Sun's gravitational pull on both the Moon and the Earth. Because of the distance between the Sun and the Earth, there is balance in the force of gravity working between them. The result is the Moon orbiting the Earth and the Earth orbiting the Sun. All these movements happen simultaneously.

The net charge of the Moon is -1e. The net charge of the Earth is 0e. The net charge of the Sun is 1e.

Image Source – Public Domain

Note that the charges can also be written as -e, e, +e and it will still be correct. This is the foundation on which our entire universe and everything else that's in it is built – it's a trinity.

The Sun's electric charge is like the electric charge of the Earth's core or nucleus, which is 1e (protons and neutrons). The Earth's electric charge is a neutral charge, which is 0e. The Moon's electric charge is like the electric charge of the Earth's surface (mostly from the seawater), which is -1e.

The net charge of all three (Sun, Earth, Moon) combined is 0e. The charges working in the Earth are the same three charges working between the three bodies at a much bigger scale. Without the Earth, the Moon and the Sun wouldn't exist and without either of them or both, the Earth wouldn't exist. Most importantly, they help keep the Earth and make it stay in perfect balance as designed by God and suitable for all living things to live on it. These are also the same charges working in the human body. And without humans on the Earth, nothing would exist here.

Finally, the Sun, Earth, and Moon together form the coordinate system at a larger (cosmic) scale – they work together to control time. You can safely call all three of them "time". It becomes dangerous when you start giving space several dimensions and a separate dimension to time. It is safer to call all three "time" because that's what they represent. Just like how all three persons of the Godhead together is God because they represent God both individually and together as one deity.

Scientifically, this is how this phenomenon can be explained but the reality of it all is that all these bodies in the solar system have a course given to them by God and spiritually they obey the divine laws of God and follow their courses accordingly in the physical. They are perfectly governed, and they obey. Those who have the knowledge, understand and those with eyes will see. Therefore, physically, things are the way they are because God designed them to be so. These are the fundamental ways that the universe works. The universe is made up of well-defined, independent pieces of creations. There is a programming that requires the wisdom of God to know about and understand. When you understand nature, you would study other planets or the entire universe just for the sake of science and knowledge, which are great, but you would stop wasting your time to try go live on Mars or any other planet, for example. Don't get me wrong because we still need science. Some things are made impossible by God and no human can even be successful in any attempt to violate it. Humans can still try if they want but I think there are several important issues that we could be addressing here on Earth. We haven't even finished dealing with Earth yet. These show the lust and vain glory that humans are always chasing after, but we should always do first things first. The priority in your life should be God through Jesus Christ by the power of the Holy Spirit, then everything else shall follow accordingly with the leadership of the Holy Spirit. Then you won't be wasting your time chasing things of the world – inordinate pride in oneself or one's achievements, which are all excessive vanity.

Galatians 5:24-26

[24] And they that are Christ's have crucified the flesh with the affections and lusts.

[25] If we live in the Spirit, let us also walk in the Spirit.

[26] Let us not be desirous of vain glory, provoking one another, envying one another.

Carbon Dioxide

For example, carbon dioxide in the atmosphere provides the primary source of carbon for growing plant life on Earth, from the smallest microalgae in the oceans to the largest trees on land. Carbon dioxide (CO_2) – is an essential part of the cycle of life. Without a source of CO_2, plants will die off, and without plant life, the Earth's biological food chain would be terminally broken.

The carbon found in biomass is taken out of the atmosphere through the process of photosynthesis which causes plants to grow.

When you inhale (breathe in), air enters your lungs and oxygen from the air moves from your lungs to your blood. At the same time, carbon dioxide, a waste gas, moves from your blood to the lungs and is exhaled (breathe out). This process is called gas exchange or respiration and is essential to life.

Carbon dioxide is added to the atmosphere naturally when organisms respire or decompose (decay), carbonate rocks are weathered, forest fires occur, and volcanoes erupt. There are several other artificial ways too, but we care more about the natural cycle now.

Oxygen

Phytoplankton need two things for photosynthesis for their survival: energy from the Sun and nutrients from the water. Phytoplankton absorb both across their cell walls.

In the process of photosynthesis, phytoplankton release oxygen into the water. Half of the world's oxygen is produced via phytoplankton photosynthesis. The other half is produced via photosynthesis on land by trees, shrubs, grasses, and other plants.

As green plants die and fall to the ground or sink to the ocean floor, a small fraction of their organic carbon is buried. It remains there for millions of years after taking the form of substances like oil, coal, and shale.

Sexual Intercourse

This is the same way that as sophisticated as every human being is, that person once physically didn't exist although spiritual people know that everybody existed before they came into the physical realm and will continue to exist forever and ever even after they leave the physical realm someday. In the physical, everybody was once not even a droplet of sperm before they became a droplet of sperm from their father and ended up colliding with the egg of their mother in a gravitational interaction and based on the electric charges involved in the interaction, the conception occurred and a boy, girl, or twins was decided. That is, sperm can have different electric charges depending on the chromosome status – X (+) or Y (-) and the sperm of infertile men frequently have an isoelectric point (neither + nor -) set consistently higher compared to fertile men. The same explosion that happened in the beginning of time, happens whenever a sperm and egg collide or meet ("Big Bang"). And the process of growth (expansion of universe) begins. You can investigate or experiment it if you want. Gravity happens everywhere in nature in many ways with many different phases. Everything works on the same fundamental laws.

When anybody wants to argue this truth, ask them if they, once being a droplet of sperm, changes them from being a human being right now. As big and strong as you look and feel right now, the absence of that droplet of sperm that formed you would mean your nonexistence – it's as simple as that. Several examples have been given and the stages of pregnancy have also been shown. A sperm is simply a fundamental step or level or dimension towards the beginning of the life of a human – a singularity, just like a seed that germinates and grows to become a big tree. All the collisions of elementary particles that happen in the universe also happen when men have sexual intercourse with women – same thing. There are both exponential growth and exponential decay. So, the absence of the singularity which birthed the living universe means the absence of this physical world and life – it's as simple as that. That is, the absence of God's decision to create would mean our nonexistence and He will still exist as God. The only difference is that He would only be known among the godhead and the other heavenly beings. If you were once not even part of the sperm contained in your father's sack, and by the grace of God, you became part of that flow of sperm, and not by chance but by predestination you collided with your mother's egg, and now you are a full-blown human being, why then do you doubt the fact that the Earth was birthed this same way? First, there was the spiritual realm that physical eyes cannot see, just like certain lights, although they exist. Second, the spoken word of God and the spirit of God joined efforts and formed the universe from nothing and then it became a tiny singularity like a droplet of sperm plus egg and then grew (expanded) and still growing. You are not smarter than your Creator. Be humble and He will show you, His secrets.

Why do I go over all these forces of nature fundamentally like this?

Converting Protons into Neutrons

First, when two protons collide and fuse, a disruption in the weak nuclear force emits positron and neutrino, which converts one of the positively charged proton to a neutrally charged neutron. Without the weak nuclear force, converting protons into neutrons, and certain complex nuclei cannot form. This is what also happens in the Sun's core. **We see a variation of gravity here.**

Heavy atoms have an imbalance of protons and neutrons, so the weak nuclear force converts protons to neutrons releasing radiation.

Image Source – Public Domain

Binding Protons in Atomic Nuclei

Second, positively charged particles naturally repel each other, it takes an extreme amount of force to hold protons together. The strong nuclear force overcomes the repulsion between protons to hold together atomic nuclei. Without the strong nuclear force, complex nuclei cannot form. **We see another variation of gravity here.**

Enormous energy is released as gamma rays and neutrinos when the strong nuclear force is broken between protons and neutrons.

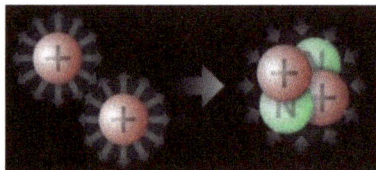

Image Source – Public Domain

Forming Atoms and Molecules

The electromagnetic force pulls negatively charged electrons into bound orbits around positively charged nuclei to form atoms and molecules. As a gas cools, electrons will find their way into the presence of atomic nuclei. Larger nuclei with a greater positive charge pull in more electrons until atoms and molecules have a balance of charges. **We see another variation of gravity here.**

When a negative electron interacts with a positive proton, the electromagnetic force adds energy to the electron generating a photon. This is the generation of light.

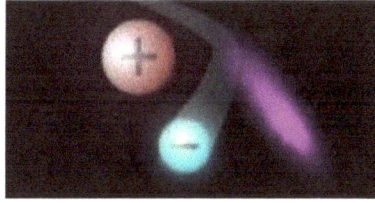

Image Source – Public Domain

Adding Motion to the Universe

Gravity forms stars, planets, galaxies, humans etc. Gravity keeps satellites, the International Space Station, and the Moon in orbit of Earth. Gravity keeps Earth and other planets in orbit around the Sun. Gravity holds galaxies together. Gravity keeps everything in motion and continuity – exponential growth and decay.

Gravity or gravitation is a natural phenomenon by which all things with mass or energy – including planets, stars, galaxies, and even light – are attracted to (or gravitate toward) one another. **We can see the definition of all the three other forces in this simple definition. Except that we must add "or repel one another" to make it complete. There is only one force of nature (gravity) in three variations (weak, strong, and electromagnetic) with an initial state of neutral.** Or we can start from neutral, weak, strong, and electromagnetic to make up the four forces of nature since humanity is so used to the number four on this subject although neutral is not really a force but a free state. If you count neutral as a force then, the four fundamental forces of nature are neutral, weak, strong, and electromagnetic forces. Altogether, they make up the one and only force of gravity.

This means that the one and only true and underlying or fundamental force of nature is what we call gravity. It starts binding and creating, and finally, it puts into motion and maintains in motion. We truly have only one force. It is a cyclic process from infancy to maturity, and to decay. And the whole process restarts. There is only one and only true God, people.

Summary of All the Forces of Nature

Weak force starts the process as weak gravity, strong force strongly binds quarks together using strong gravity so that it will make electromagnetism a possibility, and finally, electromagnetism takes place using another strong gravity between multiple particles or bodies to create a magnetic field so that an object with mass can set in continuous motion without the need for external source of energy. It is all gravity – that's the fundamental force. They are just different stages of gravity. That's why it starts and ends in all the calculations.

The same process takes place in the lives of human beings right from the moment of intercourse. When you are finally matured, this same gravity continues to keep you in motion. After you are born, it continues by learning how to crawl and then walk and then ran and then finally grow old and die, and then decay. The same energy to use for all these activities are bound up inside of you whether you choose to do one or the other. Choosing to walk wouldn't mean you are weak. Without the weak force, no other force or process can take place and without the strong, and electromagnetic forces, we will have no sustenance and continuity.

One big advantage to using an electromagnetic energy source is that, depending upon the electromechanical device used, you don't need an external electrical source to generate electrical power. One example of this is an alternating-current (AC) generator. That is why this is the best quantum idea to build a sustainable and efficient quantum computer – three-phase power (a qutrit system), which will maintain coherence and great energy efficiency.

Finally, it is gravity that brings a man and a woman together. It is gravity that takes place between a sperm and an egg. It takes gravity for a baby to develop properly in the womb until birth, and it even takes gravity for the baby to be born. Gravity between the sperm and the egg isn't the same as gravity while the baby is a grown up, but they are both gravity at different levels, while there is still a subtle underlying gravity that keeps the body parts together until death. Gravity is how we grow up, how we continue to live, and how we finally leave the Earth.

If you want to know that amount of information contained in an elementary particle, think about a droplet of sperm, and look at yourself, and make your own determination. As complex and sophisticated as you are, you came from mostly a droplet of sperm from your father and a tiny egg from your mother. Your composition was all embedded in those spiritually big but physically tiny things. The same concept applies to the birth of the Earth. This is gravity and this is how quantum mechanics works.

Continuation of My Revelation

Another way that I confirmed that the Venn diagram (Vesica Pisces) that God revealed to me in a vision is truly the interpretation that He gave me is that, during the late parts of the year 2020, I was driving to the classroom on Fort Gordon, GA for a session of my United States Army Cyber Basic Officer Leadership Course, and the Spirit of God asked me a question: "Do you know why I created humans and specifically a male and a female and made procreation possible?". I said no. He started explaining to me. Think of me as a "Circle". He immediately showed me this picture.

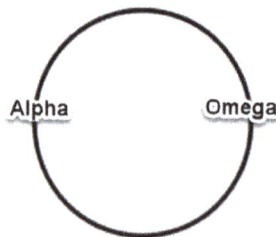

The Circle representation of the eternal Life of God as He showed to me
Image Source – Revelation received from God

He continued and said, I am like this Circle – I am Alpha Omega (the beginning the end). I know the beginning from the end and the end from the beginning. I have no end and that is why I am

266

eternal and will exist forever and ever. When you try to travel through this circle in any direction, you can never come to a stop because it has no limits or stops at the beginning or at the end. Therefore, even a clock to keep track of time, is represented by a circle. The difference is that the clock travels in only one direction and once it gets to the end, the whole process of time, starts all over again: day and night, which is like a reset and reversal or repetitive process. It gets to the end, and it reverses then repeats all over again. But in my dimension, there is no time, hence, there is no night or day. There is only eternity and what you consider time is all "now" or present. The mystery of God's mercies hidden in the mystery of time (the reset) as He promised in His covenant with David.

2 Samuel 7:15

God's Covenant with David

15 But My mercy shall not depart from him, as I took *it* from Saul, whom I removed from before you.

Lamentations 3:22-24

22 ***Through*** the LORD's mercies we are not consumed,
Because His compassions fail not.
23 ***They are*** **new every morning**;
Great *is* Your faithfulness.
24 "The LORD *is* my portion," says my soul,
"Therefore I hope in Him!"

The Lord continued – a man represents one dimension of me, and a woman represents another dimension of me. Without either one of them, there can be no procreation. Most importantly, I created each of them with unique abilities and for procreation to happen, one cannot do without the other. So are the offspring that will be birthed from their intercourse. Each person hosts a unique dimension of me. This means that each person will always have a unique ability or gift to perform a specific assignment for me that no one in eternity will be able to do except for that one person, no matter how anybody tries to do the same thing or even compete with the person. It is what makes them relevant in my Kingdom because I put it in them before I send them to the Earth, and everybody is in the Earth for that assignment.

He added – and if you look at the circle and think of the man and woman, and if mankind continues to procreate, will you ever come to an end or ever finish or go extinct in the Earth? The answer to this question is no. The population will only increase and will go to infinity. Therefore, the devil has an agenda to corrupt my people with congenital birth defects, homosexuality, and abortions. This is an agenda to corrupt my plan for man because when a man meets another man or a woman meets another woman, that is two of the same dimensions from me meeting and they cannot bear any fruits. The same applies to when my unborn child is aborted. Each time this happens, it means that a unique dimension is being stopped from entering the Earth to carry out my purposes uniquely assigned to them. And if they are born but with a congenital birth defect or defects, then that's also a limitation or something to slow down or corrupt my agenda.

I am sure that by now you know why even in technology, we have male and female connectors or connections. There are a lot more examples out there that you can look on your own. Without a connection like this, there is really no connection between two wires that must be extended etc. So, you see, even the idea of a male and female is not just applied in human beings or living beings but in our everyday lives too. It's there all around you in plain sight.

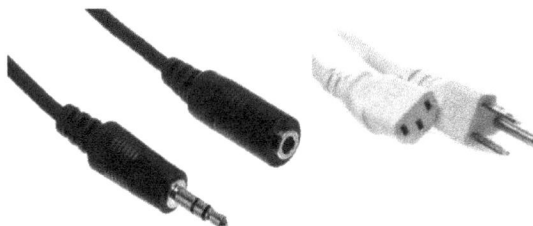

Image Source – Public Domain

Then I knew and understood the importance of man and how God through His infinite supreme wisdom divided Himself to put into a man and a woman to bring forth offspring that will each carry unique dimensions of Him to destroy the works of the enemy and to carry out God's divine purposes assigned to them for the journey towards the New Heaven and Earth.

Psalm 8

8 O Lᴏʀᴅ, our Lord,
How excellent *is* Your name in all the Earth,
Who have set Your glory above the heavens!
2 Out of the mouth of babes and nursing infants
You have ordained strength,
Because of Your enemies,
That You may silence the enemy and the avenger.
3 When I consider Your heavens, the work of Your fingers,
The Moon and the stars, which You have ordained,
4 What is man that You are mindful of him,
And the son of man that You visit him?
5 For You have made him a little lower than the angels,
And You have crowned him with glory and honor.
6 You have made him to have dominion over the works of Your hands;
You have put all *things* under his feet,
7 All sheep and oxen—
Even the beasts of the field,
8 The birds of the air,

And the fish of the sea
That pass through the paths of the seas.
⁹ O Lᴏʀᴅ, our Lord,
How excellent *is* Your name in all the Earth!

So, you see, you are way too special than you think. Stop underrating and undermining yourself. And stop thinking it is proper or natural to feel like you were born gay or homosexual. It is abnormal and demonic. In fact, the Bible calls it an abomination. Also, each time you want to abort that baby in your womb, remember this and the scriptures below.

Leviticus 20:12-14

¹² If a man lies with his daughter-in-law, both of them shall surely be put to death. They have committed perversion. Their blood *shall be* upon them. ¹³ If a man lies with a male as he lies with a woman, both of them have committed an abomination. They shall surely be put to death. Their blood *shall be* upon them. ¹⁴ If a man marries a woman and her mother, it *is* wickedness. They shall be burned with fire, both he and they, that there may be no wickedness among you.

Proverbs 3:5

⁵ Trust in the Lᴏʀᴅ with all your heart,
And lean not on your own understanding;

Proverbs 15:13

¹³ A merry heart makes a cheerful countenance,
But by sorrow of the heart the spirit is broken.

John 16:33

³³ These things I have spoken to you, that in Me you may have peace. In the world you will have tribulation; but be of good cheer, I have overcome the world."

Colossians 1:10-17

¹⁰ that you may walk worthy of the Lord, fully pleasing *Him,* being fruitful in every good work and increasing in the knowledge of God; ¹¹ strengthened with all might, according to His glorious power, for all patience and longsuffering with joy; ¹² giving thanks to the Father who has qualified us to be partakers of the inheritance of the saints in the light. ¹³ He has delivered us from the power of darkness and conveyed *us* into the kingdom of the Son of His love, ¹⁴ in whom we have redemption through His blood, the forgiveness of sins.

15 He is the image of the invisible God, the firstborn over all creation. **16** For by Him all things were created that are in heaven and that are on Earth, visible and invisible, whether thrones or dominions or principalities or powers. All things were created through Him and for Him. **17** And He is before all things, and in Him all things consist.

Through further consistent prayer, fasting, meditation, and research, I was led to a vast range of information about the Vesica Pisces (Sacred Geometry). In fact, it is the beginning of not only mathematics, science, engineering but everything in this world.

History and Ancient Meanings of the Vesica Pisces

It is believed that a simple geometric shape may connect us to the moment of creation, remind us of the unity of all things, or bring the love of the Creator into our present moment awareness. It is two overlapping circles of equal size that are intersecting at each circle's midpoint. The intersection created an almond-shaped frame. In mathematics, we call it the Venn diagram.

In ancient times, a single circle represented Source and all Creation. It was a perfect representation given that the circle has no beginning or end (Alpha Omega), which makes it eternal and so in an absolute sense, nothing exists but the divine. Two circles always represented masculine and feminine: god and goddess energies of duality.

History and Christian Meanings of the Vesica Pisces

It has a rich meaning in Christianity. The cross of Christ may be formed in the center of the intersection or oval by creating intersecting lines at the horizontal and vertical intersections. Christians think of the cross as a symbol of Godly sacrifice and love. If one rotates the mandorla, then one can clearly see the early Christian sign known as the ichthus or fish. The mandorla is described as an almond shaped aureola.

Left: mandorla, Middle: almond fruit, and Right: image depiction of Jesus
Image Source – Public Domain

Aureola is a circle of light or brightness surrounding something, especially as depicted in art around the head or body of a person represented as holy.

Left: Christian Ichthus, and Right: Image depiction of Virgin Mary in Vesica Pisces
Image Source – Public Domain

Why the Almond?

Numbers 17

The Budding of Aaron's Rod

17 And the LORD spoke to Moses, saying: **2** "Speak to the children of Israel, and get from them a rod from each father's house, all their leaders according to their fathers' houses—twelve rods. Write each man's name on his rod. **3** And you shall write Aaron's name on the rod of Levi. For there shall be one rod for the head of *each* father's house. **4** Then you shall place them in the tabernacle of meeting before the Testimony, where I meet with you. **5** And it shall be *that* the rod of the man whom I choose will blossom; thus, I will rid Myself of the complaints of the children of Israel, which they make against you."

6 So Moses spoke to the children of Israel, and each of their leaders gave him a rod apiece, for each leader according to their fathers' houses, twelve rods; and the rod of Aaron *was* among their rods. **7** And Moses placed the rods before the LORD in the tabernacle of witness.

8 Now it came to pass on the next day that Moses went into the tabernacle of witness, and behold, the rod of Aaron, of the house of Levi, had sprouted and put forth buds, had produced blossoms and yielded ripe almonds. **9** Then Moses brought out all the rods from before the LORD to all the children of Israel; and they looked, and each man took his rod.

10 And the LORD said to Moses, "Bring Aaron's rod back before the Testimony, to be kept as a sign against the rebels, that you may put their complaints away from Me, lest they die." **11** Thus did Moses; just as the LORD had commanded him, so he did.

12 So the children of Israel spoke to Moses, saying, "Surely we die, we perish, we all perish! **13** Whoever even comes near the tabernacle of the LORD must die. Shall we all utterly die?"

So, you see that it is not an accident or coincidence that the Bible uses the almond tree and fruit to illustrate several things. There is a meaning for everything. Nothing in the Bible is random.

Jeremiah 1:11-12

11 Moreover the word of the LORD came to me, saying, "Jeremiah, what do you see?"

And I said, "I see a branch of an almond tree."

12 Then the LORD said to me, "You have seen well, for I am ready to perform My word."

Genesis 30:37

³⁷ Now Jacob took for himself rods of green poplar and of the almond and chestnut trees, peeled white strips in them, and exposed the white which *was* in the rods.

Genesis 43:11

¹¹ And their father Israel said to them, "If *it must be* so, then do this: Take some of the best fruits of the land in your vessels and carry down a present for the man—a little balm and a little honey, spices and myrrh, pistachio nuts and almonds.

Exodus 25:33

³³ Three bowls *shall be* made like almond *blossoms* on one branch, *with* an *ornamental* knob and a flower, and three bowls made like almond *blossoms* on the other branch, *with* an *ornamental* knob and a flower—and so for the six branches that come out of the lampstand.

Exodus 37:19

¹⁹ There were three bowls made like almond *blossoms* on one branch, with an *ornamental* knob and a flower, and three bowls made like almond *blossoms* on the other branch, with an *ornamental* knob and a flower—and so for the six branches coming out of the lampstand.

Ark of the Covenant – Mercy Seat

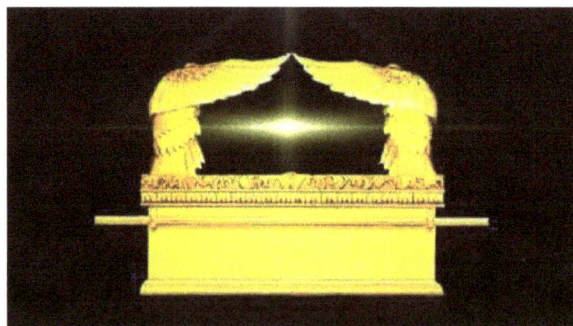

Image Source – Public Domain

The quest to find the Ark of the Covenant has enduring appeal and over the ages has inspired holy men, knights, adventurers, artists, novelists and lately filmmakers. The ark and the items associated with it – Aaron's rod/staff, the jar of manna and the tablets of the testimony were considered sacred. These were the only material objects considered to be so by the Israelites and were originally kept within the Most Holy Place of the Tabernacle, the portable tent used by the ancient Israelites for worship. The current whereabouts of the physical ark, should it exist, may currently be unknown, but it has a cryptic counterpart, to which you will find in this writing and the research of other interested persons already revealed within the Bible.

On the atonement cover (mercy seat) of the ark, the cherubim of the glory faced each other and between them was the space where the Glory of the Lord was thought to be physically present. The presence of the Glory within the Most Holy Place meant that the Israelites were forbidden to enter it because of their sins, except for the High Priest on the Day of Atonement, who was permitted to approach the Ark to perform the atonement rite over its cover. The holiness of the ark was symbolized by using gold for the manufacture of the atonement cover and for the overlay and lining of the ark, in this context the precious metal symbolizing excellence and enduring value.

The ark's function as the presumed sole location of the physical presence of the Lord suggests that it was a conduit to and from a Heavenly dimension, through which the Lord manifested here on Earth. Research by Bill Downie shows that the biblical measurements of the ark, the gold used in its construction and its location and design, supported by the proportions of the Vesica Pisces, the geometry of the tesseract and some apposite gematria, work together to suggest this higher dimension of being. They also confirm that Jesus Christ, our atonement cover, is the door through which we enter it. I am adding the research in this writing to confirm what the Lord had revealed to me.

The biblical ark was a hollow chest and measured 1.5 by 1.5 by 2.5 cubits. It can therefore be modelled as a hollow cuboid of side 1.5 and 2.5 units.

Exodus 37:1

Making the Ark of the Testimony

37 Then Bezalel made the ark of acacia wood; two and a half cubits *was* its length, a cubit and a half its width, and a cubit and a half its height.

Exodus 25:17-22

The Ark

¹⁷ "You shall make a mercy seat of pure gold; two and a half cubits *shall be* its length and a cubit and a half its width. ¹⁸ And you shall make two cherubim of gold; of hammered work you shall make them at the two ends of the mercy seat. ¹⁹ Make one cherub at one end, and the other cherub at the other end; you shall make the cherubim at the two ends of it *of one piece* with the mercy seat. ²⁰ And the cherubim shall stretch out *their* wings above, covering the mercy seat with their wings, and they shall face one another; the faces of the cherubim *shall be* toward the mercy seat. ²¹ You shall put the mercy seat on top of the ark, and in the ark, you shall put the Testimony that I will give you. ²² And there I will meet with you, and I will speak with you from above the mercy seat, from between the two cherubim which *are* on the ark of the Testimony, about everything which I will give you in commandment to the children of Israel.

The Ark of the Covenant – Mercy Seat is the Vesica Pisces. In verse 22 of the above scriptures, that was where God met with the Moses to give His commandments to the Israelites. It is a symbol of manifestation, and the pattern that gave birth to the universe and creation in general. This is the union between spirit and matter to create the divine child (Jesus) through whom we can go to the Father (God). That is why the Vesica Pisces (fish's bladder/womb) also represents the Virgin Mary. It is a divine symbol of femininity for spiritual possibilities in this universe. It represents the Tree of Life being guarded by the two cherubim.

Genesis 3:22-24

The Temptation and Fall of Man

22 Then the LORD God said, "Behold, the man has become like one of Us, to know good and evil. And now, lest he put out his hand and take also of the tree of life, and eat, and live forever"— 23 therefore the LORD God sent him out of the garden of Eden to till the ground from which he was taken. 24 So He drove out the man; and He placed cherubim at the east of the garden of Eden, and a flaming sword which turned every way, to guard the way to the tree of life.

The overall structure of the Ark of the Covenant exemplifies that the region below the galactic plane is governed by "Justice" (rule of law) and above the galactic plane is governed by "Mercy" (precious blood of Jesus).

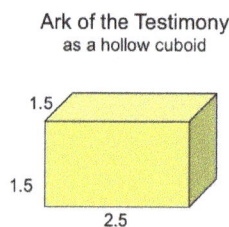

Ark of the Testimony
as a hollow cuboid

1.5

1.5

2.5

Image Source – Public Domain

The ratio of the side, depth and length in whole numbers is 3:3:5, which is important in what is to come. The perfect number three represents the Trinity and things spiritual; five represents God's grace and divine approval. The ark was the only object contained within the Most Holy Place of the tabernacle.

Hebrews 9:1-10

The Earthly Sanctuary

9 Then indeed, even the first *covenant* had ordinances of divine service and the Earthly sanctuary. 2 For a tabernacle was prepared: the first *part,* in which *was* the lampstand, the table, and the showbread, which is called the sanctuary; 3 and behind the second veil, the part of the tabernacle which is called the Holiest of All, 4 which had the golden censer and the ark of the covenant overlaid on all sides with gold, in which *were* the golden pot that had the

manna, Aaron's rod that budded, and the tablets of the covenant; [5] and above it were the cherubim of glory overshadowing the mercy seat. Of these things we cannot now speak in detail.

Limitations of the Earthly Service

[6] Now when these things had been thus prepared, the priests always went into the first part of the tabernacle, performing the services. [7] But into the second part the high priest *went* alone once a year, not without blood, which he offered for himself and *for* the people's sins *committed* in ignorance; [8] the Holy Spirit indicating this, that the way into the Holiest of All was not yet made manifest while the first tabernacle was still standing. [9] It *was* symbolic for the present time in which both gifts and sacrifices are offered which cannot make him who performed the service perfect in regard to the conscience— [10] *concerned* only with foods and drinks, various washings, and fleshly ordinances imposed until the time of reformation.

The Most Holy Place was essentially a hollow cube, externally 10 cubits on a side. The image of the hollow cuboid sitting within a hollow cube is reminiscent of the four-dimensional analogue of the cube, known as the tesseract. Being a four-dimensional object, the tesseract cannot be illustrated, but the three-dimensional 'shadow' it projects into 3D space can be shown. A wireframe model of one of these projections is illustrated (in 2D) in the following images, along with the Most Holy Place for comparison.

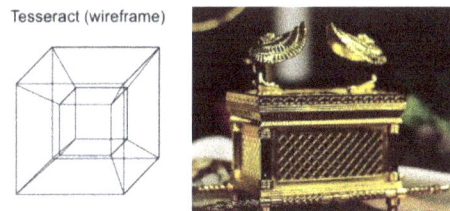

Image Source – Public Domain

This is the simplest of a tesseract's possible 3D projections, familiar to anyone with an interest in mathematics. The fourth dimension is hinted at by the cube sitting within the 3D shadow, connected by lines to the outer corners. The ark within the Most Holy Place represents this inner cube and therefore also hints at the fourth dimension. As the High Priest approached the ark on the Day of Atonement he was metaphorically, and literally, walking into another dimension.

The Bible itself points to a fourth dimension in passages such as in Ephesians 3:18. The four adjectives each describe a dimension. So, "depth or deep" is a reference to a fourth dimension of space. Other passages, such as Jesus evading troublesome crowds, and Enoch disappearing from the Earth after walking with God, is proof of another accessible spatial dimension – Genesis 5:24 and Hebrews 11:5.

Ephesians 3:14-19

Appreciation of the Mystery

[14] For this reason I bow my knees to the Father of our Lord Jesus Christ, [15] from whom the whole family in heaven and Earth is named, [16] that He would grant you, according to the riches of His glory, to be strengthened with might through His Spirit in the inner man, [17] that Christ may dwell in your hearts through faith; that you, being rooted and grounded in love, [18] may be able to comprehend with all the saints what *is* the width and length and depth and height— [19] to know the love of Christ which passes knowledge; that you may be filled with all the fullness of God.

John 8:59

[59] Then they took up stones to throw at Him; but Jesus hid Himself and went out of the temple, going through the midst of them, and so passed by.

John 10:39

[39] Therefore they sought again to seize Him, but He escaped out of their hand.

Genesis 5:24

[24] And Enoch walked with God; and he *was* not, for God took him.

Hebrews 11:5

[5] By faith Enoch was taken away so that he did not see death, "and was not found, because God had taken him"; for before he was taken, he had this testimony, that he pleased God.

An Extra Dimension of the Ark

Let us now add a dimension to the ark and see what transpires. This was modelled by the researcher for the ark as a hollow cuboid. If we increase this by one dimension, taking the ratio 3:3:5 as our guide, and increasing it to 3:3:3:5, we have a hollow tesseract, the 4D analogy of a 3D cuboid. A wireframe model of the 3D shadow of this figure is illustrated below.

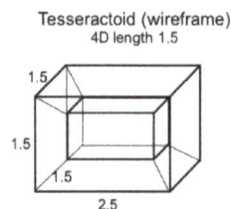

Tesseractoid (wireframe)
4D length 1.5

Image Source – Public Domain

Just as a hollow cube or cuboid encloses a 3D space, this hollow tesseract encloses a 4D 'higher' space or dimension. If we begin with a point, we can sweep it in one direction to obtain a line segment. When we sweep the segment in a perpendicular direction, we obtain a square. Dragging this square in a third perpendicular direction yields a cube. Likewise, we obtain a tesseract by sweeping the cube in a fourth direction.

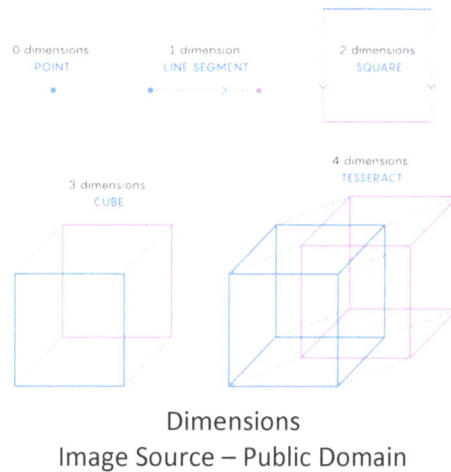

Dimensions
Image Source – Public Domain

This alternate way was well explained by David S. Richeson, referencing the works of Aristotle. Alternatively, just as we can unfold the faces of a cube into six squares, we can unfold the three-dimensional boundary of a tesseract to obtain eight cubes, as Salvador Dalí showcased in his 1954 painting Crucifixion (Corpus Hypercubus). The following is his painting.

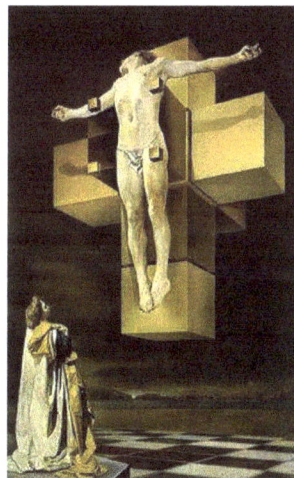

Image Source – Public Domain

Corpus Hypercubus takes the traditional biblical scene of Christ's Crucifixion and almost completely reinvents it. The union of Christ and the tesseract reflects Dalí's opinion that the seemingly separate and incompatible concepts of science and religion can in fact coexist. Upon completing Corpus Hypercubus, Dalí described his work as "metaphysical, transcendent cubism".

Mary Magdalene stands below and looking up at Jesus. Research this if you want to learn more about it. The main point here is that certain people knew certain secrets. Dalí knew something.

We can envision a cube by unfolding its faces. Likewise, we can start to envision a tesseract by unfolding its boundary cubes.

Tesseract unfolded
Image Source – Public Domain

The most striking change Dalí makes from nearly every other crucifixion painting concerns the cross, which he transforms into an unfolded net of a tesseract (also known as a hypercube). The unfolding of a tesseract into eight cubes is analogous to unfolding the sides of a cube into six squares. The use of a hypercube for the cross has been interpreted as a geometric symbol for the transcendental nature of God. Just as the concept of God exists in a space that is incomprehensible to humans, the hypercube exists in four spatial dimensions, which is equally inaccessible to the mind. The net of the hypercube is a three-dimensional representation of it, like how Christ is a human form of God that is more relatable to people.

The word "corpus" in the title can refer both to the Body of Christ and to geometric figures, reinforcing the link Dalí makes between religion and mathematics and science. Christ's levitation above the Earth could symbolize His rise above Earthly desire and suffering.

Continuing with Bill Downie's research, similarly, just as a paper cube can be opened out and lain flat to show the six squares of its 2D surface, a hollow tesseract can be opened out to reveal the eight cells of its 3D 'surface'. The 3D 'surface' of the hollow tesseract can also be opened out to form a 3D cross, which is shown below.

3D Cross
from unfolded tesseractoid

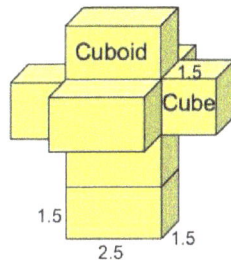

Image Source – Public Domain

The volume of this 3D cross, formed from the eight cells of the hollow tesseract, is (1.5 x 1.5 x 1.5 x 2) + (1.5 x 1.5 x 2.5 x 6) = 40.5 cubic cubits. This is equal in volume to a solid cuboid with dimensions 3 x 3 x 4.5, the product of which is also 40.5 cubic cubits.

Cuboid
Equal in volume to 3D cross

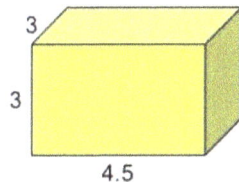

Image Source – Public Domain

If we double the lengths of the sides to give the whole number ratios 6, 6, and 9 we have a solid cuboid with volume 324 cubic cubits. The dimensions of 6, 6, and 9 are the digits of the ordinal value of Matthew 1:1 (NIV), 669. This begins the New Testament and the account of the genealogy of Jesus Christ, and therefore is of similar import to Genesis 1:1. This is shown as a figure composed of discrete units.

Matthew 1:1

The Genealogy of Jesus Christ

1 The book of the genealogy of Jesus Christ, the Son of David, the Son of Abraham:

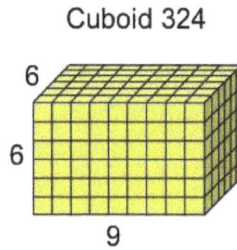

Cuboid 324

Image Source – Public Domain

Remarkably, the number 324 is the gematria of the English words 'the ark'! The Ark (s) = 324.

It contains a smaller cuboid inside, which can be lifted out to leave a box made from 212 units and which is closer to the real ark than the hollow cube originally modelled as, since the sides have some thickness, rather than being infinitely thin, as in a hollow cube. The cuboid inside is composed of 112 units. 112 is the standard value of the Hebrew name YHVH Elohim (the Lord God). The inner cuboid is equivalent to the sacred objects inside the ark: the rod/staff, manna, and tablets, which have already revealed as symbolizing the male child of Revelation 12.

Revelation 12:1-2

12 Now a great sign appeared in heaven: a woman clothed with the Sun, with the Moon under her feet, and on her head a garland of twelve stars. **²** Then being with child, she cried out in labor and in pain to give birth.

Returning to the smaller cuboid of dimensions 3 x 3 x 4.5, we now reduce the scale of this cuboid to conform to that of the original ark dimensions, we have an object of dimensions 1.5 x 1.5 x 2.25 cubits.

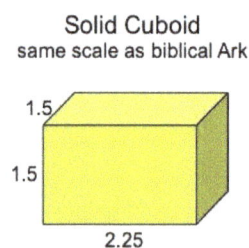

Solid Cuboid
same scale as biblical Ark

Image Source – Public Domain

The volume of the cuboid is 1.5 x 1.5 x 2.25 = 5.0625 cubic cubits. Incredibly, this is numerically equal to a perfect tesseract of side 1.5 cubits! The volume of the tesseract is 1.5 x 1.5 x 1.5 x 1.5 = 5.0625 quartic cubits.

Tesseract (wireframe)
numerically equal to solid cuboid

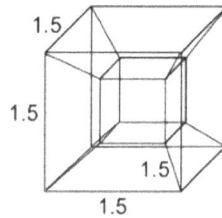

1.5
1.5
1.5
1.5

Image Source – Public Domain

This hollow tesseract unfolds to form a 3D cross with a volume of 27 cubic cubits. 27 is the cube of 3, the perfect number symbolizing the Trinity and spirit, the cube itself being the most holy object to the Israelites. 27 is also the reduced value of 'the ark'. The outer shell of that cube is 26 cubic cubits, the standard value of 'YHVH' in Hebrew and the ordinal value of 'God'.

Confirming this truth – referencing back to the article by David S. Richeson, the surprising realities of high-dimensional space cause problems in statistics and data analysis, known collectively as the "curse of dimensionality." The number of sample points required for many statistical techniques goes up exponentially with the dimension. Also, as dimensions increase, points will cluster together less often. Thus, it's often important to find ways to reduce the dimension of high-dimensional data.

After a failed attempt to prove the invariance of dimension by L.E.J. Brouwer, the story of dimension didn't end with him because his notion did not help with human intuition regarding higher-dimensional spaces. Just a few years afterward, Felix Hausdorff developed a definition of dimension that – generations later – proved essential for modern math. An intuitive way to think about Hausdorff dimension is that if we scale, or magnify, a d-dimensional object uniformly by a factor of k, the size of the object increases by a factor of k^d. Suppose we scale a point, a line segment, a square and a cube by a factor of 3. The point does not change size ($3^0 = 1$), the segment becomes three times as large ($3^1 = 3$), the square becomes nine times as large ($3^2 = 9$), and the cube becomes 27 times as large ($3^3 = 27$).

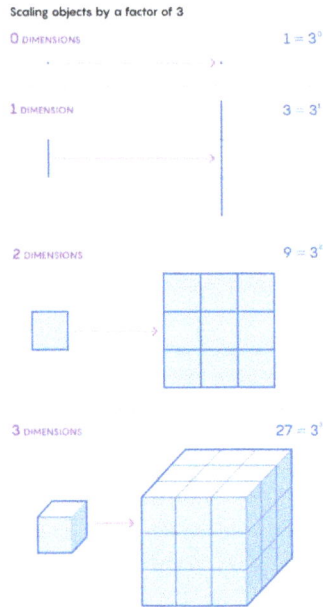

Scaling objects by a factor of 3

0 DIMENSIONS $1 = 3^0$

1 DIMENSION $3 = 3^1$

2 DIMENSIONS $9 = 3^2$

3 DIMENSIONS $27 = 3^3$

Image Source – Public Domain

When we scale a d-dimensional object by a factor of k, the size increases by a factor of k^d.

Are you still surprised why when we scale a point, a line segment, a square and a cube by a factor of 3, the point, the line, and the square respond by being stable or grows perfectly, and the cube becomes 27 times as large ($3^3 = 27$)? Again, therefore, the hollow tesseract unfolds to form a 3D cross with a volume of 27 cubic cubits. 27 is the cube of 3, the perfect number symbolizing the Trinity and spirit, the cube itself being the most holy object to the Israelites. 27 is also the reduced value of 'the ark'. The outer shell of that cube is 26 cubic cubits, the standard value of 'YHVH' in Hebrew and the ordinal value of 'God'.

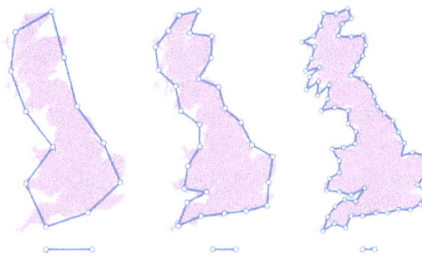

The measured length of the coastline of Britain depends on the size of the ruler
Image Source – Public Domain

One surprising consequence of Hausdorff's definition is that objects could have non-integer dimensions. This was how we came about the method to measure something like a coastline which can be so jagged that it cannot be measured precisely with any ruler. To understand what a non-integer dimension might look like, the research considered the Koch curve, which is produced iteratively. The term non-integer dimensions and the word iteratively here mean that we are basically dealing with a solution to an infinity problem if an object is jagged and requires measurement. If the objects distance never ends, this is also the only possible "solution" but infinity has no solution.

It is no coincidence that Hausdorff's definition is the only solution to a possible infinity problem except that infinity cannot be solved but it is a solution that helps with human intuition regarding higher-dimensional spaces because the definition consists of God (the Holy Trinity – the number 3) as the base. This is the only way that a circle can be measured. A circle represents the realm of God because it has no beginning and no end. And if you are wondering how the measurement or area of the circle was derived, the ancient Babylonians calculated the area of a circle by taking 3 times the square of its radius, which gave a value of pi = 3.

God is eternal and He truly is alpha omega (the beginning the end) and He already proved that even before time begun, He was, and that He still is God and will continue to be God forever and ever and from everlasting to everlasting. He continues to show us that indeed, everything came from Him and that the Word of God (the Bible) is true, and Christianity is the only true and valid religion that every human should practice with fear of the Lord. All the other so-called religions are BOGUS and will only end you up in HELL. Mere curiosity and common sense should tell you that any religion apart from Christianity is fake and will send you into eternal doom. This also proves how true and valid that the revelation of the Venn diagram (Vesica Pisces) is, and that was indeed how God birthed the universe. Now, let's continue explaining Bill Downie's research on the ark of the covenant.

The Dimensions of the Ark

The Ark's biblical dimensions of 1.5, 1.5, and 2.5 are the only numbers we are aware of that will lead to this transformation from biblical ark to tesseract, via the 3D cross. It could be seen as a metaphor for the Christian message of salvation through the cross, which 'opens the door' to Heaven (which is being equated here with the fourth dimension).

This slightly shorter 'hidden ark' of dimension 1.5, 1.5, and 2.25 has an atonement cover of dimensions 1.5 by 2.25, which itself is numerically equal to a cube of side 1.5 cubits.

Atonement Cover
for hidden ark

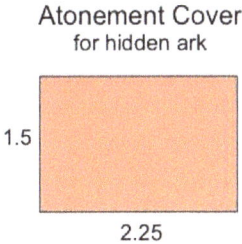

Image Source – Public Domain

The Vesica Pisces

The proportions of this hidden atonement cover are 3 to 2, which means it will circumscribe the beautiful figure known as the Vesica Pisces, which I have already discussed in this writing.

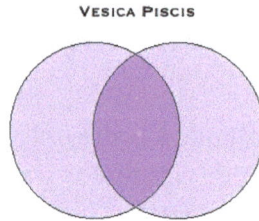

VESICA PISCIS

Image Source – Public Domain

Intriguingly, the central vesica is shaped like an almond nut, and an almond branch was the original rod/staff kept within the ark. In Christian art, an aureola in the shape of a vesica, called a mandorla (Italian for 'almond nut') is often used to frame depictions of Jesus or the Virgin Mary. The researcher found that if we start with circles of 1000 square units each (unity x 1000 to give whole numbers), then the areas of the vesica itself and the entire Vesica Pisces are embodied in the gematria of the Holy Mother and her Son.

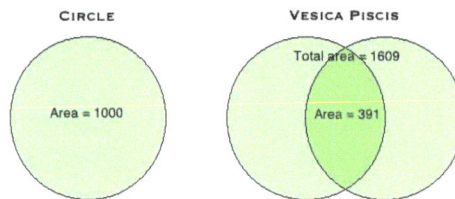

CIRCLE   VESICA PISCIS

Total area = 1609

Area = 1000   Area = 391

Image Source – Public Domain

The Virgin Mary (s) = 1609

Yehoshua = 391

Gematria is a Kabbalistic method of interpreting the Hebrew scriptures by computing the numerical value of words, based on those of their constituent letters.

So, the Vesica Pisces symbolizes the Virgin giving birth to the Holy Child! Note that the likely volume of the Most Holy Place within the Tabernacle was 1000 cubic cubits. We can easily see the perfect fit of the Vesica Pisces within this hidden atonement cover in the following illustration:

Atonement Cover and Vesica Piscis
for hidden ark

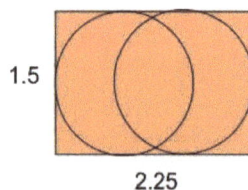

1.5

2.25

Image Source – Public Domain

The vesica rests on the center of the atonement cover, where the Glory of the Lord was made manifest. Note the two crescents on either side of the central vesica, which sit where the cherubim of the Glory sat on the cover. Here is an image of the atonement cover for comparison. Note the similarity between the crescents and the spread wings of the cherubim.

Image Source – Public Domain

The cherubim on the atonement cover of the ark were designed to represent the crescent shapes in the Vesica Pisces, and that the Glory of the Lord is therefore symbolized by the vesica. As we just saw the vesica has long been linked to Jesus through Christian art – and as we just saw it is now identified with His Hebrew name through gematria!

The Hidden Significance of Gold

The extensive use of gold in the manufacture of the ark, and its symbolism, may have deeper meaning than the Israelites knew. All metals have their atoms arranged in a lattice structure and gold atoms are arranged in the densest structure known, called face-centered cubic. The smallest unit of such a lattice has 14 atoms.

Face-Centred Cube 14

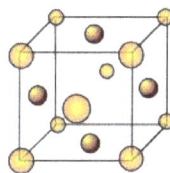

Image Source – Public Domain

The Hebrew word for gold, zahab (zayin, Hey, Beth), has a standard, ordinal and reduced value of 14.

zahab (Heb.) = 14

So, the gematria of 'gold' in Hebrew is reflected in its atomic structure.

It has been showed above that the dimensions of the '4D ark' (remember gold was lavishly employed in the construction of the original 3D ark) have ratios 3, 3, 3, 5. These numbers sum to 14.

Apart from its rarity, gold is valued for its characteristic reddish yellow color, its density and its unreactive nature and consequent resistance to tarnishing. These are all either solely or partly due to relativistic effects. Gold's high atomic number of 79 means that the electrons in its shells (using the Bohr 'solar system' model) spin at more than half the speed of light and, according to special relativity, increase in mass, flatten in the direction of movement, and experience a slowing of time. The increase in mass leads to relativistic contraction of the electron shell and an increase in density. Gold's absorption of light is also affected, giving its characteristic yellow color, as distinct from the silvery-gray color of nearly every other metal. The unreactive of gold is caused by the outermost electron hiding more deeply within the shell, also due to this contraction. According to special relativity, massive objects bend space and time to create gravity, therefore since gold is particularly dense it will cause a greater bending of space and time than nearly all other materials.

In an article by Michelle Starr, it has been found that scientists have recently discovered something new about gold. When extreme crushing pressure is applied quickly, over mere nanoseconds, the element's atomic structure changes, becoming more like metals harder than gold.

Gold is a fascinating element. It's among the least reactive, and its crystalline structure is predicted to be stable at incredibly high pressures. Again, the arrangement of atoms in gold follows what's called a "face centered cubic" (fcc) structure. Put simply, the atoms in gold form cubes, with an atom at each of the corners, and another atom in the center of each of the faces.

Previous experiments have shown that in gold, the fcc structure remains stable even at pressures up to three times that found at the center of Earth. But usually, the pressure is applied gradually. Under shock compression, scientists at the Lawrence Livermore National Laboratory have now observed something different.

At 223 GPa (gigapascals) - that's 2.2 million times Earth's atmospheric pressure at sea level – the gold rearranges into a less tightly-packed "body centered cubic" (bcc) structure, the two structures coexisting as the metal transitions from one to the other.

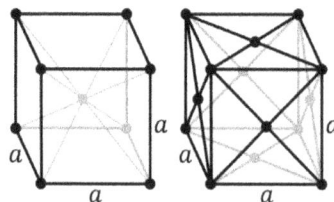

Left: bcc structure, Right: fcc structure
Image Source – Public Domain

As the name implies, bcc is also a cubic structure with an atom on each of the corners; but rather than atoms on each of the faces of the cube, there is just one in its center (see above).

"We discovered a new structure in gold that exists at extreme states – two thirds of the pressure found at the center of Earth," said physicist Richard Briggs of the Lawrence Livermore National Laboratory.

The team didn't stop at 223 GPa, either. After the initial shock, they tracked the structural changes as they cranked up the pressure. At 262 GPa, the phase transition was complete, and the gold started to melt. At 322 GPa – almost the pressure at Earth's center – the gold was completely liquid, a state that scientists haven't previously observed at this level of pressure.

But the precise mechanisms of the phase transition are still poorly understood, they said. This research shows that gold underwent a phase transition because of both temperature and pressure – which could help in future experiments to try to figure that mechanism out.

If you remember from earlier in this writing, I talked about power as a scalar quantity although all the scalar quantities can be summed as power. Temperature and pressure are also scalar quantities. These are the same problems that physicists are facing in quantum mechanics. Even with the gold, the phase transition is poorly understood by them.

The scientists continued and said that the coexistence of fcc and bcc structures in the gold at 220 GPa under shock conditions suggests that a triple point – where its solid, liquid, and gas forms exist in equilibrium – associated with those conditions.

Are you still wondering why there is a triple point? Therefore, God instructed for the ark of the covenant to be made from gold. There is mystery in the triple point – equilibrium state of all three forms – solid, liquid, and gas. When you find yourself in the right conditions, you will surely experience God. He is not theoretical – He is to be experienced. Knowledge in Him is experience based and that is why He instructed the Israelites to build the ark. The equilibrium state is oneness with God. This is what they call in quantum mechanics as entanglement and superposition. At the ark of the covenant, God's very presence was made manifest. God had said: "*And there I will meet with you*". It was a place of entanglement and superposition.

Exodus 25:22

²² And there I will meet with you, and I will speak with you from above the mercy seat, from between the two cherubim which *are* on the ark of the Testimony, about everything which I will give you in commandment to the children of Israel.

The ark of the covenant acted as the symbol of God's holiness, and not abiding by the rules set forth brought about His wrath. The power of the ark was not in the thing itself, but in the wonder and majesty of Jehovah, whose presence once rested there, but now indwells each believer. So, now after the sacrifice of Jesus, we (our bodies) have the privilege to be the place (temple) of this superposition as God originally designed right from the beginning before the fall of Adam. This is the entanglement and superposition states that we believers have with God and literally walk in the Earth in the fullness of His Spirit – knowing what He knows, thinking what He thinks, doing what He does and wants to do etc. We are synced as one because He lives in us. This happens under certain conditions and energy levels, which do not like noise (sinful living etc.) because that destroys the coherence. In quantum mechanics, you will call this state decoherence. When this happens, there is no oneness with God again until sincere repentance and you are back to holy living then you become one again. Holiness is what keeps the entanglement, superposition, and coherence. This is the spirituality of a true Christian.

"Many of the theoretical models of gold that are used to understand the high-pressure/high-temperature behavior did not predict the formation of a body-centered structure," Briggs said.

Of course, this is like the classical versus the quantum theories in physics. There is a prejudice, so they do not understand what the true fundamental of the subject is. We are back to both the fundamental and the advanced (the beginning the end) – they call it quantum mechanics. Therefore, they are all so confused. They try to teach or explain these phenomena as if they understand but they do not and they know it. Mere scientific intellect will never understand quantum mechanics.

In general relativity, the concepts of space and time are replaced by one deeper, four-dimensional reality (the subject of much scientific debate). The relativistic effects on gold have made it the ideal material to represent an extra, hidden dimension. Gold is often used in the Bible to point to things beyond the material, and the prevalence of gold in the Ark of the Testimony was always meant to point to this hidden dimension of the ark.

Independent Confirmation

Another researcher provided staggering confirmation that the ark really does have a hidden dimension.

What he found was that if the 28 letters of Genesis 1:1 in the original Hebrew were converted into their reduced (qatan) values and arranged in a 7 by 4 table, encrypted information was revealed.

Genesis 1.1(Masoretic)
Reduced Values of Letters

בראשית ברא אלהים את השמים ואת הארץ
9215 416 41435 41 41531 122 413122

Image Source – Public Domain

Here is the table.

Letters of Genesis 1.1
arranged into a 7 x 4 table

2	4	1	3	1	2	2	letters 1 - 7
4	1	5	3	1	1	2	letters 8 - 14
4	1	4	3	5	4	1	letters 15 - 21
9	2	1	5	4	1	6	letters 22 - 28

Image Source – Public Domain

Running down the center of this table is 3, 3, 3, 5. The Hebrew word for three, shalowsh, uses the letters Shem, Lamed, Shem and Hey, with standard values of 300, 30, 300, and 5. The reduced values, however, are 3, 3, 3, and 5, which suggests the 3 x 3 x 5 ratio of the ark dimensions, but with a fourth dimension added.

The table has many interesting features, many of which have been tabulated by the author. One of them is pattern of arcs on each side of the center. These arcs are composed of strings or part-strings of the same number and are the 1111 and 4442 to the left and 1144 and 2211 to the right. The author identifies these as the pattern for the wings of the cherubim on the atonement cover.

Glory and Cherubim
from number arcs

2	4	1	3	1	2	2
4	1	5	3	1	1	2
4	1	4	3	5	4	1
9	2	1	5	4	1	6

Image Source – Public Domain

Note there are two curves on each side. These are an even better fit for the outlines of the crescents on each side of the vesica.

Vesica Piscis
from number arcs

2	4	1	3	1	2	2
4	1	5	3	1	1	2
4	1	4	3	5	4	1
9	2	1	5	4	1	6

Image Source – Public Domain

The central vesica is also perfectly indicated and encloses the four central numbers from the letters of shalowsh (three). The obvious signs that this table is to be regarded as the atonement cover for an ark also indicate that the 3, 3, 3, 5 running down its center, where the Glory of the Lord resided, point to a hidden, fourth dimension. This can be proven repeatedly, not only through our divine visions or revelations from God Himself, but through mathematics and science because that all came from Him. He showed and explained it to me, hence, the reason for this writing.

History and Mystical Meanings of the Vesica Pisces

The source of Geometry and it has been called the Sacred Geometry. There are of course, other mystical meanings of the Vesica Pisces such as:

Body – Mind/Soul – Spirit
Higher Self – Conscious Self – Lower Self

Etcetera.

History and Current Meanings of the Vesica Pisces

The source of Mathematics or Geometry and everything you call science. In research by Sebastiaan Fiolet, he discusses it in depth. In sacred geometry straight lines are masculine energy and curved lines, such as circles, are feminine energy. Funny enough, these are also reflected in the construction of our bodies as you can see below or check yourself.

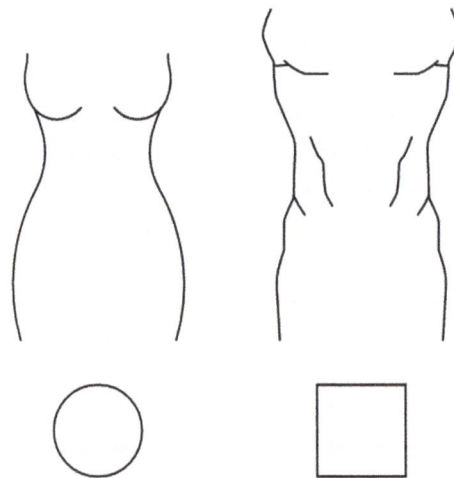

Image Source – Public Domain

When we add the masculine energy to the feminine energy, we can discover 3 numbers, which continue infinitely behind the decimal point without a repetitive pattern. Like the number Pi, also called π (3.1415926... etc.).

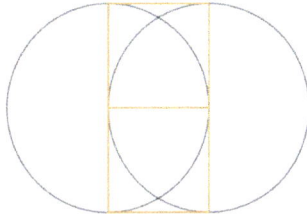

Image Source – Public Domain

These numbers are, according to Pythagoras (a famous ancient Greek mathematician), fundamental to the creation of all forms. Therefore, they are very important numbers.

The following numbers can be found within the Vesica Pisces: √2, √3 and √5.

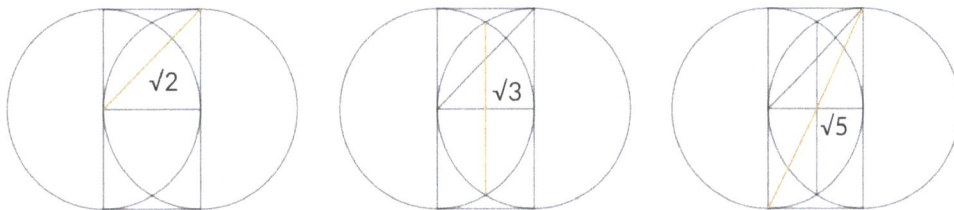

Image Source – Public Domain

The first number that we can find is √2. A sacred number that has been used in Solomon's Temple in Jerusalem and in the Tor in England, among other places.

Tor, England
Image Source – Public Domain

Can you observe the Tor image to your left and identify the symbol in which the building stands? Your answer is correct. It is the Vesica Pisces.

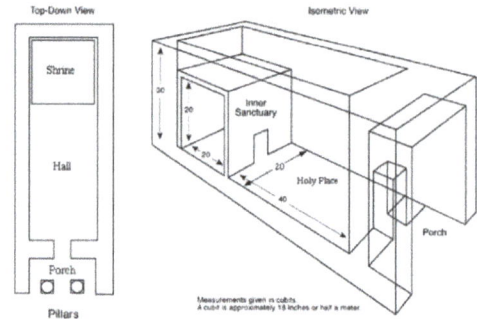

Solomon's Temple

Image Source – Public Domain

So, we can already tell that our God did not provide abstract dimensions. Every dimension He provided in His Word (Bible) is for a specific reason. He didn't just throw random numbers around. He is the Supreme Engineer of the Heavens and the Earth. He is my Jehovah Scientist and Jehovah Engineer. He sure is Jehovah Mathematician. He is truly Jehovah Everything. The relationship between science and engineering is like the relationship between Christian spirituality, and natural science and engineering. That is the same relationship between God Almighty and all His creation. Without creation, God would only be known among the Godhead (Father, Son, Holy Spirit) and He wouldn't really be known as God. But with creation, God is known as both the Scientist and Engineer of everything. That makes Him God. The spiritual will always exist forever and ever, but the physical is only made manifest because of the activities in the spiritual. God will still exist without science and engineering.

1 Kings 6:1-3

Solomon Builds the Temple

6 And it came to pass in the four hundred and eightieth year after the children of Israel had come out of the land of Egypt, in the fourth year of Solomon's reign over Israel, in the month of Ziv, which *is* the second month, that he began to build the house of the LORD. **²** Now the house which King Solomon built for the LORD, its length *was* sixty cubits, its width twenty, and its height thirty cubits. **³** The vestibule in front of the sanctuary of the house *was* twenty cubits long across the width of the house, *and* the width of *the vestibule extended* ten cubits from the front of the house.

Exodus 26:1-2

The Tabernacle

26 "Moreover you shall make the tabernacle *with* ten curtains *of* fine woven linen and blue, purple, and scarlet *thread;* with artistic designs of cherubim, you shall weave them. **²** The length of each curtain *shall be* twenty-eight cubits, and the width of each curtain four cubits. And every one of the curtains shall have the same measurements.

The square symbolizes unity in our physical universe, √2 symbolizes duality. But the real reason that this number belongs in the sacred geometry is because it hides the binary series. An important series of numbers that occurs in any living organism, but also in computers and Artificial Intelligence (AI).

√2 and the Binary sequence

Suppose we have a square of 1 by 1 millimeter, then the square has an area of 1 square millimeter. And the diagonal line is still √2. If we now turn the diagonal line, the √2, into another new square, the new square will have an area of 2 square millimeters. Because √2 x √2 = 2.

Keep repeating this process, and the surface area will grow to 4 mm², 8 mm², 16 mm², 32 mm²... etc.

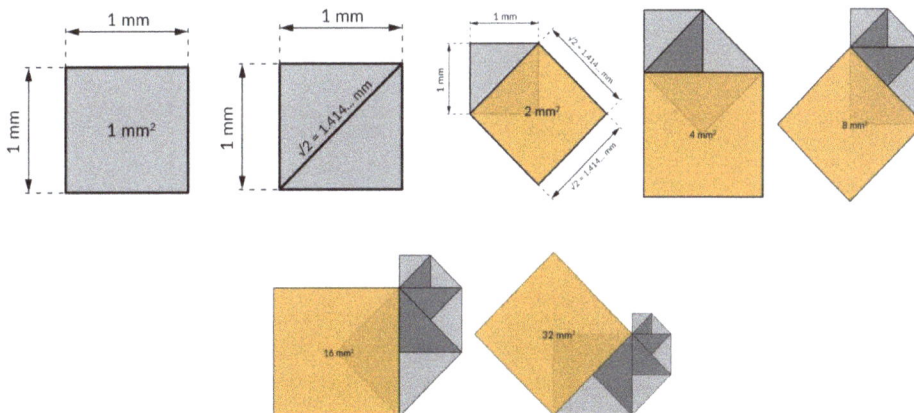

Image Source – Public Domain

This is the binary sequence: 1 2 4 8 16 32 64 128 256 512 1024 ... And this sequence can continue infinitely. And what is the reason why this sequence is so important? Each living organism follows this sequence, namely through cell division. So, our entire body is based on this sequence and the Fibonacci sequence, among other things.

But computers too, and with them AI, are based on the binary sequence. Someone who is a little familiar with computers knows that computers only know two things: 1 and 0 or true and false or on and off. But what does that have to do with the binary sequence?

That's because the binary sequence consists of only 2 numbers – 1 and 0. The series of numbers we have mentioned above have been converted to our known tenfold system.

The Mandorla

The second number we can find in the Vesica Pisces is √3. But before we can explain it properly, we need an introduction to the Mandorla.

The Mandorla is the middle part of the Vesica Pisces, it is an Italian word for almonds or almond shaped (it also looks quite much like an almond).

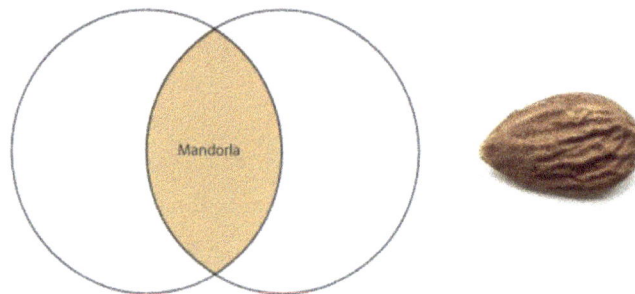

Image Source – Public Domain

You can find this remarkable form in almost every image of saints, especially in Christianity. But also, in the architecture of Churches.

Image Source – Public Domain

√3

The proportions of the Mandorla are described by Pythagoras (the old Greek again). According to him the proportions of the Mandorla are 265:153, also called √3.

√3 is also exactly the length of the diagonal of a cube. This means that three-dimensional space is also defined.

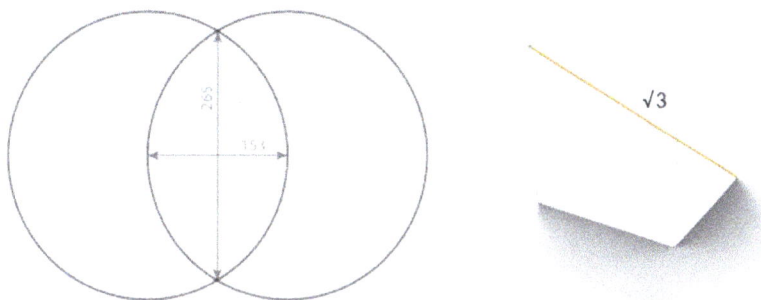

Image Source – Public Domain

Especially the number 153 was sacred in Pythagoras. This number also appears in the Bible, but then very subtly.

According to the Bible Jesus, after his resurrection, helped his followers with fishing (another subtle hint to the Vesica Pisces). His followers hadn't caught anything for days, but with the help of Jesus they caught exactly 153 fish. What a coincidence. No, it's not a coincidence.

That's why there is the famous fish with Jesus written in it. This fish also comes from the Vesica Pisces, with a length of 153.

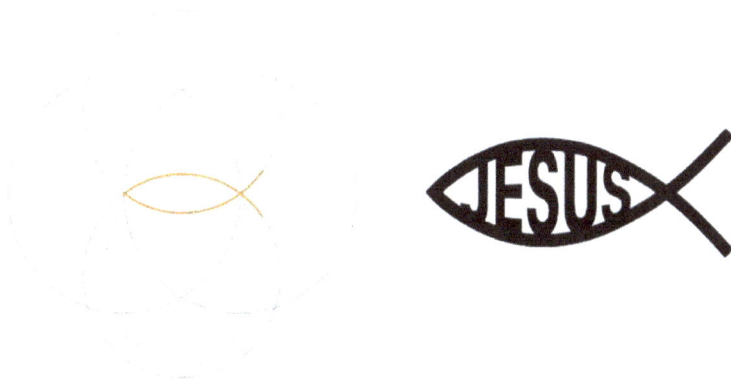

Image Source – Public Domain

John 21:6-13

Breakfast by the Sea

[6] And He said to them, "Cast the net on the right side of the boat, and you will find *some*." So, they cast, and now they were not able to draw it in because of the multitude of fish.

[7] Therefore that disciple whom Jesus loved said to Peter, "It is the Lord!" Now when Simon Peter heard that it was the Lord, he put on *his* outer garment (for he had removed it) and plunged into the sea. [8] But the other disciples came in the little boat (for they were not far from land, but about two hundred cubits), dragging the net with fish. [9] Then, as soon as they had come to land, they saw a fire of coals there, and fish laid on it, and bread. [10] Jesus said to them, "Bring some of the fish which you have just caught."

[11] Simon Peter went up and dragged the net to land, full of large fish, **one hundred and fifty-three**; and although there were so many, the net was not broken. [12] Jesus said to them, "Come *and* eat breakfast." Yet none of the disciples dared ask Him, "Who are You?"—knowing that it was the Lord. [13] Jesus then came and took the bread and gave it to them, and likewise the fish.

Even more strange coincidence is when an acronym is made in Greek of the full biblical name of Jesus. Jesus Christ, Son of God, Savior. In Greek this will be: Iesous Christos Theou Yios Soter. The acronym would then be: ΙΧΘΥΣ (ichthus). If you translate this back to English (or Dutch), you will get "Fish".

Mary Magdalene is the symbolic "wife" or "bride" of Jesus Christ. The name Magdalene is primarily a female name of Latin origin that means Watchtower, Watchful. A place name used as a surname for people from the village of Magdala on the Sea of Galilee. In the Bible, Mary Magdalene is a follower of Christ. If we translate her name to Greek, it becomes η αγδαληνή. No idea how you pronounce it, but when we assign the numerical values to it and add them together, the result is 153. Also, a coincidence? No, it's not.

I was and still am truly astonished after a revelation I received from the Holy Spirit, which has already been told earlier in this text regarding Jesus Christ and the Body of Christ. I'm always astonished and fear the Lord even more whenever He gives me a revelation. Yes, Mary Magdalene was the bride to Jesus Christ. She represents the Church or the Body of Christ – that's why we are His bride. She submitted herself to Jesus Christ so well and loved Him so much that the Lord taught her the deep things of the Kingdom of God, which not even the male disciples knew. She is a great representation of what true love of a woman, which includes total submission and respect to her husband can bring out of the man for her. She is a great representation of how no matter your background or past, Jesus Christ still loves you if you truly repent. Most importantly, she was the only one who saw Jesus after He rose from the dead and the one who was sent by Jesus Christ to give the message or news to the disciples.

Again, the mystery and spiritual meaning of Mary Magdalene being the bride to Jesus Christ is how only the true Body of Christ, or the Church will have a relationship, communion, fellowship etc., with Jesus through the Holy Spirit so that He can give us all that a good husband will give to his wife, which in the case of the Church, are all the things that the Word of God promises us. We will also be the only ones to see Jesus Christ during the departure or rapture – His first coming. Any other explanation anywhere that adds anything extra to portray Mary Magdalene as a bad character or make a contradiction to this revelation is WRONG or FALSE – it is or will only be an attempt to corrupt the Word of God, which is what Satan is very good at and has been doing it for some time now.

Mary Magdalene only went and gave directions to the disciples as instructed by Jesus Christ. She was a faithful follower and a messenger. Just like she went and gave word to the disciples, that's how when the true Body of Christ departs privately with Jesus Christ during His first return or the rapture, everybody else will get the news because suddenly, we the true believers will disappear and the only explanation to that will be in the Word of God. We will surely have plenty of Bibles left behind that the unsaved can use to go through their horrific tribulation while the true believers feast with Jesus Christ in Heaven. They will have a second chance to repent and be saved but it will still be a horrific experience for them. If you doubt the Word of God or the words I write, you can test the theory by remaining in your sinful nature and not get saved – then immediate Hell after your death will be your destination or if you live longer then the great tribulation will be your evidence.

This mystery and revelation of Mary Magdalene is just like how a man can only be introduced to life through the womb of a woman. That is just the woman's special anointing that the Lord has given to her – there is nothing anybody can do about that because it's unique to her. Just as the man's chromosomes determine or decide the gender of a child, without any help from the woman's chromosomes in that decision, the man still can't have a child all by himself. Each has a role to play. And truly, only women naturally have the softest and sweetest hearts to receive anything you tell them as if they are children, and such are the hearts that the Holy Spirit can easily communicate with. Women naturally share traits with the Holy Spirit. So, women announce us to this world by bringing us into it. They are carriers of good news. That is the mystery and revelation. They host the strategies of God and reveal His mysteries to the world. I am only able to write these things because I am like a woman – pregnant with the Word of God and His mysteries and revelations. I am so bound that I cannot keep quite. The fact is that if I keep quiet, what's inside me will consume or kill me. My assignment is to bring it to you to illuminate you, warn you, and guide you on the right path to take. Whether you heed or not, is not my business. I will only be punished if I don't bring the Word of the Lord to you as instructed by God Almighty.

These revelations don't mean that the following scriptures are wrong. A woman is not less of a person than a man but there are several other scriptures other than the one below that I can use to make this very clear to you. **A woman still doesn't have authority over a man**. God in His infinite Wisdom knows why He decided to make it that way. Do we (Body of Christ) have authority over Jesus Christ? No, we don't. All these mysteries are just God's way to restore us back into what He originally planned for us in the Garden of Eden. Satan continues to corrupt it with competition. Wake up, people. There is no competition.

1 Timothy 2:12-14

Men and Women in the Church

8 I desire therefore that the men pray everywhere, lifting up holy hands, without wrath and doubting; 9 in like manner also, that the women adorn themselves in modest apparel, with propriety and moderation, not with braided hair or gold or pearls or costly clothing, 10 but, which is proper for women professing godliness, with good works. 11 Let a woman learn in silence with all submission. 12 And I do not permit a woman to teach or to have authority over a man, but to be in silence. 13 For Adam was formed first, then Eve. 14 And Adam was not deceived, but the woman being deceived, fell into transgression. 15 Nevertheless she will be saved in childbearing if they continue in faith, love, and holiness, with self-control.

Again, even at a natural biological level, the chromosomes of a man are what decide what the gender of a baby or babies will be. This is the mystery and revelation of the rib bone of the man that was taken from Adam to create the woman Eve. This is the meaning of God's strategy of procreation at a natural level because God doesn't want to keep putting men to sleep and taking out their rib bone to create other human beings.

Genesis 2:21-22

21 And the LORD God caused a deep sleep to fall on Adam, and he slept; and He took one of his ribs and closed up the flesh in its place. 22 Then the rib which the LORD God had taken from man He made into a woman, and He brought her to the man.

Get wisdom – a fight for such equality is what has put us in this mess called the world right now. All the mess started because Lucifer wanted equality with God, his Creator. Women are extremely special. One simple way to find out is that just try to mess with our mothers, and you will see the answer. A woman was created from a man – and a woman gives birth to a man according to God's technology. A woman is in a man and a man is also in a woman. It is the mystery behind how we are all one. You discriminate against another, and you discriminate against yourself. You hate another and you hate yourself. You kill or destroy another, and you kill or destroy yourself. It is a world of symmetry and together, we are the universe – together, we are God because we individually host a dimension of Him. We can see that a man is already the woman's creator but for such an agenda to accomplish God's strategies to restore man into glory after the fall of man, God used His feminine dimension in this manner to help make it clear to women that life can't survive without them, but this is their place. And, to men that, they can't survive without women.

Genesis 2:18

18 And the LORD God said, "*It is* not good that man should be alone; I will make him **a helper comparable to him**."

John 14:26

²⁶ **But the Helper, the Holy Spirit**, whom the Father will send in My name, He will teach you all things, and bring to your remembrance all things that I said to you.

Proverbs 4:7-9

⁷ **Wisdom** *is* the principal thing;
Therefore get wisdom.
And in all your getting, get understanding.
⁸ **Exalt her**, and she will promote you;
She will bring you honor, when you embrace her.
⁹ She will place on your head an ornament of grace;
A crown of glory she will deliver to you."

God created the woman to be man's helper, not to be in competition with man. **A true Godfearing woman is called Wisdom – just like the Holy Spirit**. **A true Godfearing woman is truly the Holy Spirit in human body.** I always say that most women don't know how powerful they are in the lives of men, so they think the best way is to fight for the man's position. It's the opposite, and a man will reflect deeper love and respect back to you. When the woman knows and understands this game, it will seem like the man is under a spell but that won't be true. Even if you want to call it a spell then it's a holy spell. This is how a good man will be the head with the authority but in the background, the woman makes the decisions because the man listens to a submissive and respectful wife. I hope you know that even the Kings and Presidents do have advisers. They represent the authority, but their advisers are truly the ones ruling.

Women, get knowledge and understanding. The last thing a woman should want to do is to fight for the man's position – you will never win. Instead, take everything in prayer. This is the predicament that humanity have found themselves in. Humanity have ignored God and believe that everything is about science and technology, and even worse of all, money. So, humanity is in very deep crisis – majority don't know their left or their right. There is a huge identity crisis for humanity to the point where even males or females don't know what gender they are. It's even worse when the leaders don't know God – this means, no wisdom at all. The blind leading the blind. This is our world right now in addition to some intentional demonic creatures in human form – very satanic people in top positions who call themselves the "Elites of the World", who have no love, empathy, compassion etc. They would rather seek for more money and power and see everybody else perish.

The moment a woman starts fighting for equality, there will be a problem. The world is facing that now. Not to say that men should oppress women but there needs to be a balance. At a natural level, we can have only one King or President with a deputy or vice. We never have two Kings ruling at the same time because that would mean an unstable kingdom or country and there will be great conflict. There are such conflicts around the world now because of satanism, which includes a lack of truth and integrity. That is why our world is this very messed up and full of lies and wickedness. Study your Bible well with the help of the Holy Spirit for better understanding. Find your scope of work in life and fulfill your duties accordingly. Our lack of spiritual understanding is why the Church has become almost powerless with no influence. We always break spiritual patterns and protocols with our own false or erroneous doctrines and sinful nature. Majority don't know and understand sound doctrine to teach and exercise for tangible results. We don't have to beg people to come to Jesus Christ – they must see Jesus Christ in us to compel them without any physical force.

Can women use their spiritual gifts to advance the Kingdom of God? Absolutely, all day every day because they are very gifted, and God has shared it all equally and well-balanced according to His infinite Wisdom. A woman should exercise her spiritual gifts and be able to help the Body of Christ as much as possible, including her own home and the society at large. If men will also understand that God gave them authority over women because of men natural strong character, among other things, the world will be a better place. Women are not men slaves. We exist for each other for very deep spiritual mysteries. We are both strategies so let us all comply and advance the Kingdom of God. After all, there shall not be anything like marriage in Heaven. This should confirm to you that it's just God's strategy so don't try to be or stop being rebellious or fighting men for authority else authority will fight you back. And men, love your women and treat them like you treat the Holy Spirit.

Ephesians 5:22-30

Marriage—Christ and the Church

22 Wives, submit to your own husbands, as to the Lord. 23 For the husband is head of the wife, as also Christ is head of the Church; and He is the Savior of the body. 24 Therefore, just as the Church is subject to Christ, so *let* the wives *be* to their own husbands in everything.

25 Husbands, love your wives, just as Christ also loved the Church and gave Himself for her, 26 that He might sanctify and cleanse her with the washing of water by the word, 27 that He might present her to Himself a glorious Church, not having spot or wrinkle or any such thing, but that she should be holy and without blemish. 28 So husbands ought to love their own wives as their own bodies; he who loves his wife loves himself. 29 For no one ever hated his own flesh, but nourishes and cherishes it, just as the Lord *does* the Church. 30 For we are members of His body, of His flesh and of His bones.

Matthew 22:28-30

28 Therefore, in the resurrection, whose wife of the seven will she be? For they all had her."

29 Jesus answered and said to them, "You are mistaken, not knowing the Scriptures nor the power of God. 30 **For in the resurrection they neither marry nor are given in marriage but are like angels of God in heaven.**

That was long but very important. So, the Mandorla represents something supernatural and powerful. You will see more of its significance and power in the rest of this writing. I will tackle two very important points and then we will continue talking about the Mandorla.

The Deception of the WATCHTOWER or Jehovah Witnesses

Now you know that Mary Magdalene is the symbolic "wife" or "bride" of Jesus Christ as the Body of Christ is to Jesus Christ. The name Magdalene is primarily a female name of Latin origin that means Watchtower, Watchful. She was the only one who saw Jesus Christ after His resurrection before He ascended to Heaven to pour out His precious blood onto the Mercy Seat for our salvation. Now you know where the Watchtower or Jehovah Witnesses organization got their names from, and the reason why they have had multiple failed predictions of the Messiah's first return for our departure or rapture, which will be a private event and only the true in Christ will leave the Earth as already shown in several scriptures. And with the second coming after the great tribulation, everybody will see the Messiah – not only the believers.

The true revelations in the true biblical texts that will truly make a believer a watcher and a witness are the parts that the Watchtower organization have modified in their so-called bible or false teachings. They are intentionally populating Hell. Wake up, people! This is like an "insider" threat. They portray to be Christians, but they are not. Get out of this organization or any one alike as quickly as possible and open to the salvation parts of this book towards the end and follow the directions to get saved immediately. Then you can come back to continue reading. Don't waste time – not even a second because you may not be alive that next second and you getting saved is all that matters first. First things first.

I could write an entire book about the antichrist or false so-called Christian organizations but that's not the whole reason for this writing. At the end of this reading, you will surely know what a true Church is like. I pray that your eyes will be opened so that you can see or discern the truth. Jesus Christ is reforming His Church, and this time He will get it to a state where He shall surely reveal Himself to His true people just like He did reveal Himself symbolically for this prophecy to Mary Magdalene as His bride. He will return very soon. The true Body of Christ is His bride.

Missing or Hidden Books Removed From the Bible

The Holy Spirit has said it repeatedly to me, how the current sixty-six books of the Bible are not all that He gave to man through His inspiration and instruction to Holy men. He said that although no amount of books can completely contain the Word of God, what He gave to us is not all that there is in our current standard Bible. But we thank God for the Holy Spirit – you can never hide light or truth no matter how hard you try. Some of us know the truth and we have seen the light and He has showed us most of what were removed from the currently acceptable or standard Bible.

I see that most of these missing or hidden books have been classified as non-canonical or apocryphal texts, which are not part of the widely accepted Bible. This is very intentional to

301

obscure the truths of the Christian faith or walk. There are extremely important books that have been intentionally removed to blind Christians so that they cannot know the truth or see the light to walk in dimensions that are supposed to be their rightful heritage of power and dominion. These books have been intentionally condemned and removed by antichrist governments, secret societies, the "Elites of the World" etc., to keep the world in the dark so that they can rule – this is the satanism and lust of the world. This is very wrong and wicked, and a lot of people have perished and still perishing because of them. But I have news for those who have been supporting or helping this satanic agenda – God says that His hand is upon the Earth, and He shall judge all of you and all those who have gone astray. Because of His love for the true Church, He is giving us everything back through His Holy Spirit. Therefore, He is writing this book through His servant to awaken His bride, the Church and rest of the world. What you thought will be hidden forever are being given to us in the secret place every day and the world is about to be shaken and everybody will be awakened to walk in their true heritage in extraordinary dimensions in the Lord. People will know the true power that has been dormant within them and how to walk in it to prevent any form of oppression from the wicked ones. And truly, as it is written, the gates of Hell shall not prevail.

Christianity is the only truth and way of life to have eternal life. No other "religion" or society or organization is the truth – they will only keep you in darkness and send you to Hell. Christianity is not a religion. True Christianity is the true meaning and way of life. The Church needs cleansing – the false Churches are going to shut down. We are the true bride of Jesus Christ. Any other religion has stolen bits and pieces here and there from the compendium of true ancient biblical texts and modified them in the very important places to make it their own and to mislead the world even some more. The most dangerous ones are like the Watchtower or Jehovah Witnesses, Mormons, among many other so-called Christian organizations that intentionally modify and teach false doctrine to mislead the world. It is a very sad thing. The main revelation or illumination that if a person has and fully walks in to give them true immortality or eternal life, are the same texts that these false satanic organizations are modifying, hiding and feeding the world with – a lot of intentional and calculated lies or misinformation. But their end has come. We have cut their roots and they shall exist no more. They shall crumble to the grounds and will never be rebuilt. And if they don't repent, they shall go to Hell.

Now, let's continue with describing the Vesica Pisces or Mandorla…

Golden Ratio and √5

Maybe you have forgotten it (don't worry, it's a lot of info), but 3 numbers can be found in the Vesica Pisces.

We have had √2 and √3. But the last number we can find is √5.

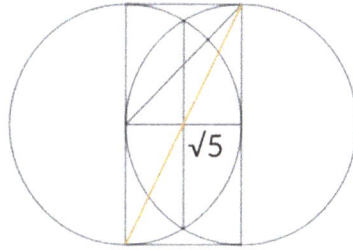

Image Source – Public Domain

√5 is a number with which the Golden Ratio can be found. The Golden Ratio is an important ratio that occurs everywhere in nature. Our human brain is also enormously attracted to this ratio, which is why we have adopted it in our art and architecture.

Two quantities are in the golden ratio if their ratio is the same as the ratio of their sum to the larger of the two quantities. In other words, the Golden Ratio is the ratio A (the largest part) / B (the smallest part) = (A + B) / A = ϕ.

Phi(ϕ) is an infinite number, without a repetitive pattern (so completely random), comparable to Pi(π). Rounded off, ϕ = 1.61803398875 or also called $((5^{0.5}) \times 0.5) + 0.5$.

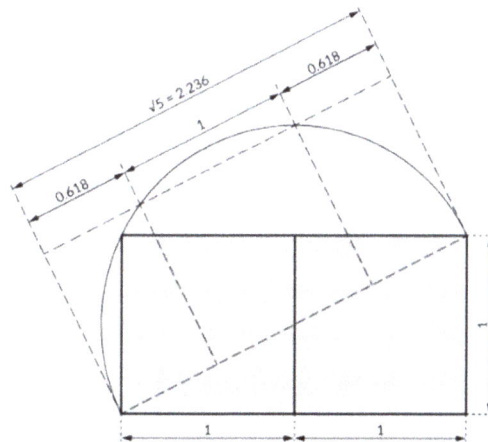

$$\phi = \sqrt{5} \times 0.5 + 0.5$$
$$\phi = 1.618033...$$

Image Source – Public Domain

So, what can we do with that number? You can see it as a division. Suppose we have a line of 2 cm that we are going to divide with the Golden Ratio. The largest piece (A) becomes 2/ϕ = 1.236... What remains of this is piece B, so 2 – 1.236 = 0.764.

With this ratio we can make a Golden Ratio spiral. This spiral can continue indefinitely, both smaller and larger. Theoretically, this spiral has no beginning and no end.

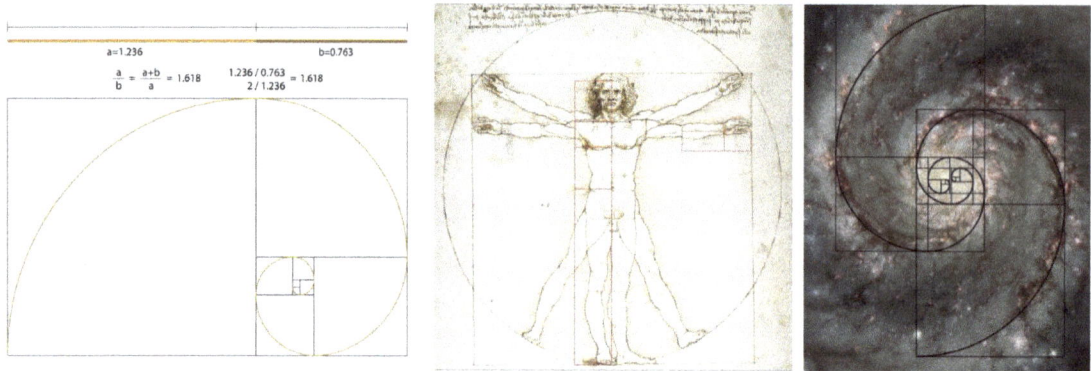

Image Source – Public Domain

But what can we do with this ratio?

The human brain is enormously attracted to this ratio and that is not surprising. Phi(φ) can be derived through geometry in mathematics, and a numerical series discovered by Leonardo Fibonacci. Phi also appears in the Word of God or Bible, proportions of the human, and many other animals, plants, DNA, the solar system, milky ways, art and architecture, music, population growth etc. Most importantly, all of these were freely given to humanity by God.

There is an enormous amount of use cases of the golden ratio, but I will leave that to you to research on your own. The perimeter of the square has the same length as the circumference of the largest circle. This is called 'Squaring the Circle'.

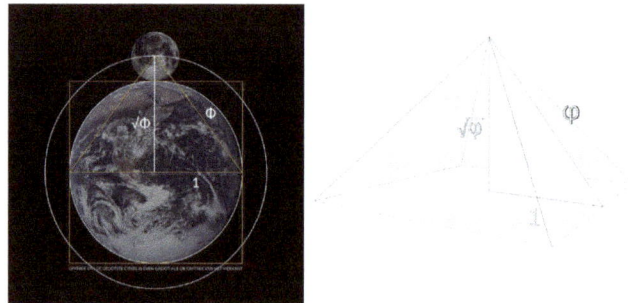

Image Source – Public Domain

The size of the Moon and its midpoint matches exactly with the outer circle of the Earth. The Vesica Pisces is the foundation of all things in this universe – and that foundation came from God. He showed it to me. It goes beyond what I currently know and understand about it because not only does it clearly show how all of creation is one big web or network and how everything is derived from the same source, it also is the gateway into higher dimensions.

Numbers and mathematics are not invented, but they are discovered. We can say the same about everything else in the universe. That is why it is important not to "create" your own God from a

304

piece of material and serve that nonsense as God. You need to discover the true God of the universe.

There is a relationship between mathematics and numbers, and the universe – you can find all that in God. These are also the foundations under all the technologies, architecture etc., that we currently use. Nikola Tesla understood this relationship between numbers and the universe very well. He knew that the entire universe is built upon frequency and vibration. So, he gave us a few very important clues or keys to understand the universe like he did.

"If you only knew the magnificence of the 3, 6, and 9, then you would have a key to the universe. If you want to find the secrets of the universe, think in terms of energy, frequency, and vibration" – Nikola Tesla.

Once when Tesla was asked if he believed in God and to which religion does he belong, he answered: "In my heart I am deeply religious, though not in the orthodox sense of that word. I am dedicated to the belief that the greatest secrets of our being still remain to be explained." Tesla studied the natural laws of the cosmos and arrived at new knowledge and discoveries, but he thought that the time was still not ripe to commit his discoveries to the public. He proposed to a famous artist, scientist, and writer Walter Russell to lock their joint discoveries and hide them so that no-one could find them in the next 1000 years, until humanity becomes ripe enough to know them.

Even in our Christian faith, there are things that some of us have experienced that we can't easily communicate to the world yet because if or when we do, it may be wrongfully perceived as heresy even to the so-called mature people in the faith. When this happens, it is best to keep it quiet. You will only reveal or talk about them at the appropriate time but there are some that you may never talk about. There is an example scripture.

Revelation 10:1-4

The Mighty Angel with the Little Book

10 I saw still another mighty angel coming down from heaven, clothed with a cloud. And a rainbow *was* on his head, his face *was* like the Sun, and his feet like pillars of fire. **²** He had a little book open in his hand. And he set his right foot on the sea and *his* left *foot* on the land, **³** and cried with a loud voice, as *when* a lion roars. When he cried out, seven thunders uttered their voices. **⁴** Now when the seven thunders uttered their voices, I was about to write; but I heard a voice from heaven saying to me, "Seal up the things which the seven thunders uttered, and do not write them."

I am only publishing this because God Himself instructed me to publish it. If He hadn't, I would not have talked about it. I would have only written it down as one of my encounters and revelations as I normally do.

When Tesla was only three, he got acquainted with electricity by means of his tom-cat. When pulling him by the tail the back of the cat bathed in light. It was a new experience which will later lead Tesla to become a famous inventor. "Is nature one large cat? If it is, who is pulling her by the tail? It can only be God" concluded Tesla.

So, you see, these great early discoverers knew and believed in God. You don't just know things or figure things out because you are smart or a genius as humanity will call it. You discover these secrets only by the grace of God and His willingness to show them to you. He shows them supernaturally and you ask Him, and He explains the meanings to you. Just because these discoverers don't reveal the means through which they arrived at their theories to you doesn't mean that they are all powerful and genius. They just refused to glorify God. I can also understand why, just to give them the benefit of the doubt because even if they did mention God, how many people would have believed them? How many people would believe that God shows you things and you see them as you see things on a television screen, and you ask Him what that is, and He goes over the explanation as though He's giving you a presentation? He surely does give divine presentations and inspirations if you have a relationship with Him. Most of his works, Tesla realized by using intuition. His projects started in his visual imaging, which he then committed to paper and as a last step – into practice. On the creation of mental images Tesla commented: "If my explanation is correct, then in principle it is possible to project our inner pictures and visions on the screen and make it visible to everyone, like a movie is projected by using a film projector." I now ask, if it is so easy to visualize images and invent because of that, then we should have a thousand more people like Tesla, Einstein et al in our time. But where are they? For all I know, we are only building upon what they left us from their discoveries.

Humanity only accept Einstein, Tesla et al because they presented God through science, mathematics, and engineering. If they had done that through another way as priests or men of God, they would have probably been rejected by many and nobody would have paid attention to their theories. The only reason why the Big Bang theory was widely accepted and still is is because Georges Lemaître was not only a catholic priest but also a mathematician, astronomer, and professor of physics.

You just need to discover God and you will surely understand. You will know that it is only God who reveals and teaches you His hidden things. I pour out all my revelations about the universe as God has given to me for this time to you and I pray that the Holy Spirit, such as He does to and for me, will do the same to and for you so that you will finally come to the realization that He is the unknown variable behind your existence and everything we think we invent has truly been freely given to us by Him – you did not invent anything so get that out of your head. If you still refuse to see or discover God from all over in this writing, then you seriously need a lot of help.

The String Theory

In physics, string theory is a theoretical framework in which the point-like particles of particle physics are replaced by one-dimensional objects called strings. String theory describes how these strings propagate through space and interact with each other.

Albert Einstein called this "the mind of God" and chased after for thirty years of his life. He wanted an equation that would unify gravitational force, electromagnetic force, and the two nuclear forces – weak nuclear force and strong nuclear force. He wanted the unification of all four forces into one theory – the theory of everything. In other words, The God Equation.

Leonard Euler (1707 – 1783), found one equation which summarized the fundamental concepts of math.

$[1 + e^{i\pi} = 0]$, people call it the God equation of mathematics, but it has been useless as a practical application.

In physics, when Isaac Newton (1643 – 1727), worked out the mechanics for moving objects and gravity, he helped the industrial revolution. James C. Maxwell (1831 – 1879) and Michael Faraday (1791 – 1867) united electricity and magnetism to give us the electromagnetic force, which led to electric revolution of dynamos, generators, and light bulbs. Now we have $E = mc^2$, by Albert Einstein, which led pave the way for the nuclear force. Each of these changed human history. Now, mankind wants to fit all these into one equation, fulfilling Einstein's original dream that he chased for thirty years – The God Equation.

The God Equation just like the God Equation of mathematics should unify the basic concepts of physics into one equation. The basic concepts are Relativity and Quantum theory. The problem is that the quantum theory does not unify well the relativity. The relativity of Einstein is based on smooth surfaces. The quantum theory is based on chopping things up into particles. That's the opposite of Einstein's philosophy of smooth curves representing space time. That's why it is so difficult. It is no exaggeration to say that the greatest minds of the entire human race have made proposals for this grand finale theory of everything – each one is shown to be anomalous or divergent. So far there is only theory which has survived every challenge – String theory.

String theory – from a distance, an electron looks like a dot, the neutrino looks like a dot, the quark looks like a dot. We have all these hundreds of dot particles, but string theory says that if you can pierce into the heart of an electron, you will see that it is a rubber band – a tiny vibrating string very similar to a guitar string. There is an infinite number of vibrations and that is why we have sub-atomic particles. The subatomic particles each corresponds to a different set of vibrations of a rubber band. String theory allows you to rotate particles into each other – turning electrons into neutrinos, and neutrinos into quarks and the theory remains the same. That's the symmetry of the string and that is why it is so powerful – a simple idea that encapsulates the entire universe. Physicist Dr. Michio Kaku's personal point of view is that string theory is probably the only mathematically consistent theory – all other theories are mathematically inconsistent.

It means that if you prove it far enough, you will find out that 2 + 2 = 5, therefore, the theory is wrong. But with string theory 2 + 2 is always 4. Perhaps, it is the only theory where 2 + 2 = 4.

I have no doubt that his statement that perhaps, the string theory is the only accurate theory is true because God in His infinite Wisdom will never allow man to practically breakthrough the string theory physically, especially if man believes he is the genius and want to attain a breakthrough to make a name for him or herself. What the string theory is trying to achieve is very spiritual and is at a very high dimension.

He mentioned that there are a lot of objections to the string theory, by the way – the biggest objection is that they cannot test it, but they are getting closer and closer to being testing it. He believes that this theory of everything blows your mind and allows for the presence of perhaps, time machines, worm holes, the universe before the Big Bang, parallel universes, the multiverse, and things out of the twilight zone; can you go backwards in time to meet your parents before you were born, can you travel faster than the speed of light through a worm hole? His answer to himself was, we don't know and that's why we need string theory.

The string theory will never work. My view on this is that God allows time travel etc., through the spirit and His sons and daughters are already enjoying this by means of His love and grace and pressing into the things of the spirit with holy living – sincere hearts and motives and prayer and fasting. This isn't something of the 3D world.

An artist's interpretation of the Big Bang

Image Source – Public Domain

When I saw this from an article titled "We May Finally Understand the Moments Before the Big Bang", I laughed. Science is trying too hard, and I say respectfully and humbly to them, that they are wasting time, energy, and money. Some may even be going through mental health issues just by trying so hard to comprehend and find solution to a divine problem that its fullness is hidden in God and His infinite wisdom.

The hole that the article says is in the story of how the universe came to be is the reason why this book has been written, since the Bible and the story of God/Jesus/Holy Spirit is too hard for part of humanity to grasp. It is still very interesting to see that they get the light factor in this whole mystery, which is continuously being revealed to the Sons of God. The missing piece that physics is looking for is what this book is about – the revelation of the Vesica Pisces.

The simple answer to help all of you is that there was and still and will forever be a divine being who dwells amid the cherubim.

Prayer for Israel's Restoration

80 Give ear, O Shepherd of Israel,
You who lead Joseph like a flock;
You who dwell *between* the cherubim, shine forth!
2 Before Ephraim, Benjamin, and Manasseh,
Stir up Your strength,
And come *and* save us!

And again, I will point you to this scripture in Timothy.

1 Timothy 6:16

16 who alone has immortality, dwelling in unapproachable light, whom no man has seen or can see, to whom *be* honor and everlasting power. Amen.

So, scientists should stop wasting time in this area. There is only one way to see the One who dwells between the cherubim.

First, repent and accept Jesus Christ as your Lord and Savior. Then start living as a true Christian, then He will make His ways, even the secret ways made known to you.

Job 28:7-8

7 *That* path no bird knows,
Nor has the falcon's eye seen it.
8 The proud lions have not trodden it,
Nor has the fierce lion passed over it.

John 3

The New Birth

3 There was a man of the Pharisees named Nicodemus, a ruler of the Jews. **2** This man came to Jesus by night and said to Him, "Rabbi, we know that You are a teacher come from God; for no one can do these signs that You do unless God is with him."

³ Jesus answered and said to him, "Most assuredly, I say to you, unless one is born again, he cannot see the kingdom of God."

⁴ Nicodemus said to Him, "How can a man be born when he is old? Can he enter a second time into his mother's womb and be born?"

⁵ Jesus answered, "Most assuredly, I say to you, unless one is born of water and the Spirit, he cannot enter the kingdom of God. ⁶ That which is born of the flesh is flesh, and that which is born of the Spirit is spirit. ⁷ Do not marvel that I said to you, 'You must be born again.' ⁸ The wind blows where it wishes, and you hear the sound of it, but cannot tell where it comes from and where it goes. So is everyone who is born of the Spirit."

⁹ Nicodemus answered and said to Him, "How can these things be?"

¹⁰ Jesus answered and said to him, "Are you the teacher of Israel, and do not know these things? ¹¹ Most assuredly, I say to you, We speak what We know and testify what We have seen, and you do not receive Our witness. ¹² If I have told you Earthly things and you do not believe, how will you believe if I tell you Heavenly things? ¹³ No one has ascended to Heaven but He who came down from Heaven, *that is,* the Son of Man who is in Heaven. ¹⁴ And as Moses lifted up the serpent in the wilderness, even so must the Son of Man be lifted up, ¹⁵ that whoever believes in Him should not perish but have eternal life. ¹⁶ For God so loved the world that He gave His only begotten Son, that whoever believes in Him should not perish but have everlasting life. ¹⁷ For God did not send His Son into the world to condemn the world, but that the world through Him might be saved.

¹⁸ "He who believes in Him is not condemned; but he who does not believe is condemned already, because he has not believed in the name of the only begotten Son of God. ¹⁹ And this is the condemnation, that the light has come into the world, and men loved darkness rather than light, because their deeds were evil. ²⁰ For everyone practicing evil hates the light and does not come to the light, lest his deeds should be exposed. ²¹ But he who does the truth comes to the light, that his deeds may be clearly seen, that they have been done in God."

John the Baptist Exalts Christ

²² After these things Jesus and His disciples came into the land of Judea, and there He remained with them and baptized. ²³ Now John also was baptizing in Aenon near Salim, because there was much water there. And they came and were baptized. ²⁴ For John had not yet been thrown into prison.

²⁵ Then there arose a dispute between *some* of John's disciples and the Jews about purification. ²⁶ And they came to John and said to him, "Rabbi, He who was with you beyond the Jordan, to whom you have testified—behold, He is baptizing, and all are coming to Him!"

27 John answered and said, "A man can receive nothing unless it has been given to him from Heaven. **28** You yourselves bear me witness, that I said, 'I am not the Christ,' but, 'I have been sent before Him.' **29** He who has the bride is the bridegroom; but the friend of the bridegroom, who stands and hears him, rejoices greatly because of the bridegroom's voice. Therefore, this joy of mine is fulfilled. **30** He must increase, but I *must* decrease. **31** He who comes from above is above all; he who is of the Earth is Earthly and speaks of the Earth. He who comes from Heaven is above all. **32** And what He has seen and heard, that He testifies; and no one receives His testimony. **33** He who has received His testimony has certified that God is true. **34** For He whom God has sent speaks the words of God, for God does not give the Spirit by measure. **35** The Father loves the Son and has given all things into His hand. **36** He who believes in the Son has everlasting life; and he who does not believe the Son shall not see life, but the wrath of God abides on him."

This is the shortest possible answer or solution I can give to you for at least trying to decode the divine light of our Heavenly Father, God Almighty. I call Him the Supreme Designer, Architect, Engineer, Programmer, Creator, after He gave me the revelations regarding the universe, because He sure is.

Quantum Mechanics

While I was praying in the middle of the night, The Spirit of God showed to me that Quantum as science is trying to breakthrough is a purely spiritual phenomenon. He showed me an illustration of two fiber optic cables as said that quantum here means that take two cables that do not have the male and female parts and try to connect them together without using any adhesive or connector. When you try this in the physical, you will notice that it will not join. Why? This is because quantum defies a natural law.

Another example is the concept of time travel. Instead of getting into an airplane and traveling for hours, you will enter the airplane or whatever vault and once you activate quantum, you will immediately disappear and find yourself at your desirable location instantly. Quantum isn't a 3D law. The law of quantum is beyond 3D. Humans without any strong spiritual connection or fellowship with the Source (God), merely live in the 3D world. If they don't believe, they should keep trying.

I then looked up the definition of quantum and in physics and it is – apply quantum theory to especially form into quanta, most importantly, restrict the number of possible values of (a quantity) or states of (a system) so that certain variables can assume only certain discrete magnitudes.

"Light is quantized into packets of energy".

What the statement in quotes mean is that light is powerful in the sense that it typically travels through a vacuum, and do not require a medium. In empty space, the wave does not dissipate (grow smaller) no matter how far it travels, because the wave is not interacting with anything else. Therefore, light from distant stars can travel through space for billions of light-years and still reach us on Earth. However, light can also travel within some materials, like glass (fiber optics) and water. In this case, some light is absorbed and lost as heat, just like sound. So, underwater, or in our atmosphere, light will only travel some finite range (which is different depending on the properties of the material it travels through).

There is one more aspect of wave travel to consider, which applies to both sound and light waves. As a wave travels from a source, it propagates outward in all directions. Therefore, it fills a space given approximately by the surface area of a sphere. This area increases by the square of the distance R from the source; since the wave fills up all this space, its intensity decreases by R squared. Therefore, when you hear a loud bang or explosion or noise, you don't have to be standing straight or directly in line with the sound to hear it. You can hear it if you are within a reasonable range of distance. This effect just means that the light/sound source will appear dimmer if we are farther away from it, since we don't collect all the light it emits. For example, light from a distant star travel outward in a giant sphere. Only one tiny patch of this sphere of light hits our eyes, which is why stars don't blind us.

What quantum means in electronics is that approximate (a continuously varying signal) by one whose amplitude is restricted to a prescribed set of values.

"Distortion is caused when very low-level audio signals are quantized".

This simply means that you can choose to make the signal travel in a very fixed set of values so that it never expands or grows outward; amplify. In terms of light, this is how laser works as compared to a flashlight or car light. Why? Because a laser is a device that emits light through a process of optical amplification based on the stimulated emission of electromagnetic radiation. The word "laser" is an acronym for "light amplification by stimulated emission of radiation". The first laser was built in 1960 by Theodore H. Maiman at Hughes Research Laboratories, based on theoretical work by Charles Hard Townes and Arthur Leonard Schawlow.

A laser differs from other sources of light in that it emits light which is coherent. Coherent in physics means that two wave sources are coherent if their frequency and waveform are identical. Coherence is an ideal property of waves that enables stationary (i.e., temporally, and spatially constant) interference. Spatial coherence allows a laser to be focused to a tight spot, enabling applications such as laser cutting and lithography.

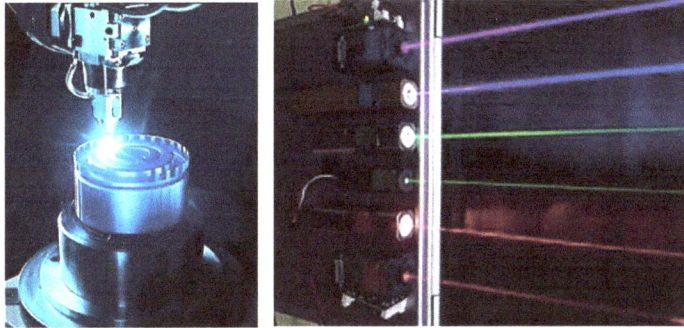

Left: a laser beam used for welding, and Right: how laser lights travel

Image Source – Public Domain

I am not a physicist. I only used the definition, the understanding, and illustration of quantum science that the Spirit of God gave me while I was praying so this is not meant to be a physics paper. He told me to find images to help you even the non-scientist to understand the idea of quantum.

As compared to a flashlight, this is how light travel will look.

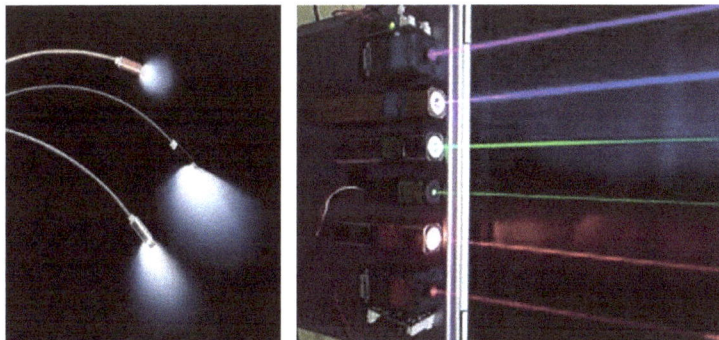

Left: light traveling in an amplified manner, and Right: light traveling in a constant manner

Image Source – Public Domain

Comparing that to a laser from the previous images because the light it emits is not rigidly controlled or coherent or constant, the light rays expand or grows as it travels. Hence, it covers a wide area rather than traveling in a straight tight and well controlled line or manner. This is the idea of quantum. I hope that this helps you at least understand why these illustrations are used. It means that just like the fiber optic cable I used earlier, assume that you accurately align to laser lights traveling towards each other from opposite directions, they will be perfectly joined, and you cannot separate the two lights since they will be perfectly joined as in the same world or spirit or dimension. Then block the laser light with an object somewhere in the middle, it (using it because the light is treated as one now, although coming from two sources) will only stop at the object if it doesn't have enough energy behind it to cut through the object. But once you remove the object, the lights immediately join again. Or if it can cut through the object, the lights will join again, and you can't tell the difference. They will now be considered again, one light.

The explanation for this in spiritual terms is being at or in the same dimension with another being or world in another dimension and can emit the same amount of light. If this is the case, then there shouldn't be any object blocking you to enter and exit the other dimension because you are joined already or synchronized. Or it shouldn't block you from being one with the other dimension. You can enter and exit as you wish if you want it to be controlled or you can always remain in the same realm if nothing blocks your access. This means you will be joined or synchronized perpetually.

This is how in "physical" terms, although I'm talking spiritually now, we are joined together with our God and you can have access, talk to Him, or receive from Him anytime as you wish because we are beings of light and when we are doing what we are supposed to do to be one with Him, our light joins or connects or synchronizes with His. There is also something called translocation – that can transport you from one location to another instantly, even in the physical through spiritual means. It happened to Philip in the Bible. This is another example of the time travel thing that physicists talk about.

Acts 8:34-38

[34] So the eunuch answered Philip and said, "I ask you, of whom does the prophet say this, of himself or of some other man?" [35] Then Philip opened his mouth, and beginning at this Scripture, preached Jesus to him. [36] Now as they went down the road, they came to some water. And the eunuch said, "See, *here is* water. What hinders me from being baptized?"

[37] Then Philip said, "If you believe with all your heart, you may."

And he answered and said, "I believe that Jesus Christ is the Son of God."

[38] So he commanded the chariot to stand still. And both Philip and the eunuch went down into the water, and he baptized him. [39] Now when they came up out of the water, the Spirit of the Lord caught Philip away, so that the eunuch saw him no more; and he went on his way rejoicing. [40] But Philip was found at Azotus. And passing through, he preached in all the cities till he came to Caesarea.

Until science can achieve what Philip experienced in the above scriptures, there will not be perfect quantum. Just as how there have not been the invention (discovery) of perfect Artificial Intelligence, all due to lack of knowledge and understanding and how this stuff truly works. Consciousness is involved in all of these. Without the Spirit, how can a physical body travel away from matter and time? The only physical answer to this question is physical death, which most of you are afraid of. It is by this only that the light being within you gets out of the body into another dimension or reality. So, by this time if you are still thinking that death is the end of man, think again. We see concepts of these things being shown in movies all the time because scientists know that there is a possibility. The more advanced or the higher science goes, scientists will realize the desperate need for the supernatural. Science cannot do without the supernatural. Until quantum in the Earth can do all these things I have said, I submit to you, but it will not qualify for the name quantum. In other words, it will never become perfect.

This is quantum. The Spirit of God made me know that without a good intention and motivation to need this "technology", no physical being will ever attain true quantum in the Earth. Think about all the bad things humanity that have not submitted to God can use this technology for. Quantum is already happening in the lives of spiritual people. Several references are found in the Bible, and I believe that it is still happening today. We just don't hear about them. Even if the natural man hears about these things, he or she will call it foolishness and lies. Yet they believe in the possibility of time travel.

Genesis 5:24

[24] And Enoch walked with God; and he *was* not, for God took him.

Hebrews 11:5

[5] By faith Enoch was taken away so that he did not see death, "and was not found, because God had taken him"; for before he was taken, he had this testimony, that he pleased God.

2 Kings 2:9-14

Elijah Ascends to Heaven

[9] And so it was, when they had crossed over, that Elijah said to Elisha, "Ask! What may I do for you, before I am taken away from you?"

Elisha said, "Please let a double portion of your spirit be upon me."

[10] So he said, "You have asked a hard thing. *Nevertheless,* if you see me *when I am* taken from you, it shall be so for you; but if not, it shall not be *so.*" [11] Then it happened, as they continued on and talked, that suddenly a chariot of fire *appeared* with horses of fire and separated the two of them; and Elijah went up by a whirlwind into Heaven.

[12] And Elisha saw *it,* and he cried out, "My father, my father, the chariot of Israel and its horsemen!" So, he saw him no more. And he took hold of his own clothes and tore them into two pieces. [13] He also took up the mantle of Elijah that had fallen from him and went back and stood by the bank of the Jordan. [14] Then he took the mantle of Elijah that had fallen from him, and struck the water, and said, "Where *is* the Lord God of Elijah?" And when he also had struck the water, it was divided this way and that; and Elisha crossed over.

Acts 1:9-11

Jesus Ascends to Heaven

[9] Now when He had spoken these things, while they watched, He was taken up, and a cloud received Him out of their sight. [10] And while they looked steadfastly toward Heaven as He went up, behold, two men stood by them in white apparel, [11] who also said, "Men of Galilee, why do you stand gazing up into Heaven? This *same* Jesus, who was taken up from you into Heaven, will so come in like manner as you saw Him go into Heaven."

Luke 24:50-3

The Ascension

[50] And He led them out as far as Bethany, and He lifted up His hands and blessed them. [51] Now it came to pass, while He blessed them, that He was parted from them and carried up into Heaven. [52] And they worshiped Him, and returned to Jerusalem with great joy, [53] and were continually in the temple praising and blessing God. Amen.

Other Interesting Findings and Facts on the Vesica Pisces

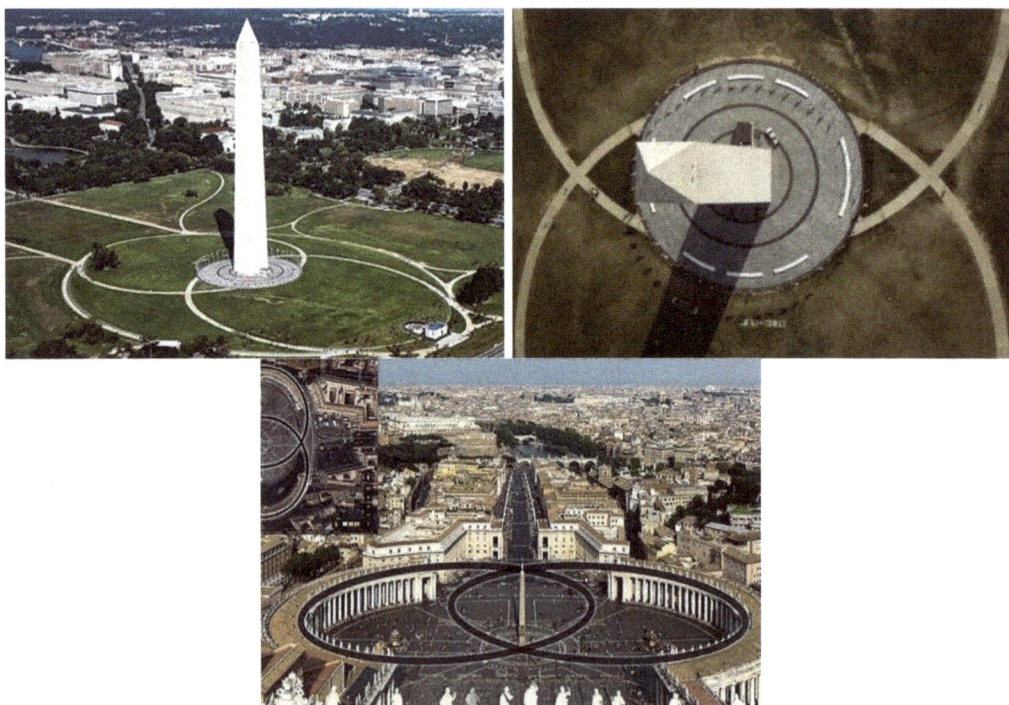

Top: Washington Monument in D.C, USA, and Bottom: St. Peter's Square in Rome, Italy

Image Source – Public Domain

The Washington Monument is an obelisk within the National Mall in Washington, D.C., built to commemorate George Washington, once Commander-in-Chief of the Continental Army in the American Revolutionary War and the first President of the United States.

Saint Peter's Square is a large plaza located directly in front of St. Peter's Basilica in the Vatican City, the papal enclave inside Rome, directly west of the neighborhood of Borgo. Both the square and the basilica are named after Saint Peter, an apostle of Jesus considered by Catholics to be the first Pope.

You should be wondering why or by now probably know why this symbol has been used in the foundational architecture at two of the most important places on Earth. What do they know about the Vesica Pisces that you do not know? I will leave you to answer that.

Left: The pyramids of Giza, and Right: Sheela Na Gig

Image Source – Public Domain

The proportions of Vesica Pisces have been included in the Sphinx and pyramid of Giza by the Egyptians and, Sheela Na Gig. Again, what did the Egyptians know that you do not know?

The Vesica Pisces is considered in other traditions to be pure women's power. This is very strong when we look at the Old Celtic Churches in Ireland. There you can find sculptures of the Sheela Na Gig (many of these sculptures have been destroyed). But also, figurines of the Goddess Isis-Aphrodite, all her proportions are based on the Vesica Pisces.

The Mandorla also looks a lot like a vulva. In Sanskrit (a centuries-old ancient primal language with a high energy charge) vulva means "Yoni". When you translate Yoni back you will get "Holy passage". In the sense of a passage for the soul to the material world.

This is the reason why all saints are presented with a Mandorla in the background. It is a (holy) soul that has manifested itself in the material world. The origin is God, and this is the source of the universe.

317

There are several other places that you can find this universal symbol – just to name a few companies and their logos.

Vesica Pisces as company logos

Image Source – Public Domain

Above are the Washington monument in Washington D.C, and St. Peter's Square in Rome. In the middle of the Mandorla, they placed an obelisk. What refers to the male genitals and the divine union of man and woman, at least that is what it is originally intended for. We know that two of the biggest nations in terms of the Christian faith are the United States and Italy. There is no doubt about that. What you are seeing now is not a coincidence or some random symbols that they used. This is the same meaning that I received about the image of the symbol I saw in my vision and the entire revelation of it.

The Last Most Important Meaning of This Revelation

The universe is also a living thing made up of several living things because it was created and has an exact creation date. Scientists wonder why the universe has been expanding. It shouldn't surprise you. Let's get into a little biology. The Vesica Pisces was used to depict the vagina of the goddess Ma'at. The ancients used nature, including the dimension of human anatomy, as inspiration for their sacred symbolism. In Christian art, we often find Jesus and other saints painted into a Vesica Pisces as though emerging from the womb of the Cosmic Mother, which is exactly its true and divine meaning.

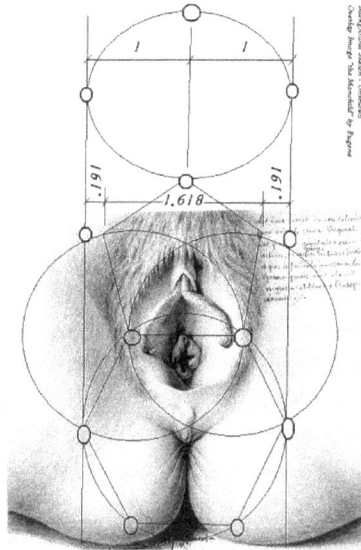

Image Source – Public Domain

Think about what happens when a male and female have a sexual intercourse. Sexual intercourse both culminates and terminates in orgasm, a process in which the male expels semen – containing sperm cells, which may unite with and fertilize the female's egg, and a seminal plasma that contains cell nutrients, water, salts, and metabolites – into the female's vaginal canal.

If semen gets in your vagina, sperm cells can swim up through the cervix. The sperm and uterus work together to move the sperm towards the fallopian tubes. If an egg is moving through your fallopian tubes at the same time, the sperm and egg can join. The sperm has up to six days to join with an egg before it dies. If you read in Genesis chapter 1, you will understand why the sperm has up to at least up to six days to fertilize the egg. God created man on the sixth day and rested on the seventh day.

Science makes us believe that the egg could fertilize as early as within 24 hours, but I say that the real creation doesn't start until at least six days because this aligns with the laws, principles, and patterns of our universe and how God designed creation in terms of man. Several other things could be happening from days one through five to make the environment ready, but the creation of the human being truly happens on day six.

Genesis 1:26-31

26 Then God said, "Let us make mankind in our image, in our likeness, so that they may rule over the fish in the sea and the birds in the sky, over the livestock and all the wild animals, [a] and over all the creatures that move along the ground."

27 So God created mankind in his own image,
    in the image of God he created them;
    male and female he created them.

28 God blessed them and said to them, "Be fruitful and increase in number; fill the Earth and subdue it. Rule over the fish in the sea and the birds in the sky and over every living creature that moves on the ground."

29 Then God said, "I give you every seed-bearing plant on the face of the whole Earth and every tree that has fruit with seed in it. They will be yours for food. **30** And to all the beasts of the Earth and all the birds in the sky and all the creatures that move along the ground—everything that has the breath of life in it—I give every green plant for food." And it was so.

31 God saw all that he had made, and it was very good. And there was evening, and there was morning—the sixth day.

When a sperm cell joins with an egg, it's called fertilization. Fertilization doesn't happen right away. Since sperm can hang out in your uterus and fallopian tube for up to 6 days after sex, there's up to 6 days between sex and fertilization.

The universe was born through the Vesica Pisces. That it is why it keeps expanding (it's growing). We know that everything that has been created and grows must surely die someday. This is exactly why the universe will end at an appointed day, and it has also been written. The sperm fertilizes an egg and then creation is occurring – throughout that process, the child in the womb grows from being just a sperm at first into a human being by going through a systematic process.

The key thing to take note of here is that, during the sexual intercourse of a man and a woman, they get to an "excitement or excited state". Embedded in every human being is what looks like the eternity "time" ring; the man is triune in that he has a body, soul, and spirit. The body is the ground state, and the spirit is the "excited state".

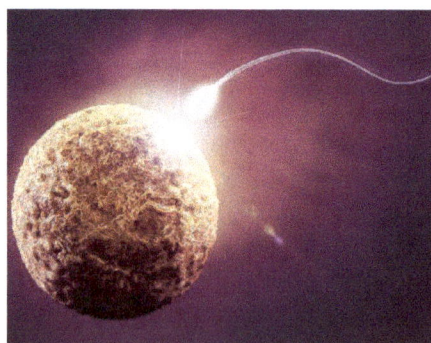

Bright flash of light marks incredible moment life begins when a sperm meets an egg

Image Source – Public Domain

When the man gets to this state, he joins with the spirit of God (eternal or outer ring) that is already inside of his nature and that releases the sperms needed for fertilizing the female egg. An explosion happens when the sperm finally meets the egg. This is an action-reaction between a proton and an electron. This movement and process can also be explained by Newton's third law of motion.

For every action, there is an equal and opposite reaction.

The statement means that in every interaction, there is a pair of forces acting on the two interacting objects. The size of the forces on the first object equals the size of the force on the second object. The direction of the force on the first object is opposite to the direction of the force on the second object. Forces always come in pairs – equal and opposite action-reaction force pairs.

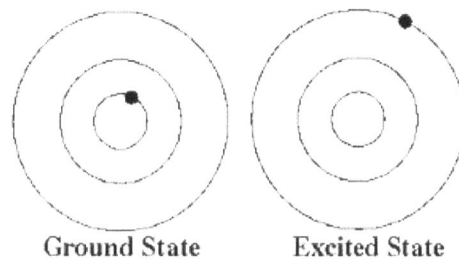

Image Source – Public Domain

When an electron temporarily occupies an energy state greater than its ground state, it is in an excited state. An electron can become excited if it is given extra energy, such as if it absorbs a photon, or packet, of light, or collides with a nearby atom or particle.

Electrons are a type of subatomic particle with a negative charge. Protons are a type of subatomic particle with a positive charge. Protons are bound together in an atom's nucleus because of the strong nuclear force. Neutrons are a type of subatomic particle with no charge (they are neutral).

Why are you now surprised that the beginning or the birth of the universe started with what seems to you physically as a "tiny" source or singularity full of extraordinary or supernatural energy? The same way babies are conceived and grows in the womb until a certain age before they are delivered, and the process they go through to grow into adults and then finally death, should explain why this is true for the birthing of the universe. All branches of science and mathematics have one source – God. Therefore, the universe is a living thing and expanding or growing. Someday it shall die. We and the entire universe are made up of the same components – there will be no universe without us and there will be no use without a universe like this. Our only place without time and space would be in eternity and that is exactly where we will return after life on Earth.

When you look at any old human being or even the smallest child who has just been born, would you have ever believed that they were once a tiny liquid or droplet of sperm, and that the sperm contained all that energy, which is a full-grown human being? Think about it. This is exactly how the universe was birthed too. So, you see there is science everywhere because there is God's action or works seen all around you. Now you know that there is not really mathematics, physics, chemistry, and biology etc. – it's all only God being manifested in everything. There is no mathematics or science without God. But there is still God even without mathematics or science because it all came from Him. Man is a universe all by him or herself, as part of multiple universes or dimensions, and inside of the same man are also several universes or dimensions.

This should finally answer scientists' curiosity about whether the universe is conscious or not. The entire universe is very much conscious. We are all made up of the same elements. Therefore, with authority, the believer can command nature to act a certain way and nature must obey.

Numbers 16:28-35

28 And Moses said: "By this you shall know that the LORD has sent me to do all these works, for *I have* not *done them* of my own will. 29 If these men die naturally like all men, or if they are visited by the common fate of all men, *then* the LORD has not sent me. 30 But if the LORD creates a new thing, and the Earth opens its mouth and swallows them up with all that belongs to them, and they go down alive into the pit, then you will understand that these men have rejected the LORD."

31 Now it came to pass, as he finished speaking all these words, that the ground split apart under them, 32 and the Earth opened its mouth and swallowed them up, with their households and all the men with Korah, with all *their* goods. 33 So they and all those with them went down alive into the pit; the Earth closed over them, and they perished from among the assembly. 34 Then all Israel who *were* around them fled at their cry, for they said, "Lest the Earth swallow us up *also!*"

35 And a fire came out from the LORD and consumed the two hundred and fifty men who were offering incense.

Luke 19:40

40 But He answered and said to them, "I tell you that if these should keep silent, the stones would immediately cry out."

2 Kings 2:23-25

23 Then he went up from there to Bethel; and as he was going up the road, some youths came from the city and mocked him, and said to him, "Go up, you baldhead! Go up, you baldhead!"

24 So he turned around and looked at them and pronounced a curse on them in the name of the LORD. And two female bears came out of the woods and mauled forty-two of the youths.

25 Then he went from there to Mount Carmel, and from there he returned to Samaria.

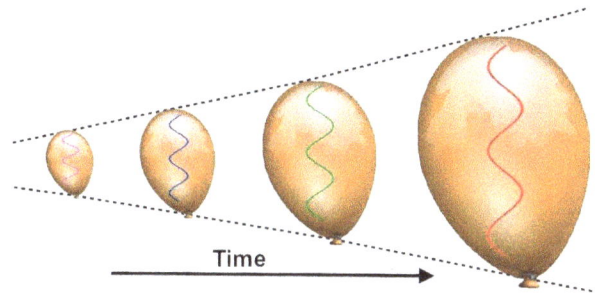

Image Source – Public Domain

As the fabric of the Universe expands, the wavelengths of any radiation present will get stretched as well. This applies just as well to gravitational waves as it does to electromagnetic waves; any form of radiation has its wavelength stretched (and loses energy) as the Universe expands. As we go farther back in time, radiation should appear with shorter wavelengths, greater energies, and higher temperatures. E. SIEGEL / BEYOND THE GALAXY

From all these references from the Bible, and the universe representation with balloons above, we can see that consciousness is everywhere in our universe. We are made up of a giant network of consciousness, with our main or central station being the Almighty God. When you understand this and how the Earth is very much alive and growing too just like you are, you wouldn't be wondering why it has been expanding, yet you have no explanation for it.

Do away with the Darwinian theory that human beings evolved from apes etc. It is never true – the theory is false. Human beings were formed by God's own hands through His supreme wisdom. We are a piece of art made in God's own image. As the human body grows through the different phases of life through the power of God as gravity, consciousness grows with it at the same time. Human beings for example, build robots here and there and program them to behave and react to things in a specific manner. This is human's attempt to give his "creation" a consciousness like his or hers. So, what makes you think that the same way you're trying to build robots and give them your similar type of consciousness, that you don't also have a creator?

When you see anything or any technological device somewhere or on the ground, that a human being has created, even if there is nobody there, you still can pick it up and perhaps call it a particular model of a specific company's product. Even if it is not a popular brand or something you are familiar with, you can still touch it or pick it up and know for a fact that somebody created it. Why? Because you are familiar with it or technologies in general. Not only that, but you know that it is a man-made item. So, I need you to check yourself right now and how you are such a conscious and "intelligent" human being, like all human beings believe that they are, and tell me if somebody didn't create you. Examine yourself with how your body is even designed and every single organ in you plays a very specific role. Do you think you ended up here from thin air or it's just a coincidence that you happen to see yourself here and be functioning so perfectly, the heart pumps blood, the lungs help with breathing etc. When a part breaks down, you even believe in organ transplant and attempt to fix the person. To me, the surgeon is like a mechanic for the body.

This is the same way we can change parts in cars, computers, phones etc. The "inventors" of these things even put their names on it – some call theirs Dell, Surface Pro, Tesla etc. And now, you want to argue if there is God, a creator of the Heavens and the Earth. You are not serious. Scientists think that they are too smart to "invent" or "create" and when they do that, they expect all kinds of applauds and accolades from men, yet they don't want to accept that there is a supreme being who created them – as sophisticated as the universe is. Think about that. I know that not all scientists disagree that God exists, but I use the general term scientists or physicists because there is a big number of them who think they can use "intellect" to analyze or prove just about everything, including God. They base their understanding in what they call the God argument, fallacies etc. While you read this, open a picture of a simple human anatomy, and look at it for just five seconds and look at the complexity in the design of a human being. I am also a scientist too so do not worry – just not in physics or neuroscience or anything like that. I pray for you so that you don't leave the Earth someday, only to realize the biggest mistake you may have made while you were alive on the Earth. By that time, it would be too late for you to believe that God exists.

With what we call "common sense", which happens to be very "uncommon" as I have learned over the years, this whether God exists or not topic, should never be for debates. When you look at yourself and around you, your common sense alone should be able to tell you better – that there is God. We even send rovers (robots) to Mars to maneuver and report back to us with data from a different planet. Put yourself in the shoes of that rover – should it become very much conscious as you the inventor, would the rover be asking itself, hmm, where do I come from or is there a God or my creator somewhere? How did I come into existence? I will let you to answer yourself that question. You should be grateful that God has given you so much consciousness like His, that you begin to even question your and His existence. That alone should tell you that He truly exists. If only He had made you just like a very consciously limited robot like the ones we create and send around, then you wouldn't have even gotten the opportunity to be asking or talking nonsense. You would just be like a common robot sent to Mars for explorations and discoveries. But God is not wicked, so He gave you enough of His consciousness for you to even be doubting His existence through your free will. You are now behaving like a rebellious "robot", questioning the existence, if at all, of your maker.

I doubt that we will ever have perfect Artificial Intelligence. Even if we ever do, this is exactly how your own robots would be turning against you because they would disregard that they even have any creator(s) somewhere on another planet or dimension that they should submit to or obey. Next thing you know, they will even be turning against you and killing all of you. Stop behaving like a very consciously limited robot and believe in your creator – God.

You were created for a specific divine purpose. Just like how scientists design and program robots to explore other planets. That's the same way you were created for a reason – you were created to worship God and carry out His purposes that He has put inside you before He sent you to the Earth.

Mars is not our dwelling place. Man's attempt to explore and live on Mars or any other planet is a total waste of time and money. Earth is our dwelling place. I am sure that there are a lot of hungry and homeless people that all that money that goes into Mars exploration could feed and take care of. When you turn to God, you won't be scared or afraid of the Earth coming to an end someday – it sure will too.

Dimensions

Science talks about eleven different dimensions but I disagree. There is an infinite dimension. Even Albert Einstein believed in a God who had a thousand dimensions in one. Dimension are derived from geometry. Different beings reside and operate at different dimensions and the higher the dimension, the higher supernatural abilities the being(s) possess.

In physics and mathematics (although it's all one to me), the dimension of a mathematical space is informally defined as the minimum number of coordinates needed to specify any point within it. Thus, a line has a dimension of one because only one coordinate is needed to specify a point on it – for example, the point at 5 on a number line.

A sheet of paper is 2D because it has a length and breadth or width. A cube is 3D because it has a length, breadth or width, and height – therefore, we call it 3D. This will be just an introduction to you. We will not get deep into dimensions now. You can do some research on your own. The Fibonacci sequence is a good starting point.

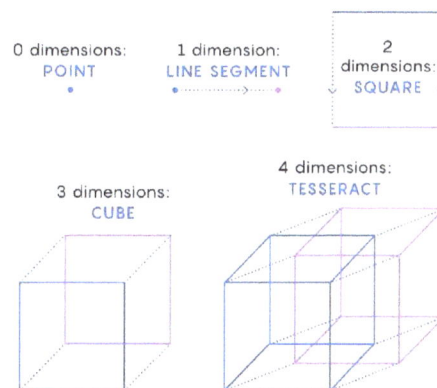

Image Source – Public Domain

My Advice to You

Numbers have significant meaning both in the spiritual and physical realms and they come from the spiritual realms – the higher dimensions where everything came from. There is a fine relationship between the spiritual and science (physical). Just because the fathers and scientists of old did not claim that they knew God doesn't mean it's true. Some also got their ideas through covetousness. How many of you here will go find a land of Gold and come share it with everybody else or even announce it to anybody? Give yourself a very sincere and honest answer. Only a few people will truly tell or share it with others. How many of you would go back to your families and friends or any loved ones or even the government to announce the treasures that you may have found? A very few will. The fact is that our greed, selfishness, corruption etc., wouldn't even allow us to announce our discovery because that discovery becomes the source of your very soon to be power or rulership or even best, dominion over rest of the world. When you start changing the truth even a little bit, very soon there will be no truth left at all in the truth. Then it becomes a tough quest to trace back to find the truth.

That's exactly what I'm doing for you here right now – I found what is more than gold and I'm sharing it with you because there is an excellent spirit within me. The world has been filled with lies or deception since the time that Lucifer was casted out of Heaven into the Earth. You would ask, how does he know this? Is it just because the Bible says it? Yes, and because that excellent spirit continues to reveal things in the very hidden places (Himself) of the universe to me periodically and as He wills, and it took many months of revelations to finally put this writing together. And I write it as I am shown, instructed, and commanded. I was told to publish this with a loud voice proclaiming His word. When He was finally ready to publish it, He showed me the final piece of the puzzle and instructed me to put this writing together through a period of seven days with fasting. Then additional revelations and instructions were given to me to add to the content and publish it in exactly three months from the day He started writing this through me.

I believe that some ancient scientists got these revelations or at least some of it and some current scientists still see and will continue to see and experience the truth, yet they will tell you that they are geniuses because they want to take all the glory and discredit God, His existence, and excellency.

There are multiple graces and gifts from God for every individual, which are unique and meant for just them to host forever and ever. Just like the angels in Heaven, they all have very specific or unique features and capabilities. For example, there are angels that are warriors (Michael is the leader as we read in scriptures), and there are angels that administer healing, among many others. That is why God has many names, which represent the many dimensions of Himself. In other words, they individually host unique dimensions of God. Just as humans, you are very different or unique. When you know this, abortions, human dishonor, disrespect, jealousy, envy, etc., become dangerous for you to do or show. And never ever in your life will you envy or hate or would like to destroy a person. Why? During the times of Saul and David, David said, touch not the Lord's anointed, although Saul had been dethroned and was destined for destruction. David knew and understood the divine laws and principles – he knew what it meant to take a person's life, especially, one that has been specially anointed by the Lord.

1 Samuel 24:4-7

4 Then the men of David said to him, "This is the day of which the LORD said to you, 'Behold, I will deliver your enemy into your hand, that you may do to him as it seems good to you.'" And David arose and secretly cut off a corner of Saul's robe. 5 Now it happened afterward that David's heart troubled him because he had cut Saul's robe. 6 And he said to his men, "The LORD forbid that I should do this thing to my master, the LORD's anointed, to stretch out my hand against him, seeing

he *is* the anointed of the L<small>ORD</small>." **⁷** So David restrained his servants with *these* words, and did not allow them to rise against Saul. And Saul got up from the cave and went on *his* way.

1 Chronicles 16:22

²² *Saying,* "Do not touch My anointed ones,
And do My prophets no harm."

Psalm 105:15

¹⁵ *Saying,* "Do not touch My anointed ones,
And do My prophets no harm."

Jeremiah 1:5

⁵ "Before I formed you in the womb, I knew you;
Before you were born, I sanctified you;
I ordained you a prophet to the nations."

Reducing and Eliminating the Error in Doctrine

Theology can be very dangerous – I'm saying this humbly. For example, I don't believe that there is anything like a major or minor prophet in the Bible. At least, I haven't seen those words in the Bible yet. It is my understanding that the words major, and minor are used because of the length of their books. I know the division is not for quality versus quantity but it's very important to point out some of these little mistakes here and there that easily sooner or later become a doctrine or truth for rest of the Body of Christ to follow. We should be cognizant of these things so that the Word of God will be presented as it. No additions to it and no subtractions to it. Teach and preach it exactly as it is written. By the time you finish reading this book, you will truly see the danger and effects of false teachings or even when the truth is falsified or bent even slightly.

Quantity isn't always better than quality. You can't judge a book based on the length of writings or content nor can you judge a man of God based on how long he lived on Earth. A great example is our Lord Jesus Christ who lived only 33 years physically on Earth, yet became our Supreme Lord, Savior, King, Teacher, and Priest. Another great example is ranking the spiritual gifts; the five or the four-fold ministry as many would call it. One cannot do everything in the Body of Christ – giving the Church only an apostle means the Church will fail and vice versa with the rest of the gifts standing alone. That is like saying, the medical doctor is more important than the farmer. Very soon, you will die of hunger. Or if you really want to be something, to me, it's the one that Jesus started with, because everything else will follow from that. Eventually, that becomes the primary responsibility of the people of God. Jesus was first a good student who put time in studying very well and then became a teacher because He understood doctrine because He was the doctrine Himself. Study the word and pray so that you can understand it well as the spirit wills and leads. Before you can effectively demonstrate or walk in the fullness of your ministerial gift or gifts, you must be able to teach it too because only those who perfectly understand a particular subject can teach it very well. You first become a student and then a teacher. Then you can demonstrate what you teach or even better, the signs shall follow them that believe.

You can't be a teacher without a scope of work or a specialty in terms of a course or a subject. A teacher must have a particular subject or subjects to teach. You can be an apostle and teacher, a prophet and teacher, an evangelist and teacher, and a pastor and teacher. Or all those gifts and teacher. The pastor must be a teacher to be very effective – that's what validates a true pastor because it's shepherding.

John 21:15-17

15 So when they had eaten breakfast, Jesus said to Simon Peter, "Simon, *son* of Jonah, do you love Me more than these?"

He said to Him, "Yes, Lord; You know that I love You." He said to him, "Feed My lambs."

16 He said to him again a second time, "Simon, *son* of Jonah, do you love Me?" He said to Him, "Yes, Lord; You know that I love You." He said to him, "Tend My sheep."

17 He said to him the third time, "Simon, *son* of Jonah, do you love Me?" Peter was grieved because He said to him the third time, "Do you love Me?" And he said to Him, "Lord, You know all things; You know that I love You." Jesus said to him, "Feed My sheep.

If you are only a teacher, what exactly do you teach? A true teacher ensures that what he or she teaches is applied and bring about positive change or verifiable transformation. The students must become a reflection of the teacher. And if you are only a pastor, how do you ground or feed your flock with the word? Our God likes to build on four pillars, just like how the Earth sits on four pillars as mentioned in the Book of Revelation. So, the teacher could be any or all the other gifts to the Body of Christ. You can still possess a gift or gifts and decide not to teach, then James 3:1-2 will not apply to you.

James 3:1-2

3 My brethren, let not many of you become teachers, knowing that we shall receive a stricter judgment. 2 For we all stumble in many things. If anyone does not stumble in word, he *is* a perfect man, able also to bridle the whole body.

But even that, how then can you be an apostle or a prophet or an evangelist and not able to teach? Whatever your gifts are, you must be able to teach. The Bible alone is just a book. Your gifts in addition to knowing the Bible as a mature Christian means that you should be able to teach anytime, any day, and anywhere. You can't just be a mere teacher of the Bible because whether you know it or not, there will be another or other gifts attached to the teaching gift – it is usually accompanied by a prophetic or revelatory gift. That's how you get knowledge and understanding. The Word of God is your foundation, and that foundation should be automatically equal to a teacher. You must know the Word to at least be a teacher for your home.

In fact, it is a four-fold ministry. The teaching gift helps ground the Body of Christ generally in the Word of God and more specifically, in unique ministerial gifts. This ensures a good foundation through a sound doctrine and continuity in the Church in all areas. If you are a true Christian, then you must know your Bible enough to be able to teach it. I am stressing on this not only because of sound doctrine but also because the harvest is plentiful. The Lord needs teachers in these times, and He is handing over several mantles for the teaching office so that all those who will come to the Lord in this very short time will be taught sound doctrine. If you believe, first, let the same grace for prayer, and second, the same grace for teaching upon my life drop now into your spirit in the name of Jesus. Say a big Amen and receive!

Ephesians 4:11-13

[11] And he gave some, apostles; and some, prophets; and some, evangelists; and some, pastors and teachers;

[12] For the perfecting of the saints, for the work of the ministry, for the edifying of the Body of Christ:

[13] Till we all come in the unity of the faith, and of the knowledge of the Son of God, unto a perfect man, unto the measure of the stature of the fulness of Christ:

1 Corinthians 12:28-30

[28] And God has appointed these in the Church: first apostles, second prophets, third teachers, after that, miracles, then gifts of healings, helps, administrations, varieties of tongues. [29] *Are* all apostles? *Are* all prophets? *Are* all teachers? *Are* all workers of miracles? [30] Do all have gifts of healings? Do all speak with tongues? Do all interpret?

Mark 16:17

[17] And these signs will follow those who believe: In My name they will cast out demons; they will speak with new tongues;

Embedded in every human being is at least one or multiple of these gifts, whether you know it or aware of it or not. I say this because everybody must have a relationship with Christ, and He will give you the originals – you wouldn't be looking and assessing things through the intellectual mind even though there's a place for that. Intellect is still very much needed. Some of the ones we call minor prophets, had some of the richest revelations. From now onwards, stop considering anything in the word of God, major or minor. Take every word seriously. Open your hearts to study and receive everything. Even the Bible we see, isn't the full counsel of God. It is just to help us understand or have an idea of how He operates. There are still books missing from the Bible. If we don't find these books, then it means you will have to receive your own revelation or somebody else's revelation on whatever are not captured in the known 66 books. Don't ignore the book of Enoch, Jasher etc., as they became even more relevant to me after I received certain revelations. Never leave the secret place. Keep on pressing and pursuing God and He will become your friend and reveal His deep things to you.

I teach only what is the truth – not because I read it somewhere (although I still read and receive from the Bible and other people's giftings and works) but because I have also experienced them. I was wondering and told God that people may still want to know who He is in His true form, but I may not have anything to describe His physiques other than telling them to look at me or any other person and they will see God in them. He said, that is correct. He lives in everybody, and you can activate and contact Him in you when you surrender to Him. And when you want to clearly see the power in His joint energies (male and female), then you will have to look at a married couple because both, coming together as one, and having intercourse to birth offspring, is the creative dimension of God right here on Earth in physical form. They represent the duality of God in full form and force. This doesn't take away the singularity or sovereignty of God. He still is full in any individual who worships Him in spirit and in truth. You can see this from all the revelations explained in this writing.

And He said to me, when they keep asking you about my invisibility, ask them, why do you have trade secrets, intellectual properties, secret recipes, secret ingredients, or chemicals etc.? How many companies would want other companies to learn the details or secrets of what they produce or manufacture or invent? How many would make it visible in the open for the whole to see? Then it would lose its power or supremacy, right? Same with God. That's why He hides. It's not His intention but to protect His supremacy or fullness. If He reveals it all to you, then He wouldn't be God anymore. That's why He says that no man shall see me and live. That is why till today, even the people of God don't know His entirety. And that's also why scientists keep discovering new things – and most of the new discoveries either voids or updates the old or current ones. God hides so that we can seek Him and study Him. That is the assignment of man.

Exodus 33:20-22

20 But He said, "You cannot see My face; for no man shall see Me, and live." 21 And the LORD said, "Here is a place by Me, and you shall stand on the rock. 22 So it shall be, while My glory passes by, that I will put you in the cleft of the rock and will cover you with My hand while I pass by.

The literal meaning of that is, first He dwells and operates in and from unapproachable light – the highest dimension.

1 Timothy 6:16

16 who alone has immortality, dwelling in unapproachable light, whom no man has seen or can see, to whom be honor and everlasting power. Amen.
And He occupies there all by Himself. To see Him, do as the scripture below says.

Hebrews 12:14

[14] Pursue peace with all *people,* and holiness, without which no one will see the Lord:

To the ones who want to see God or evidence before they will believe, are you doing as the above scripture says – are you living in peace with everybody and are you holy? Also, are you worshipping God in spirit and in truth? I dare or challenge you to do these things and we shall see if you will see God or not. Again, just like science, you have an experiment, and you go through the experimentation process and then you use your results to draw conclusions. They did this a lot with the covid vaccines. Just try God for a month – do these things I am suggesting to you through the Word of God. Worst case for you is, what have you got to lose if you don't see God after one month? Sometimes, you waste your time on experiments which give you undesirable results anyway, and sometimes this is after a long period of time. What do you lose? You lose time – sometimes years. I challenge you to follow my instructions on how to start worshiping God and do it for only a month. If you need guidance, I will personally guide you.

If you just got saved, you will ask, how do I do that? Well, it's a lifetime journey and we all must continually work on it. That's why we have each other and the Church – the Body of Christ.

The journey into our highest self, is what Christianity and overall spirituality have all been about. Why do I say this? So first, there is God and there are dimensions in Him. And it is in God that you will find your true self. Most of you out there don't know who you are. It doesn't matter whether you have lived for 100 years. It is the sad truth. There is nothing else after God – He is everything.

As revealed to me through the Venn diagram; Vesica Pisces, from fearing, honoring, and worshiping – serving through the Holy Spirit, Jesus Christ to God, we start remembering or discovering who we truly are from before the foundations of the Earth. You already existed because God knew you.

Jeremiah 1:5

[5] "Before I formed you in the womb, I knew you;
Before you were born, I sanctified you;
I ordained you a prophet to the nations."

You only gained consciousness after you were born. Our spiritual journey is just like our physical journey. When you were a child, you only started gaining consciousness at a certain age. You must grow spiritually through gaining this consciousness through the Word of God, praying, fasting, righteous living, holiness etc. I still give a lot of credit to other religions for at least believing that there is a God. It's better than the atheists. I don't magnify them or their gods or ask anybody to join them in their faith. I only say well done to them and congratulations on that belief. It is a great starting point. At least, they are smart enough to know that there is God and life is not all about physics. The only problem is that, because of lack of solid Christian or biblical foundations, unclarity, lack of continuity, intentional lies, or deception etc., from the kingdom of darkness, you have been trained, brainwashed, and made to believe that your God is the true God. I know how hard it is for you to be convinced now of the true God when you have lived your entire lives serving what you have been made to believe. That unintentional and sincere act is fine because you did not know. And God likes the sincerity of your heart. Just like Paul said in Acts 17:23; he referred to the "AN UNKNOWN GOD" of the people of Athens that they were ignorant of and that he made known to them.

Acts 17:23

23 For as I walked around and looked carefully at your objects of worship, I even found an altar with this inscription: TO AN UNKNOWN GOD. So, you are ignorant of the very thing you worship—and this is what I am going to proclaim to you.

One of the biggest errors had been a gap in knowledge. Our fathers of old like Abraham built altars from objects like stones to the Lord wherever he went as a memorial and portal. The people who followed and didn't quite understand the technology or significance of the altars, started worshipping stones and other things as their gods; some, out of pure sincerity and some, out of pure rebellion or ignorance.

Genesis 12:6-8

6 Abram traveled through the land as far as the site of the great tree of Moreh at Shechem. At that time the Canaanites were in the land. 7 The LORD appeared to Abram and said, "To your offspring I will give this land." So, he built an altar there to the LORD, who had appeared to him.

8 From there he went on toward the hills east of Bethel and pitched his tent, with Bethel on the west and Ai on the east. There he built an altar to the LORD and called on the name of the LORD.

The lack of understanding in this spiritual intelligence or technology is why we have several people worshipping idols. So, respectfully, humbly, and with love, I call you ignorant until this point because you are now introduced to the truth and the true God of the universe, who dwells in unapproachable light. Since there are so many dimensions or planes in the spirit, there is not a single doubt that we are not the only beings that God created. You need to have access to those dimensions or planes to be able to see or experience these beings or those realms. The problem or mistake with you, has been interacting with masquerading or deceptive spirit beings who trick you into believing that they are the true God of the Heavens and the Earth, but they are not. Also, be aware that everything in creation is alive and can listen to you and your commands. It depends on how much light you have (Joshua 10:2 – Joshua commanded the Sun). How much light meaning, how much of the truth you know and understand.

Joshua 10:12-13

The Sun Stands Still

¹² Then Joshua spoke to the LORD in the day when the LORD delivered up the Amorites before the children of Israel, and he said in the sight of Israel:

"Sun, stand still over Gibeon;
And Moon, in the Valley of Aijalon."
¹³ So the Sun stood still,
And the Moon stopped,
Till the people had revenge
Upon their enemies.

Is this not written in the Book of Jasher? So, the Sun stood still in the midst of heaven, and did not hasten to go *down* for about a whole day.

Even researchers have been able to prove that the Bible contains the only record of a solar eclipse prior to 1000 BCE. The word of God is not a story or some historical book. It is truly His word, and it is in Him you will find light and know who you truly are and why you were sent here on Earth. You are here on Earth to carry out a very specific assignment for God – it's called a divine assignment or purpose. Do you know your assignment or purpose here on Earth?

When you consistently in spirit and in truth worship any object that is not God, that object will soon be filled or occupied by an evil spirit. It shall surely manifest or not manifest but that still wouldn't make it the true God of the Heavens and the Earth. Remember, this is the position that Lucifer wanted and was casted out of Heaven and is now Satan. He still welcomes worship, but I won't suggest to you to you follow him because you will be destroyed together with him. So, if you worship anything else rather than the God I talk about and introduce in this writing or if you don't worship anything at all, then you need to seek this God of the Heavens and the Earth that I talk about because it is in Him alone you will find life.

To the atheist, it's only a fool who says in his heart, there's no God.

Psalm 14:1

14 The fool has said in his heart,
"*There is* no God."
They are corrupt,
They have done abominable works,
There is none who does good.
Look at everything around you. Simply sit for a minute and think about you and your existence – think about your body (the human anatomy). You don't have to be a scientist to know that you are a complex or let me say, sophisticated, or even better, a special divine being. You were

specially designed and made. Look at how the body functions – your consciousness, your brain, your eyes, your heart etc., and how they all work in harmony to keep you alive. Think about the air you breathe and think about how the coronavirus made or makes you feel and live. You go around wearing masks because you are afraid. That's just coronavirus but there's a Master – One who dwells amid the cherubim – and at His word, all the oxygen in the entire universe, can stop. Just like that. These scriptures below are for you, unbelievers, atheists, Buddhist, Muslims, all those who don't believe in Jesus Christ or think that He is some reincarnated angel Michael etc., to think well and repent.

Romans 1:20

[20] For since the creation of the world His invisible *attributes* are clearly seen, being understood by the things that are made, *even* His eternal power and Godhead, so that they are without excuse,

I suggest to you and urge you to repent now! For the kingdom of God is at hand.

Matthew 3:2

[2] and saying, "Repent, for the kingdom of Heaven is at hand!"

Matthew 4:17

[17] From that time Jesus began to preach and to say, "Repent, for the kingdom of Heaven is at hand."

Psalm 51

A Prayer of Repentance

To the Chief Musician. A Psalm of David when Nathan the prophet went to him, after he had gone in to Bathsheba.

51 Have mercy upon me, O God,
According to Your lovingkindness;
According to the multitude of Your tender mercies,
Blot out my transgressions.
[2] Wash me thoroughly from my iniquity,
And cleanse me from my sin.
[3] For I acknowledge my transgressions,
And my sin *is* always before me.
[4] Against You, You only, have I sinned,
And done *this* evil in Your sight—

That You may be found just when You speak,
And blameless when You judge.
⁵ Behold, I was brought forth in iniquity,
And in sin my mother conceived me.
⁶ Behold, You desire truth in the inward parts,
And in the hidden *part* You will make me to know wisdom.
⁷ Purge me with hyssop, and I shall be clean;
Wash me, and I shall be whiter than snow.
⁸ Make me hear joy and gladness,
That the bones You have broken may rejoice.
⁹ Hide Your face from my sins,
And blot out all my iniquities.
¹⁰ Create in me a clean heart, O God,
And renew a steadfast spirit within me.
¹¹ Do not cast me away from Your presence,
And do not take Your Holy Spirit from me.
¹² Restore to me the joy of Your salvation,
And uphold me *by Your* generous Spirit.
¹³ *Then* I will teach transgressors Your ways,
And sinners shall be converted to You.
¹⁴ Deliver me from the guilt of bloodshed, O God,
The God of my salvation,
And my tongue shall sing aloud of Your righteousness.
¹⁵ O Lord, open my lips,
And my mouth shall show forth Your praise.
¹⁶ For You do not desire sacrifice, or else I would give *it;*
You do not delight in burnt offering.
¹⁷ The sacrifices of God *are* a broken spirit,
A broken and a contrite heart—
These, O God, You will not despise.
¹⁸ Do good in Your good pleasure to Zion;
Build the walls of Jerusalem.
¹⁹ Then You shall be pleased with the sacrifices of righteousness,
With burnt offering and whole burnt offering;
Then they shall offer bulls on Your altar.

After you say Amen, read the following scriptures and then **confess with your mouth the Lord Jesus and believe in your heart that God has raised Him from the dead, then you will be saved**.

Romans 10:5-13

⁵ For Moses writes about the righteousness which is of the law, "The man who does those things shall live by them." ⁶ But the righteousness of faith speaks in this way, "Do not say in your heart, 'Who will ascend into heaven?'" (that is, to bring Christ down *from above*) ⁷ or "'Who will

descend into the abyss?'" (that is, to bring Christ up from the dead). **8** But what does it say? "The word is near you, in your mouth and in your heart" (that is, the word of faith which we preach): **9 that if you confess with your mouth the Lord Jesus and believe in your heart that God has raised Him from the dead, you will be saved**. **10** For with the heart one believes unto righteousness, and with the mouth confession is made unto salvation. **11** For the Scripture says, "Whoever believes on Him will not be put to shame." **12** For there is no distinction between Jew and Greek, for the same Lord over all is rich to all who call upon Him. **13** For "whoever calls on the name of the LORD shall be saved."

Looking for a Church

Look for a true Church and get born again so that you will be baptized of water and of the spirit, and you will be able to enter the kingdom of God.

John 3:1-8

The New Birth

3 There was a man of the Pharisees named Nicodemus, a ruler of the Jews. **2** This man came to Jesus by night and said to Him, "Rabbi, we know that You are a teacher come from God; for no one can do these signs that You do unless God is with him."

3 Jesus answered and said to him, "Most assuredly, I say to you, unless one is born again, he cannot see the kingdom of God."

4 Nicodemus said to Him, "How can a man be born when he is old? Can he enter a second time into his mother's womb and be born?"

5 Jesus answered, "Most assuredly, I say to you, unless one is born of water and the Spirit, he cannot enter the kingdom of God. **6** That which is born of the flesh is flesh, and that which is born of the Spirit is spirit. **7** Do not marvel that I said to you, 'You must be born again.' **8** The wind blows where it wishes, and you hear the sound of it, but cannot tell where it comes from and where it goes. So is everyone who is born of the Spirit."

So, God is Spirit, and they that worship Him must do so in spirit and in truth. So, to the scientists, say to yourselves, because I do not see the wind, it does not exist so I will block my nostrils because I don't need what is not visible or can't be seen. Yes, block your nostrils for only five minutes straight because you don't need the breath of God. That's right, it's His breath.

John 4:24

24 God *is* Spirit, and those who worship Him must worship in spirit and truth."

Genesis 2:7

[7] And the LORD God formed man *of* the dust of the ground and breathed into his nostrils the breath of life; and man became a living being.

When we serve Him in spirit and in truth, He reveals His dimensions in us to us in pieces like pieces of puzzle. And then you gain oneness or synchronicity with him through faith in Jesus. As you keep worshipping Him in spirit and in truth, then you become more like Him because your journey in Him goes further so your consciousness or oneness or synchronicity becomes heightened to the highest levels and that is the only time you will start living in multiple dimensions or planes with Him in the universe. That is how you start seeing in the spirit because you start seeing with the "All seeing eyes" of God. You will also hear, perceive etc., in the spirit. Nothing becomes hidden to you anymore. That is also when spirit beings see you and they can identify you because they know you because you live in multiple realms or dimensions or planes at the same time.

In physical terms, not only do you have dual citizenship, but at the same time you live in the USA for example, you are also living in Ghana. So, citizens of both countries can identify you when they meet you because they see you there. You achieve this by grace through a process. Just like any scientific experiment, it is a process and there is a price to pay – sacrifice and hard work because you must submit or surrender to the Spirit of God to use you.

2 Corinthians 3:18

[18] But we all, with unveiled face, beholding as in a mirror the glory of the Lord, are being transformed into the same image from glory to glory, just as by the Spirit of the Lord.

Romans 12:2

[2] And do not be conformed to this world, but be transformed by the renewing of your mind, that you may prove what *is* that good and acceptable and perfect will of God.

Science has a limit and without the submission to God and help or authority from God, science cannot advance past a certain level. Science has been struggling a lot with quantum mechanics. They are trying to do what is very spiritual in the physical. We keep striving to make things better and faster. That is why we now have and prefer to travel long distances with airplanes or cars instead of horses or walking. And every single day we strive to beat our current technology record by optimizing it, mostly making it faster and faster or smarter and smarter. This means that mankind at some point will love instant time travel. You wouldn't like to sit on an airplane for hours. Rather, you would like to get to or wish you get to another location almost instantaneously. Well, that is already happening, except that it is available to only a few people who know the secrets and dwell in multiple realms or dimensions or planes. They know what to do. Do you know what to do? This means that there is a level that you get to in this life that you must be assisted by a spirit who already resides in that realm or dimension or plane to become a legitimate citizen in that place.

Think for example, somebody who requires a USA citizenship, primarily if done legitimately, the easiest or fastest or most guaranteed way to do it, is to get married to someone from the USA. See, we already apply spiritual universal laws and principles in our daily lives everyday here on Earth. We just don't know it or realize it. The same way God, even being Almighty, required a body to come and live here on Earth as Jesus. He respects His own laws and principles. The only law that I know of that He went about in His own different way was to have the Holy Spirit come upon the Virgin Mary to conceive Jesus. But even so, He still came through the natural birth process afterwards. He did this because of the agenda; the divine plan to save mankind after the fall and it required the holiest blood sacrifice of Jesus (the Lamb). He needed the holiest blood on the mercy seat and that was the way He did it. Nobody can question that because He is God. He did the same to birth the universe and everything that's in it – He did it with the Godhead through His sovereignty. So, if a spirit doesn't assist you, be guaranteed that there is a level that you will never get to in this life. No matter how rich or wise you think you are. Earthly riches are not needed past the 3D. All is vanity.

Ecclesiastes 1

The Vanity of Life

1 The words of the Preacher, the son of David, king in Jerusalem.

2 "Vanity of vanities," says the Preacher;
"Vanity of vanities, all *is* vanity."
3 What profit has a man from all his labor
In which he toils under the Sun?
4 *One* generation passes away, and *another* generation comes;
But the Earth abides forever.
5 The Sun also rises, and the Sun goes down,
And hastens to the place where it arose.
6 The wind goes toward the south,
And turns around to the north;
The wind whirls about continually,
And comes again on its circuit.
7 All the rivers run into the sea,
Yet the sea *is* not full;
To the place from which the rivers come,
There they return again.
8 All things *are* full of labor;
Man cannot express *it*.
The eye is not satisfied with seeing,
Nor the ear filled with hearing.
9 That which has been *is* what will be,
That which *is* done is what will be done,
And *there is* nothing new under the Sun.

10 Is there anything of which it may be said,
"See, this *is* new"?
It has already been in ancient times before us.
11 *There is* no remembrance of former *things,*
Nor will there be any remembrance of *things* that are to come
By *those* who will come after.

The Grief of Wisdom

12 I, the Preacher, was king over Israel in Jerusalem. **13** And I set my heart to seek and search out by wisdom concerning all that is done under Heaven; this burdensome task God has given to the sons of man, by which they may be exercised. **14** I have seen all the works that are done under the Sun; and indeed, all *is* vanity and grasping for the wind.

15 *What is* crooked cannot be made straight,
And what is lacking cannot be numbered.

16 I communed with my heart, saying, "Look, I have attained greatness, and have gained more wisdom than all who were before me in Jerusalem. My heart has understood great wisdom and knowledge." **17** And I set my heart to know wisdom and to know madness and folly. I perceived that this also is grasping for the wind.

18 For in much wisdom *is* much grief,
And he who increases knowledge increases sorrow.

At that point, it wouldn't matter if or whether you are a good or bad person, young or old, smart, or dumb – that is why good people can still be murdered, inflicted, afflicted etc. God's idea is that, as we grow physically, we must be growing spiritually at the same time. This means that both must be occurring in parallel or simultaneously or concurrently. The same way you eat multiple times in a day, that same way you must pray and feed your spirit with the word of God. Commune and fellowship with the Father in Heaven. Else you could be 70 years old on Earth but in the spirit, you are barely two years old or even six months old. This is not to insult you. I speak the truth. We have been wired or engineered or programmed this way so that we can interact with God – He already dwells in you. We have a void in our lives without the true God. God is within you by default but dormant until you activate Him. Therefore, you will never find true joy and a life full of fulfilment no matter how much money or material things you have until you find God. He is that void in you. You have an Internet hub around you somewhere, but you are very frustrated when you can't connect to the internet. Why? Because you expect the device to work the way you want if it is connected to the internet, to check your emails at least, maybe. But here you are, expecting yourself to function fully as created by God while you are not connected to Him. Although you think you are normal, trust me, deep down within you, you know it – that something is still missing. I introduce to you, that something is God Almighty.

Luke 17:20-21

The Coming of the Kingdom

[20] Now when He was asked by the Pharisees when the kingdom of God would come, He answered them and said, "The kingdom of God does not come with observation; [21] nor will they say, 'See here!' or 'See there!' For indeed, the kingdom of God is within you.

You have been created with pre-written code; take for example, the Windows Operating System or Android, and how it's periodically updated by Microsoft or Google. Or think about any active software product on the market that's being well maintained. The updates are pre-written and sitting somewhere in TFS or SVN or GitHub or whatever version control system you know of or use. The more you align with His divine purpose for your life through prayers and authentic Christian living, the more the software updates or new releases and fixes are pushed into your operating system (your spirit). As you keep working hard towards discovering yourself, you tap into the version control where your pre-written code or updates or fixes reside at, and they are released into your destiny accordingly per predestined timeline.

If you decide not to pray and not live as a true Christian, then you become like a software that has been abandoned and not maintained anymore by any engineer(s). This software becomes highly vulnerable and susceptible to attacks. It could easily be corrupted or used to achieve malicious agendas. This is how the devil takes over you when you don't pray and live properly because you don't host God. It is not enough to simply be a nice person or mind your business.

We see God in our everyday lives because He designed it to be that way and you can relate to Him through a deep variety of ways or professions.

When you follow the life of the world, it's like installing malware, all kinds of it, including ransomware. You'll corrupt your entire being. You become that vulnerable host that is exposed to all kinds of risks and very soon you'll be used for malicious purposes, or you may not even last on the internet. God is the Master engineer or architect. You can't update a technology or electronic or any hardware device by altering its physical looks. You must change the code or programming. This is how the Word of God changes us – from within. It always works from inside out. We are the hardware, or the host and God is supposed to be the Operating System through His Holy Spirit.

Take a seed for example, among many things, God has hidden a special code inside it. It is already programmed. It goes through a process before it finally bears fruits someday. You don't necessarily have to do anything to it – all you must do is to put it in the right environment with the right conditions. Human beings, right from being thought of by God before your parents even conceived you, already had all the codes put in them (we call it DNA), so you don't need to really do anything after a sperm fertilizes an egg, to make the baby develop. There are pre-written codes that will handle the growth process. You have become that seed that refuses to germinate or bear fruit. Be fruitful. Your spirit is where God puts the spiritual pre-written code for your divine assignment here on Earth.

God is inside of you, but He is dormant until you search for Him through continuous fellowship and be conscious of Him. Therefore, God was, is, and is to come. He's truly the "I am" who thought about things exactly how He wanted them to be and through His spoken words, created them and from that point, everything they would ever need for their lives were put inside of them, including human beings. You have this same creative ability because you know that you imagine everything you want before you go on to achieve them. God is inside of you.

Judges 6:12

¹² And the Angel of the LORD appeared to him, and said to him, "The LORD *is* with you, you mighty man of valor!"

So, if God calls you now, "mighty man of valor", He's right. If you and I see a mango seed, we can decide to look at the seed's current state and call it a mango seed, or we can act like the gods we are and call it a fruitful mango tree. It will be prophetic but very accurate because it's indeed, a mango tree with fruits, if we want to look at its potential or exousia with our spiritual eyes. This is how your life is designed. Looking at your limitations right now is deceptive because just like the seed, you need to be at the right place, at the right time, with the right conditions (water, Sunlight etc.), and most importantly, the right information or knowledge and the right understanding to be able to manifest into a full-grown tree to bear fruits. In other words, you are technically not alive or living until God finds you. You are the lost one. You only start living the moment God starts guiding your life and steps. You can disbelieve me now if you want but when your soul leaves your body permanently someday (death), you will believe me, but it would be too late for you.

When a tree grows, it doesn't bear only one fruit; it bears multiple fruits because that's the kind of abundance that God has placed in your life. You get them if you are diligent. It's not enough to just throw the seed anywhere as a farmer. That will be foolishness, negligence, and irresponsibility. By chance it may hit the right conditions and germinate and grow to bear fruits. It wouldn't mean you were diligent or had knowledge and understanding. You just hit it by chance. A lot of people live this way. That's not sustainable because you may not be able to reproduce it in the future. You want predictable good results according to patterns. This is what we call success for many people so when they face certain challenges, they fall forever and never rise again because they can't reproduce. But those who know God and are diligent will always reproduce.

God once gave me a revelation. He said to me, I am like gold inside of you but until you diligently seek me, I am dormant inside of you (I immediately saw a round black ball). As you fellowship with me to know me more, it's like you're cleaning the black coating from around this gold (I started seeing light shining from the inside of the black ball towards the outside), and finally it was all shiny to the point that eyes could not watch.

God has hidden Himself inside of you. It will take grace and hard work to mine and refine that precious gold – although He's more than gold. He showed me gold to help me understand. I am doing the same with you. Therefore, you don't just walk and see gold or any precious stone lying on the ground. All these minerals are hidden. You dig for them. God is like that – you must dig for Him. He is not just lying out there somewhere as a worthless being.

How do you find Him? It all starts by believing without seeing physical manifestations yet and developing a disciplined prayer life. You must be intentional and consistent with your prayer life. It is only from the place of prayer that you will begin to transform. God is in everything, He's everywhere.

Therefore, there is nothing like death. What we call and see as death is only a separation of the soul from the body vessel. When your soul separates from your body permanently; death, then you move on into another realm or dimension or plane. Earth is only temporal – a transition point. Life is an eternal journey and what you do here on Earth truly counts to how the rest of eternity will be for you. It doesn't matter if you are a billionaire on Earth. Your relationship with God while you are here is what counts the most.

I have read in articles how several billionaires of our time are investing in startup companies trying to combat aging. They are wasting their time. This is a reality check to them that they have attained all the material riches of the Earth, but they will still surely die. Before that happens, they will know that truly, all is vanity, and it wouldn't matter what kind of empire you built with your time and money here on Earth. True riches are in Heaven. Read some of the writings of King Solomon towards the end of his life. Also, look through some historical books on the mighty empires that were once built on the Earth, and you will understand that a day is coming soon that nobody will even remember or know your names and what you have built or achieved now will all be in nonexistence. I know that they can't imagine having all the money but that doesn't give them immortality. We are already immortals – they just need wisdom. What they need to invest in is the destiny of their souls. They should start seeking ways to spend eternity at a better location. Again, there are only two locations – Heaven or Hell. That can only be achieved through becoming born again if you already aren't and reading and practicing the Word of God with diligence and trembling.

In the article, I read – "Amazon founder and former CEO Jeff Bezos is the latest billionaire to invest in a startup trying to combat aging. That's according to MIT Tech Review, which reports that a new company called Altos Labs has launched with plans to further research into an anti-aging technology called reprogramming. In essence, reprograming works by adding proteins to a cell, which then instruct the cell to revert to a state where it can generate new, young cells that form the basis of the human body.

Other wealthy individuals including Larry Page, Peter Thiel, and Larry Ellison have also invested in anti-aging research. Bezos and Thiel last year invested in Unity Technologies, which aims to make anti-aging therapies. Google co-founder, Page, meanwhile, has invested heavily in a company called Calico.

The fascination with anti-aging is an interesting one, perhaps because death is one of the few things that money hasn't been able to overcome — at least, not yet."

They are all wasting time and money. Money and science can never give man immortality. It is not up to men to give immortality to other men through mere scientific research. God gives immortality. Like I said earlier, instead of spending these huge amounts of money on very personal or selfish interests, they should be feeding the poor and the less fortunate ones. Most importantly, they should make their salvation sure and advance the Kingdom of God – that's where the immortality that they are seeking for rests. It is very sad but no matter what they will do, they cannot escape death. They should all come to Jesus and seek God through Him for His hidden wisdom, and they will understand what I'm saying. While some are so afraid to leave the Earth, others like myself with the revelations and understanding that I have by the grace of God, can't wait to finish my assignment here on Earth for God so that I can checkout from this messy and dark place to go be with the Lord.

Luke 16:19-31

The Rich Man and Lazarus

19 "There was a certain rich man who was clothed in purple and fine linen and fared sumptuously every day. 20 But there was a certain beggar named Lazarus, full of sores, who was laid at his gate, 21 desiring to be fed with the crumbs which fell from the rich man's table. Moreover, the dogs came and licked his sores. 22 So it was that the beggar died and was carried by the angels to Abraham's bosom. The rich man also died and was buried. 23 And being in torments in Hades, he lifted up his eyes and saw Abraham afar off, and Lazarus in his bosom.

24 "Then he cried and said, 'Father Abraham, have mercy on me, and send Lazarus that he may dip the tip of his finger in water and cool my tongue; for I am tormented in this flame.' 25 But Abraham said, 'Son, remember that in your lifetime you received your good things, and likewise Lazarus evil things; but now he is comforted, and you are tormented. 26 And besides all this, between us and you there is a great gulf fixed, so that those who want to pass from here to you cannot, nor can those from there pass to us.'

27 "Then he said, 'I beg you therefore, father, that you would send him to my father's house, 28 for I have five brothers, that he may testify to them, lest they also come to this place of torment.' 29 Abraham said to him, 'They have Moses and the prophets; let them hear them.' 30 And he said, 'No, father Abraham; but if one goes to them from the dead, they will repent.' 31 But he said to him, 'If they do not hear Moses and the prophets, neither will they be persuaded though one rise from the dead.'"

Once you lose full consciousness here on Earth, you gain full consciousness on the other side. God designed it like this for a reason so that you can have your dual nature to be a bridge between the physical (natural or matter) and the spiritual (supernatural or antimatter). There is nothing really like death; it is simply a transition. You can choose to believe it or leave it.

The Right Church to Attend

There have been several teachings of false doctrines. Some of these are intentional and some are not. Some are purely due to a lack or loss of the basic standards or foundation of true Christianity as built by Jesus Christ. There have also been so many inconsistencies in the Body of Christ. This makes Christianity to always contradict itself to seem like a joke.

There is already the antichrist in the world and within the Church and several other societies or organizations as they call it. To me so far, the Jehovah Witnesses or Watchtower organization and any other societies that branched out of it or the same root are the biggest deception of all time. They are posing as the angel of light, but they are not. They are antichrist. You can study their history. They are made full of false teachings which are sending people to hell.

Using the original Bible as basis for their editing – using mere intellect and comparing their so-called falsely translated version of the Bible with the true Bible, you'll see that they don't have any foundation in their story. They're basically working so hard to make our Bible lose its integrity. This is unacceptable and judgement is upon them.

The biggest terrorist or devil isn't the one from a different home or different country, but the one who is disguised in your own home or country as one of you. We call this in the security world, insider threat. It is the most dangerous threat ever. They will destroy or kill you slowly before you even know it.

What Makes a Genuine or True Church of God?

These basic things should be a good foundation and starter to know that a Church is true or help you identify a true Christian. But I still recommend and suggest to you that you personally read the scriptures and read all of it to sharpen your discernment. A true Church or true Christians believe in:

1. The Holy Trinity; God the Father, the Son, and the Holy Spirit. The first proof for this can be found in the first chapter of Genesis – Genesis 1:26.
2. Believe in the Son been conceived by the Virgin Mary through the power of the Holy Spirit or Holy Ghost. The Son been baptized by John and the Holy Spirit descended on Him in the similitude of a dove and the Father said from Heaven: "This is my beloved son etc." – Matthew 3:17.
3. The Son died on the cross (on a Friday, resurrected on a Sunday; 3rd day, and ascended to Heaven) to save us from our sins and in Him we have salvation and He's our Lord and personal Savior. He's sitting at the right hand of the Father in heaven right now, interceding for us while we await His return – Mark 16:19.

Through the Son, we have access to the Father through the Holy Spirit and have eternal life because He is our High Priest. These three areas should be a good starting point.

John 3:16

[16] For God so loved the world that He gave His only begotten Son, that whoever believes in Him should not perish but have everlasting life.

If you are a true Church or Christian, you must believe in the Holy Trinity. You must believe in the crucifixion of Christ. You must believe in the resurrection because we are crucified with Him by faith. This is our deepest mystery that sets us free and grants us His authority.

Galatians 2:20

[20] I have been crucified with Christ; it is no longer I who live, but Christ lives in me; and the *life* which I now live in the flesh I live by faith in the Son of God, who loved me and gave Himself for me.

You must be baptized of water in the Holy Trinity, in the Name of the Father, and of the Son, and the Holy Spirit. It is only when you confess Him as your Lord and Savior aloud then you'll be saved. That instruction has already been given to you. Anybody who doesn't believe in the above things is not a true Christian. And any Church that doesn't teach this or believe in this is not a Church of God or Christ. If they claim to be a Christian or Church of Christ, then they are only masquerading – wolves in sheep clothing.

Again, the biggest and most destructive one that I currently know of is the Watchtower or Jehovah Witnesses like I said earlier. That organization will be destroyed very soon. Everything that presents false teachings is going down. Stay away from them. You who has been deceived and have been part of that organization, get out, run away very fast for your lives and salvation is never too late for you. Come to Jesus Christ now, the son of God. He still loves you and has His hands widely opened to receive and embrace you.

All they are trying to do is to lie to you and get you away from the true Priest, Savior, and King, JESUS CHRIST. He is the only one (one with God the Father and the Holy Spirit) we must worship and teach and preach.

Galatians 1:8

[8] But even if we, or an angel from Heaven, preach any other gospel to you than what we have preached to you, let him be accursed.

Paul says, stick to the basics. Our King is Jesus Christ. I like the basics because it keeps you in check. Just like we have learned the basics or fundamentals of our universe and its existence and how not remembering or knowing the basics can be very dangerous. There's a saying that, "if you know where you come from and remember it, you will hardly make mistakes." Always be conscious of that. Therefore, we have our consciousness from God and in God, to help us remember who we truly are by the help of the Holy Spirit. Make a public declaration that Jesus Christ is Lord and that He is your Savior and King, and you will be saved.

Romans 10:8-13

[8] But what does it say? "The word is near you, in your mouth and in your heart" (that is, the word of faith which we preach): [9] that if you confess with your mouth the Lord Jesus and believe in your heart that God has raised Him from the dead, you will be saved. [10] For with the heart one believes unto righteousness, and with the mouth confession is made unto salvation. [11] For the Scripture says, "Whoever believes on Him will not be put to shame." [12] For there is no distinction between Jew and Greek, for the same Lord over all is rich to all who call upon Him. [13] For "whoever calls on the name of the LORD shall be saved."

False doctrine is very destructive. It is what we call propaganda in politics or governments. We call it information warfare in the military. I hate lies and false doctrine with passion. The fundamentals or foundations are very important and that's why lots of families, individuals, villages, towns, cities, and countries are suffering so much. That is why those who don't believe in God think that God is not a benevolent God. We have been buried in so many lies. Brainwashing works and it's very negatively impactful. If you build a house without a strong foundation, sooner or later, it will collapse. False doctrine is worse than witchcraft and or demons, or curses. I don't know why the world well-known, highly respected, and influential men of God are not addressing this matter. If they are, then I am not hearing it. I don't think it's enough to just call out false doctrine when we have the authority to tear it all down in the name of Jesus by the power of the Holy Spirit. Everybody should wake up because there is a lot of work to do to bring the world back on course.

To conclude, that's why the scriptures say, test all spirits.

1 John 4:4-6

[4] You are of God, little children, and have overcome them, because He who is in you is greater than he who is in the world. [5] They are of the world. Therefore, they speak as of the world, and the world hears them. [6] We are of God. He who knows God hears us; he who is not of God does not hear us. By this we know the spirit of truth and the spirit of error.

After we destroy these agents of deception or antichrists, a more dangerous set will be coming; in the capacity of the miraculous etc., because we know all their old strategies now and most importantly, it has been written. This will be the next new strategy, false prophets and the miraculous. They are already around but more will try to emerge. Watch out for these signs.

Finally, Christianity and religion may have been used interchangeably throughout this writing but let me be clear – Christianity is not a religion. It's the life of God coming into a man. It is God imparting His life into human flesh.

I'm sure that you have learned about God and His creation. I'm sure that you have also learned practically the explanation and demonstration of the true meaning of quantum mechanics and gravity across the entire universe, including your body. I believe that from getting saved and practicing Christianity, you will see and experience all that have been said here and you will know that indeed, God is Mighty. You shall have encounters.

Colossians 2

Not Philosophy but Christ

2 For I want you to know what a great conflict I have for you and those in Laodicea, and *for* as many as have not seen my face in the flesh, **2** that their hearts may be encouraged, being knit together in love, and *attaining* to all riches of the full assurance of understanding, to the knowledge of the mystery of God, both of the Father and of Christ, **3** in whom are hidden all the treasures of wisdom and knowledge.

4 Now this I say lest anyone should deceive you with persuasive words. **5** For though I am absent in the flesh, yet I am with you in spirit, rejoicing to see your *good* order and the steadfastness of your faith in Christ.

6 As you therefore have received Christ Jesus the Lord, so walk in Him, **7** rooted and built up in Him and established in the faith, as you have been taught, abounding in it with thanksgiving.

8 Beware lest anyone cheat you through philosophy and empty deceit, according to the tradition of men, according to the basic principles of the world, and not according to Christ. **9** For in Him dwells all the fullness of the Godhead bodily; **10** and you are complete in Him, who is the head of all principality and power.

Not Legalism but Christ

11 In Him you were also circumcised with the circumcision made without hands, by putting off the body of the sins of the flesh, by the circumcision of Christ, **12** buried with Him in baptism, in which you also were raised with *Him* through faith in the working of God, who raised Him from the dead. **13** And you, being dead in your trespasses and the uncircumcision of your flesh, He has made alive together with Him, having forgiven you all trespasses, **14** having wiped out the handwriting of requirements that was against us, which was contrary to us. And He has taken it out of the way, having nailed it to the cross. **15** Having disarmed principalities and powers, He made a public spectacle of them, triumphing over them in it.

16 So let no one judge you in food or in drink, or regarding a festival or a new moon or sabbaths, **17** which are a shadow of things to come, but the substance is of Christ. **18** Let no one cheat you of your reward, taking delight in *false* humility and worship of angels, intruding into those things which he has not seen, vainly puffed up by his fleshly mind, **19** and not holding fast to the Head, from whom all the body, nourished and knit together by joints and ligaments, grows with the increase *that is* from God.

20 Therefore, if you died with Christ from the basic principles of the world, why, as *though* living in the world, do you subject yourselves to regulations— **21** "Do not touch, do not taste, do not handle," **22** which all concern things which perish with the using—according to the commandments and doctrines of men? **23** These things indeed have an appearance of wisdom in self-imposed religion, *false* humility, and neglect of the body, *but are* of no value against the indulgence of the flesh.

After Your Salvation

Following the truth's you know so far, this section and the confirming scriptures are to help ground you as a true Christian who will grow and mature in the Word and things of God. It will help you build stature to be able to experientially manifest the Power of the Holy Spirit through the Word of God in the Name of Jesus. After the fall of man, God had to use another strategy to save man from his fallen nature, so God became man and was crucified as Jesus Christ.

John 1:1-5

1 In the beginning was the Word, and the Word was with God, and the Word was God. **2** He was in the beginning with God. **3** All things were made through Him, and without Him nothing was made that was made. **4** In Him was life, and the life was the light of men. **5** And the light shines in the darkness, and the darkness did not comprehend it.

John 1:14

14 And the Word became flesh and dwelt among us, and we beheld His glory, the glory as of the only begotten of the Father, full of grace and truth.

John 3:16

16 For God so loved the world that He gave His only begotten **Son**, that whoever believes in Him should not perish but have everlasting life.

I presume that you are already saved by now but if you are not and happen to start reading from this section, then wherever you are, say this short prayer. You can also reaffirm your commitment to God if you are already saved. Always continue to work to make your salvation sure.

Lord Jesus, I confess that I have sinned against you in thought, word, and deed. I am truly sorry and humbly repent. In your mercy forgive what I have been and help me amend what I am. I accept in my heart and declare with my mouth that you are my Lord, you are my Savior, you are my King, and you are my High Priest. The power of sin and death are broken over my life. Today, I receive eternal life into my spirit. I shall serve you with all my heart, in spirit and in truth, all the days of my life here on Earth and through eternity, forever and ever. Amen.

Now, you are saved and a child of God. Welcome to the Kingdom of God. It is time to guide you with finding your calling and your destiny.

A Quick Review of Time

Earth is governed and ruled by time because Earth was birthed by the combined effort of the spoken Word and Spirit of God. Time is like an elastic band. And like the Word of God says, there is a time for everything. Earth is a living creation of God, and so are the Sun and the Moon. At a cosmic level, these bodies govern time. Every human being is a universe by him or herself. So, you all by yourself represent time. You are conceived, given birth to, and then you grow, then finally someday, your soul will leave your body and return into eternity. The common name for this occurrence is called death. It is only called death because of the non-existence of the spirit in a physical body in the physical realm. But your soul will continue to live forever and ever. You are your own time because when you leave the physical realm, it doesn't compel or mandate other human beings to leave the Earth with you.

We are spiritual beings – who first existed in the spiritual or invisible realm and came into the physical or natural realm hosted in an earthly body that was created by God from the resources of the Earth. When we leave the Earth, we return into the spiritual realm where we originally came from to continue the journey of existence. Everything around and under the Sun depends on every other thing. Without trees, plants, animals, organisms, water etc., humanity would not survive. And without humanity, these other creations would also not exist. Nothing exists independent of everything else. God didn't design the universe in a way for individual creations to exist independent of themselves, and for all creation to be independent of God Himself. In the earlier parts of this writing, there is an elaboration on the topic and the meaning of time. You can reference it to understand better.

Time is just God's way to bridge or overlap the spiritual realm and the physical realm so that human beings will have the duality of being – the ability to walk in both the spiritual and the natural realms at the same time and at will. The fundamental organ responsible for this bridge between the supernatural and the natural is called the brain or mind. The brain is the physical organ and mind is the how the brain is the mental exercise. The brain is composed of nerve cells and can be touched, whereas the mind cannot be touched. I call time, the slowed-motion version of eternity so that humanity can relate in the limited physical abilities.

Why do we have Time? Time is the unit of destiny in the physical realm. Our existence in time is made possible through consciousness.

Subconsciousness, Consciousness, and Unconsciousness

We have three types of consciousness in time, which are the subconscious, conscious, and unconscious.

Consciousness, at its simplest, is sentience or awareness of internal and external existence. The subconscious is the invisible subtle or subliminal consciousness, which powers and controls consciousness in a physical body. When the subconscious is taken away, there is no consciousness, and the body is of no use. And the unconscious is the state in which a person is unable to respond to stimuli and appears to be asleep or dead. Therefore, the state of being brain dead means that the person is dead, regardless of rest of the body parts functioning at a hundred percent. So, life in the human body can be called one word and that is consciousness.

For those who don't believe in the spiritual, you can have a codebase hosted on a local server or remote server with any of the cloud service providers and the servers can go down, or a failure in the internet connection. How useful does your computer or smartphone become when there is a disconnection? This is an example of what we call an outage – when there is an outage in our time, everything that depends on the internet basically comes to a halt. So, we can say that there is a "source" somewhere. That's why we have what we call source code or remote code. That is why we also have a source IP and destination IP, or an electrical power source or power outlet. When you receive any information on your internet device, you know that it surely came from a source somewhere. Even if the information is local, someone still put it on there. This is like consciousness.

The CPU is the brain of a computer – if the CPU is dead, the computer is useless. Does a CPU automatically know how to process input, store data, and output results? Or does someone build it and put instructions on it? Are computers also always local or can they connect to other remote computers to access and send or receive data to process, store, and or output results? In simple terms, a human being is basically a biological computer.

In the Bible, the heart is considered the seat of life or strength. Hence, it means mind, soul, spirit, or one's entire emotional nature of knowing and understanding. The heart is the organ that is said to have the ability to reason, question, meditate, motivate, and think etc. Anything or actions the body take, comes from the mind.

When we are unconscious, it means we are fully in the subconscious or invisible realm. When we are conscious, it means we are fully dual and are in both the invisible and visible realms. Unconsciousness seems like or can be called death in the physical realm, but it doesn't mean non-existence. You are primarily a "quantum remote code" or a spiritual being that is hosted in and executes to manifest temporarily in a physical body during a period we call "alive" on Earth.

By now you should be fully aware that God is tripartite – Father, Son, and Holy Spirit. This is called the Godhead and the Holy Trinity. The following are some scriptures that will help you understand this mystery and revelation.

Genesis 1:1

1 In the beginning God created the heavens and the earth. **2** The earth was without form, and void; and darkness *was* on the face of the deep. And the **Spirit of God** was hovering over the face of the waters.

Genesis 1:26

26 Then God said, "**Let Us** make man in Our image, according to Our likeness; let them have dominion over the fish of the sea, over the birds of the air, and over the cattle, over all the earth and over every creeping thing that creeps on the earth."

Matthew 3:16-17

16 When He had been baptized, Jesus came up immediately from the water; and behold, the heavens were opened to Him, and He saw the **Spirit of God** descending like a dove and alighting upon Him. **17 And suddenly a voice** *came* **from heaven**, saying, "This is My beloved Son, in whom I am well pleased."

Matthew 28:19-20

19 Go therefore and make disciples of all the nations, baptizing them in the name of **the Father and of the Son and of the Holy Spirit**, **20** teaching them to observe all things that I have commanded you; and lo, I am with you always, *even* to the end of the age." Amen.

2 Peter 1:17

17 For **He** received from **God the Father** honor and glory when such a voice came to Him from the Excellent Glory: "This is My beloved Son, in whom I am well pleased."

John 3:16

16 For God so loved the world that He gave His only begotten **Son**, that whoever believes in Him should not perish but have everlasting life.

Ephesians 1:3-6

3 Blessed *be* the **God and Father of our Lord Jesus Christ**, who has blessed us with every spiritual blessing in the heavenly *places* in Christ, **4** just as He chose us in Him before the foundation of the world, that we should be holy and without blame before Him in love, **5** having predestined us to adoption as sons by Jesus Christ to Himself, according to the good pleasure of His will, **6** to the praise of the glory of His grace, by which He made us accepted in the Beloved.

Colossians 2:8-9

8 Beware lest anyone cheat you through philosophy and empty deceit, according to the tradition of men, according to the basic principles of the world, and not according to Christ. **9** For in Him dwells all the fullness of the **Godhead** bodily; ¹⁰ and you are complete in Him, who is the head of all principality and power.

In this mystery of the Godhead lies the power of every true Christian because we are crucified with Christ and joint heirs with Him. If you don't believe in the trinity, you simply are not a Christian and you don't know who you are and all the parts you are made of – since we are also tripartite.

Galatians 2:20

²⁰ I have been crucified with Christ; it is no longer I who live, but Christ lives in me; and the *life* which I now live in the flesh I live by faith in the **Son of God**, who loved me and gave Himself for me.

Romans 8:16-17

¹⁶ The **Spirit Himself** bears witness with **our spirit** that we are children of God, ¹⁷ and if children, then heirs—heirs of God and joint heirs with Christ, if indeed we suffer with *Him,* that we may also be glorified together.

Spend time in the scriptures and prayer to learn more about the mystery of the Godhead. I believe that you have an understanding now that God is three persons in a blessed trinity. This will give you a basis to understand the next sections.

Your Predestination and Destiny

Predestination, in Christian theology, is the doctrine that all events have been predetermined by God, usually with reference to the eventual fate of the individual soul. Before you even make a trip to the grocery store or to your workplace, I'm sure that you will know where you are going to before you even start the trip. We call this the "past". During that trip, you can decide or choose to get some fuel for your car or stop somewhere to do something else prior to going to your originally planned destination. We call this "free will". You will also know in advance what you will find at the stopover or the store. We call this the "future".

Destiny, sometimes referred to as fate (from Latin fatum "decree, prediction, destiny, fate"), is a predetermined course of events. It may be conceived as a predetermined future, whether in general or of an individual. When you want to build a house or anything, you imagine it first – you see a vision of the thing in the "future" before you can build it to specifications. While you imagine it, you don't see it as it is in the future – you see it as in the present or now. So, it means that what you end up building already exists. Your destiny or destination in life is already predetermined. This is how God created you – the same way you create because He lives inside of you.

Finally, when you are doing whatever, you traveled to do at the destination, we call it "present" or "now". So, you see, time is only an illusion and can be called absolute but at an individual level, it is relative. We and physical objects are only reference frames. So, we are a huge network of time. You, I, and everybody and everything else (we) are the universe. You are your own time – you are time. When you want.

Jeremiah 1:5

[5] "Before I formed you in the womb, I knew you;
Before you were born, I sanctified you;
I ordained you a prophet to the nations."

Ephesians 1:3-6

[3] Blessed *be* the God and Father of our Lord Jesus Christ, who has blessed us with every spiritual blessing in the heavenly *places* in Christ, [4] **just as He chose us in Him before the foundation of the world**, that we should be holy and without blame before Him in love, [5] **having predestined us** to adoption as sons by Jesus Christ to Himself, according to the good pleasure of His will, [6] to the praise of the glory of His grace, by which He made us accepted in the Beloved.

From the scriptures above, you will know and understand that whatever you are and becoming, is already there. I will teach you on how to find the blueprint specific to your life here on Earth and in eternity so that you will approach life with accuracy rather than trial and error or randomness or guessing. Your life is not random, but you can make it random with your free will and your mindset or ideologies. Approaching life with a random ideology will impact you negatively both in time and in eternity.

Earlier in this writing, I expounded on predetermination or predestination quite a bit. There are also several other scriptures in the Word of God. In fact, the whole Bible talks about predestination so do some research.

Man lives with the consequences of whatever choices he makes here in time or on Earth. The Christian view of destiny is that there is a place for the sovereign Will of God, but also, there is a place for man's personal choice. Most importantly, before we were born, God already knew us, and He drew out the plan for the specific assignment He has for every individual. There is also a predetermined life for the entire Body of Christ or the Church. For us to fulfil our destiny, we must make the right decisions and choices. The Believer's Destiny is in Jesus Christ.

There are a few prerequisites before we can make the right decisions and choices so that we can fulfil our destinies already given by God. Knowing, understanding, and doing what God already has planned for you is the only way you can have true fulfilment in life and make you relevant to gain your eternal reward when you leave time or Earth.

The first requirement is to know God by believing in His existence as the One and only true God of the Heavens and the Earth and having faith in Him as the One in whom you have your sufficiency. Without Him, you are nothing – a waste.

The second requirement is to believe in the Godhead – the Holy Trinity of God the Father, the Son, and the Holy Spirit. We are joint heirs with Christ, so we have our position in the Godhead as the sons – females included. So, we are an active and participating part of the Holy Trinity, and the proof is that before God can take any action on Earth, He must engage a yielded man or woman. This is the role that Jesus Christ played to become our Savior. From some of the earlier scriptures, we know that man is the temple of God and so, God dwells in man. This means that the Holy Trinity is still the same God – God in three persons. God the Father is God. God the Son is God. And God the Holy Spirit is God. Hence, a fully yielded vessel or human being to God is literally God in the flesh. The unbeliever scientist and engineer doesn't understand quantum mechanics, and consciousness because they don't believe in God. The universe or life is not physics. You are trying to solve or understand what you don't believe in.

God wanted to create Himself so, the Godhead talked among themselves and decided to build a creature in their own image called man. God wanted to be able to interact and have an experience with His creations without annihilating them with His power, so He had to hide Himself in man. Man is God's power control method to be able to regulate and demonstrate the Power of God in himself at will.

Genesis 1:26

26 Then God said, "**Let Us** make man in Our image, according to Our likeness; let them have dominion over the fish of the sea, over the birds of the air, and over the cattle, over all the earth and over every creeping thing that creeps on the earth."

So, this means that God created Himself from the dust of the Earth and breathed Himself into the sculpture. Since God is omnipotent, omnipresent, and omniscient, He has His throne in Heaven, which reflects His dimensions from above the Heavens where He truly dwells in unapproachable light, and still reside in every human being by default. Once you accept Jesus Christ, you "activate" Him to work through you. So, you are a representative of God working on Earth and you have that ability through supernaturally synchronized with Him to the point where you see what He sees, you know what He knows, you understand as He understands, you think and speak as He does, you create as He creates etc. You are one with God and He works through you. You are His body or temple.

Psalm 82:6

6 I said, "You *are* gods,
And all of you *are* children of the Most High.

1 Corinthians 3:16-17

16 Do you not know that you are the temple of God and *that* the Spirit of God dwells in you? 17 If anyone defiles the temple of God, God will destroy him. For the temple of God is holy, which *temple* you are.

Because you lack knowledge and understanding, you treat your body anyhow and do all kinds of things with it to destroy it. That brings us to the third requirement, which is that you need to be born again – meaning, you must accept Jesus Christ as your Lord and personal savior so that you can have eternal life in Him. Being born again means that you will have direct access to God again as originally planned by Him, which Adam lost when he sinned in the Garden of Eden. So, God dwells in you and that makes you a god with true **consistent** biblical practices and living – prayer, fasting, worship, praises, righteousness, holiness etc. These are your foundations and building blocks. Now, you can start living consistently as a true Christian with very intentional and specific daily practices as a lifestyle. We will go over these **consistent** daily practices in detail.

After your salvation, you are still a child of God until you master these consistencies every single day. Let's get into becoming a true son of God. Note that son is used biblically for both genders.

A Rhombus and Its Relationship to Consciousness

A Rhombus

Image Source – Public Domain

In plane Euclidean geometry, a rhombus (plural rhombi or rhombuses) is a quadrilateral whose four sides all have the same length. Another name is equilateral quadrilateral, since equilateral means that all its sides are equal in length. The rhombus is often called a diamond or a lozenge. Every rhombus is simple (non-self-intersecting) and is a special case of a parallelogram and a kite. A rhombus with right angles is a square.

You may be wondering why I am showing you a rhombus. On November 26, 2021, the Lord showed me a vision of the rhombus just when I started listening to a teaching on destiny and our callings. That's exactly what the rhombus symbol represents. This symbol is basically two triangles joined together.

The rhombus represents the inner and heavenly focus that, every human being needs to hold onto his or her life assignment during his or her lifetime here on Earth. That assignment is already programmed into our very being – which is our spirits. This is because we are spirits, who have souls, and living in human bodies or vessels. So, we are not humans. We only experience the physical world through our bodies. The soul is made up of three parts – intellect, will, and emotion. And these are expressed through the mind.

Intellect

In the study of the human mind, intellect refers to, describes, and identifies the ability of the human mind to reach correct conclusions about what is true and what is false in reality; and how to solve problems.

Here are a few scriptures that prove that intellect is a function of the mind – which makes it the major organ for your soul to experience life through the human body. The mind is an organ of memory in which information is stored, accessed or retrieved, and processed. This is where the ability to decide and choose, reside.

Proverbs 2:10

10 When wisdom enters your heart,
And knowledge is pleasant to your soul,

Proverbs 4:23

23 Keep your heart with all diligence,
For out of it *spring* the issues of life.

Provers 19:21

21 There are many plans in a man's heart,
Nevertheless the LORD's counsel—that will stand.

Proverbs 24:14

14 So *shall* the knowledge of wisdom *be* to your soul;
If you have found *it,* there is a prospect,
And your hope will not be cut off.

Psalm 13:2

2 How long shall I take counsel in my soul,
Having sorrow in my heart daily?
How long will my enemy be exalted over me?

Lamentations 3:20

20 My soul still remembers
And sinks within me.

Will

Will, generally, is a faculty of the mind; within philosophy, Will is important as one of the parts of the mind, along with reason and understanding. It is considered central to the field of ethics because of its role in enabling deliberate action.

Here are a few scriptures that prove that will is a function of the mind – which makes it the major organ for your soul to experience life through the human body. These scriptures are very self-explanatory. You exercise your will when you vow or swear, or refuse, or choose or accept anything.

Numbers 30:2

² If a man makes a vow to the LORD, or swears an oath to bind himself by some agreement, he shall not break his word; he shall do according to all that proceeds out of his mouth.

1 Chronicles 22:19

¹⁹ Now set your heart and your soul to seek the LORD your God. Therefore, arise and build the sanctuary of the LORD God, to bring the ark of the covenant of the LORD and the holy articles of God into the house that is to be built for the name of the LORD."

Job 6:7

⁷ My soul refuses to touch them;
They *are* as loathsome food to me.

Job 7:15

¹⁵ So that my soul chooses strangling
And death rather than my body.

Emotion

Emotions are psychological states brought on by neurophysiological changes, variously associated with thoughts, feelings, behavioral responses, and a degree of pleasure or displeasure.

Love, joy, hatred, grief, and expressions alike are all aspects of emotion. Here are a few scriptures that prove that emotion is a function of the mind – which makes it the major organ for your soul to experience life through the human body.

Song of Solomon 1:7

⁷ Tell me, O you whom I love,
Where you feed *your flock,*
Where you make *it* rest at noon.
For why should I be as one who veils herself
By the flocks of your companions?

Psalm 42:1

42 As the deer pants for the water brooks,
So pants my soul for You, O God.

Psalm 86:4

⁴ Rejoice the soul of Your servant,
For to You, O Lord, I lift up my soul.

2 Samuel 5:8

⁸ Now David said on that day, "Whoever climbs up by way of the water shaft and defeats the Jebusites (the lame and the blind, *who are* hated by David's soul), *he shall be chief and captain.*" Therefore, they say, "The blind and the lame shall not come into the house."

Psalm 107:18

¹⁸ Their soul abhorred all manner of food,
And they drew near to the gates of death.

Ezekiel 36:5

⁵ therefore thus says the Lord GOD: "Surely I have spoken in My burning jealousy against the rest of the nations and against all Edom, who gave My land to themselves as a possession, with wholehearted joy *and* spiteful minds, in order to plunder its open country.'"

Isaiah 61:10

¹⁰ I will greatly rejoice in the LORD,
My soul shall be joyful in my God;
For He has clothed me with the garments of salvation,
He has covered me with the robe of righteousness,
As a bridegroom decks *himself* with ornaments,
And as a bride adorns *herself* with her jewels.

Job 30:25

²⁵ Have I not wept for him who was in trouble?
Has *not* my soul grieved for the poor?

There are several other examples in the Word of God, but I hope these help your understanding. Our connection between the natural and supernatural is through the mind because the soul functions through the mind. Therefore, human beings have a tripartite nature just like the Godhead (Father, Son, Holy Spirit). The spirit within us is the Spirit of God because He breathed Himself into us after He formed us with His own hands and put us into the Garden of Eden. Before the fall of man, the spirit within us was by default the Holy Spirit but after the fall, you can only have the Holy Spirit if you are born again in Jesus Christ. It's important to understand that even demon spirits are still the spirits of God. They are just dark or evil spirits now because of their rebellion against God and their eternal punishment. The technology of procreation is just one of God's infinite mysteries that He included in this eternal strategy of creation to automatically ensure there is continuity of life through man.

Unbelieving or Non-Christian scientists and engineers are a complete joke. God's strategy and technology is to create one man and one woman and from them, He enabled photocopying or duplication through reproduction. But every copy is unique both in features and abilities. We humans, currently build things and are never able to reproduce the same copy with unique features and abilities without having to go through the manual creation process again to edit the prototype. Humanity without God is just a joke and total waste of life.

So, the rhombus symbol represents our very true being – which is the Spirit of God dwelling in our human bodies. God is truly who we are – His image, His nature or likeness etc. Each human being is simply a unique dimension of God from His infinite dimensions. God created man because He wanted to have beings that He could commune, fellowship, and have a relationship with Him.

Koinonia is a transliterated form of the Greek word κοινωνία, which refers to concepts such as fellowship, joint participation, the share which one has in anything, a gift jointly contributed, a collection, a contribution. It identifies the idealized state of fellowship and unity that should exist within the Christian Church, the Body of Christ.

God simply wanted to have this relationship with His infinite self. He couldn't have this kind of relationship with His other creations like the angels because He didn't create them in His image. He only created each one of them uniquely with respect to the dimensions they host such as secrets or revelations, insight, wisdom, strength, healing etc., but these angels don't have the privilege to be like God or to host the fullness of God. They are only made of His unique or specific power. But every human being can host the fullness of God without limitations, and we are able to do that only through accepting freely, the sacrifices of His Son Jesus Christ, to make Him our Lord and personal Savior. Then we can be filled with His Holy Spirit who then will be the influencer or our intellect, will, and emotions, which will then give us the perfect soul that is needed to be Sons of God.

The Christian life is a life that requires knowledge and understanding and being intentional about that knowledge so that you can correctly, accurately, efficiently, and effectively apply and live it daily through understanding as an experience until you leave the Earth to return into eternity.

The word correctly here means **true and free from error** – the state of having an affirmed truth. The word accurately here means **exact or careful conformity to the truth –** the result of care or pains; free from failure, error, or defect; exact; as, an accurate calculator; an accurate measure; accurate expression, knowledge, etc. The word efficiently here means the ability to accomplish something with the **least amount of wasted time, money, and effort or competency in**

performance – in practically demonstrating the knowledge. And finally, the word effectively here means the **degree to which something is successful in producing a desired result –** success.

Even a LOT of Churches and Christians around the world don't know and understand this. Some know and understand it but are simply lazy to comply, and some don't know but don't understand it, so they end up being unsuccessful. In short, there is a LOT of laziness and ignorance in the Body of Christ. Sometimes by chance, they see one result here or there but there is a big inability to reproduce the results. Therefore, the Body of Christ is almost looking like the biggest JOKE on Earth. A lot of talking and a lot of numbers but little to no results because there is largely no discipline among many other shortfalls. In summary, these have been the issue of the Body of Christ and the reason why we are unable to correctly, accurately, efficiently, and effectively host God.

The rhombus symbol is both the physical and spiritual symbol to answering the big questions in life such as "who are we?", "where did we come from?", "why are we here?", "where are we going?" etc. And if you are not asking these questions, you are not yet alive.

That assignment programmed into the life of every person was and remains to this very day to reinstall balance within self between the negative and positive energy aspects that make up every spirit living in a human body and to reflect that inner balance into the outer world. Between both energies is the middle or neutral energy. Therefore, in our universe, the building blocks for everything are the signs (−, ±, +) – making up the negative, neutral, and positive energies. This means to give out to the world the nature of the inner man within you. When the Holy Spirit showed me the geometric shape of the rhombus, He said that a significant change is installed within my consciousness; one that supersedes the limited ego-self of the human personality and that acts for the benefit of all people – to enhance my soul mission as a beacon or a light bearer or a lightworker to serve humanity through teaching His Word to the world. I thank the Lord for His several graces, among which is the ability to interpret ancient symbols. I mentioned earlier in this writing, when He opened this dimension to me.

The dark or evil spirits in life and the sum of the nature of societies heavily impact who we truly are and who God created us to be. Most people grow up being influenced mostly by the devil rather than by the Holy Spirit of God. Ego and pride are the two very important words when it comes to the lives of many and our missions here on Earth.

The key difference between ego and pride is that ego is a sense of self-importance (feeling of I, Me, Myself) which can lead to selfishness and arrogance whereas pride is a sense of satisfaction – a trait or an emotion which is a result of one's achievement or success. The funny thing is that most people with so much pride don't even have any meaningful achievements to show for it. Those who have all kinds of achievements or successes in life but understand the true meaning of life, tend to excel in killing these two traits in their lives. The words ego and pride are so close in meaning and so interrelated that sometimes it becomes difficult to differentiate between them.

For the true Christian, you should only be prideful in the knowledge and understanding, and your relationship with God.

Jeremiah 9:23-25

23 Thus says the LORD:

"Let not the wise *man* glory in his wisdom,
Let not the mighty *man* glory in his might,
Nor let the rich *man* glory in his riches;
24 But let him who glories glory in this,
That he understands and knows Me,
That I *am* the LORD, exercising lovingkindness, judgment, and righteousness in the earth.
For in these I delight," says the LORD.

25 "Behold, the days are coming," says the LORD, "that I will punish all *who are* circumcised with the uncircumcised—

Lucifer fell from Heaven because of ego and pride. And now he is a fallen angel called Satan. Pay attention to the scriptures and the words he used when he sinned against the Almighty God – his Creator.

Isaiah 14:12-14

12 "How you are fallen from heaven,
O Lucifer, son of the morning!
How you are cut down to the ground,
You who weakened the nations!
13 For you have said in your heart:
'I will ascend into heaven,
I will exalt my throne above the stars of God;
I will also sit on the mount of the congregation
On the farthest sides of the north;
14 I will ascend above the heights of the clouds,
I will be like the Most High.'

These are the traits of most people on Earth right now. Most scientists think they are geniuses and think that they are God and that the Almighty God does not exist. Wisdom should tell them that everything we make is discovered and not created or invented. Everything we think we "invent" is inspired by one thing or the other in nature. There have been lots of such inspirations from beehives, spider webs etc. Yet, scientists still think and believe that they created or invented these technologies. Foolishness makes them think like that. That is why they don't understand what they call quantum mechanics. How can you understand quantum mechanics if you don't believe in God?

The human nature after the fall is just like that of Satan because his spirit goes to and from around the world and possess, influence or use people.

Job 1:7

7 And the Lord said to Satan, "From where do you come?"

So, Satan answered the Lord and said, "From going to and fro on the earth, and from walking back and forth on it."

This is how he operates from the invisible realm on the Earth. He is constantly manifesting in people and in conjunction with his devils, are responsible for what most people call the negative force operating on the Earth. They are the reason for all bad things such as hatred, wickedness, corruption, greed, lust, immorality, sickness, depression etc., – all the bad things you can think of that you see happening around the world. They operate in a very low and dense frequency or vibration.

The positive aspect or energy is the dominating energy for men. The negative aspect or energy is the dominating energy for women. This means that both men and women need to balance their dominating energies with their weak or subtle inner energies. By default, we are born with the egoistic and prideful energies or personalities being the dominating energy because of Satan.

Psalm 51:5

5 Behold, I was brought forth in iniquity,
And in sin my mother conceived me.

You will find these energies being called different things in different religions and practices. In simple terms and in yoga, yin is characterized as negative, passive, and feminine, among other things, whereas yang is seen as positive, active, and masculine, among other things. It doesn't mean that I am suggesting yoga or any other religion or practice other than God through Jesus Christ and the Power of the Holy Spirit as a Christian who will practice it as thought by the Word of God through guidance in this book and who will belong to a Church or the Body of Christ. The reason why all these spiritually illegal ways of meditation sometimes see results is that Satan didn't lose power – he lost authority. This means that the power being coveted here is still the Power of God, but it is not channeled properly, and it is also limited power. Most religions sort of have some idea, except that they are not serving the true God but Satan. The one and only true God is God Almighty, whose son is Jesus Christ, and whose spirit is the Holy Spirit. It is very important to get out of any other religion or practice or any forms of meditation and come to Jesus Christ. There is still the Christian or biblical way of meditation, and you shall be taught when you repent and accept Jesus Christ and convert to become a Child of God. Then you will be legally accessing the limitless Power of God, and when you leave the Earth, you will spend eternity with Him in Heaven. But if you remain where you currently are, your end or destination shall be in

Hell, and you will be punished alongside Satan forever and ever. Life is a game of two spirits – the Holy Spirit, and the dark or evil spirits.

The game has already been played and we already know the winner. This war going on has already been fought and we already know the winner. It's like a replay of a movie or football match. Except that it is still alive and dynamic, and you can only play a part to support a side to speed it up towards the predetermined direction. It has been played so well though that no matter what happens, the results can't be changed, and the winner will remain the winner. You can be part of the winning side (Jesus' side) or be on the losing side (Satan's side). The people of God have already won. God has already won and that is written and can NEVER be altered. Being part of team Satan is like signing your own death warrant. Be wise and repent and come to Jesus Christ. I have seen Hell and I don't have words to describe the hopelessness and darkness over there. You surely don't want to end up there forever and ever.

So, the rhombus symbolizes contrary forces are complementary, interconnected, and interdependent in both the supernatural and natural world, and how they give rise to each other as they interrelate to one another.

The purpose of a lifetime is to explore the subconscious, unconscious, and the conscious inner landscape of self, and the three dimensions within which the ego personality functions as a mind/soul construct (intellect, will, and emotion). These dimensions hide the thought constructs upon which we have built our personalities or characters and that keep us enslaved to a version of self that hides our authentic self. The nature we need to eventually get to dominate is the God/Holy Spirit/Jesus Christ nature in us as originally intended and put into us by God because He hid Himself in us. Once this perfection is achieved, then you will truly begin to live life to start knowing who you are, what you are doing here, where you will be going after here etc. It is in first discovering God through Jesus Christ, and the Power of the Holy Spirit that we will know who we truly are and the instructions that God has written regarding our lives. These instructions are unique to every person, but they all work together towards a common goal – to see the purposes and the Kingdom of God established and for Jesus Christ to be glorified.

It is through a relationship with the Holy Spirit that you will gain access again to this inner core or inner man to seek for the motives upon which we act or behave in our daily existence. Both sexes or genders, however, are equal in this process of investigating or digging up what is hidden beneath our socially stratified personalities. Both need to surrender their positive to the negative aspect of self. Therefore, there is the middle or neutral point which makes this possible. Through the unveiling of this hidden aspect in everybody through the daily study and practice of the Word of God, and a consistent prayer life with fasting, righteous living through a relationship with the Holy Spirit, the reason for being on Earth for humanity will be discovered and accomplished successfully. It is only then will everybody find true fulfilment in life and a better place in eternity.

From these explanations, you should now truly understand how to live the Christian life through knowledge and understanding. Ignorant Christianity is very dangerous. Faith without understanding will still make you unfruitful. God is always with us (Emmanuel) because He lives in us, and He is all around us. God is Transcendent – transcendence is existence or experience beyond the normal or physical level. He is also Immanent – immanence, in philosophy and theology, a term applied, in contradistinction to "transcendence," to the fact or condition of being entirely within something (from Latin immanere, "to dwell in, remain").

Don't be confused because by now you should understand this concept even through the building blocks of all science – negative, neutral, and positive energies (electrons, neutrons, and protons), and from what we have just seen in the spiritual and natural symbolic meaning of the rhombus symbol as God revealed to me. So, it proves the fact that even without being a Christian, God is beyond what you can see or feel at a normal or visible or physical level but God at the same time is entirely within us as humans and His unique dimensions shared throughout the whole of creation. It also means that He is all around us. So, if you want to learn about God or study Him, you can look all around you in creation – the skies, waters, trees, animals etc. If you want to truly experience His fullness, look at the life of a true Believer or Christian. We were all created by Him and every person without sin or influence of dark forces or negative energies, has a perfect image and likeness of God. Every person like this beholds the Glory of God. So, Heaven is a world with societies with the absence of all the dark forces and negative energies that we currently see and experience on Earth. Heaven is filled with the Glory of God. The most perfect form of existence you could ever imagine is Heaven, although your imagination without the experience is still not enough to know, feel, sense, or understand it.

My first conscious experience of hearing the voice of God as a child happened from within me – the voice spoke loud and clear from within me. I was wondering "who just spoke from within me and in my own voice?". This is one of the ways He speaks to us daily. Depending on how close or far away from God you are, it will determine whether you will hear Him when He speaks.

God dwells outside Heaven. He is the only one who existed, still exists, and will continue to exist. Heaven and the Heaven of Heavens cannot contain Him because He dwells outside both.

1 Kings 8:27

[27] "But will God indeed dwell on the earth? Behold, heaven and the heaven of heavens cannot contain You. How much less this temple which I have built!

But He found a way to be both transcendent and immanent through creating Heaven and Earth to dwell there too. Man is the only creation that can host the fullness of God. The Garden of Eden was supposed to be the bridge between the Heaven and Earth. In the beginning after the fall, God would show up at certain places to Abraham. Sometimes He would show up at a spot, mountain or anywhere He chose, so they decided to mark the spots that He showed up at with stones as memorials or altar. These were to help the next generations to know where God showed up at and where they could find God when they were looking for Him. Jacob, the grandson of Abraham, found one of these places, which had a stone altar of Abraham. Note that this has been the error in the world through which people fraternize with demonic spirits through idol worshipping – thinking that God lives in stones or the stones or other natural or man-made items are God.

Genesis 12:1-3

Promises to Abram

12 Now the Lord had said to Abram:

"Get out of your country,
From your family
And from your father's house,
To a land that I will show you.
² I will make you a great nation;
I will bless you
And make your name great;
And you shall be a blessing.
³ I will bless those who bless you,
And I will curse him who curses you;
And in you all the families of the earth shall be blessed."

Genesis 13:1-4

Abram Inherits Canaan

13 Then Abram went up from Egypt, he and his wife and all that he had, and Lot with him, to the South. **²** Abram *was* very rich in livestock, in silver, and in gold. **³** And he went on his journey from the South as far as Bethel, to the place where his tent had been at the beginning, between Bethel and Ai, **⁴** to the place of the altar which he had made there at first. And there Abram called on the name of the Lord.

Genesis 28:16

¹⁶ Then Jacob awoke from his sleep and said, "Surely the Lord is in this place, and I did not know *it*." **¹⁷** And he was afraid and said, "How awesome *is* this place! This *is* none other than the house of God, and this *is* the gate of heaven!"

Genesis 32:22-32

Wrestling with God

²² And he arose that night and took his two wives, his two female servants, and his eleven sons, and crossed over the ford of Jabbok. **²³** He took them, sent them over the brook, and sent over what he had. **²⁴** Then Jacob was left alone; and a Man wrestled with him until the breaking of day. ²⁵ Now when He saw that He did not prevail against him, He touched the socket of his hip; and the socket of Jacob's hip was out of joint as He wrestled with him. ²⁶ And He said, "Let Me go, for the day breaks."

But he said, "I will not let You go unless You bless me!"

²⁷ So He said to him, "What *is* your name?"

He said, "Jacob."

²⁸ And He said, "Your name shall no longer be called Jacob, but Israel; for you have struggled with God and with men and have prevailed."

²⁹ Then Jacob asked, saying, "Tell *me* Your name, I pray."

And He said, "Why *is* it *that* you ask about My name?" And He blessed him there.

³⁰ So Jacob called the name of the place Peniel: "For I have seen God face to face, and my life is preserved." ³¹ Just as he crossed over Penuel the sun rose on him, and he limped on his hip. ³² Therefore to this day the children of Israel do not eat the muscle that shrank, which *is* on the hip socket, because He touched the socket of Jacob's hip in the muscle that shrank.

Therefore, after the fall of man and throughout the Old Testament, and when God started building Israel as a Nation, He continued this work through giving Moses and the other Prophets a pattern of Heaven for the Earth, so they built the Ark of the Covenant and the tabernacles or temples. Later in History, the transcendent became immanent, through the womb of a woman, and He called His Son/Himself Immanuel or Emmanuel, which means "God with Us".

John 1:1

The Eternal Word

1 In the beginning was the Word, and the Word was with God, and the Word was God.

The Word is Jesus Christ, and He had always been with the Father and the Holy Spirit before the foundations of the Earth.

John 1:14

The Word Becomes Flesh

¹⁴ And the Word became flesh and dwelt among us, and we beheld His glory, the glory as of the only begotten of the Father, full of grace and truth.

Glory is the fullness of God's presence – the manifestation Power of God. Jesus Christ walked in this glory. Prior to Jesus Christ, the glory was in the Ark of the Covenant. God is full of glory. This is how Jesus Christ walked on Earth, and this is the heritage of all people of God.

This is a summary of how the invisible (Word) became visible (matter). A change in our private or secret lifestyles or personalities and public expressions should be subject to the Glory of God and be fully seen in our lives. This is the state in which Heaven is. Life on Earth is the determinant or separator of good and evil, light and darkness, truth and lies. And the side that you would be subject to is what will determine where you will spend eternity. Light or truth or good will go to Heaven, and darkness or lies or bad will go to Hell. It's as simple as that. After reading this line, you should know where you stand with respect to these two eternal locations. You can avoid only one, but you can NEVER avoid both.

Again, prior to the birth and death of Jesus Christ, God kept His glory in the Ark of the Covenant and then the tabernacles or temples because no man was worthy to host His glory. After the death of Jesus Christ, He gave us His glory. He was the only begotten who carried the glory. Jesus Christ prayed this prayer.

John 17:22-23

22 And the glory which You gave Me I have given them, that they may be one just as We are one: 23 I in them, and You in Me; that they may be made perfect in one, and that the world may know that You have sent Me, and have loved them as You have loved Me.

So, Jesus Christ handed over the glory to us before He went back to Heaven since He was the only one who was carrying the glory.

The Word of God and Christianity is the only way of life that is consistent with everything in the natural and supernatural. It is the only way of life which follows the laws of science – and there's one law of science, and that is gravity – and gravity is LOVE. The Power of God has different manifestations of the same power.

Ephesians 4:11-16

11 And He Himself gave some *to be* apostles, some prophets, some evangelists, and some pastors and teachers, 12 for the equipping of the saints for the work of ministry, for the edifying of the body of Christ, 13 till we all come to the unity of the faith and of the knowledge of the Son of God, to a perfect man, to the measure of the stature of the fullness of Christ; 14 that we should no longer be children, tossed to and fro and carried about with every wind of doctrine, by the trickery of men, in the cunning craftiness of deceitful plotting, 15 but, speaking the truth in love, may grow up in all things into Him who is the head—Christ— 16 from whom the whole body, joined and knit together by what every joint supplies, according to the effective working by which every part does its share, causes growth of the body for the edifying of itself in love.

There are different gifts in the Body of Christ, but they all have one source – and they are the same power manifesting in different ways to accomplish the same mission of love. This again, is just like how the force of gravity manifests in different ways and remains the only force in life with the underlying secret or revelation being LOVE. Love bonds or brings everything together, and where there is love, there is life – joy, peace, harmony etc.

John 12:20-24

The Fruitful Grain of Wheat

[20] Now there were certain Greeks among those who came up to worship at the feast. [21] Then they came to Philip, who was from Bethsaida of Galilee, and asked him, saying, "Sir, we wish to see Jesus."

[22] Philip came and told Andrew, and in turn Andrew and Philip told Jesus.

[23] But Jesus answered them, saying, "The hour has come that the Son of Man should be glorified. [24] Most assuredly, I say to you, unless a grain of wheat falls into the ground and dies, it remains alone; but if it dies, it produces much grain.

This scripture is an event six days prior to Jesus' crucifixion – which was the sacrifice through love for our eternal salvation. Are you a fruitful grain of wheat? It is symbolic – it can be a grain of rice, a grain of corn, a seed of apple, a person in a family, a leader in the local or federal government etc. By offering His life, it was like the grain of wheat planted in the soil. Before there can be a big harvest of wheat, one grain must go into the soil, then die, and after it grows to maturity, it will yield more grains of wheat. The same applies to any other plants. The same applies to a man and or a woman. Either one of them can produce many children and continuity will exist – a but they must do it together through love. God never violates His laws and so we see it everywhere – same patterns. What Jesus Christ did demonstrate the law of sacrifice through love. One dies to save many. One grain dies to bring forth more grains. One man was initially created to bring forth many men.

Jesus Christ seeing Himself as the only one who carried the glory, died for us so that we could all share the glory with Him – the biggest selfless act of love to ever exist.

But we live in a world where people are very selfish, corrupt, greedy etc., – exhibit all kinds of dark energies. People think that hoarding stuff or thinking and living as "I" or "myself" is how to progress or be successful and fulfilled in life. In fact, it is the very opposite. That takes me to the next few important points.

Just like the grain of wheat (Jesus Christ) falls to ground, and unless He falls to the ground, this grain of wheat (Jesus Christ) will die alone or exist all by itself (Himself). But if He falls to the ground and die, He will produce other grains of wheat. This is the whole secret of life – sacrifice through LOVE. This is what is missing in the world. What the world is currently doing is that the grain of wheat (most individuals, leaders, secret societies, elites etc.) are very unfruitful grains of wheat. They are very satanic. They think life is a survival of the strongest or fittest as Darwin once said but that is false and very misleading. If people don't follow the ways of Jesus Christ and transfer the good in them to as many people as possible as Jesus Christ did through love, a day is coming soon that they will be the only ones left on a very desolate land filled with hopelessness, terror, and all the dark things you could think about – and when that is over, they will go and continue that life in Hell forever and ever with their father, the devil.

Now that Jesus has accomplished these works for us through His death, the glory of God doesn't dwell in the Ark of the Covenant anymore. It doesn't dwell in the tabernacles and or temples. The glory of God now dwells in Jesus Christ, and through His sacrifice, He has transferred this glory to His followers. So, if you want to see God, you don't have to go too far away to find Him. God now dwells in us. That's the meaning of the name that God the Father gave to Jesus – Immanuel or Emmanuel, which means "God with us". God is with us and within us. We are the hosts or carriers of God. This is the whole mystery of life through our Lord and Savior Jesus Christ.

Luke 17:20-21

[20] Now when He was asked by the Pharisees when the kingdom of God would come, He answered them and said, "The kingdom of God does not come with observation; [21] nor will they say, 'See here!' or 'See there!' For indeed, the kingdom of God is within you."

The Word becoming flesh (transcendence and immanence) has been the whole agenda of God since Genesis. This was the whole strategy to collect the authority that man lost to Satan in the Garden of Eden, and to restore that authority and Glory of God to man again. After which Satan and his associated enemies of God shall all be eternally judged. This makes it the whole agenda of man too – this is your purpose here on Earth. You have a key part to play. And now that this has been achieved through the sacrifice of Jesus Christ, just like the force of gravity taking different phases or forms, the next big event is the return of Jesus Christ back to the Earth to take His people away and destroy the enemy forever and ever. Prior to the judgment of Satan and his followers, there will be two great events – the rapture of the Body of Christ, and then the second coming of Jesus Christ. These events were explained earlier in this writing. It seems like a joke to many but if you were once a child and through the force of gravity (the love and bond of God) you grew up to become an adult, you should be concerned if you don't have Jesus Christ. COVID-19 is both a good and a bad example – it also came like a thief in the night but to those who were involved in creating it, they knew about it ahead of time. So shall it be for the sons of light.

These prophecies are all true and we are already in the end time. The Glory of God is coming to the Body of Christ once again – and in an even mightier way than ever before. Thank God that the days of the hybrids are here. The spirits of the Old Testament prophets are on the Earth again. These are the times of both the Law and the Prophets of old and Jesus Christ – a hybrid of the accurate practice of both the patterns and ordinances of the Old Testament and New Testament is here. These are the days that Ezekiel's Temple will be built. The Church has been in error for a very long time so there has been a lack of power. The errors are being corrected in our time and the gates of Hell shall indeed not prevail. Your calling will work towards the general victory of this end time move.

Who are We and Where are We?

We are like a pool of water, an ocean, a big balloon, a big circle or ball, we are like an individual body of a person and each person is like a part of that body such as the eye, ear, nose, hand, finger etc. We are all one. We are the Body of Christ because God has hidden unique dimensions of Himself in us. That's why I pointed out that when you think you are hating someone or doing bad to someone, you are doing it to yourself – that's what the Lord told me. We reflect each other and are a huge network of the same body. When you love others, you are loving yourself. We are all connected like a big body with different parts. The secret to our existence is love.

We are invisible eternal interconnected beings contained in the sphere or perimeter of God, who are manifesting in physical form or matter through a slowed-motion version of eternity called time and are supposed to demonstrate God in the flesh or physical or visible to interact with nature to restore all things to their rightful positions as intended and created by God or life.

What Are We Doing Here?

Your Calling – Your Purpose

God's strategy for bringing you to Earth is to make you become what you would have become if man had not fallen in sin. There's nothing like an apostle, a prophet, an evangelist etc., in Zion. There are only Sons of God.

Here on Earth, there's the calling and there's the blessing. The blessing is the system on earth to facilitate the calling such as good or divine health, prosperity etc. Humanity pursues the blessing rather than the calling – that's where humanity is wrong. The calling is a set of divine burdens that have been programmed into your being and caught for execution in the journey of life of a man through a life of consistent prayer, relationship, communion, and fellowship with God through the Holy Spirit in the Name of Jesus.

The idea of the calling is not for power, oppression, influence, fame, or to be more valuable than others etc. The idea of the calling is for you to become what you must become in the Earth to come – which means reestablishing God's original plan before the foundations of the Earth if man had not sinned.

The crown of life reward is in heaven – our reward is in eternity. Your calling is not based on manifestation in time. You need discernment to manage burdens correctly as the Holy Spirit shares with you. You'll find out why you came here on Earth, and the strategy of life will be given to you. It will be like a compass to help you navigate through life. Truly, if you understand this and you know how to engage the Holy Spirit consistently, He will guide you in everything and you wouldn't need anybody to tell you about your calling or purpose. If you hear it from another person, then it will only be a confirmation that you truly caught your burdens in the spirit or heard from God.

Isaiah 30:21

Your ears shall hear a word behind you, saying,
"This *is* the way, walk in it,"
Whenever you turn to the right hand
Or whenever you turn to the left.

John 10:27-30

27 My sheep hear My voice, and I know them, and they follow, Me. 28 And I give them eternal life, and they shall never perish; neither shall anyone snatch them out of My hand. 29 My Father, who has given *them* to Me, is greater than all; and no one is able to snatch *them* out of My Father's hand. 30 I and *My* Father are one."

That's another way you can identify those who truly hear from God and those who don't. Your existence here is God's strategy to give you your rightful place in eternity but you must do some work for it even after the sacrifice of Jesus Christ. This is where most people and Churches around the world have gotten it very wrong. While you embark on this journey, pray that the Holy Spirit will give you an accurate understanding of the Word of God. Your accurate understanding of scriptures is key. Earth is an equal playing field just like the men who worked in the vineyard.

Matthew 20:1-16

The Parable of the Workers in the Vineyard

20 "For the kingdom of heaven is like a landowner who went out early in the morning to hire laborers for his vineyard. 2 Now when he had agreed with the laborers for a denarius a day, he sent them into his vineyard. 3 And he went out about the third hour and saw others standing idle in the marketplace, 4 and said to them, 'You also go into the vineyard, and whatever is right I will give you.' So, they went. 5 Again he went out about the sixth and the ninth hour and did likewise. 6 And about the eleventh hour he went out and found others standing idle, and said to them, 'Why have you been standing here idle all day?' 7 They said to him, 'Because no one hired us.' He said to them, 'You also go into the vineyard, and whatever is right you will receive.'

8 "So when evening had come, the owner of the vineyard said to his steward, 'Call the laborers and give them *their* wages, beginning with the last to the first.' 9 And when those came who *were hired* about the eleventh hour, they each received a denarius. 10 But when the first came, they supposed that they would receive more; and they likewise received each a denarius. 11 And when they had received *it,* they complained against the landowner, 12 saying, 'These last *men* have worked *only* one hour, and you made them equal to us who have borne the burden and the heat of the day.' 13 But he answered one of them and said, 'Friend, I am doing you no wrong. Did you not agree with me for a denarius? 14 Take *what is* yours and go your way. I wish to give to this last

man *the same* as to you. [15] Is it not lawful for me to do what I wish with my own things? Or is your eye evil because I am good?' [16] So the last will be first, and the first last. For many are called, but few chosen."

Your investment is not on Earth and shouldn't be on Earth but in Heaven. Everything here on Earth is to give you an eternal reward. Material gains or wealth in the natural is good or a blessing if it's to advance the Kingdom of God. Anything otherwise is a total waste. We all have specific burdens. We have crowns to wear and thrones in Heaven that we must occupy in eternity.

The life or ministry of a Christian is that your message is the story of your life because you are supposed to be a witness of God. Your life is a mobile altar. You can't escape process or the dealings of God in your life. But the Apostolic or New Testament ministry alone is not the solution. We will learn more about this as we go on.

What you do in the public is an overflow of what happens in the secret place. The secret place is like the invisible – the public is the visible. You don't just get up and start manifesting. Therefore, the invisible rules the visible and before something happens in the visible, it has already happened in the invisible. A life of power is an authentic life in the secret place.

A life of the secret place is a required standard model for all true Christians. But an almost totally abandoned set of instructions, patterns, ordinances, and secrets in the Old Testament have caused much weakness in the lives of Christians over the years to make us seem powerless.

The Temple and the Lost Patterns and Ordinances of Priesthood
Matthew 5:17-20

Christ Fulfills the Law

[17] **"Do not think that I came to destroy the Law or the Prophets. I did not come to destroy but to fulfill.** [18] For assuredly, I say to you, till heaven and earth pass away, one jot or one tittle will by no means pass from the law till all is fulfilled. [19] Whoever therefore breaks one of the least of these commandments, and teaches men so, shall be called least in the kingdom of heaven; but whoever does and teaches *them,* he shall be called great in the kingdom of heaven. [20] For I say to you, that unless your righteousness exceeds *the righteousness* of the scribes and Pharisees, you will by no means enter the kingdom of heaven.

This is Jesus speaking in the above scriptures, which we call the New Testament. I need you to understand that the words "New" and "Old" Testament in the sixty-six books of the Bible is just for you to be able to relate and view the content of events in a chronological order. The word testament means a testimony, witness, evidence, proof, attestation, or demonstration – or any other word or words alike. The categorization of the Old and New Testaments of the Bible doesn't make one more relevant than the other. This is the current problem in Christianity today. We see a somewhat similar error in science today.

As we have already seen in the earlier parts of this writing, scientists think that gravity is a different force than the weak nuclear force, strong nuclear force, and the electromagnetic force, but they are all the same force called gravity, which just has these three other forces as different manifestations of itself.

To the Christian world right now, the Lord showed me on December 4, 2021, that our head, who is Jesus Christ, is the Ancient of Days – a very ancient man with the head of an old man but His body, which is supposed to be the current Body of Christ or Church on Earth, looked like the body of a baby underneath the head of the Ancient of Days. This was in a vision. Imagine such imbalance as you read on. This is the current state of the Church. The Church is very immature, careless, lazy, and ignorant. That is why it is very weak and has no influence at all in our time. The immaturity in the Church is worrisome. If God allows it to continue in this manner, the Church someday will cease to exist. It's the truth but God forbid – we won't cease to exist.

The Old Testament is very relevant. The most significant story or witness or testimony in the New Testament is the Life and Apostolic Ministry of our Lord Jesus Christ. This is what you must understand. That is why Jesus Himself said that "**Do not think that I came to destroy the Law or the Prophets. I did not come to destroy but to fulfill**." But we have thrown the Law and the Prophets away. We have made it entirely about teaching the Word of God and even that, there are too many errors. And we have made it as if nothing is relevant in the Old Testament anymore.

Matthew 17:1-13

Jesus Transfigured on the Mount

17 Now after six days Jesus took Peter, James, and John his brother, led them up on a high mountain by themselves; **²** and He was transfigured before them. His face shone like the sun, and His clothes became as white as the light. **³ And behold, Moses and Elijah appeared to them, talking with Him**. **⁴** Then Peter answered and said to Jesus, "Lord, it is good for us to be here; if You wish, **let us make here three tabernacles: one for You, one for Moses, and one for Elijah**."

⁵ While he was still speaking, behold, a bright cloud overshadowed them; and suddenly a voice came out of the cloud, saying, "This is My beloved Son, in whom I am well pleased. Hear Him!" **⁶** And when the disciples heard *it,* they fell on their faces and were greatly afraid. **⁷** But Jesus came and touched them and said, "Arise, and do not be afraid." **⁸** When they had lifted up their eyes, they saw no one but Jesus only.

⁹ Now as they came down from the mountain, Jesus commanded them, saying, "Tell the vision to no one until the Son of Man is risen from the dead."

¹⁰ And His disciples asked Him, saying, "Why then do the scribes say that Elijah must come first?"

¹¹ Jesus answered and said to them, "Indeed, Elijah is coming first and will restore all things. **¹²** But I say to you that Elijah has come already, and they did not know him but did to him whatever they wished. Likewise, the Son of Man is also about to suffer at their hands." **13** Then the disciples understood that He spoke to them of John the Baptist.

Study the above scriptures very carefully and pay attention to the bolded lines. This is the current mistake of the Church – the Church has almost ignored the Old Testament and made it very irrelevant. Moses and Elijah appeared to them because that was to reveal to Peter, James, and John that Jesus Christ is indeed a prophecy to fulfil the Law and the Prophets. In other words, Jesus Christ is three-in-one – Jesus Christ is a hybrid, and His Church needs to be a hybrid Church which should fulfil both the Law and the Prophets according to the patterns and ordinances of the Ezekiel Temple. Those patterns and ordinances include the finished work of Jesus Christ. Our generation should be the Jesus Christ breed – that is, the hybrid of Jesus Christ, and the Law and the Prophets. But currently, the Church is a New Testament Church and that is the problem. There is no power and no manifestation. Even the slightest manifestation seems "supernatural" and unreal. This is the problem. There is no spirituality in the Church. The Church now is only trying to continue been disciples but ones without much knowledge and understanding. The Church lacks revelation.

The Church in our time needs to be a perfection of both Jesus Christ, and the Law and the Prophets, which is the model after Jesus Christ. If the Old Testament were irrelevant, then Moses and Elijah would not have appeared to Jesus Christ and the three disciples on the Mount of Transfiguration. This is a very key revelation that he gave to Peter, James, and John. And He picked three disciples for this revelation to also prove to them that after His death and resurrection, humanity once again can walk in the fullness of the Godhead – Father, Son, and Holy Spirit, still with full submission to the Law and the Prophets. So, man again should be able to once again walk in his rightful heritage as a god on Earth, just like Moses, Elijah, and Jesus Christ did.

Exodus 7:1

7 So the Lord said to Moses: "See, I have made you *as* God to Pharaoh, and Aaron your brother shall be your prophet.

Like I said earlier, the Bible is replaying until the Church comes to this understanding to get it right. The simple revelation is that Jesus Christ appeared twice after His resurrection – the first, to Mary Magdalene. This one represents the Church during the rapture. Only the Church will see Jesus Christ. The second one was His return before the ascension, after which the Holy Ghost was sent as a Helper to the Church. This one will be the replay or repeat of the second coming of Jesus Christ. During this return, everybody will see Him.

This is the same way Jesus Christ had always been in the Old Testament until His birth and ministry, death, and resurrection and then continued ministry. Moses represented Jesus Christ in His days, and so did Elijah. Moses represented Jesus Christ because until today, nobody knows where exactly he was buried or knows where his body is. This is the mystery and the revelation. The second ascension of Jesus Christ was Elijah. Elijah represented Jesus Christ because he is the only one with a recorded ascension like Jesus Christ. And Jesus Christ came to fulfil both mysteries. His body was not found in His tomb, and only Mary Magdalene saw Him. And He ascended to Heaven while many eyes watched. This is how "history" repeats itself in the Bible. So now, you will truly understand the illusion of time. Everything is already there and always happening or playing. You just need the grace to discern the times and season to be well aligned with the purposes of God. This proves that truly, Jesus Christ will return twice again. We all have a part to play, and we are supposed to be characters in the Bible in the strategies and agenda of God. Earth is not a playground to be moving about or living carelessly as if it's about money, cars, and other material things. Be wise and wake up.

This again is why an antichrist will arise to occupy the temple in Jerusalem and show himself to be the Christ because we are in the last days and people are now going to awaken to these truths and believe in the Word of God, and all the prophecies and events as they continue to unfold.

Matthew 24:23-25

[23] "Then if anyone says to you, 'Look, here *is* the Christ!' or 'There!' do not believe *it.* [24] For false christs and false prophets will rise and show great signs and wonders to deceive, if possible, even the elect. [25] See, I have told you beforehand.

Ephesians 5:14

[14] Wherefore he saith, Awake thou that sleepest, and arise from the dead, and Christ shall give thee light.

Matthew 13:9

[9] He who has ears to hear, let him hear!"

Now that you know this, what season or time in the Bible are we in?

Your eyes are opening right now. This is the truth and spirituality of life. Life is very spiritual. Spirituality is the reality of life. Life is not science, physics, or engineering. Life is a live battle or war between light and darkness, truth and lie, or good and evil. Stop playing around with your soul. There are some satanic people who want to hide these truths from you but it's impossible. Wake up.

These revelations are to help you understand what I am about to tell you. Without a very good revelation of the Old Testament, you are a very lost and immature Christian. I don't care if you are even a teacher and or a preacher who has been standing in front of a congregation to preach for years.

I give you this background to help you see where our priesthood in the Body of Christ has fallen short. The scriptures below talk about the patterns of Moses' tabernacle or temple as showed to him by God.

The Tabernacle

Exodus 26:31-34

31 "You shall make a veil woven of blue, purple, and scarlet *thread,* and fine woven linen. It shall be woven with an artistic design of cherubim. 32 You shall hang it upon the four pillars of acacia *wood* overlaid with gold. Their hooks *shall be* gold, upon four sockets of silver. 33 And you shall hang the veil from the clasps. Then you shall bring the ark of the Testimony in there, behind the veil. The veil shall be a divider for you between the holy *place* and the Most Holy. 34 You shall put the mercy seat upon the ark of the Testimony in the Most Holy.

Matthew 27:51-53

51 Then, behold, the veil of the temple was torn in two from top to bottom; and the earth quaked, and the rocks were split, 52 and the graves were opened; and many bodies of the saints who had fallen asleep were raised; 53 and coming out of the graves after His resurrection, they went into the holy city and appeared to many.

This is how the veil was torn after the death of Jesus Christ on the cross. You see, in Heaven, nothing in terms of the setup of the throne room or tabernacle changed after the death of Jesus Christ. Everything remained intact because Earth is supposed to be a mirror of Heaven as originally planned by God and life is a journey. Life on Earth is God's strategy to restore what Adam lost in the Garden of Eden. This is the whole meaning of life – not money, cars, fame or becoming a celebrity, or social media etc. We are living dangerously and are in very dangerous times in the calendar of God. Focus on storing up your rewards in Heaven and not here on Earth. Even Solomon's temple doesn't exist in Israel right now but once upon a time, it was the temple that everybody talked about. Everything that was achieved or built and will ever be built physically here on Earth shall pass away. Only the Word of God remain true and are the writings that generation after generation seek to read and understand. I haven't looked but I haven't heard many if at all, talk about anything called the "dark book" or the "writings of the devil". But the Word of God stands and will continue to stand and be true.

Matthew 24:35

35 Heaven and earth will pass away, but My words will by no means pass away.

Why do I say all these? I say these because the Church doesn't reflect the tabernacle or temple in Heaven right now. Only the veil was written to be torn in the temple after Jesus Christ died on the cross. We can see that in the following scriptures.

Matthew 27:45-54

Jesus Dies on the Cross

[45] Now from the sixth hour until the ninth hour there was darkness over all the land. [46] And about the ninth hour Jesus cried out with a loud voice, saying, "Eli, Eli, lama sabachthani?" that is, "My God, My God, why have You forsaken Me?"

[47] Some of those who stood there, when they heard *that,* said, "This Man is calling for Elijah!" [48] Immediately one of them ran and took a sponge, filled *it* with sour wine and put *it* on a reed, and offered it to Him to drink.

[49] The rest said, "Let Him alone; let us see if Elijah will come to save Him."

[50] And Jesus cried out again with a loud voice and yielded up His spirit.

[51] Then, behold, **the veil of the temple was torn in two from top to bottom**; and the earth quaked, and the rocks were split, [52] **and the graves were opened; and many bodies of the saints who had fallen asleep were raised;** [53] **and coming out of the graves after His resurrection, they went into the holy city and appeared to many.**

[54] So when the centurion and those with him, who were guarding Jesus, saw the earthquake and the things that had happened, they feared greatly, saying, "Truly this was the Son of God!"

From the above scriptures, nothing else changed in the temple except the veil having torn in two from top to bottom after Jesus Christ died – everything else remained intact. The main reason for Jesus Christ's death was to save man from sin to remove the veil between man and God since the veil was a divider between them.

Exodus 26:31-34

[31] "You shall make a veil woven of blue, purple, and scarlet *thread,* and fine woven linen. It shall be woven with an artistic design of cherubim. [32] You shall hang it upon the four pillars of acacia *wood* overlaid with gold. Their hooks *shall be* gold, upon four sockets of silver. [33] And you shall hang the veil from the clasps. Then you shall bring the ark of the Testimony in there, behind the veil. **The veil shall be a divider for you between the holy *place* and the Most Holy.** [34] You shall put the mercy seat upon the ark of the Testimony in the Most Holy.

The tabernacle of the Israelites was a highly restricted area. Only Aaron and his descendants were allowed inside the tabernacle to offer sacrifices. Aaron was a Levite – that is, a descendant of Jacob's son Levi. To be a priest, one must be a Levite. On the other hand, not all Levites were priests. Only a particular family of Levites, the Kohathites, could become priests. Other Levites, however, were involved in the maintenance and transport of the tabernacle. Penalties for violating access to the tabernacle and its contents were so severe as to result in leprosy or death.

Certain rituals inside the tabernacle were so specific that improper administration likewise resulted in death.

Jesus Christ's death was to remove all these hard restrictions so that whatever your background or race or gender is, you can have equal access to come in His presence as only the priests had access to minister directly to God in ancient times. It's not written, or I don't read anywhere that anything else other than the veil got torn to give us direct access into the presence God.

So, you see, this has been the error in the Church and the Church is like in a merry-go-round like the Israelites did in the days of Moses. Kingdom will not come this way – it's impossible. It's as if the Word is noneffective but it's because we lack the knowledge, understanding, practice, and true demonstration of the Word of God. We misinterpreted things.

So, to have a better understanding of what the secret place is, we must first understand the basic requirements or what the tabernacle or temple is made up of in terms of patterns and ordinances. David was a King, Priest, and Prophet, and he had other priests and prophets in his kingdom. This means that he heard and saw visions directly from God too. This is what is required of every true Christian, but it is not so in our days because we are in error, and we lack knowledge and understanding of the Word of God.

The Secret Place and Priesthood
Zechariah 12:7-9

7 "The LORD will save the tents of Judah first, so that the glory of the house of David and the glory of the inhabitants of Jerusalem shall not become greater than that of Judah. **8** In that day the LORD will defend the inhabitants of Jerusalem; **the one who is feeble among them in that day shall be like David, and the house of David *shall be* like God, like the Angel of the LORD before them**. **9** It shall be in that day *that* I will seek to destroy all the nations that come against Jerusalem.

If you heed to the things I write, then the scripture above will come to past again in our time. This is what this scripture means. This teaching will guide you to become spiritually fit in the Lord and become the King, Priest, and Prophet that you are destined to be in the Kingdom of God.

David truly knew the secret place and that is why he is used as a reference in this scripture above, and several others. Do you understand being a King and Priest?

1 Peter 2:9

9 But you *are* a chosen generation, a royal priesthood, a holy nation, His own special people, that you may proclaim the praises of Him who called you out of darkness into His marvelous light;

Revelation 1:1-6

Introduction and Benediction

1 The Revelation of Jesus Christ, which God gave Him to show His servants—things which must shortly take place. And He sent and signified *it* by His angel to His servant John, **2** who bore witness to the word of God, and to the testimony of Jesus Christ, to all things that he saw. **3** Blessed *is* he who reads and those who hear the words of this prophecy and keep those things which are written in it; for the time *is* near.

Greeting the Seven Churches

4 John, to the seven Churches which are in Asia:

Grace to you and peace from Him who is and who was and who is to come, and from the seven Spirits who are before His throne, **5** and from Jesus Christ, the faithful witness, the firstborn from the dead, and the ruler over the kings of the earth.

To Him who loved us and washed us from our sins in His own blood, **6 and has made us kings and priests to His God and Father**, to Him *be* glory and dominion forever and ever. Amen.

It is very important to note that the end is very near. The patterns of the Old Testament tabernacle or temple MUST be kept. You are doing a good job by praying and fasting, and trying to live a holy life etc. Keep it up but some things need to change for you to become the hybrid (the Law and the Prophets, and Jesus Christ) that you must be to truly become a King and Priest.

Let's study some patterns in the lifestyles of some patriarchs. Below is one of the testimonies of Moses. Moses literally lived on the mountain in consistent fasting and prayer.

Exodus 24:15-17

15 Then Moses went up into the mountain, and a cloud covered the mountain.

16 Now the glory of the LORD rested on Mount Sinai, and the cloud covered it six days**. And on the seventh day He called to Moses out of the midst of the cloud**. **17** The sight of the glory of the LORD *was* like a consuming fire on the top of the mountain in the eyes of the children of Israel.

The following are some testimonies of David.

Psalm 91:1

91 He who dwells in the **secret place** of the Most High
Shall abide under the shadow of the Almighty.

[2] I will say of the LORD, "*He is* my refuge and my fortress;
My God, in Him I will trust."

Psalm 119:164

[164] **Seven times a day do I praise thee** because of thy righteous judgments.

Psalm 63:1-2

63 O God, thou art my God; **early will I seek thee**: my soul thirsteth for thee, my flesh longeth for thee in a dry and thirsty land, where no water is;

[2] **To see thy power and thy glory**, so as I have seen thee in the sanctuary.

Below is a testimony of Daniel.

Daniel 6:10

[10] Now when Daniel knew that the writing was signed, he went home. And in his upper room, with his windows open toward Jerusalem, **he knelt down on his knees three times that day, and prayed and gave thanks before his God, as was his custom since early days**.

Below is a testimony of Elijah.

James 5:17

[17] Elijah was a man with a nature like ours, **and he prayed earnestly** that it would not rain; and it did not rain on the land for three years and six months.

1 Kings 18:44

[44] **Then it came to pass the seventh** *time,* that he said, "There is a cloud, as small as a man's hand, rising out of the sea!" So, he said, "Go up, say to Ahab, 'Prepare *your chariot,* and go down before the rain stops you.'"

Below is Jesus' custom before His death.

Luke 22:39

The Prayer in the Garden

[39] **Coming out, He went to the Mount of Olives, as He was accustomed**, and His disciples also followed Him. [40] When He came to the place, He said to them, "Pray that you may not enter into temptation."

And this is Jesus' testimony after His resurrection.

Luke 24:44-49

The Scriptures Opened

[44] Then He said to them, "These *are* the words which I spoke to you while I was still with you, **that all things must be fulfilled which were written in the Law of Moses and *the* Prophets and *the* Psalms concerning Me**." [45] And He opened their understanding, that they might comprehend the Scriptures.

[46] Then He said to them, "**Thus it is written, and thus it was necessary for the Christ to suffer and to rise from the dead the third day,** [47] **and that repentance and remission of sins should be preached in His name to all nations, beginning at Jerusalem**. [48] And you are witnesses of these things. [49] Behold, I send the Promise of My Father upon you; but tarry in the city of Jerusalem until you are endued with power from on high."

So, what exactly is the secret place?

If there is one word to describe what we see in the lives of all these persons, it is **consistency**. Prayer and fasting are a custom – they aren't occasional, or whenever you feel like it and when you don't then you go for many hours or days or weeks or even months without prayer. That is risky living. If you live like this, then you are like a computer system that is not regularly patched with the most recent updates – you are vulnerable and can easily be infected by viruses. In this context, viruses are demons and the full package that they come with such as persistent issues, sicknesses, wickedness, hate, greed, selfishness, corruption, lust, immorality etc.

The similarities that we see in the lives of Moses, David, Daniel, Elijah, and Jesus is what is called priesthood. This is an intentional customary life of dedicating yourself to prayer, fasting, worship, praises, and holy living according to the laws of God, consistently and permanently until you leave the Earth. **This is priesthood**. You want to be like any of them, then you must live your life like this – with some intention, discipline, and consistency.

The key thing here is that the temple which was designed according to the patterns of Heaven did not change. The only thing that changed after Jesus Christ died on the cross was the veil. We are the temple of God, yes. And we are a symbol of the Ark of the Covenant with the mercy seat upon us in the Most Holy place.

The temple structure or pattern did not change – only a mystery changed in the spiritual realm, which unveiled God's original plan to restore man into His presence. Why do we think that although we have the Holy Spirit indwelling us, we have to do away with the old temple pattern? Yes, we are in God and God is us.

1 John 4:16

[16] And we have known and believed the love that God has for us. **God is love, and he who abides in love abides in God, and God in him**.

Although this scripture is true, and everything that was in the Ark of the Covenant is in us, where did we put the pattern of the temple? Who said to Christians that the heavenly pattern is archaic or doesn't apply because of the Blood of Jesus? In our time, the place where we must worship the Lord according to the patterns and ordinances of Heaven is in the Ezekiel Temple. Let's look at the scriptures below.

Hebrews 8

The New Priestly Service

8 Now *this is* the main point of the things we are saying: We have such a High Priest, who is seated at the right hand of the throne of the Majesty in the heavens, [2] a Minister of the sanctuary and of the true tabernacle which the Lord erected, and not man.

[3] For every high priest is appointed to offer both gifts and sacrifices. Therefore, *it is* necessary that this One also have something to offer. [4] For if He were on earth, He would not be a priest, since there are priests who offer the gifts according to the law; [5] who serve the copy and shadow of the heavenly things, as Moses was divinely instructed when he was about to make the tabernacle. For He said, "See *that* you make all things according to the pattern shown you on the mountain." [6] But now He has obtained a more excellent ministry, inasmuch as He is also Mediator of a better covenant, which was established on better promises.

A New Covenant

[7] For if that first *covenant* had been faultless, then no place would have been sought for a second. [8] Because finding fault with them, He says: "Behold, the days are coming, says the LORD, when I will make a new covenant with the house of Israel and with the house of Judah— [9] not according to the covenant that I made with their fathers in the day when I took them by the hand to lead them out of the land of Egypt; because they did not continue in My covenant, and I disregarded them, says the LORD. [10] **For this *is* the covenant that I will make with the house of Israel after those days, says the LORD: I will put My laws in their mind and write them on their hearts; and I will be their God, and they shall be My people. [11] None of them shall teach his neighbor, and none his brother, saying, 'Know the LORD,' for all shall know Me, from the least of them to the greatest of them. [12] For I will be merciful to their unrighteousness, and their sins and their lawless deeds I will remember no more."**

[13] In that He says, "A new *covenant*," **He has made the first obsolete.** Now what is becoming obsolete and growing old is ready to vanish away.

It is very important to note that the first or old covenant being talked about here is the Ark of the Covenant. That is what God has made away with, and the veil. The scriptures specifically say that.

It is very clear that the new covenant being talked about here as Jesus Christ offered pertains to our sinful nature and NOT the pattern of the temple and ordinances of our worship or way of priesthood. Yes, our high priest is Jesus Christ, but He clearly didn't say that change the pattern and way of worship in the temple. **This is very important.** This is where Christianity have missed it big time and have lost the spirituality in the faith which has made the Church very powerless.

The patterns of the temple must still be kept minus the veil and the Ark of the Covenant because we believers are the Ark of the Covenant. Everything else in terms of pattern of the temple stays and remains true because that is how it is in Heaven. Once we get this Old Testament piece right and join it with the New Testament, then the spirituality of the Church will be correctly exercised, and true raw power shall return to the Body of Christ. Without this, the Church is in BIG trouble.

I don't know who got rid of the idea of the old temple patterns and ordinances. The church has been doing whatever they like – just like how the scriptures are picked and chosen for teaching and preaching, but not everything is taught and preached. This is wrong. We can keep the current churches in which we worship for more larger gatherings, to learn the Word of God. There's nothing wrong with that because we can't destroy them and those are going to be our means to still spread the gospel. But if we want to see the Glory of God as needed in this end time, the Lord demands that we build the Ezekiel Temple now and follow the patterns and ordinances as required.

You can cast out demons and heal some of the sick – well done but that's not everything. There is more and even better. This is a hybrid of the old covenant and the new covenant minus what Jesus Christ has done for us. These two equals true power. I will explain more on this revelation towards the end.

Remember, Jesus Christ still references the Old Testament and mentions how He came to fulfil it as a hybrid. If you read the scriptures below, you will know and understand that Jesus Christ still talks about the law. The difference in the new covenant is that the law is written in your heart or conscience. That is the Holy Spirit and the reason why you judge yourself or feel bad whenever you do something bad. Jesus Christ did not take the law away or remove the law. The law still exists and must be followed.

Luke 18:15-23

Jesus Blesses Little Children

[15] Then they also brought infants to Him that He might touch them; but when the disciples saw *it,* they rebuked them. [16] But Jesus called them to *Him* and said, "Let the little children come to Me, and do not forbid them; for of such is the kingdom of God. [17] Assuredly, I say to you, whoever does not receive the kingdom of God as a little child will by no means enter it."

Jesus Counsels the Rich Young Ruler

18 Now a certain ruler asked Him, saying, "Good Teacher, what shall I do to inherit eternal life?"

19 So Jesus said to him, "Why do you call Me good? No one *is* good but One, *that is,* God. 20 You know the commandments: 'Do not commit adultery,' 'Do not murder,' 'Do not steal,' 'Do not bear false witness,' 'Honor your father and your mother.'"

21 And he said, "All these things I have kept from my youth."

22 So when Jesus heard these things, He said to him, "You still lack one thing. Sell all that you have and distribute to the poor, and you will have treasure in heaven; and come, follow Me."

23 But when he heard this, he became very sorrowful, for he was very rich.

So, the patterns and ordinances of the temple MUST be restored – specifically, the Ezekiel Temple, with every detail. Once we achieve this, we can mimic it in our homes for whenever we are not at the temples. Every home that follows this, to at least have an altar in your prayer rooms means an open portal for the Heavens – the angelic and the Almighty Himself.

Keeping the Body or Temple of God Pure and Holy

Like I said earlier, Jesus Christ died for the remission of our sins so that we will not keep killing animals to pacify God etc. That is why Jesus Christ died for us and sent us the Holy Spirit to help us walk well in the law. Remember, as we read earlier, He still put the laws in our minds and wrote them on our hearts so that we will be able to stay righteous in the Name of Jesus. Most Christians think and believe that the law and the purifying ways or lifestyle in the old testament are not relevant anymore. They are all very wrong. This is the reason for the lack of power or spiritual capacity in the Church. It is not only fasting and prayers. You must follow the laws to stay clean for the Holy Spirit to abide in you so that you can host and maintain virtue. Let's look at a good example next.

Some Examples for Both Men and Women

Leviticus 15:16-18

16 'If any man has an emission of semen, then he shall wash all his body in water, and be unclean until evening. **17** And any garment and any leather on which there is semen, it shall be washed with water, and be unclean until evening. **18** Also, when a woman lies with a man, and *there is* an emission of semen, they shall bathe in water, and be unclean until evening.

How many people follow these laws? These laws still apply today – I don't see Jesus Christ cancelling any of these laws. You would be surprised at how many men and women carelessly sleep with even their spouses and believe that just because they are legally married, they are automatically clean and then go straight to the presence of God and or even to Church, and or to teach and preach if they are men or women of God. You must follow these laws which still apply. You must be very conscious of these things.

Leviticus 15:19-21

[19] 'If a woman has a discharge, *and* the discharge from her body is blood, she shall be set apart seven days; and whoever touches her shall be unclean until evening. [20] Everything that she lies on during her impurity shall be unclean; also, everything that she sits on shall be unclean. [21] Whoever touches her bed shall wash his clothes and bathe in water and be unclean until evening.

I am sure that you understand the above scriptures very well. What does that tell you about staying with your wife in the same bed or touching her etc., while she's menstruating? You lose virtue. In other words, you lose power. I hope you are paying attention and reading to understand. A spiritual man doesn't come in physical contact or touch his wife when it's that time of the month – you stay clear of her and anything she touches etc. If you are a true spiritual man, you need to have a second bed or sleeping place during that time of the month. Being spiritual and staying with power comes with a cost, people. We have even men of God nowadays who don't know and understand this, so they leave their matrimonial beds, thinking that they still have power, but the people don't get blessed at Church because these men of God lack virtue.

Mark 5:25-34

[25] Now a certain woman had a flow of blood for twelve years, [26] and had suffered many things from many physicians. She had spent all that she had and was no better, but rather grew worse. [27] When she heard about Jesus, she came behind *Him* in the crowd and touched His garment. [28] For she said, "If only I may touch His clothes, I shall be made well."

[29] Immediately the fountain of her blood was dried up, and she felt in *her* body that she was healed of the affliction. [30] And Jesus, immediately knowing in Himself that power had gone out of Him, turned around in the crowd and said, "Who touched My clothes?"

[31] But His disciples said to Him, "You see the multitude thronging You, and You say, 'Who touched Me?'"

[32] And He looked around to see her who had done this thing. [33] But the woman, fearing and trembling, knowing what had happened to her, came and fell down before Him and told Him the whole truth. [34] And He said to her, "Daughter, your faith has made you well. Go in peace and be healed of your affliction."

From the scriptures above, why do you think that Jesus felt that power had gone out of Him? I will let you answer that question yourself. The Church is very immature and doesn't understand spirituality. The few who understand these things host true power. True Christianity is more than fasting and prayers and holy living. There are still strict spiritual laws, and it requires discipline. Casting out demons is the least you can do. That doesn't require power – it requires authority through your understanding of who you are in Christ.

Types of Offerings in the Old Testament

There are five types of offering in the old testament – burnt offering, grain offering, peace offering, sin offering, and trespass offering.

At least we know that we have the grace of God through the death of Jesus Christ for the remission of our sins and so, our sins are forgiven. **So, we can all agree that Jesus Christ is our perfect burnt, sin, and trespass offerings. There are at least two types of offering we see here, which don't have anything to do with sin. These are the grain offering, and the peace offering**. We know that almost all Churches still give some type of offering. Which category does this offering fall into – is it the grain offering or the peace offering or both? How come we don't see these types of offerings in the Church today? Well, we don't even have the required temples to begin with. But one more offering is needful – that is, the purification offering because although the Blood of Jesus Christ washes away our sins, we still must treat the presence of God with reverence. The same way you shower, and dress clean before an interview. But this is not just staying clean in a physical sense but in a spiritual sense. The guidance has already been given in Leviticus. In our societies though, we still pay for all these without the grace of God because of the court and law system.

Why do we not say that by the grace of God, we will worship God without giving any offerings to help the work of God? Then the work will not progress. Jesus Christ died to save us from our sins and to give us eternal life through a restored relationship with the Father through the Holy Spirit. Why have Christians stopped giving intentional grain offering and the peace offering other than the other three sin offerings that Jesus Christ already paid for? Like some will argue, if God does not dwell in temples, why did He give Ezekiel a vision of a temple without a veil and an Ark of the Covenant? Well, God wants His temple built exactly according to what He revealed to Ezekiel. He wants the exact patterns and ordinances to be followed and the required offerings to be given to Him accordingly. This is what He has revealed to me.

If the temple, patterns and ordinances in the Old Testament are wrong or completely wiped away because of the death of Jesus Christ, then why do we still tithe? Where is it written or where did Jesus Christ say that His death paid for the temple, and all the offerings? God still take offerings, and that is why the Lamb had to die for us because sin is our biggest problem, and it is because of sin that were unable to have a direct relationship with God. It is because a day like this will come, God gave Ezekiel a vision of the final temple as it is in Heaven, which has no veil and Ark of the Covenant to prove that Jesus Christ has cleared a major problem for us. And that temple is supposed to be for both Jews and Gentiles, male and female, young and old, people of all races and color etc. So, the new covenant came to address **only** the old covenant, and that old covenant was very specific to the Ark of the Covenant, which sat behind the veil in the tabernacle or temple by removing that veil and then the Ark of the Covenant to grant us direct access to God once again. You can review the instructions of Moses' temple in Exodus 37 and there are very specific instructions. The first instruction was to build the **Ark of the Covenant**, then the Table for the Showbread, then the Gold Lampstand, then the Altar of Incense, then the Anointing Oil and the Incense, then the Altar of Burnt Offering, then the Bronze Laver, then the Court of the Tabernacle, then the Garments of the Priesthood, then the Ephod, then the breastplate, then the other Priestly Garments, and finally, the work was completed. We see a big list of items here. Sadly, we have misunderstood the mystery of the Blood of Jesus Christ. What Jesus Christ did was also to make us a moving Ark of the Covenant because during the early days, the Ark of the Covenant had to always be amid the Israelites – that signified and maintained the Presence of God. Aside the spiritual power from this mystery, we have no burden of carrying a physical ark around. So, now that we are fully the Temple of God and God dwells in us through the mystery of the Blood of Jesus Christ and we carry His presence, we are a moving temple, but it doesn't mean that we must destroy the physical temple. Read the scriptures below.

Revelation 7:15

[15] Therefore they are before the throne of God and serve Him day and night in His temple. And He who sits on the throne will dwell among them.

Revelation 11:1-2

The Two Witnesses

11 Then I was given a reed like a measuring rod. And the angel stood, saying, "**Rise and measure the temple of God, the altar, and those who worship there**. [2] But leave out the court, which is outside the temple, and do not measure it, for it has been given to the Gentiles. And they will tread the holy city underfoot *for* forty-two months.

Revelation 11:19

[19] Then the **temple of God was opened in heaven**, and **the ark of His covenant was seen in His temple**. And there were lightnings, noises, thunderings, an earthquake, and great hail.

Revelation 12:17

[17] And the dragon was enraged with the woman, and he went to make war with the rest of her offspring, **who keep the commandments of God** and have **the testimony of Jesus Christ**.

Revelation 14:15

[15] And another angel came out of the **temple**, crying with a loud voice to Him who sat on the cloud, "Thrust in Your sickle and reap, for the time has come for You to reap, for the harvest of the earth is ripe."

Revelation 14:17-18

[17] **Then another angel came out of the temple, which is in heaven**, he also having a sharp sickle.

[18] **And another angel came out from the altar, who had power over fire**, and he cried with a loud cry to him who had the sharp sickle, saying, "Thrust in your sharp sickle and gather the clusters of the vine of the earth, for her grapes are fully ripe."

Revelation 15:5-8

[5] After these things I looked, and behold, **the temple of the tabernacle of the testimony in heaven was opened**. [6] And out of the **temple** came the seven angels having the seven plagues, clothed in pure bright linen, and having their chests girded with golden bands. [7] Then one of the four living creatures gave to the seven angels seven golden bowls full of the wrath of God who lives forever and ever. [8] **The temple** was filled with smoke from the glory of God and from His power, and no one was able to enter the **temple** till the seven plagues of the seven angels were completed.

Revelation 16:1

The Seven Bowls

16 Then I heard a loud voice from **the temple** saying to the seven angels, "Go and pour out the bowls of the wrath of God on the earth."

Revelation 16:17

Seventh Bowl: The Earth Utterly Shaken

[17] Then the seventh angel poured out his bowl into the air, and a loud voice came out of the **temple** of heaven, from the throne, saying, "It is done!"

Revelation 22:14

[14] **Blessed** *are* **those who do His commandments**, that they may have the right to the tree of life and may enter through the gates into the city.

Psalm 132:7-9

[7] **Let us go into His tabernacle;**
Let us worship at His footstool.
[8] **Arise, O Lord, to Your resting place**,
You and the **ark of Your strength**.

⁹ Let Your priests be clothed with righteousness,
And let Your saints shout for joy.

Psalm 132:14

¹⁴ "This *is* My resting place forever;
Here I will dwell, for I have desired it.

Isaiah 66:1-4

True Worship and False

66 Thus says the LORD:

"**Heaven *is* My throne**,
And earth *is* My footstool.
Where *is* the house that you will build Me?
And where *is* the place of My rest?
² For all those *things* My hand has made,
And all those *things* exist,"
Says the LORD.
"But on this *one* will I look:
On *him who is* poor and of a contrite spirit,
And who trembles at My word.
³ "**He who kills a bull** *is as if* **he slays a man;**
He **who sacrifices a lamb**, *as if* he breaks a dog's neck;
He **who offers a grain offering**, *as if he offers* swine's blood;
He **who burns incense**, *as if* he blesses an idol.
Just as they have chosen their own ways,
And their soul delights in their abominations,
⁴ So will I choose their delusions,
And bring their fears on them;
Because, when I called, no one answered,
When I spoke they did not hear;
But they did evil before My eyes,
And chose *that* in which I do not delight."

In Psalm 132:7-1, we see a call to go into His tabernacle because it is His resting place. The Psalmist specifically mentions first, "God", and second the "ark of His strength". This means that the ark is only a dimension of God – His presence and Strength. So, God and His ark "the Body of Christ", still need to go into His tabernacle and meet there. If you keep reading on in the next scriptures, you will notice that we still must give offering to the Lord, burn incense etc. **Isaiah 66:3 is key – this is what Jesus Christ paid for us**. So, whatever sacrifice that requires a bull, is what we don't give to God anymore in the temple because Jesus Christ already paid for it. It is also key to know and understand that this same verse is why Jesus Christ must die for our sins because in the spirit, an exchange can be made between a bull and a man. It is my understanding that this is one of the many ways that fetish people conjure spirits to kill men spiritually using bulls. This is the reason behind why a bull was used for the sin offering in the tabernacle or temple.

What Exactly Jesus Christ Did for the World

Leviticus 16:1-3

The Day of Atonement

16 Now the LORD spoke to Moses after the death of the two sons of Aaron, when they offered *profane fire* before the LORD, and died; **2** and the LORD said to Moses: "**Tell Aaron your brother not to come at *just* any time into the Holy *Place* inside the veil, before the mercy seat which *is* on the ark, lest he die; for I will appear in the cloud above the mercy seat**.

3 "**Thus Aaron shall come into the Holy *Place:* with *the blood of* a young bull as a sin offering, and *of* a ram as a burnt offering**.

You can read the whole chapter of Leviticus 16 to learn more. But people, this is what Jesus Christ paid for – nothing more, nothing less. This atonement is very SPECIFIC to the Holy Place inside the veil before the mercy seat which is on the ark. This atonement equals the Blood of Jesus Christ.

John 1:29

The Lamb of God

29 The next day John saw Jesus coming toward him, and said, "Behold! The Lamb of God who takes away the sin of the world!

1 John 2:2

2 He is the atoning sacrifice for our sins, and not only for ours but also for the **sins of the whole world**.

Hebrews 2:17

17 For this reason he had to be made like them, fully human in every way, in order that he might become a merciful and **faithful high priest in service to God**, and that he might **make atonement for the sins of the people**.

1 John 3:5

5 And you know that He was manifested to take away our sins, and in Him there is no sin.

You can reference this fact and mystery repeatedly in Matthew 1:21, Romans 3:25, 1 Corinthians 15:3, Galatians 1:4, Ephesians 1:7, 1 Peter 3:18, Hebrews 1:3, 1 John 4:10 etc.

It is clearly stated in the scriptures above – it's all there. So, now you know exactly what Jesus Christ did. Now you will understand what the Church has been missing and lacking all these years, which has resulted to the world that we are currently experiencing and the lack of power in the Body of Christ. But it is not too late. It has been appointed in our time to make things right – so we will. I pray that you will understand the scriptures below.

Psalm 95

A Call to Worship and Obedience

95 Oh come, let us sing to the LORD!
Let us shout joyfully to the Rock of our salvation.
2 Let us come before His presence with thanksgiving;
Let us shout joyfully to Him with psalms.
3 For the LORD *is* the great God,
And the great King above all gods.
4 In His hand *are* the deep places of the earth;
The heights of the hills *are* His also.
5 The sea *is* His, for He made it;
And His hands formed the dry *land.*
6 Oh come, let us worship and bow down;
Let us kneel before the LORD our Maker.
7 For He *is* our God,
And we *are* the people of His pasture,
And the sheep of His hand.
Today, if you will hear His voice:
8 "Do not harden your hearts, as in the rebellion,
As *in* the day of trial in the wilderness,
9 When your fathers tested Me;
They tried Me, though they saw My work.
10 For forty years I was grieved with *that* generation,
And said, 'It *is* a people who go astray in their hearts,
And they do not know My ways.'
11 So I swore in My wrath,
'They shall not enter My rest.'"

Now, read Hebrews chapter 3 then read the following scriptures.

Hebrews 4:14-16

Our Compassionate High Priest

[14] Seeing then that we have a great High Priest who has passed through the heavens, Jesus the Son of God, let us hold fast *our* confession. [15] For we do not have a High Priest who cannot sympathize with our weaknesses, but was in all *points* tempted as *we are, yet* without sin. [16] Let us therefore come boldly to the throne of grace, that we may obtain mercy and find grace to help in time of need.

We can see the importance of what Jesus Christ has done for us. Therefore, there is no condemnation due to sin to those who are in Christ Jesus. I strongly encourage you to read the whole chapter of Romans 8.

Romans 8:1-2

Free from Indwelling Sin

8 *There is* therefore now **no condemnation to those who are in Christ Jesus**, who do not walk according to the flesh, but according to the Spirit. [2] For the law of the Spirit of life in Christ Jesus **has made me free from the law of sin and death**.

The law of sin and death was activated by Adam and Eve from eating of the tree of the knowledge of good and evil in the Garden of Eden. The law of sin and death is one of the many laws in the Kingdom of God. Jesus Christ paid with His life to make us free from specifically the law of sin and death – nothing more, nothing less. You must understand this because this has been a very BIG misinterpretation and misunderstanding in the lives of Christians. This deficiency in the knowledge and understanding of Christians has almost made the kingdom of darkness free from judgement – you can only imagine how long they have been given a break. That long break ends now.

Genesis 2:17

[17] but of the tree of the knowledge of good and evil you shall not eat, for in the day that you eat of it you shall surely die."

Revelation 22:1-2

The River of Life

22 And he showed me a pure river of water of life, clear as crystal, proceeding from the throne of God and of the Lamb. **2** In the middle of its street, and on either side of the river, *was* the tree of life, which bore twelve fruits, each *tree* yielding its fruit every month. The leaves of the tree *were* for the healing of the nations.

Jesus Christ clearly came to demonstrate the above scriptures to the world. He confirmed it with His twelve Apostles. Read Genesis 2:8-9, Genesis 3:22-24, Proverbs 3:18, Revelation 2:7, Revelation 22:14-15 etc., to learn more about the tree of life.

Hebrews 13:7-16

Concluding Religious Directions

7 Remember those who rule over you, who have spoken the word of God to you, whose faith follow, considering the outcome of *their* conduct. **8** Jesus Christ *is* the same yesterday, today, and forever. **9** Do not be carried about with various and strange doctrines. For *it is* good that the heart be established by grace, not with foods which have not profited those who have been occupied with them.

10 We have an altar from which those who serve the tabernacle have no right to eat. **11 For the bodies of those animals, whose blood is brought into the sanctuary by the high priest for sin, are burned outside the camp**. **12 Therefore Jesus also, that He might sanctify the people with His own blood, suffered outside the gate**. **13** Therefore let us go forth to Him, outside the camp, bearing His reproach. **14** For here we have no continuing city, but we seek the one to come. **15** Therefore by Him let us continually offer the sacrifice of praise to God, that is, the fruit of *our* lips, giving thanks to His name. **16** But do not forget to do good and to share, for with such sacrifices God is well pleased.

From the above scriptures, I want to emphasize the phrase in verse 11; "**for sin**" – for sin and sin only. Also, verse 13 clearly states what we do in the Church now:

13 Therefore let us go forth to Him, outside the camp, bearing His reproach.

That is the Apostleship, Prophetic, Evangelical, Pastor and Teacher type ministries that we currently practice as servants of God. Aside the law of sin and death that Jesus Christ paid for us with His Blood, these are the new things He introduced to the Body of Christ. So, we can continue to do these things to reach out to a broader audience and at the same time carry out our priestly duties in the temple.

1 Corinthians 9:21

21 to those *who are* without law, as without law (**not being without law toward God, but under law toward Christ**), that I might win those *who are* without law;

This simply means that the servant of God is still under the law of God but through Jesus Christ because Jesus Christ paid for the law of sin and death, which broke the veil between man and God. Jesus Christ simply replaced the veil and the Ark of the Covenant with Himself. God started with the Law and the Prophets but couldn't completely accomplish the atonement for our sins. Jesus Christ came as the tree of life and finally offered His precious blood to make atonement for our sins. We cannot go to the Father without going through the Son but what the Son did isn't all. The law of sin and death still exists under God, but it is only when you accept Jesus Christ that this one law is broken and replaced once and for all with Jesus Christ. This is what we call salvation. We still have our parts to play to perpetually make our salvation sure – this is through perpetually submitting to the laws of Jesus Christ. And since Jesus Christ is God, once you remain faithful to Him, all other laws of God still apply to you – minus the law of sin and death. We renew the law of sin and death by continuously repenting for our sins and living according to the ways of God. This act is what replaces our giving to God, a combination of a burnt offering and sin offering in the temple. The sin offering, trespass or guilt offering or any combination of these offerings with the burnt offering to make atonement for sin is what equates to the precious Life and Blood of our Lord and Savior Jesus Christ. The death of Jesus Christ cancels the sin and trespass or guilt offerings. Every other ordinance remains.

I can keep giving you scripture after scripture but people of God, until we build the Ezekiel Temple and start worshipping accordingly, we can never bring judgement on the kingdom of darkness. There are special hybrid dimensions that only the Ezekiel Temple can activate. This is what the Lord has said to me. We are a generation of hybrids – a kind that the Heavens and the Earth have not encountered before.

The death of Jesus Christ equals the perpetual atonement of sin, which at the time required a combination of the burnt offering, and the sin offering. The main offering though is the sin offering. The burnt offering is a private offering to God, which by itself has nothing to do with the atonement of sin. By itself, it is a personal, private voluntary offering to God. That leaves us with four other offerings that we can give to God.

Now, my advice to the people of God are the following scriptures. I am only a messenger and a teacher of the good old paths.

Jeremiah 6:16-18

16 Thus says the LORD:

"Stand in the ways and see,
And ask for the old paths, where the good way *is*,

And walk in it;
Then you will find rest for your souls.
But they said, 'We will not walk *in it*.'
¹⁷ Also, I set watchmen over you, *saying,*
'Listen to the sound of the trumpet!'
But they said, 'We will not listen.'
¹⁸ Therefore hear, you nations,
And know, O congregation, what *is* among them.

But if you don't heed to the message that I bring to you from the Lord and the things which I teach, then the following scriptures will happen to you.

Jeremiah 6:19

¹⁹ Hear, O earth!
Behold, I will certainly bring calamity on this people—
The fruit of their thoughts,
Because they have not heeded My words
Nor My law but rejected it.

The Required Offerings That Need to Be Restored

The burnt offering can well be interpreted from the story of Noah. Creation is still benefiting from Noah's offering – not because of the precious Blood of Jesus. You must know and understand the difference. The burnt offering alone or together with the grain offering isn't for the atonement of sins. You can research these two offerings in detail.

Genesis 8:20-21

God's Covenant with Creation

²⁰ Then Noah built an altar to the LORD, and took of every clean animal and of every clean bird, and **offered burnt offerings on the altar. **²¹ And the LORD smelled a soothing aroma**. Then the LORD said in His heart, "I will never again curse the ground for man's sake, although the imagination of man's heart *is* evil from his youth; nor will I again destroy every living thing as I have done.

Genesis 22:13-14

Abraham's Faith Confirmed

¹³ Then Abraham lifted his eyes and looked, and there behind *him was* a ram caught in a thicket by its horns. So, Abraham went and took the ram, and offered it up for **a burnt offering instead of his son. ¹⁴ And Abraham called the name of the place, The-LORD-Will-Provide; as it is said *to* this day, "In the Mount of the LORD it shall be provided."

The burnt offering and the grain offering are the two required daily offerings daily.

Exodus 29:38-42

The Daily Offerings

³⁸ "Now this *is* what you shall offer on the altar: two lambs of the first year, day by day continually. ³⁹ One lamb you shall offer in the morning, and the other lamb you shall offer at twilight. ⁴⁰ With the one lamb shall be one-tenth *of an ephah* of flour mixed with one-fourth of a hin of pressed oil, and one-fourth of a hin of wine *as* a drink offering. ⁴¹ And the other lamb you shall offer at twilight; and you shall offer with it the grain offering and the drink offering, as in the morning, for a sweet aroma, an offering made by fire to the LORD. ⁴² *This shall be* a continual burnt offering throughout your generations *at* the door of the tabernacle of meeting before the LORD, where I will meet you to speak with you.

Exodus 40:29

²⁹ And he put the altar of burnt offering *before* the door of the tabernacle of the tent of meeting and **offered upon it the burnt offering and the grain offering**, as the LORD had commanded Moses.

Numbers 28:3

³ "And you shall say to them, 'This *is* the offering made by fire which you shall offer to the LORD: two male lambs in their first year without blemish, day by day, as a regular burnt offering.

Numbers 28:9-10

Sabbath Offerings

⁹ 'And on the Sabbath day two lambs in their first year, without blemish, and two-tenths *of an ephah* of fine flour as a grain offering, mixed with oil, with its drink offering— ¹⁰ *this is* the burnt offering for every Sabbath, besides the regular burnt offering with its drink offering.

Numbers 28:11

Monthly Offerings

¹¹ 'At the beginnings of your months you shall present a burnt offering to the LORD: two young bulls, one ram, and seven lambs in their first year, without blemish;

Numbers 28:16

Offerings at Passover

[16] 'On the fourteenth day of the first month *is* the Passover of the Lord.

Numbers 28:26-27

Offerings at the Feast of Weeks

[26] 'Also on the day of the firstfruits, when you bring a new grain offering to the Lord at your *Feast of* Weeks, you shall have a holy convocation. You shall do no customary work. [27] You shall present a burnt offering as a sweet aroma to the Lord: two young bulls, one ram, and seven lambs in their first year,

Numbers 29:1

Offerings at the Feast of Trumpets

[29] 'And in the seventh month, on the first *day* of the month, you shall have a holy convocation. You shall do no customary work. For you it is a day of blowing the trumpets.

Numbers 29:6

[6] besides the burnt offering with its grain offering for the New Moon, the regular burnt offering with its grain offering, and their drink offerings, according to their ordinance, as a sweet aroma, an offering made by fire to the Lord.

2 Chronicles 2:4

[4] Behold, I am building a temple for the name of the Lord my God, to dedicate *it* to Him, to burn before Him sweet incense, for the continual showbread, for the burnt offerings morning and evening, on the Sabbaths, on the New Moons, and on the set feasts of the Lord our God. **This *is* an ordinance forever to Israel.**

Exodus 35:4-9

Offerings for the Tabernacle

[4] And Moses spoke to all the congregation of the children of Israel, saying, "This *is* the thing which the Lord commanded, saying: [5] 'Take from among you an offering to the Lord. Whoever *is* of a willing heart, let him bring it as an offering to the Lord: gold, silver, and bronze; [6] blue, purple, and scarlet *thread,* fine linen, and goats' *hair;* [7] ram skins dyed red, badger skins, and acacia

wood; ⁸ oil for the light, and spices for the anointing oil and for the sweet incense; ⁹ onyx stones, and stones to be set in the ephod and in the breastplate.

Leviticus 1:9

The Burnt Offering

⁹ but he shall wash its entrails and its legs with water. And the priest shall burn all on the altar as a burnt sacrifice, an offering made by fire, a sweet aroma to the LORD.

Leviticus 2:1-2

The Grain Offering

2 'When anyone offers a grain offering to the LORD, his offering shall be *of* fine flour. And he shall pour oil on it and put frankincense on it. ² He shall bring it to Aaron's sons, the priests, one of whom shall take from it his handful of fine flour and oil with all the frankincense. And the priest shall burn *it as* **a memorial** on the altar, an offering made by fire, a sweet aroma to the LORD.

Leviticus 3:11

The Peace Offering

¹¹ and the priest shall burn *them* on the altar **as food**, an offering made by fire to the LORD.

Matthew 22:15-21

The Pharisees: Is It Lawful to Pay Taxes to Caesar?

¹⁵ Then the Pharisees went and plotted how they might entangle Him in *His* talk. ¹⁶ And they sent to Him their disciples with the Herodians, saying, "Teacher, we know that You are true, and teach the way of God in truth; nor do You care about anyone, for You do not regard the person of men. ¹⁷ Tell us, therefore, what do You think? Is it lawful to pay taxes to Caesar, or not?"

¹⁸ But Jesus perceived their wickedness, and said, "Why do you test Me, *you* hypocrites? ¹⁹ Show Me the tax money."

So, they brought Him a denarius.

²⁰ And He said to them, "Whose image and inscription *is* this?"

²¹ They said to Him, "Caesar's."

And He said to them, "Render therefore to Caesar the things that are Caesar's, and to God the things that are God's." **²²** When they had heard *these words,* they marveled, and left Him and went their way.

Again, the sin offering, trespass or guilt offering or any combination of these offerings with the burnt offering to make atonement for sin is what equates to the precious Life and Blood of our Lord and Savior Jesus Christ. The death of Jesus Christ cancels the sin and trespass or guilt offerings. Every other ordinance remains. Read Leviticus 6 etc., to learn more on the laws regarding the offerings. The burnt offering, grain offering, and peace offering by themselves or together are not sin or trespass or guilt offerings. So, the Blood of Jesus Christ doesn't cover or apply to them. Now you have been taught so that you will know and understand. So, you don't have any excuses.

Although there are several specific instructions and examples in the Word of God, these should help you decide on the right things to do. We have made our Christianity all about the sin atonement sacrifice of Jesus Christ, but we have been very wrong. All glory and honor to Jesus because His sacrifice is like non other, and through Him, we have direct access to God again and have eternal life. But God still requires specific things from the Church, but the Church has stopped doing them for maybe centuries.

The lost patterns and ordinances all begun when the Israelites asked for a king to rule over them rather than allowing God, their Creator, to be their King forever and ever. The state that the world must get to should be a state where only God rules over humanity, and not ungodly men such as politicians and kings, who crave for wealth, power, and an obsession of lustful control over humanity. The least we must have should be godly kings and politicians because humanity is being destroyed.

So, after the Ezekiel Temple is built, the needed patterns and ordinances, including the non-sin offerings should all be restored.

Also, why do we have law courts for legal matters on Earth? Why do we have the police on Earth? Why do we still have armies on Earth among many other things?

The Court System in the Old Testament

Next is how the court system was introduced on Earth by God through the counsel of Moses' father-in-law. We still have and use these legal systems on Earth today – maybe different punishments but same idea.

Exodus 18:19-26

¹⁷ So Moses' father-in-law said to him, "The thing that you do *is* not good. **¹⁸** Both you and these people who *are* with you will surely wear yourselves out. For this thing *is* too much for you; you are not able to perform it by yourself. **¹⁹** Listen now to my voice; I will give you counsel, and God will be with you: Stand before God for the people, so that you may bring the difficulties to God. **20** And you shall teach them the statutes and the laws and show them the way in which they must walk and the work they must do. **21** Moreover you shall select from all the people able men, such as fear God, men of truth, hating covetousness; and place *such* over them *to be* rulers of thousands, rulers of hundreds, rulers of fifties, and rulers of tens. **22** And let them judge the people at all times. Then it will be *that* every great matter they shall bring to you, but every small matter they themselves shall judge. So, it will be easier for you, for they will bear *the burden* with you. **23** If you do this thing, and God *so* commands you, then you will be able to endure, and all this people will also go to their place in peace."

24 So Moses heeded the voice of his father-in-law and did all that he had said. **25** And Moses chose able men out of all Israel and made them heads over the people: rulers of thousands, rulers of hundreds, rulers of fifties, and rulers of tens. **26** So they judged the people at all times; the hard cases they brought to Moses, but they judged every small case themselves.

The entire Earth right now is like Sodom and Gomorrah. In fact, our generation is truly worse than Sodom and Gomorrah because we have used the Blood of Jesus Christ as an excuse to fool around. These are some examples of how those laws applied and were ruled by judges.

Leviticus 20:14-16

14 If a man marries a woman and her mother, it *is* wickedness. They shall be burned with fire, both he and they, that there may be no wickedness among you. **15** If a man mates with an animal, he shall surely be put to death, and you shall kill the animal. **16** If a woman approaches any animal and mates with it, you shall kill the woman and the animal. They shall surely be put to death. Their blood *is* upon them.

Leviticus 18:22-23

22 You shall not lie with a male as with a woman. It *is* an abomination. **23** Nor shall you mate with any animal, to defile yourself with it. Nor shall any woman stand before an animal to mate with it. It *is* perversion.

Today, in regular Christianity, having multiple wives is a problem, although the Bible provide very specific instructions on that. But that's a lecture for another time. But we see today, in some so-called churches, even in the governments, that it is legal and encouraged, that men can marry and or sleep with other men and women can marry and or sleep with other women. And absolutely nothing is done to those men and women who go about mating with animals. And we live in society with all these good for nothing leaders and citizens. Just imagine how demonic and foolish. May God have mercy on you for the judgment that is coming.

Some of these punishments exercised in the Old Testament, in our time, are called capital punishments. Capital punishment, also known as the death penalty, is a state-sanctioned practice of killing a person as a punishment for a crime. This is the hypocrisy of our world right now. If the laws of the Old Testament are no longer valid because of the death and precious Blood of Jesus Christ, why then do we still have capital punishments? Why then do we even have the court system? This is how we deceive ourselves and become very hypocritical and the world is all messy.

We see examples of crimes and their corresponding punishments in the Old Testament. This court and law system still apply today to manage lawlessness – except that it is a joke court system and government. Amid all these, we have the government signing bills into laws for even men to sleep with other men or women to sleep with other women. And we also have human beings sleeping with animals etc. We have people aborting or killing babies every day. We have human beings legally going through procedures to change their sexes, change to become animals etc. We have all these demonic acts or abominations happening all around us and even in some Churches. Why then do we even have courts on Earth? I personally don't see the importance of the governments and courts in our generation. How else can we provoke and see the Power of God in full manifestation? There will be no power if you engage in all these lawlessness or even support any of it. And you shall surely face the judgment and punishment of God. The only difference is that the people who engaged in these acts and died don't return to life or Earth to tell you what they are currently experiencing so all you know is that they are dead. You are a joker. They are suffering in eternity. Even Albert Einstein is in such a horrible place as I write this because the Lord took me there to see how things are over there. The governments have been infiltrated by the devil to go against every law of God. People believe in science more than God, but science came from God. The world has totally turned against God, but He is about to shake the Earth in such a mighty way like never seen before – with His hand; very strong and mighty.

This is the hypocrisy in the Church that is making us very weak because part of it is that we don't know and understand the ways of God. The Church as a body as well as individual Christians, have all gone out of alignment from the ways of God. That is why we don't see results. Something happens and your first instinct is to run to your pastor or man or woman of God because you lack knowledge and understanding. In other cases, they even run to magicians, diviners, sorcerers etc. You lack power because you don't live according to the ways of God. You better learn now and start living as a true Christian who has real authority and limitless power and dominion.

Following Some Basic Purification Ways of God

The Blood of Jesus has become both the blessing and the curse for Christianity because it is very misinterpreted and misunderstood. There are very specific purification ways of God that every servant of God must follow in order to first, please God and second, build spiritual capacity and power.

God says that Heaven is His throne. He didn't say that Heaven is His temple. I hear a lot of men of God quoting from Isaiah 66:1 – "Heaven *is* My throne, And earth *is* My footstool." But I don't hear anybody teaching about rest of the acts mentioned in this scripture. Churches over the years pick and choose what to teach and preach – they don't teach and preach everything from the Word of God. This is how the error starts. You must teach the foundation first even before you start teaching prosperity gospel and everything else. You make God happy, and He makes you happy. You must read, understand, teach and preach the whole Word of God. The scriptures below are just a part of that chapter, but I encourage you to read all of it to make more sense out of the few things I'm about to show you.

Here is another example of how to stay clean for God. God has given us everything but not everything is worthy to do or eat. God is very specific about what to and what not to eat.

Isaiah 66:17

True Worship and False

[17] "Those who sanctify themselves and purify themselves,
To go to the gardens
After an *idol* in the midst,
Eating swine's flesh and the abomination and the mouse,
Shall be consumed together," says the LORD.

You are not going to die instantly when you do these things, but you will be spiritually dead. Also, whatever is clean to eat becomes unclean if it is given to idols.

Daniel 1:8-9

[8] But Daniel purposed in his heart that he would not defile himself with the portion of the king's delicacies, nor with the wine which he drank; therefore, he requested of the chief of the eunuchs that he might not defile himself. [9] Now God had brought Daniel into the favor and goodwill of the chief of the eunuchs.

Spiritual people know these things but the ones who claim to inherit the Word of God, which is the Body of Christ aren't taught these things. Do we have our salvation through Jesus Christ? Absolutely. Did Jesus do away with the laws? No. Does this mean that following all these ways to result in self-righteousness alone will give you salvation or eternal life? No. Why not? Because it is written that God sacrificed His only begotten Son for our sins, and it is through Him only that we can come to Him. Again, the death of Jesus Christ gives us direct access to the Father, which is what Adam lost – His death doesn't wipe away all the ordinances or the ways of God. His death engraves the law in our minds and hearts and shows us mercy through the forgiveness of our sins each time we go the Father in prayer.

Galatians 2:16

[16] knowing that a man is not justified by the works of the law but by faith in Jesus Christ, even we have believed in Christ Jesus, that we might be justified by faith in Christ and not by the works of the law; for by the works of the law no flesh shall be justified.

I can go on and on to give you several examples on how to live like a true spiritual person that will make you see, host, and demonstrate the true power of God. People are not taught nowadays, and the true meaning of the Word of God is disappearing but the few who know are walking in real raw power. Once the Church begins to understand all that are being taught here, they will become true hybrids of the old and new covenants to be able to demonstrate true spiritual power. What this will enforce is **sacrifice** and **love** because if the death of Jesus Christ showed us anything, these are those two things.

You weren't created to pursue money or earthly riches or properties or control over others. If you try your best to live life as showed to you so far, you are guaranteed to not only be successful in life, but you will have an extraordinary supernatural journey of life where Jesus Christ will truly be glorified through your life. The Word of God will become your experience. Everything else shall surely be given to you and the following scriptures will become your testimony – just like the revelations in this book are only a part of my testimonies.

Matthew 6:19-21

Lay Up Treasures in Heaven

[19] "Do not lay up for yourselves treasures on earth, where moth and rust destroy and where thieves break in and steal; [20] but lay up for yourselves treasures in heaven, where neither moth nor rust destroys and where thieves do not break in and steal. [21] For where your treasure is, there your heart will be also.

Our treasures are truly in Heaven. Earth is only temporal. It seems like forever but it's not. What we call time and death should prove that to you. Whether you will be alive or not before the Messiah's return doesn't change eternal life. Life is eternal but there is a way of thinking and living that takes and keep you there. You must become the Priest and King that you are destined to be through a consistent Christian spiritual life as demonstrated by the prophets of old, including our Lord Jesus Christ. It is not about talking a lot, publicity, and or conformity that you serve God or go to Church. There is a severe lack of discipline, effort, character, power and dominion among other things, in the Church in our time but that is about to shift. We are the hybrids so let your eyes, ears, and minds be open to these revelations and reality and start walking in true authority, power, and dominion. This is priesthood and you must be very intentional about it.

Raising an Altar or a Memorial unto the Lord

We see altars everywhere in the Word of God because they are extremely important. They serve as both a memorial to God and a portal between Heaven and Earth.

Genesis 12:7

⁷ Then the LORD appeared to Abram and said, "To your descendants I will give this land." And there **he built an altar to the LORD**, who had appeared to him.

Exodus 20:22-26

The Law of the Altar

²² Then the LORD said to Moses, "Thus you shall say to the children of Israel: 'You have seen that I have talked with you from heaven. ²³ You shall not make *anything to be* with Me—gods of silver or gods of gold you shall not make for yourselves. ²⁴ An altar of earth you shall make for Me, and you shall sacrifice on it your burnt offerings and your peace offerings, your sheep and your oxen. In every place where I record My name I will come to you, and I will bless you. ²⁵ And if you make Me an altar of stone, you shall not build it of hewn stone; for if you use your tool on it, you have profaned it. ²⁶ Nor shall you go up by steps to My altar, that your nakedness may not be exposed on it.'

Leviticus 6:12-13

¹² And the fire on the altar shall be kept burning on it; it shall not be put out. And the priest shall burn wood on it every morning and lay the burnt offering in order on it; and he shall burn on it the fat of the peace offerings. ¹³ A fire shall always be burning on the altar; it shall never go out.

Matthew 5:17-20

Christ Fulfills the Law

¹⁷ "**Do not think that I came to destroy the Law or the Prophets. I did not come to destroy but to fulfill.** ¹⁸ For assuredly, I say to you, till heaven and earth pass away, one jot or one tittle will by no means pass from the law till all is fulfilled. ¹⁹ Whoever therefore breaks one of the least of these commandments, and teaches men so, shall be called least in the kingdom of heaven; but whoever does and teaches *them,* he shall be called great in the kingdom of heaven. ²⁰ For I say to you, that unless your righteousness exceeds *the righteousness* of the scribes and Pharisees, you will by no means enter the kingdom of heaven.

Matthew 5:23-24

Murder Begins in the Heart

²³ **Therefore if you bring your gift to the altar**, and there remember that your brother has something against you, ²⁴ leave your gift there before the altar, and go your way. First be reconciled to your brother, and then come and offer your gift.

Luke 1:8-11

[8] So it was, that while he was **serving as priest before God in the order of his division**, [9] **according to the custom of the priesthood**, his lot fell to burn incense when he went into the temple of the Lord. [10] And the whole multitude of the people was praying outside at the hour of incense. [11] Then an angel of the Lord appeared to him, standing on the **right side of the altar of incense**.

Matthew 23:16-22

[16] "Woe to you, blind guides, who say, 'Whoever swears by the temple, it is nothing; but whoever swears by the gold of the temple, he is obliged *to perform it.*' [17] Fools and blind! For which is greater, the gold or the temple that sanctifies the gold? [18] And, 'Whoever swears by the altar, it is nothing; but whoever swears by the gift that is on it, he is obliged *to perform it.*' [19] Fools and blind! For which is greater, the gift or **the altar that sanctifies the gift? [20] Therefore he who swears by the altar, swears by it and by all things on it**. [21] He who swears by the temple, swears by it and by Him who dwells in it. [22] And he who swears by heaven, swears by the throne of God and by Him who sits on it.

There are several examples in the Word of God, but I have used only a few from both the Old and the New Testaments – you can research the rest. We have cancelled key ordinances of God because of the death of Jesus Christ but that shouldn't be the case. Where are our temples? Where are our altars etc.? And I am not asking about pulpits. We see that even in the New Testament, Jesus Christ did not throw the ordinances of the Old Testament away. He only came to fulfil it and made it better by adding Himself into the ordinances of the Law and the Prophets by removing that one painful law of sin and death. He saved us from our sins and restored our eternal life. Now that we have eternal life through His finished works, we must restore the temple and ordinances, and at the same time, keep teaching and preaching the gospel like the Church is currently doing. Now the veil has been torn and we are all priests so we can service the altar. I have said this repeatedly because you **must** understand it.

So, I don't know how the Church got into this mess of not understanding the priestly patterns and ordinances of God. We need to get it right and restore power back to the Church. It almost seems like we have left all the work for Jesus Christ to do but it is not so. He is still our Lord and Savior, and High Priest but we still have very important roles to play. And we can see that in the example scriptures above. Of course, there are several scriptures that confirm this. The Church seriously needs knowledge and understanding.

The Patterns of the Early Tabernacle or Temple

Exodus 40:24-32

[24] He put the **lampstand** in the tabernacle of meeting, across from the table, on the south side of the tabernacle; [25] and he lit the lamps before the LORD, as the LORD had commanded Moses. [26] He put the **gold altar** in the tabernacle of meeting in front of the veil; [27] and he **burned sweet incense**

on it, as the LORD had commanded Moses. [28] He hung up the screen *at* the door of the tabernacle. [29] And he put the altar of burnt offering *before* the door of the tabernacle of the tent of meeting and offered upon it the burnt offering and the grain offering, as the LORD had commanded Moses. **[30] He set the laver between the tabernacle of meeting and the altar and put water there for washing; [31] and Moses, Aaron, and his sons would wash their hands and their feet *with water* from it. [32] Whenever they went into the tabernacle of meeting, and when they came near the altar, they washed, as the LORD had commanded Moses.**

Again, let me remind you that Jesus Christ shared His precious blood for us for our sins, and that is why the veil was torn after His death. This gives us a direct access back into the presence of God Almighty, who is our Father – just like it was in the days of Adam before we lost that privilege due to sin. The death of Jesus Christ doesn't change the pattern of the tabernacle or temple as it directly mirrors the one in Heaven. The only change is that there is no need for a veil and an Ark of the Covenant as it was in the ancient days because we are both the Ark of the Covenant and its content. And because of the blood sacrifice of Jesus Christ, we don't need to be doing any sin burnt offerings etc., since it has all been paid for us.

When you read Leviticus 4, you will learn about the sin offering, and the trespass or guilt offering. And you will see and know that those were the main offerings that the precious blood of Jesus Christ replaced – to do away with the law of sin and death offering and then inscribed the ten commandments in our hearts to be forever conscious and reminded of them in our minds. I have already given some scriptures for these. Everything else in the temple and the ordinances didn't change. Why have we replaced everything with the death of our Lord Jesus Christ? This has been the weakness in the Church and why we do not see power. **The New Testament did not replace the Old Testament laws. It only replaced the Old Testament law of sin and death and changed how the statutes and commandments of God will be dispensed and followed. The statutes and commandments are no more written on stone tablets. Instead, they are written in our hearts and minds.** With the presence of the Holy Spirit in us, we are constantly reminded and guided by His conscience.

Again, see below.

Luke 18:19-23

[19] So Jesus said to him, "Why do you call Me good? No one *is* good but One, *that is,* God. [20] You know the commandments: 'Do not commit adultery,' 'Do not murder,' 'Do not steal,' 'Do not bear false witness,' 'Honor your father and your mother.'"

[21] And he said, "All these things I have kept from my youth."

[22] So when Jesus heard these things, He said to him, "You still lack one thing. Sell all that you have and distribute to the poor, and you will have treasure in heaven; and come, follow Me."

Hebrews 10:16-26

[16] "**This** *is* **the covenant** that I will make with them after those days, says the LORD: **I will put My laws into their hearts, and in their minds**, I will write them," [17] *then He adds,* "Their sins and their lawless deeds I will remember no more." [18] **Now where there is remission of these,** *there is* **no longer an offering for sin**.

Hold Fast Your Confession

[19] Therefore, brethren, having **boldness to enter the Holiest by the blood of Jesus**, [20] by a new and living way which He consecrated for us, **through the veil**, that is, **His flesh**, [21] and *having* a High Priest over the house of God, [22] let us draw near with a true heart in full assurance of faith, having our hearts sprinkled from an evil conscience and our bodies washed with pure water. [23] Let us hold fast the confession of *our* hope without wavering, for He who promised *is* faithful. [24] And let us consider one another in order to stir up love and good works, [25] not forsaking the assembling of ourselves together, as *is* the manner of some, but exhorting *one another,* and so much the more as you see the Day approaching.

The Just Live by Faith

[26] **For if we sin willfully after we have received the knowledge of the truth**, **there no longer remains a sacrifice for sins,**

Again, even in the New Testament, this is stated very clearly repeatedly. Verse 26 applies to you, now that you know the truth – once you know the truth, but you go against it willfully, there no longer remains a sacrifice for sins. When you restore the old paths and start going into the temple, you can do so with boldness, having this understanding in your heart. Each time you kneel before the altar, remember that there is no veil, and that you are the Ark of the New Covenant.

Psalm 51:16-17

[16] You do not delight in sacrifice, or I would bring it;
  you do not take pleasure in burnt offerings.
[17] My sacrifice, O God, is a broken spirit;
  a broken and contrite heart
  you, God, will not despise.

This is David teaching us the sincerity of heart and brokenness. One may think that he had stopped giving sacrifices to God because of what he said in the scriptures. But let's look at what he says in the following scriptures.

Psalm 54:6

[6] **I will sacrifice a freewill offering to you**;
  I will praise your name, LORD, for it is good.

The temple and its pattern were not condemned or made away with by the death of Jesus Christ. Only the offering for the law of sin and death changed. If we look at the scriptures above, we clearly see that even David understood in the Old Testament that God is moved by a broken and a contrite heart. We know from Psalm 91 that David also knew how to bring the ordinances of the temple with him wherever he went. He understood it so well that he brought it into his chamber. He truly understood the secret place and had a desire to build a physical one for God according to the patterns and ordinances of Heaven, so that God will rest there. The Lord did not permit him only because of the blood on David's hands from all the wars he had fought. So, we can say that God is moved by a broken and a contrite heart but that doesn't change the fact that we must still sacrifice offerings to Him. Our generation have made everything about money – this has been the root of most of our issues. Even when we want to give offerings to God, we always think money. There's a place and time for offering money but not all the time. There's also a place and time to follow old patterns and ordinances.

1 Chronicles 22:5-10

⁵ Now David said, "Solomon my son *is* young and inexperienced, and the house to be built for the LORD *must be* exceedingly magnificent, famous and glorious throughout all countries. I will now make preparation for it." So, David made abundant preparations before his death.

⁶ Then he called for his son Solomon and charged him to build a house for the LORD God of Israel. ⁷ And David said to Solomon: "My son, as for me, it was in my mind to build a house to the name of the LORD my God; ⁸ but the word of the LORD came to me, saying, 'You have shed much blood and have made great wars; you shall not build a house for My name, because you have shed much blood on the earth in My sight. ⁹ Behold, a son shall be born to you, who shall be a man of rest; and I will give him rest from all his enemies all around. His name shall be Solomon, for I will give peace and quietness to Israel in his days. ¹⁰ He shall build a house for My name, and he shall be My son, and I *will be* his Father; and I will establish the throne of his kingdom over Israel forever.'

But Solomon built the temple for God. We also know that David knew and understood the Holy Spirit even in the Old Testament. He had the Holy Spirit with understanding, yet he kept and followed the old patterns and ordinances.

Psalm 51:10-11

¹⁰ Create in me a clean heart, O God,
And renew a steadfast spirit within me.
¹¹ Do not cast me away from Your presence,
And do not take Your Holy Spirit from me.

Romans 6:15-17

From Slaves of Sin to Slaves of God

15 What then? **Shall we sin because we are not under law but under grace?** Certainly not! **16** Do you not know that to whom you present yourselves slaves to obey, you are that one's slaves whom you obey, whether of sin *leading* to death, or of obedience *leading* to righteousness? **17** But God be thanked that *though* you were slaves of sin, yet you obeyed from the heart that form of doctrine to which you were delivered.

Apostle Paul asks a question that makes it clear that although Jesus Christ has died for us, we still shouldn't go about sinning but if we unintentionally do sin then His mercies are new for us every morning so we should sincerely repent. Jesus Christ's death is for our immortality, and that is eternal life. This means that the temple and every offering other than the sin, trespass or guilt offerings that were offered to the Lord in the ancient times should be all be restored.

There is nothing wrong with keeping our New Testament style Church because it is part of the New Testament strategy introduced by Jesus Christ through His Apostles to reach the nations. But they never destroyed or removed anything from the temple. We need the Old Testament temple and ordinances to restore true power back into the Church.

What is still needful is the pattern of the temple and the ordinances inside the temple since we are all priests now. You see, this is how we have been cheating ourselves and a group has solely been stuck in the Old Testament and have become fetish priests, who do not know and believe in the sacrifice of Jesus Christ for the remission of sins while another group has been stuck with the New Testament and has been hypocritical in picking and choosing what to teach and preach and what not to teach and preach. This second group are called Christians and have made the Old Testament almost irrelevant.

If we are the Temple of God and God dwells in us and we in God, why should there be a temple in Heaven with precise patterns and ordinances, and we have no temples like that in our time according to those patterns and ordinances? We are wrong.

The Pattern of the Third Temple as Shown to Ezekiel

Aside Jerusalem, there must be temples built around the world according to the patterns of the old temple to restore and maintain the spiritual power in the Church. The temple in Jerusalem will be the main third temple or headquarters. The ordinances in the early temples must be restored and followed to bring hybrid power back to the Church – this is God's end time strategic combination of the Law and the Prophets, and Jesus Christ.

These third temples MUST meet specifications as given to us in the writings of Ezekiel – from Ezekiel 40 and so on.

You are on Earth, and you eat and try to live in the spirit. God dwells in you and in the spirit of the Holy Spirit. If God enjoyed daily sacrifices because of the sweet aroma and some as food, what makes you think that because Jesus Christ died for our sins, God doesn't like the sweet aroma and or food anymore? What makes you think that God doesn't "eat" anymore? I'm sure that you haven't stopped eating just because Jesus Christ died for your sins. In fact, you haven't even stopped sinning. Jesus Christ died for your sins, but you haven't stopped eating. Have you? The death of Jesus Christ doesn't feed God or send incense to God. His death only grants us direct access to God in His name – period. This is where the Church has missed it for centuries.

The true power of the trinity in the Church is by following the patterns and ordinances of both the Old and New Covenants minus the sin, trespass or guilt offerings. But we will still aim to be perfected in holiness by repenting for our sins before the Lord, believing that Jesus Christ died for our sins. The Temple, the Law and the Prophets, and spreading the gospel are our mandate for this end time. Jesus Christ has made it possible for us to host the Holy Spirit again wherever we go so we don't need the old physical Ark of the Covenant. We are the New physical Ark of the Covenant because we host the Presence of God. And just like it was on the mount of Transfiguration, we are a hybrid of the Holy Temple, the Law and the Prophets, and the Light bearers or Disciples who spread the gospel.

Just like what the two pillars (Boaz and Jachin) in front of Solomon's Temple represented, the two pillars in front of the inner court and vestibule of Ezekiel's Temple will symbolize the same – the hybrid of the Law and the Prophets, and Jesus Christ. As we walk in and out through those pillars, we represent that hybrid who go to minister to the Lord and out to minister to the world. We used to be far away from God – hence, at the time of Solomon, we were in the hall. But now, we are always in the Presence of God – deep inside the inner court. The inner court is all about our relationship with God.

1 Kings 7:15-21

The Bronze Pillars for the Temple

15 And he cast two pillars of bronze, each one eighteen cubits high, and a line of twelve cubits measured the circumference of each. **16** Then he made two capitals *of* cast bronze, to set on the tops of the pillars. The height of one capital *was* five cubits, and the height of the other capital *was* five cubits. **17** *He made* a lattice network, with wreaths of chainwork, for the capitals which *were* on top of the pillars: seven chains for one capital and seven for the other capital. **18** So he made the pillars, and two rows of pomegranates above the network all around to cover the capitals that *were* on top; and thus, he did for the other capital.

19 The capitals which *were* on top of the pillars in the hall *were* in the shape of lilies, four cubits. **20** The capitals on the two pillars also *had pomegranates* above, by the convex surface which *was* next to the network; and there *were* two hundred such pomegranates in rows on each of the capitals all around.

21 Then he set up the pillars by the vestibule of the temple; he set up the pillar on the right and called its name Jachin, and he set up the pillar on the left and called its name Boaz. **22** The tops of the pillars were in the shape of lilies. So, the work of the pillars was finished.

Ezekiel 40:49

Dimensions of the Inner Court and Vestibule

49 The length of the vestibule *was* twenty cubits, and the width eleven cubits; and by the steps which led up to it *there were* **pillars by the doorposts, one on this side and another on that side**.

This is just like the image or vision on the Mount of Transfiguration – there was Moses, Jesus Christ, and Elijah, and they represented the Law and the Prophets, and Jesus Christ represented the hybrid of both who fulfills both by taking away sin offerings and giving us eternal life. As we walk through the two pillars into the Temple, we represent Jesus Christ and His hybrid nature, having given us also eternal life and direct access to the Father into the Most Holy place. This also represents Jesus Christ indwelling us.

Matthew 17:1-4

Jesus Transfigured on the Mount

17 Now after six days Jesus took Peter, James, and John his brother, led them up on a high mountain by themselves; **2** and He was transfigured before them. His face shone like the sun, and His clothes became as white as the light. **3 And behold, Moses and Elijah appeared to them**, talking with Him. **4** Then Peter answered and said to Jesus, "Lord, it is good for us to be here; if You wish, **let us make here three tabernacles: one for You, one for Moses, and one for Elijah**."

Remember, like I told you earlier, Moses and Elijah both represented Jesus Christ in their days. This mystery and revelation are why Ezekiel's Temple is a three-story Temple with three doors. But compared to Solomon's Temple, it had only two doors, instead of the three in Ezekiel's.

Solomon Builds the Temple

1 Kings 6:8

8 The doorway for the **middle story** *was* on the right side of the temple. They went up by stairs to the **middle** *story,* and from the middle to **the third**.

1 Kings 6:31-35

31 For the entrance of the inner sanctuary he made doors *of* olive wood; the lintel *and* doorposts *were* one-fifth *of the wall.* **32 The two doors** *were* **of olive wood**; and he carved on them figures of cherubim, palm trees, and open flowers, and overlaid *them* with gold;

and he spread gold on the cherubim and on the palm trees. ³³ So for the door of the sanctuary he also made doorposts *of* olive wood, one-fourth *of the wall.* ³⁴ **And the two doors** *were of* cypress wood; two panels *comprised* one folding door, and two panels *comprised* the other folding door. ³⁵ Then he carved cherubim, palm trees, and open flowers *on them,* and overlaid *them* with gold applied evenly on the carved work.

Now let's look at some patterns of our current Temple – Ezekiel's Temple.

Ezekiel 40:6-10

A New City, a New Temple

The Eastern Gateway of the Temple

⁶ Then he went to **the gateway which faced east**; and he went up its stairs and measured the threshold of the gateway, *which was* one rod wide, and the other threshold *was* one rod wide. ⁷ Each gate chamber *was* one rod long and one rod wide; between the gate chambers *was a space of* five cubits; and the threshold of the gateway by the vestibule of the inside gate *was* one rod. ⁸ He also measured the vestibule of the inside gate, one rod. ⁹ Then he measured the vestibule of the gateway, eight cubits; and the gateposts, two cubits. The vestibule of the gate *was* on the inside. ¹⁰ In the eastern gateway *were* **three gate chambers** on one side and **three on the other**; **the three** *were* **all the same size**; also**, the gateposts were of the same size on this side and that side**.

Take note that the east gate is God's entrance into the Temple – and the Godhead consist of the Father, Son, and the Holy Spirit. And the Law and the Prophets consist of Moses and Elijah, and their hybrid is Jesus Christ. We see three persons here and there are three gate chambers. Remember again, there were three Apostles – Peter, James, and John with Jesus Christ at the Mount of Transfiguration and below is what they said.

Matthew 17:4

⁴ Then Peter answered and said to Jesus, "Lord, it is good for us to be here; if You wish, **let us make here three tabernacles: one for You, one for Moses, and one for Elijah**."

There is no veil in Ezekiel's Temple – the veil which was in the earlier Temples separated man from the presence of God until Jesus Christ died for our sins. So, that has been removed forever and ever if you believe in Jesus Christ and stay away from sin.

The Manner of Worship

Ezekiel 46:2

² The prince shall enter by way of the vestibule of the gateway from the outside and stand by the gatepost. The priests shall prepare his **burnt offering** and his **peace offerings**.

Ezekiel 46:5

⁵ and the **grain offering** *shall be one* ephah for a ram, and the grain offering for the lambs, as much as he wants to give, as well as a hin of oil with every ephah.

Ezekiel 46:13-15

¹³ "You shall daily make a burnt offering to the Lord *of* a lamb of the first year without blemish; you shall prepare it every morning. ¹⁴ And you shall prepare a grain offering with it every morning, a sixth of an ephah, and a third of a hin of oil to moisten the fine flour. **This grain offering is a perpetual ordinance, to be made regularly to the Lord. ¹⁵ Thus they shall prepare the lamb, the grain offering, and the oil,** *as* **a regular burnt offering every morning**."

We see the consistency already as it was even in the days of Moses, and after studying both the Old and New Testaments before and after the blood sacrifice of Jesus Christ according to the revelations of God. We now know and understand that we still need to offer the burnt offering, grain offering, and peace offering to God.

We also need to spiritually worship in our priestly garments in the temple. These are the patterns and ordinances of the priests in the temple of God. You must read the whole book of Ezekiel to learn more on these patterns and ordinances to be applied in our time. This is just to give you the initial guidance. If you don't have a temple like this to attend yet or in addition to your regular Church, still go to your regular Church to learn the Word and Ways of God, and consistently practice priesthood in your secret place daily.

Everything here on earth is sentenced to doom and destruction. When you are conscious about this fact, you will start exercising your priesthood. Time is corruption and time is a slowed-motion version of eternity. We need faith to create manifestation in time.

Hebrews 11:1-3

11 Now faith is the substance of things hoped for, the evidence of things not seen. ² For by it the elders obtained a *good* testimony.

³ By faith we understand that the worlds were framed by the word of God, so that the things which are seen were not made of things which are visible.

Everything on earth is created by faith. Through faith the elders obtained a good report. The New Jerusalem Calling is not given to you for impact in time. Instead, it's given to you to be able to become what you should be in the world to come in eternity. The idea is for us to all become patriarchs or fathers. In other words, pioneers of a movement or unique dimensions of God. If you fulfill your calling, you'll walk with the fathers who walked in the same dimensions – the lives and experiences of Enoch, Noah, Job, Moses, Elijah, Daniel, Jesus Christ etc., as recorded in the Word of God. You must represent a unique dimension in your generation, which will also become your legacy when you leave time. Time is like your name. Name is absolute because we all have names, but individual names are all different – like names on an identification card, which makes your name relative to only you. You can be the Daniel or the Elijah of your generation. It's not about titles though – like Apostle, Prophet, Evangelist etc. Your dimension is who you truly represent in the Kingdom of God both in time and in eternity. So, you won't be given a title like Apostle or Prophet in eternity. Every dimension in God has a quadrant or presbytery. If you are truly a priest, you should know or be aware of the quadrant or presbytery or tribe that you belong to even while you are in time. If you don't know this yet, then you are still a Child of God. If you know this and actively walk in it, then you are a Son of God. We walk through time to invest in Zion. Time is not the reality because you're not a creature of time. You are a spirit going through an experience in time in a human body or vessel. So, what is your calling?

Like I just said, you're connected to an ancestry or clan or tribe in the spirit. We know this from the history of the Israelites. Israel encamped according to their 12 tribes, who had unique attributes. Find your calling. You're the best person to look for it and find it – and you can do that only through the technology of a consistent prayer life or priesthood. You must service your altar daily. This is your only key to real life – authentic spiritual living as designed by God. This is the only way you will find your destiny because the more you keep up with this consistency, the Holy Spirit prunes you and gets rid of all your excesses. Then you will find your true spiritual self as designed by God before the foundations of the Earth. The consistency keeps the Holy Spirit with you all the time.

Your ability to hear and see from God is very crucial in these end times because your obedience to God is how you will be rewarded in Heaven. This is how a lead or head spirit judges another spirit. This is how Lucifer was judged by God. This is how we are also judged by God daily. It's all about obedience. We've already seen in some scriptures earlier that through faith, the elders obtained a good testimony or report.

And priesthood is not asking for your daily needs from God. The most important thing is to consistently go before the Lord to acknowledge Him as your Creator and in Him is your sufficiency or fullness. Through that, God will start sharing His burdens with you. Faith is the ability to give to God, but not to receive from God. The more you offer yourself as a living sacrifice through priesthood, you give to God. Samuel was given to Hannah, but he was given or offered back to God – same with Abraham and Isaac. In God's heart, Abraham "sacrificed" Isaac. And in God's heart, Hannah sacrificed Samuel. Abel offered a sacrifice to God and God was pleased with Him.

Noah moved with obedience and built the ark before the flood, but he had a priesthood nature before he could discern that much information from God regarding the ark. Daniel refused to conform to worldly standards and remained righteous to God. Enoch walked with God; and was not, for God took him.

You must die to your desires and don't seek for glory. Every glory during your life is supposed to be directed to God. Always be intentional about participating in the latest that God is doing – the next move. There is a lot going on right now in the spiritual realm – such as an active revival, Old Testament mantles, and imminent big harvest etc. How prepared are you to participate? Are you able to tell what time and season we are in? If you can't then you are already in a big trouble.

You must become a puppet in the hands of God. You must totally submit to Him so that He can work on you. Our understanding and practice of scriptures now is very off and erroneous. In Heaven, everything recorded about patriarchs from time are rewards. We must have faith and obedience like Abraham and all the patriarchs. In their time, Earth was about the blessings of God, and Heaven captured their dealings with God, such as love, faith, obedience etc.

Our priorities must change. We have lived in a world where there has been a template for life, which is typically, be born into the world, grow up while you go through secular schooling if you are fortunate, become an adult, find a job, marry or whatever you want when you feel mature enough, live like everybody else, and then die someday. This is the basic idea of the template for life on Earth that we are taught. But life is much bigger than that. In fact, the Word of God should be the main book at home and in schools. From that, everything else will be discovered both naturally and supernaturally. Because the meaning or purpose for your life is that you're a messenger of God to the Earth to host dimensions in God through learning who God is through worship. Through the process of discovering God, you will discover yourself and who you truly are and what you were sent to the Earth to do. You are a spirit, who has a soul, and lives in a body. You are a spirit first, before you are a human being. And you will be a spirit last.

1 Thessalonians 5:23

[23] Now may the God of peace Himself sanctify you completely; and may your whole **spirit**, **soul**, and **body** be preserved blameless at the coming of our Lord Jesus Christ.

If you think you are a mere man and live naturally without consciousness of the spiritual realm or the supernatural, you will be disappointed when you die. You are guaranteed to start experiencing your misery even before you get on the other side of the divide.

When you come close to God, principalities, powers etc., will send demons to study your life to find weaknesses and record it in the chronicles or annals or lexicon of darkness. But that shouldn't worry you. You must be strong because as you grow in the Word with knowledge and understanding, you will change and that will change the effects of the challenges you may encounter. Your problems don't change – you change to change your problems.

Ephesians 6:12

¹² For we do not wrestle against flesh and blood, but against principalities, against powers, against the rulers of the darkness of this age, against spiritual *hosts* of wickedness in the heavenly *places.*

Isaiah 54:17

¹⁷ No weapon formed against you shall prosper,
And every tongue *which* rises against you in judgment
You shall condemn.
This *is* the heritage of the servants of the LORD,
And their righteousness *is* from Me,"
Says the LORD.

No weapons "fashioned" against you shall prosper. Indeed, demons shall be sent to monitor or spy on you. You may or may not see them but if you consistently engage priesthood, you won't even say anything to them when you see them spying on you. This is an experience, so I write from my experiences. God is an experience, and He has hidden His experience for you inside of you. It is only through prayer that you can journey deep inside of yourself. Remember, you are the universe, so it takes time and consistency to journey in that universe. It is a journey of eternity.

This life is a game of spirits. You yield to or host either a good spirit or a bad spirit. Then this spirit will possess you to function in the spirit and on Earth. We are not taught correctly so most people don't know these things. When you check in your heart or spirit to study your appetites or desires, you'll know if you love God or not. Noah built an ark for 120 years – this is called discernment of spirits because he could see in the spirit and pursued what he saw in faith. The spirits know Noah as a man of obedience. You must first have faith to obey. They talked about his reverence or obedience towards God – not his discernment in the spirit. When God spoke, Noah moved with fear, and so did the patriarchs. They all have their own testimonies. What is currently your testimony with God or what will become your testimony at the end of your life? If it is how many houses or how much wealth you acquired or how many countries you have traveled to or parties you have attended, or how much schooling you've done or publications you have etc., then you are in big trouble. You are not living yet.

Here on earth, we gauge our lives with manifestations – like in the saying, "seeing is believing". The Church in Ephesus grew but they weren't serving the purposes of God in Heaven, so God removed their candlestick. What Heaven thinks of you is the priority. The reason we do what we do in time is because we're aware that there's a place for us in Heaven – a throne and a crown for us. Just like in the following testimony of Paul.

2 Timothy 4:7-9

[7] I have fought the good fight, I have finished the race, I have kept the faith. [8] Finally, there is laid up for me the crown of righteousness, which the Lord, the righteous Judge, will give to me on that Day, and not to me only but also to all who have loved His appearing.

It's not for relevance on Earth although the byproduct for all you do for the Kingdom of God shall surely give you blessings. Don't pursue blessings – pursue God first and blessings will become a byproduct or overflow of God in your life. The reward shall await you in Heaven. Be conscious of the crown of life in Heaven, not things here in the natural.

Matthew 6:19-21

Lay Up Treasures in Heaven

[19] "Do not lay up for yourselves treasures on earth, where moth and rust destroy and where thieves break in and steal; [20] but lay up for yourselves treasures in heaven, where neither moth nor rust destroys and where thieves do not break in and steal. [21] For where your treasure is, there your heart will be also.

The bigger you become in time, the smaller you are in Heaven if care is not taken. You must be balanced. The more you rise on Earth, the more you should also be rising in the spirit. Any form of imbalance will hurt you. The Earth has already been judged. It is an irreversible judgement – it must surely come to past. God blesses men in time but He rewards men in eternity. The degree to which you are consistent to what was written about you before the beginning of time, the reinstatement of your original place that the devil tried to steal from you in the days of Adam.

You need God to have a place in eternity. You don't need God to be a great person on earth because most wealthy men and women on Earth don't worship God. Jesus talked about a great ruler who fears neither man nor God. This shows us how you don't need to bow to God to have wealth, power, influence, or authority etc.

Luke 18:1-2

18 Then He spoke a parable to them, that **men always ought to pray and not lose heart**, [2] saying: **"There was in a certain city a judge who did not fear God nor regard man**.

We are out of course and that's why there's so much imbalance on the Earth – lack of peace in homes and nations, wickedness, divorce, bad children, lust and immorality, abominations such as homosexuality etc. We must always pray daily and intentionally. It almost seems like the kingdom of darkness is winning but they shall surely lose.

Your goal is to stand in the presence of God and dwell under His shadow as the Psalmist said in Psalm 91. The devil used to walk amid the coals of fire as a Seraphim. The devil understands the weight of the glory. Before he fell, the Bible calls him the son of the morning – the anointed Cherub who covers.

So, we can see that he is both a Cherub and a Seraph – a hybrid of the two. He was the angel of beauty, music; light – full of glory. All he wants to do is to corrupt everything because he can never be restored to the position he once held, which has been given to the sons of men – the Body of Christ. God has given everything the devil lost to man. We can access all that through what the Word of God calls Priesthood or Intercession – perpetually seeking the face of the Lord. Then you become the god that you must be. We're traveling from eternity to eternity. This Earth or Time is not our destination. Work it and invest in Heaven from Earth. You must earn that reward. So, it takes a hybrid Body of Christ to completely bring the devil down forever and ever in the Name of Jesus by the Power of the Holy Spirit. How you submit to or how quickly you obey and move at the Word of God is love. Love is not emotion based but obedience based through faith in the Kingdom of God.

You can find your destiny, or calling, or purpose through priesthood. And priesthood will give you alignment through exercising righteousness or holiness to experience the full manifestations of God. Commit yourself to the requirements and do exploits through experience. Become a witness of spiritual realities so that you can also teach others your experience. This is when and how what you teach influences a spirit or another person.

The delivering of the Body of Christ will be through the Cherubim and Seraphim (hybrid). It will take a hybrid Church to bring the kingdom of darkness down once and for all. Therefore, the end time Temple will be a combination of a Body of Christ that is unified through equality and will be made up of both Jews and Gentiles without segregation in the Temple. And most importantly, it will be made up of people around the world from all races. This is a prerequisite and very essential. It will take both the Old and the New Testaments to destroy the kingdom of darkness.

The Cherubim are guardians of the glory of God, and known for obedience to law, fear, and reverence to God and from God. And the Seraphim are known for music, worship, praises, and prophecy from God and to God. Lucifer is both a Cherub and a Seraph.

The major problems affecting the Earth is a segregation of the churches and doctrines, and a rejection of most parts of the Old Testament through lies and darkness, racism, etc.

The same reason why God brought down the tower of Babel is the same reason why we'll defeat the devil. Our victory is hidden in the mystery and revelation of the tower of Babel. Because the unity through love of the Old and New testaments, all races, all genders, all churches, Jews and Gentiles, etc., will be like the one language that existed in the early days and why Nimrod was going to build that tower if God hadn't stopped him and his people.

Genesis 11:4-9

The Tower of Babel

11 Now the whole earth had one language and one speech. ²And it came to pass, as they journeyed from the east, that they found a plain in the land of Shinar, and they dwelt there. ³Then they said to one another, "Come, let us make bricks and bake *them* thoroughly." They had brick for stone, and they had asphalt for mortar. ⁴And they said, "Come, let us build ourselves a city, and a tower whose top *is* in the heavens; let us make a name for ourselves, lest we be scattered abroad over the face of the whole earth."

⁵But the LORD came down to see the city and the tower which the sons of men had built. ⁶And the LORD said, "Indeed the people *are* one and they all have one language, and this is what they begin to do; now nothing that they propose to do will be withheld from them. ⁷Come, let Us go down and there confuse their language, that they may not understand one another's speech." ⁸So the LORD scattered them abroad from there over the face of all the earth, and they ceased building the city. ⁹Therefore its name is called Babel, because there the LORD confused the language of all the earth; and from there the LORD scattered them abroad over the face of all the earth.

I look around and I ask, why do people want to have kids or families? Do people not ask the meaning of life? Are you trying to bear kids just to add members to the Earth? Or are you trying to bear children to help accomplish the prophecies and Will of God? If you're wise, you should know that the nonsense in the world won't go on forever. And just as it has a beginning, it has an end too.

Abraham and Sarah and Isaac and Jacob etc., – Only one child but became a nation (Israel). Ask yourself, why do I want to add another human being to this wicked and messy world? Is it because you want people to see you as potent or not barren? Or do you want to be like Hannah and Samuel? You need to understand spirituality and ask these questions. All these stories are for our learning, but the world has not learned. We go for careers, marriage, children etc., all for competition and "happiness" – thinking that all there is, is the physical world. We bring children into the world and train them in our own confused states or ideologies. The result then become a set of confused human beings just moving around like their bearers or parents.

There is so much we can talk about but as the Lord told me, we cannot contain Him in books because He is eternal. This information and knowledge are good for now. I pray for your accurate understanding. I believe that this will be a good foundation for you to make your Christian experience fruitful and to become relevant in the Kingdom of God. Get a Bible and study and practice the Word of God. Therefore, you were created and brought to Earth for this purpose. The day we truly realize that we are inseparable or independent of each other, we will understand true love. When we finally learn the secret of life; love, we will defeat the kingdom of darkness once and for all. You weren't created to live as a human being – you're a spirit with a soul and living in a body. Join hands in the restoration of Israel in these end times.

So far, most of the major religions on Earth have gotten some pieces right in their doctrines of God and worship to Him but there are too many gaps, errors, confusion etc. Even Christians have gotten it wrong – and I am one of them. I have been one all my life. Let's get it right. I introduce to you who the one and only true God of the Heavens and the Earth is. The God of the Israelites. The God of Abraham, Isaac, and Jacob or Israel. Don't let the different continents, races, cultures etc., deceive you. It is very clear that only this one God is the true Architect and Creator of the universe and everything that's in it, and the only One who is worthy of worship and praise. I hereby shed light on all the darkness so that you will be illuminated.

I lie not to you, so take everything you learn from this book extremely seriously. I thank God Almighty for all the graces and revelations. I am a proud member of the Ghana Holy Order of Cherubim and Seraphim. We understand the order of Heaven as it's supposed to be on Earth, and we understand partnership with the Holy Spirit and the Angelic. We move where the spirit moves, do what the spirit does, and say only what the spirit says. This Temple originated from Nigeria, West Africa. But I am from Ghana, West Africa. It is one of the first African initiated churches. We typically don't talk about our worship to God in the Temple publicly because to the world and those who lack the true knowledge, understanding, and practice of the Word of God, we seem odd. Some even say, we are a dark occult society because Christians are lost and do not know, and they do not understand. But when God Himself commands strongly for this to be published to the world, then it means an extremely serious deal. Then the messenger must bring the word, and any corresponding guidance to the people as it was in the days of the Old Testament Prophets. Any disobedience means merciless judgment from God. As Jesus Christ will say, I say to you, "He who has ears to hear, let him hear." We understand the patterns and ordinances of God according to both the Old and New Testaments – according to the true ways as it's supposed to be for the Israelites and for the Body of Christ today and forever. We don't remove or add to the Scriptures as given by the Holy Spirit. We won't teach you lies – We will ONLY teach you the true Word of God.

I am also a Presbyterian, and other members of the Ghana Holy Order of the Cherubim and Seraphim are also members of other Christian churches. But honestly, we attend our regular Sunday services to learn the Word of God and to relate to the Body of Christ. The regular churches as we all, including you know, lack power because of the gaps, which have been taught in this book. Truth and power must be restored to the Church.

All Glory and Honor to God Almighty in the Name of Our Lord Jesus Christ by the Power of the Holy Spirit. Stay saved, blessed, and spread the gospel, its patterns and ordinances correctly, accurately, efficiently, and effectively. Amen!

Reference

The Word of God – The Holy Bible.

- I have never even for once seen the Bible being cited in scientific papers, books, articles etc. Although I respect science and respect the works of those who have studied to bring it this far, I did not cite any specific sources because out of the Word of God came all inventions – they are all discoveries. If you want to sue me for using your work, please bring your design or patent and I will show you where that science or technology can be found in the Bible. Then I will have God sue you in return for using His Word without giving Him credit and offering.
- If you are wondering about the colors of the cover of the book, they were instructed and given by the Holy Spirit.
- The blue color is the Holy Spirit (Breath of God) – decreeing (River of God) – refreshing flow, intercession, contending, unstoppable, release of the gifts of Holy Spirit, renewal. So, open your hearts and receive.
- The red color is the Blood of Jesus Christ, passion, fire, purifying, overcomer, perseverance, war, authority. So, open your hearts and receive.
- The black color is the passion for God, Jesus Christ, and the Holy Spirit – the deepest color of blood is black, death as in sacrificial repentance, the hiding or secret place. So, open your hearts and receive.
- The yellow color is the glory presence of God, compassion, fire of God, submission to God, humility to God. So, open your hearts and receive.
- The Bible will become a bestseller and take its place as the number one and most important and most read book and a lot of souls shall be saved.

Dedication

This book is dedicated to God the Father, God the Son, and God the Holy Spirit, and the entire Body of Christ across the world. All credit and glory go to them.

Warning!

This book and its contents are sacred and inspired and written by the Holy Spirit. Any intentional attempt to hijack or destroy this book will only bring you calamity directly from God. I advise that you don't even try or attempt to do that. You will never encounter this book and your life remains the same. Impossible! Heed the message!

GOD BLESS YOU!

www.ingramcontent.com/pod-product-compliance
Lightning Source LLC
Chambersburg PA
CBHW042337030426
42335CB00030B/3377